HALF THE PERFECT WORLD

To Fran,

I hope there is enough Leonard Cohen in here to keep your interest :)

Peace.

HALF THE PERFECT WORLD

Writers, Dreamers and Drifters on Hydra, 1955–1964

PAUL GENONI AND
TANYA DALZIELL

MONASH University Publishing

Half the Perfect World: Writers, Dreamers and Drifters on Hydra, 1955–1964

© Copyright 2018 Paul Genoni and Tanya Dalziell
All rights reserved. Apart from any uses permitted by Australia's Copyright Act 1968, no part of this book may be reproduced by any process without prior written permission from the copyright owners. Inquiries should be directed to the publisher.

Monash University Publishing
Matheson Library and Information Services Building
40 Exhibition Walk
Monash University
Clayton, Victoria 3800, Australia
www.publishing.monash.edu

Monash University Publishing brings to the world publications which advance the best traditions of humane and enlightened thought.

Monash University Publishing titles pass through a rigorous process of independent peer review.

www.publishing.monash.edu/books/hpw-9781925523096.html

ISBN: 978-1-925523-09-6 (paperback)
ISBN: 978-1-925523-10-2 (pdf)
ISBN: 978-1-925523-11-9 (epub)

Series: Biography

Design: Les Thomas

Cover image: Charmian Clift, George Johnston, Marianne Ihlen, Leonard Cohen, and Jason Johnston (foreground), at Spilia Beach, Hydra, September 1960. (James Burke)

A catalogue record for this book is available from the National Library of Australia

CONTENTS

Acknowledgements vii

A note on the text xii

Preface xiii

Introduction 1

    Chapter 1   Hydra: island and town 33

    Chapter 2   *To spiti tou* Johnston: the Australian House 55

    Chapter 3   Islands: dreaming and living 80

    Chapter 4   Comings and goings 114

    Chapter 5   *Archontiká* 165

    Chapter 6   Socialising at Katsikas 193

    Chapter 7   Singin' at Douskos, swingin' at Lagoudera 227

    Chapter 8   Tourism 246

    Chapter 9   Sailing *Stormie Seas* 280

    Chapter 10   Demetri's pool 313

    Chapter 11   At work 338

    Chapter 12   Leaving 370

Conclusion 398

Image attributions 407

A note on sources and further readings 409

Index 415

ACKNOWLEDGEMENTS

In compiling the material for *Half the Perfect World* we are deeply indebted to many people.

Our heartfelt thanks belongs to Dorothy (Dot) Wallis, widow of Redmond Frankton Wallis, for providing access to her husband's Hydra photographs and other documents. Dorothy has been an unfailingly responsive and delightful correspondent, willingly sharing her personal memories of her husband and providing carefully considered insights relating to his life before their marriage.

Equally invaluable assistance has been provided by James Burke's family—his son, the late James (Jim) Burke, and his daughters Rosemary Burke and Jean Crawford. Locating the Burke family took perseverance, guess work and all the power of Google, but it was worth every bit of time and effort. They have been endlessly helpful and considerate of our requests and unstintingly willing to share their father's legacy. Meeting Rosemary and walking with her on the streets of Hydra where James Burke worked has been one of the unforgettable delights of this project.

We were also very fortunate to make contact with Dinnie Blair. Dinnie has been generous, helpful and entertaining, and has regularly amazed us with her sparkling memories of life on Hydra in the early sixties. To meet Dinnie on her first visit in many years to the island that had been her beloved home is a treasured memory that erases the notion that some types of research are 'work'.

We experienced great generosity from many people on Hydra, none more so than Brian and Valerie Sidaway, who we owe so much for their great interest in, and contribution to, this project. Their willingness to share their knowledge of Hydra and its history has been inspiring and has given us the opportunity to meet William Pownall and learn from his memories of earlier times. Warm thanks to Michael Pelekanos, who exemplifies Hydra's reputation for hospitality and sociability and to Yanni and Micky Papapetros, who do so much to keep alive memories of Hydra's 'golden years'—please check out their invaluable *Hydra Once Upon a Time* Facebook page. In Greece, we had additional assistance from Marina Bernier-Eliades and Platon Alexis Hadjimichalis.

In Australia, Rodney Hall, Mungo MacCallum and Robert Owen all took considerable time to share their memories of Hydra and their friends George Johnston and Charmian Clift. We thank them for their generous responses to our many questions. V.A. (Del) Kolve, Klaus Merkel, Mary Jane Pease (Case) and Inge Schneier Hoffman were also munificent correspondents with lively memories of their time on Hydra in 1960, who took in their stride two Australian researchers who unexpectedly contacted them with photographs and questions about their younger selves. The list of other correspondents is long. We are exceedingly grateful to Matt Carroll, Alison Case, Christopher Case, Gloria Crespo MacLennan, Harry Fatouras, Athena Gassoumis, Helle Goldman, Adrien Heckstall, Natasha Heidsieck Mack, Marianne Ihlen, Katyuli Lloyd, Diana MacCallum, Kevin McGrath, Constantine (Dinos) Michaelides, Michael Mingos, Ira Nadel, Megan O'Connor, Polly Samson, Lawrence Sherman, Sylvie Simmons, Sarah Sparks, Heather Strang and Julian Tompkin. Ευχαριστούμε την to Christine House for the Greek translations.

We would also like to acknowledge Garry Kinnane and Nadia Wheatley, the authors of the two standard biographies of George Johnston and Charmian Clift respectively: *George Johnston: A Biography*, Melbourne: Nelson, 1986; and *The Life and Myth of Charmian Clift*, Sydney: Harper Collins, 2001. They have produced two extremely fine and thorough pieces of research that provide an indispensable foundation for our work about the couple. We have included attributed quotes from both texts, but other background information and details have also been sourced from these essential books. We thank Garry Kinnane for his personal correspondence and encouragement.

A big acknowledgement to all those colleagues who came to Hydra with us in 2016 for the *Half the Perfect World* conference. Requiring busy people to

ACKNOWLEDGEMENTS

cross hemispheres is a large ask, but, in this case, it delivered wonderful company, enlightening discussions and passionate singing. Thanks to Douskos Taverna for the loan of the guitar!

Research of this type would be considerably more difficult without the collecting institutions that do the essential work of preserving cultural memory. The Turnbull Library (National Library of New Zealand) proactively solicited the archive of Redmond Wallis when it might have been neglected and forgotten. The assistance of their reference and copying staff has been essential to our use of this material. The National Library of Australia has been extremely helpful in providing access to the archives of George Johnston and Charmian Clift and associated material, including the Hazel de Berg Collection of interviews with Australian authors and the papers and photographs of Colin Simpson. The Emory University Alumni Archive was a very helpful source of initial information relating to James Burke's life and career. We are thrilled that James Burke's personal archive has recently been housed at the Stuart A. Rose Manuscript, Archives, and Rare Book Library, Emory University.

Leonard Cohen kindly gave permission to reproduce his letters held at The University of Toronto's Thomas Fisher Rare Book Library. We thank Mr. Cohen's manager, Robert Kory, for his assistance and Jennifer Toews for sourcing the letters from the library archive. Brianna Cregle provided assistance at Princeton University in accessing the Clift and Johnston papers from the Archives of Harold Ober Associates and the papers of Gordon Merrick, both held in the library's special collections. Suzana Tamamovic at the London School of Slavonic and East European Studies Library, University College London, located images of Sam Barclay and *Stormie Seas* that helped with identifications. Helen Symington at the Manuscript Division, National Library of Scotland, assisted with access to the papers of Patrick Leigh Fermor. Jenny Hodge at the University of California Davis Special Collections, Shield Library, assisted with the Steve Sanfield Papers. Maria Victoria Fernandez facilitated the papers of Clift and Johnston housed in the David Higham Associates Collection, Harry Ransom Centre, University of Texas. Staff at the Lilly Library, Indiana University, provided access to the Bobbs-Merrill Archive containing papers relating to Clift and Johnston. Kathy Shoemaker at the Manuscript, Archives, and Rare Book Library, Emory University, provided valuable assistance in tracing the life of James Burke through his father's archive. The archivist at HarperCollins, Dawn Sinclair, made a great effort, but with little luck, to locate material relating to Clift and Johnston. Natasha Marfutenko at Archives Research, the Australian Broadcasting Corporation, sought in vain for the interview Redmond Wallis conducted with George Johnston on Hydra before Johnston returned to Australia. Siobhan Dee at the National Film and Sound Archive of Australia digitised for us audio copies of George Johnston's radio serials of the late 1940s—*Death Takes Small Bites* and *Death By Horoscope*. Regina Feiler and Amy Wong of The LIFE Picture Collection (a 'closed' archive) responded courteously to our early requests for information relating to James Burke and set us on our determined path to uncover much more than the relatively small amount of data said to be housed in that archive. Anne L. Moore, Special Collections Library, W.E.B. Du Bois Library, University of Massachusetts Amherst, helpfully provided us with copies of William J. Lederer's correspondence. At Sotheby's Australia, we are indebted to Geoffrey Smart and John Keats for arranging our use of Sidney Nolan's 'Hydra' painting; thanks to Giulia Leali at Bridgeman Images for organising copyright permissions for this painting, and Kathleen Burke and her colleagues at the National Gallery of Victoria for locating the image. Ioanna Moraiti at the Benaki Gallery, Athens, facilitated the reproduction of Nikos Hadjikyriakos-Ghika's painting 'The Studio in Hydra'. Katherine O'Brien from the Reid Library at the University of Western Australia helped in sourcing obscure articles and *The Australian Women's Weekly* image of Sidney and Cynthia Nolan on Hydra.

Nathan Hollier at Monash University Publishing has been unfailingly supportive of this book, and we thank him and his staff, particularly Les Thomas, Joanne Mullins and Sarah Cannon, for their patience, enthusiasm and professionalism. Curtin University's School of Media, Creative Arts and Social

ACKNOWLEDGEMENTS

Inquiry provided important practical assistance with the project, as did the University of Western Australia's discipline of English and Literary Studies. Thank you to the Association for the Study of Australian Literature—their support has been invaluable.

Jamie Hamilton and Eladia, Caleb and Jordi Hamilton-Dalziell have lived with the researching and writing of this book, as has Lyn Genoni. Thank you! And also a big thanks to Margot and Kevin Dalziell, and Reg Genoni, who all supported the project and book with their steadfast interest and belief.

The help and interest of all those mentioned above has been inspiring and sustaining. We realise that memories fade and distort, that photographs and texts are invariably subjective, potentially misleading, and subject to multiple (mis)interpretations. All the help and information we have received has been freely given with the intention of being accurate, and the choices made with regard to the content of *Half the Perfect World* are ours alone. We fully respect that some people declined our requests for interviews and information. We will be pleased to be corrected if obvious errors or avoidable omissions have been made.

A NOTE ON THE TEXT

Agreement on English transliterations of Greek words and names is not always easy to reach. For example, Ύδρα is most commonly translated into English as Hydra, but spellings such as Ydra, Idhra and Idra are also found. We have therefore needed to make decisions regarding a consistent form of English transliteration, mindful that variations exist. Misspellings, grammatical quirks and typographical errors in original documents have been left to stand as they are intrinsic to the originals and do not prevent a clear reading. The exception is cabled correspondence, where some idiosyncrasies unique to the form have been 'smoothed over'.

PREFACE

The polished hill
The milky town
Transparent, weightless, luminous
Uncovering the two of us
On that fundamental ground
Where love's unwilled, unleashed, unbound
And half the perfect world is found

Leonard Cohen / Anjani Thomas, 'Half the Perfect World'

We had escaped our societies. Nobody was watching us. We could be free, we could behave as we liked. We had found the meaning of our existence. The real meaning of existence was there all the time of course, in the simple pattern of the island which we had annexed as our own primitive milieu, but after a time we could not see it for the mired footprints of our own excesses.

George Johnston, *Clean Straw for Nothing*

When Leonard Cohen recalled his Greek island home of Hydra in song, it was with a sense of its singularity, a place infused with transcendence and ripe with romantic and erotic promise. When George Johnston wrote of Hydra in his autobiographical novel *Clean Straw for Nothing*, he evoked a contemporary Eden, blessedly free from the demands and scrutiny of modern urban life and full of existential possibilities, but where the "simple pattern of the island" was erased by its all-too-human realities. Johnston was pointing, as Cohen had done, to the 'half perfect' nature of this island living.

Leonard Cohen, Katsikas *kafenio*, 1964. (Redmond Wallis)

PREFACE

That Cohen and Johnston shared a vision of Hydra's exceptionalism is due, in some measure, to the fact that the two writers knew each other well and had a specific experience in common—both were part of a fabled international community of artists, authors and intellectuals that formed on Hydra in the late 1950s and early 1960s. The circumstances surrounding the formation, evolution and eventual disintegration of that community as well as the social experiences its 'members' shared are the subjects of this book.

How Cohen came to be on Hydra is a story that has been told frequently and is peddled today by those selling the island as a desirable holiday destination—after all, it is Cohen who went on to become the most famous of Hydra's international residents. As the Canadian himself has recounted, a casual conversation with a sun-tanned bank teller during a bleak London spring led him to take a plane to Athens and then a ferry to Hydra in mid-April 1960. Within months the proceeds from a timely inheritance enabled him to buy a house on the island, high above the spectacular harbour and dockside. Here, the legend goes, Cohen met and lived with his partner Marianne Ihlen in idyllic simplicity throughout the 1960s as he wrote the novels and poems, and crafted the songs, that would earn him international renown. For the years that Cohen came and went, Hydra was a sanctuary from his steadily growing fame and, thereafter, an inspiration that inflected his writing until his death in 2016.

The arrival on Hydra in 1955 of Australian Johnston and his wife, Charmian Clift—also escapees from drab postwar London—and their key role in the formation of this creative community in an unlikely location is less well known. However, as Cohen later recalled, for the young writers and artists who found their way to Hydra, Johnston and Clift embodied the romantic appeal of a life lived intensely and dedicated to the production of art.

> They had a larger-than-life, a mythical quality. They drank more than other people, they wrote more, they got sick more, they got well more, they cursed more and they blessed more, and they helped a great deal more. They were an inspiration. They had guts. They were real, tough, honest. They were the kind of people you meet less and less.

Charmian Clift and George Johnston. (James Burke)

For a generation of writers, dreamers and drifters, being on Hydra provided an opportunity to experiment, drop out, take risks and to embrace a world charged with possibilities that weren't found in the middle-class urban backgrounds that many of them shared. The place was beautiful, the living cheap, the sunshine abundant and the time needed for writing or the making of art was theirs. But no matter how enticing Hydra may have been, it was also a small, remote and underdeveloped island where the isolation intensified everyday interactions and existential anxieties in ways that were constantly challenging, and where 'freedom' could both inspire and debilitate. As Johnston noted, by escaping the usual social and moral constraints, members of the expatriate colony were eventually confronted by the "mired footprints of our own excesses".

Half the Perfect World takes Johnston and Clift's arrival on Hydra in August 1955 as a transitional moment in the development of the island's expatriate artist community and argues that, by the time the couple departed

PREFACE

in 1964, this community (at least in its initial form) was all but exhausted. But while Johnston and Clift are central to the book's focus, many other individuals, some now famous and others all but unknown, are accounted for in order to represent the broad range of experiences that living on Hydra at the time involved. In this way, *Half the Perfect World* might be called a prosopography—the story of a group of people who, by design or chance, found themselves in a shared situation, the study of which reveals insights into their individual circumstances as well as the time and place in which they lived.

Looking at both the key players and the wider Hydra 'colony' provides an understanding of not only personal lives and relationships within this now mythical moment of postwar artistic bohemianism, but also an array of phenomena that were coalescing in unpredictable ways as the 1960s dawned—phenomena that both determined who came to Hydra and why, and the nature of their experiences of the island and its artist community. Some of the factors at play included modernities of travel, tourism and leisure; fading and emerging geopolitical realities of a transformed Europe; fledgling liberal social movements and counter-cultures; technologies of communication and entertainment; incipient pop culture; the rapidly changing conditions of expatriation; and shifting moral frameworks for personal relationships.

Finding oneself on Hydra and deciding to set up house was not only an act of individual whim or will but also deeply reflective of both the disquiets and opportunities transforming western culture in the aftermath of the Second World War. In particular, it was a time when modern cities were becoming something more (or other) than an economic necessity. On one hand, they were embraced as spaces providing a wealth of personal opportunity, rich in convenience and comfort, lavish with entertainment, and enmeshed in the social and economic advantages provided by postwar technology. On the other hand, they were also seen as increasingly hostile and alienating places, undermining traditional forms of community and deadening the human spirit. Depending on one's point of view, the decision Johnston, Clift, Cohen and others took to seek out a place such as Hydra—exotic, possibly quixotic and at a considerable geographic and imaginative distance from where and what they knew best—might represent one of two motivations: a rejection of the intellectual stimulation and creative *frisson* necessary for personal enrichment and the pursuit of great art; or an embrace of a simpler, more 'authentic' style of living, which provided the time and spiritual nourishment needed to realise their creative desires.

Creative bohemianism was, of course, nothing new, nor was the inclination for creative individuals to come together into supportive enclaves that sat at the margins of social normality. It was, however, novel to build such an enclave in the mid-twentieth century on a distant, poorly serviced and economically challenged island and to live embedded in a foreign culture and language. It was, as this group was to discover, half of a perfect world.

Living half the perfect world. Marianne Ihlen and Tot (Axel Jnr), Leonard Cohen, David Goschen, George Johnston and Charmian Clift. (James Burke)

INTRODUCTION

By the time George Johnston and Charmian Clift arrived on Hydra with their children, Martin and Shane, in August 1955 (a third child, Jason, was born on the island in early 1956), they already enjoyed certain notoriety in their native Australia. Johnston was born in 1912 and raised in a working-class Melbourne family. He learnt early to rely upon his precocious facility with a pen and started submitting occasional pieces to the *Argus* newspaper while in his mid-teens. In his early twenties, he started work with the paper as a cadet reporter, where he quickly attained a reputation as the newsroom's handsome 'golden boy', before coming to national attention during the Second World War as one of the country's foremost war reporters. Receiving his war correspondent's accreditation with the rank of captain in January 1942, Johnston was immediately posted to Port Moresby to cover the Japanese advance on New Guinea. Filing regular reports that were syndicated to major Australian papers, he rapidly achieved a reputation with readers for his vivid reporting and amongst other journalists for his reliability and speed at the typewriter. He returned to Australia after three months and then travelled widely during the later years of the war.

The exact places Johnston went to remain a matter of conjecture, but he certainly spent time in the US, Britain, Italy, Greece, India, Yugoslavia, several Middle Eastern countries, Burma, China, Tibet and Japan. In addition to filling many newspaper column inches, Johnston furthered his literary ambitions by writing a number of hastily produced books based on his wartime experiences, both before and after his commission. These included titles such as *Grey Gladiator*; *Battle of the Seaways*; *Australia at War*; *New Guinea Diary*, and *Pacific Partner*. One of his final dispatches was a first-hand account of the signing of the Japanese surrender documents aboard the USS Missouri on September 2nd, 1945.

Although Johnston came to regard his non-combatant wartime role with deep ambivalence, his articles and books provided many Australians with knowledge of the war's progress; and, along the way, he cultivated an image as the young and dashing globetrotting daredevil that the public presumably wanted in a war correspondent. When Johnston returned to Australia and rejoined the *Argus* at the war's end, his prospects appeared bright. It was a future that seemed to be further cemented in March 1946 when he was appointed the inaugural editor of a new magazine, the *Australasian Post*, while working out of his *Argus* office.

Charmian Clift was over a decade younger than her husband-to-be, having been born in August 1923 in the coastal New South Wales town of Kiama. Her childhood and teenage years were spent in her schooling at Kiama and nearby Wollongong, after which she undertook a series of short-term jobs in Kiama. From an early age and fed by her love of reading, Clift had her sights set on a much bigger world and dreamt of an escape from the rural valleys and beaches of her hometown. After winning a 1941 *Pix* magazine beach-girl photographic competition, Clift left for Sydney in search of the excitement and worldly glamour she craved.

Clift briefly found independence living a single life and working as an usherette in Kings Cross, but her experience of the big city did not proceed as planned. In the early months of 1942, she found herself pregnant and with no prospect of establishing a permanent relationship with the child's father. Her daughter was born on Christmas Day and almost immediately relinquished for adoption. Clift returned to Kiama for several months to recover before joining the Australian Women's Army Service in April 1943. She trained initially as an anti-aircraft gunner before transferring to the Land Headquarters in Melbourne and was commissioned as a lieutenant in August 1944. At the same time, Clift began writing and publishing short stories in various small journals, and her literary ambitions received a boost when she was appointed to a position editing and writing for an army magazine, *For Your Information*.

Johnston and Clift first met in May 1945 when they were both still in uniform and Johnston was briefly on leave in Melbourne. The attraction was

INTRODUCTION

immediate and mutual. Johnston could not help but be impressed by the glamorous, vivacious and smart young lieutenant—Johnston's biographer, Garry Kinnane, wrote of Clift that "There was nothing coy about her: she was confident, straight-backed, and certain of her attractiveness to men"—and the accomplished, worldly and moderately-famous Johnston appealed to Clift's desire to join her life and intellect to a world larger than Sydney and Melbourne could provide.

Any chance for Johnston and Clift to immediately further their relationship was curtailed when Johnston returned to Asia to see out the remainder of the war. The couple would soon meet again, however, when, the following year, Clift started work alongside Johnston at the *Argus*. This time the outcome was explosive when they commenced an affair that rapidly became common knowledge. The scandal arose because Johnston had been married since 1938 and had a daughter, Gae, born in 1941. The *Argus* management (and presumably staff) disapproved of their star reporter's extramarital relationship with the office beauty and let him know so. But the couple was not deterred, and after they began openly living together, Clift was dismissed because of her relationship with a married man. Johnston gave the *Argus* management the choice of reinstating Clift or accepting his resignation, and they—almost certainly to his surprise—chose the latter.

Thereafter, things moved quickly for Johnston and Clift. Putting Melbourne and the notoriety of their relationship behind them, they moved to Sydney where Johnston obtained a divorce, and he and Clift married in August 1947. During this period Johnston turned his hand to writing fiction, publishing his first novel in 1948, *Death Takes Small Bites*, a thriller set on the Burma Road with a hero with the unlikely name of Cavendish C. Cavendish and a heroine, Charmian Anthony. While Johnston would later tell literary agent David Higham in a letter from July 1954 that "I consider it a pretty lousy book", the novel had moderate success in a tough postwar market. In the same letter, Johnston related that the book had been translated into French under a title that was "inexplicable", *Le Petite Feu* (The Small Fire), and that in paperback it had sold "roughly one hundred and ten thousand copies in this edition". As this self-promotion suggests, Johnston was always a keen opportunist, and the novel was eventually serialised for Australian radio (2UW) in 1950 followed by *Death By Horoscope*, a serial based on a book manuscript that never saw the light of day. (Correspondence from August and September 1951 between Johnston and Higham suggests that "complications" stemming from anticipated claims by Curtis Brown to act as an agent for the title could have been partly to blame. Victor Gollancz rejected it outright in December 1951). A second novel, *Moon at Perigee*, promptly followed, which again drew on Johnston's experience in Asia, specifically in India.

It was apparent during their early-married years in Sydney that Johnston and Clift were already planning for a life well away from the postwar Australia that frustrated them with its insularity and conservatism. Their departure was delayed by the arrival of children, with a son, Martin, born in November 1947 and a daughter, Shane, born in February 1949. To pay the bills, Johnston returned to journalism, obtaining a position with the *Sun*, but his attention was increasingly given to writing fiction, and he now began to involve Clift as a joint author. The couple targeted what was then Australia's richest literary prize of £2000 and a publication deal, offered by the *Sydney Morning Herald* for an unpublished novel. They submitted *High Valley*, another novel with a setting inspired by Johnston's wartime adventures, this time a trek he had undertaken through Tibet in 1945. The novel won the major prize, which immediately established their reputation as a literary couple while also validating their personal relationship and fuelling their dream of a life devoted to writing.

With this success achieved, Johnston and Clift in early 1951 joined the postwar exodus for London where Johnston had found a position managing the Associated Newspaper Service's office on Fleet Street. The couple were true expatriates in the sense that they envisaged, and even welcomed, the possibility of never returning to Australia. Clift in particular was marked out as the kind of expatriate who most troubled the national psyche—one who aggressively rejects her home country. As she later explained in an interview:

INTRODUCTION

> At the time I left Australia, I wanted desperately to leave. I didn't like Australia a bit. It had that very nasty feeling of post-war, I thought it was money-grubbing and greedy, all the values I thought were important didn't seem to be there anymore. … I remember sailing out and waving goodbye to the Harbour Bridge and thinking, I'll never see that again.

The Johnstons arrived in a London and were soon mixing with other artists, actors, writers, musicians and broadcasters from 'down under', such as Sidney and Cynthia Nolan, Peter Finch, Paul Brickhill, Peter Porter, Albert Arlen, Wilfrid Thomas, Colin Colahan and Cedric and Pat Flower. Initially, as Clift later recalled, they revelled in both the great metropolis and the antipodean otherness that set these Australians apart.

> I used to think that the most desirable state of being that could be imagined was to be a young and talented Australian in London. Weren't we healthier, more vital, more buoyant? And didn't we have so much enthusiasm, so much talent that it was frustrating to the point of actual discomfort to keep ourselves within decent British bounds? We kept bursting out all over the place. … We were enchanted, amused, excited, indignant, frustrated, discouraged, and sometimes contemptuous.

Gradually, the excitement the Johnstons felt at being at the heart of the Empire was tempered by the daily stress of living in a city still bedevilled by postwar reconstruction, social dislocation and rationing. When Clift later recalled her time in London, she summoned up a rollcall of anxieties about modernity and its impacts:

> the smoke pall hanging over Paddington and the grey-brown rows of smutty terraces, of crowded subways and gas bills and income-tax and telephones and the shimmer of television screens, of the grey, anxious faces crowding the streets, of the feverish neuroses of staying alive and scrabbling for contentment, of the nightly retreats into private sorrows …

HALF THE PERFECT WORLD

Today we recognise the neo-romantic rejection of modernity and urbanisation in search of simpler and more authentic living as a ubiquitous and benign trope of contemporary travel and life(style) writing. In the 1950s, however, it represented something quite different—a schism from the promises entailed in the victory of war that had seemingly scripted a future based on the triumph of national values and technological superiority. Johnston and Clift had other reasons for leaving London, including their desire to write full time (since arriving in London they had co-authored another novel, *The Big Chariot*); the need for a more amenable climate; and the dynamics of their marriage that saw Clift struggling to find space for her literary ambitions in a partnership in which she was increasingly defined as a wife and a mother. So again they moved on, leaving behind the locus of Australian literary expatriation in search of a very different experience.

There were elements of serendipity and misadventure that took Johnston and Clift to the unlikely Greek islands of Kalymnos and then Hydra, where they found themselves far removed from the editors, agents, publicists, reviewers and readers that constituted London literary life. Yet the couple saw themselves as part of a generation for whom expatriation and transience were to become totally unexceptional and indeed a right of passage for ambitious literary types. Clift, writing in her 1956 memoir, *Mermaid Singing*, of the couple's decision to uproot their family and head for Kalymnos, foresaw their future as one in which they wandered the world, untethered from home ownership.

> For we are the new nomads, the twentieth century, who wander the earth with trailing roots, our possessions portable, our dwellings temporary. Not for us the parish register, the crammed attic, great-grandmother's furniture, the field planted out for the next generation, the family vault and ancestral worms. We pay weekly for the space we take up in the world, from the moment we open our eyes in the hospital ward to the time we close them in the rented house.

But things would change by the time Clift and Johnston moved to Hydra in the late summer of 1955. With two children in school and struggling to adjust

INTRODUCTION

to their new life, and with Clift unexpectedly pregnant, a life-on-the-move was about to become much more difficult. Suddenly, they needed to be settlers rather than nomads. So the decision was made to buy a house, thereby reinforcing the couple's presence on Hydra and ensuring the near-decade they lived on the island, from 1955 to 1964, would become the centrepiece of their shared lives and myth. Their decision also marked a decisive moment in the development of Hydra's renowned expatriate colony of writers and artists who would flock to the island during the coming years and which is at the centre of *Half the Perfect World*.

While the Johnstons' arrival on Hydra was a turning point, they were not the first foreigners with literary or artistic ambitions to find their way to the island, nor would they be the first to settle there (more or less) permanently. Indeed, there had been a regular artistic presence on the island since the opening of a branch of the Athens School of Fine Arts in 1936, which was designed to entice international tourists with artistic or cultural interests. Art school visitors were also joined by a steady flow of largely British artists and intellectuals who passed through the mansion of hospitable and internationally renowned Greek modernist painter Nikos Hadjikyriakos-Ghika whose family had been on the island since the seventeenth century.

Likely the first foreigners to establish a permanent presence on the island were Frenchman Christian Heidsieck and his wife, Lily Mack, who had lived with her Russian émigré family in Athens since she was a young girl. Mack's brother Vladimir was a painter, and the family was well connected with Athenian arts circles before and during the Second World War. Following the war, Heidsieck and Mack made the decision to move to Hydra to live and work, despite the island having few services such as electricity or running water. They arrived in 1948, renting a house in Kamini, a fishing village immediately to the west of Hydra Port, where Heidsieck built a woodfired kiln and commenced his career as a ceramicist, using skills he had acquired in Italy and at Maroussi in Greece. While Heidsieck threw the pots and mixed the glazes, Lily (known to islanders as Angoulina) undertook less glamorous chores such as carrying and lighting wood for the kiln and cleaning up the

Christian Heidsieck at his potter's wheel, 1958. (Vasso Mingos)

clays at the end of each workday. Lily also supplemented the family income by making jewellery and paintings to be sold at the port. The Heidsiecks purchased a house in Kamini in 1954—which is still owned by the family—and thereby entrenched their presence on the island.

Soon after buying his island house, Heidsieck was drafted into the French services and spent two years in Algeria. When he and Lily returned to Hydra, they found that they were no longer the only foreigners living on the island—Johnston and Clift had arrived, and others had followed. Indeed, such was the growth of the foreign contingent of writers and artists on the island that it soon gathered attention. Photojournalist Vasso Mingos documented their presence in an article titled 'Island of writers', which appeared in June 1958 in the English-language magazine *Pictures from Greece*. Mingos noted that

INTRODUCTION

the Heidsiecks' "splendid isolation" on Hydra was now over and that, led by the Johnstons, "Hydra had become a writers' island during his [Heidsieck's] absence".

As recounted by Mingos, the Johnstons were followed by the Irishman and aspiring writer Patrick Greer and his Australian wife, Nancy Dignan. (This couple would live in the Heidsieck's house while Christian was absent in Algeria, and Dignan would later illustrate Clift's 1959 Hydra memoir *Peel Me a Lotus*). They were soon joined on the island by David and Angela Goschen, an artistic English couple, and their daughters, Chryssoula and Mariora; Norwegian writer Axel Jensen and his partner Marianne Ihlen; Egyptian-born Italian Paolo Tilche, his Czechoslovakian wife, Magda, and their son, Sandro; and American Gill Schwartz (who previously worked at a US airbase in Morocco as an electronics technician) and his French wife, Loetitia. As with so many others who would find themselves on Hydra, the Schwartzes turned up on a whim that unearthed latent artistic ambitions.

> They had been honeymooning around Europe when they stumbled on Hydra.
>
> 'I had been wanting to do some serious writing, and this seemed an opportune time and the place to do it', says Gill.
>
> So they settled there. Gill finds that in Hydra he is in no conflict with his surroundings, 'maybe because the place is conducive to my line of thought—introspection!'

These were the people, Mingos declared, who made up "Hydra's community of writers—a phenomenon unique in the history of this or any other Greek island".

In the same breath as Mingos announced the emergence of this "unique" international community with its sense of optimistic camaraderie, he also expressed concern that its success could be the cause of its demise.

> What is the future of the community? Will it dwindle or will it grow? Will the presence of these highly evolved intellectuals, these ultra-civilized complicated products of our age, eventually alter the atmosphere of the

An introspective Gill Schwartz, 1958.
(Vasso Mingos)

island? Will they cause it to lose its unsophisticated air, its refreshing simplicity which constitutes 90 per cent of its charm? It is difficult to say.

In the hearts of some of the older members of the community, at any rate, a fear has dawned: that their numbers will grow to such an extent that in the months and years to come as to make life on the island untenable.

To underscore Mingos's point about the island's uncertain future as a haven for creative types, a banner headline ran across two pages of the nine-page spread, "There is ever a fear in the hearts of these new 'Hydriotes': Maybe the

INTRODUCTION

Magda, Sandro and Paolo Tilche on the terrace of their Hydra home, 1958.
(Vasso Mingos)

island will attract other cosmopolitans and Hydra will lose its unsophisticated charm and become another 'tourist-besieged' Capri!"

As Mingos noted, he was not alone in his concern that Hydra was on the cusp of unwelcome change. At the time that he was putting his article together, Clift was drafting *Peel Me a Lotus*, describing not only her family's first year on the island but also her growing realisation that the poor, secluded and beautiful Greek island she and Johnston had made their writerly home was rapidly becoming a desirable tourist destination. Clift would soon bemoan the "arrival of the people with the leisure and the money and the taste to be amused by artists, and the people with the big yachts and big bank accounts who send the cost of living so high that the poor artists are forced to move on and discover another little port". Almost from the outset, a place that might have been perfect for a form of 'escape' was made half-perfect by the presence of other escapees.

In addressing itself to the changing social conditions on Hydra during the core years of its storied artist community, *Half the Perfect World* draws from a range of sources left by members of the community. Foremost among these are Charmian Clift and George Johnston themselves. It would be ill-advised to assume that the events detailed in their fiction—or in Clift's case, her memoirs—are a solemnly accurate testament to their island lives; however there is plenty to indicate that neither Clift nor Johnston was shy about writing autobiographically. Many of Johnston's own biographical details and character traits (real, desired and projected) find expression in the alter-ego character of David Meredith, who took shape in the fiction Johnston wrote on Hydra and became the central character of the autobiographical Meredith trilogy that sits at the heart of his achievement and reputation. In these and other novels Johnston wrote compulsively about the couple's relationship, including various jealousies, rivalries and betrayals. Clift was more personally circumspect, with her two artfully constructed Greek island memoirs consisting of a bedrock of verifiable fact embellished by some imaginative detail. While the couple's narratives must be weighed carefully alongside other accounts, they are nonetheless an irresistible component of any search for the 'truth' about their lives on Hydra. Clift's *Peel Me a Lotus* in particular provides an indispensable account of the island's fledgling expatriate colony.

It is also the case that Johnston's fictional counterpart, David Meredith, is articulating a desire rather than an actuality when he states of Hydra that, "Nobody was watching us". While it was true that Clift and Johnston were removed from the moral and social scrutiny that had brought them undone in Melbourne, a number of Hydra's expatriates spent a considerable amount of time watching and recording each other in letters, diaries, lightly fictionalised narratives and photographs. Johnston and Clift would both find themselves fictionalised in others' writings and not always in the most flattering

INTRODUCTION

light. Gordon Merrick, now recognised as being among the first successfully mass-marketed queer novelists, was but one of Hydra's expatriate writers who lifted 'material' from the often-tumultuous lives and relationships he witnessed. Merrick's *Forth into Light*, published in 1974—a few years after Clift and Johnston had passed away—features a dipsomaniac novelist, George Leighton, who spends too much time drunk and arguing with his wife about her suspected infidelity. It is a scenario that would have been all too familiar to the protagonist's namesake and immediately recognised by those who knew Johnston and Clift from their time on Hydra.

While *Half the Perfect World* refers to various written sources, both published and unpublished, as well as oral accounts and interviews, it is particularly indebted to two key sources, both of which come with their own intriguing backstories. The first of these is the archive of fifteen hundred black and white images that *LIFE* photographer James Burke captured of the island and its inhabitants in the late summer of 1960, none of which were published in *LIFE* magazine at the time. Burke's photographs only began to circulate publicly on the internet following a partnership forged in November 2008 between two transnational conglomerates—TimeWarner and Google. Few details beyond the photographer's name and the date of October 1960 accompany the images on the Google Arts & Culture platform, and it has been left to social media—Facebook pages, websites and blogs devoted to Australian literature, Hydra and Leonard Cohen—to provide sketchy commentary on these now digitally mobile photographs. Just how James Burke came to be on Hydra with his camera is integral to the story told in *Half the Perfect World*—a story told with the help of many of his photographs.

Burke's keenness to photograph and write a story about an 'artist colony' on Hydra was far from accidental. Burke had been friends with George Johnston since 1944 when they met in China where Johnston was covering the Sino-Japanese War, and the Shanghai-born, Mandarin-speaking Burke was attached to the US Office of War Information and operating a listening post behind Japanese lines.

George Johnston and James Burke, Tibet, 1945.
(James C. Burke Collection)

When Johnston returned to China in 1945 after a period of leave in Australia, he again met up with Burke, who was now working as a war correspondent for *Liberty*, which competed against *The Saturday Evening Post* in the lucrative US weekly magazine market. In an extraordinary wartime diversion, the two men found themselves in Tibet in July and August 1945. With time on their hands, they took a five-week trek on ponies through the high mountain valleys in order to reach the Konka Gomba lamasery, which Johnston believed was the model for the idyllic Shangri-La lamasery in James Hilton's 1933 novel, *Lost Horizon*. As Johnston later wrote of this journey in his final posthumously published novel, *A Cartload of Clay*:

> They stayed in lamaseries and strange temples and smelly stone houses but mostly in the black yurts of the yak and sheep nomads, and they rode wherever the whim took them—or the high passes allowed them—through the most beautiful country Meredith had ever seen, or even imagined.

INTRODUCTION

On the return journey, Burke fell seriously ill with a kidney infection, and Johnston saved his friend's life by ferrying him out of the mountains until, with Burke "insensible", they reached a US airstrip just in time for Johnston to fire a gun and catch the attention of the last plane as it taxied for departure from a dismantled airfield.

Johnston and Burke remained in contact after the war as Burke continued working as a journalist in a series of Asian postings. He was located in Peking (Beijing) when the communist forces overran the city in January 1949, and he and his young family were forced to remain there under a form of house arrest before being allowed to travel to the US in June. Keen to return to Asia, Burke moved his family to India in early 1950, firstly freelancing and then taking a position with *Time* magazine and progressing to the position of *Time* Bureau Chief in New Delhi.

During these years, Burke occasionally submitted his own photographs to illustrate his reports and gradually became more interested in this side of his work. As a result, he returned to New York in 1956 for formal training as a photojournalist. As it happened, Burke's first photo assignment for *LIFE* brought him into contact with a bohemian artistic enclave—similar to that which he would later encounter on Hydra—when he was sent to photograph the burgeoning number of independent artists and galleries grouped around New York's 10th Street. Between December 1956 and January 1957, Burke photographed a number of the major abstract expressionists who were at the centre of the mid-century transformation of American art, including Willem de Kooning, Franz Kline and Martin Resnick, as they worked, partied and talked in their studios, galleries and homes in the 10th Street precinct. The 10th Street galleries were more than art spaces; they were the centre of New York's avant-garde, featuring jazz, poetry readings, performance art, comedy and more. It was also the area of New York favoured by the Beat writers and where the famed Cedar Street Tavern became the preferred meeting place for both the 10th Street artists and the leading literary Beats such as Allen Ginsberg, Jack Kerouac, Gregory Corso and Frank O'Hara. By photographing on 10th Street, Burke was both learning his trade as a photojournalist and receiving

Unidentified, Russian-American actress Zina Rachevsky,
Conrad Rooks (back to camera), Greek writer Nanos Valaoritis and Gregory Corso,
Athens, 1959. (James Burke)

an education on the workings of a bohemian Beat subculture absorbed in its own art practice and social rituals, and self-consciously separate from the daily grind of life in the metropolis.

With his photojournalistic credentials secured, Burke returned to Asia for a posting in Hong Kong before moving to Athens in 1959 and into a role which gave him coverage of a broad sweep of Southern Europe, the Middle East and North Africa. It also brought him back into contact with American Beat culture as, by this time, the postwar generation of American writers and artists were an established presence in several European cities, including Athens. Exactly how the connection was made is unclear, but in September 1959, Burke photographed Beat poet Gregory Corso in several locations around Athens including at the Parthenon, at a poetry reading and having lunch at the home of aspiring American filmmaker Conrad Rooks, who would go on to make the acclaimed Beat-influenced films *Chappaqua* (1966) and *Siddhartha* (1972). (Corso and Rooks both visited Hydra. Corso visited in 1959 when, on

INTRODUCTION

a remote part of the island and likely under the influence of hallucinogens, he had a vision of 'Death', and was so entranced by the experience that he returned several times attempting to recreate the moment. Rooks's visits produced fine photographic portraits of Johnston and Clift, copies of which are held in the Johnston and Clift archive at the National Library of Australia). While Burke captured some excellent photographs of Corso, it seems the relationship between the photographer and his subject may not have always been amicable. A letter Corso wrote to Allen Ginsberg from Athens in October 1959 records that in one intemperate and alcohol-influenced incident, he flung a glass at the unfortunate Burke.

Working from Athens also allowed Burke to resume personal contact with George Johnston on nearby Hydra. Burke visited Johnston and Clift on the island on the weekend of May 21st and 22nd, 1960, and on the 26th he cabled New York with a proposal for a story for *LIFE*—a photojournalistic account that would, in effect, update the work done by Mingos two years earlier. Addressing the wire to George Caturani from the magazine's Foreign News Service, Burke made his pitch by playing up the island's Beat credentials and foregrounding the role of Johnston and Clift.

> Island of Hydra, four hours slow ferryboat across Saronic gulf from Athens, is sort of minor key Greek Majorca still cheap and not yet famous. Its year around international colony of artists and writers (largely Scandinavian and Canadian at moment) is small but summer season now beginning brings visiting stream ranging from fullbright scholars to beatniks like Gregory Corso. Atmosphere is fairly beat, with bearded barefoot types lounging about waterfront tables drinking oozo (strong Greek anisette) and talking about last nights party. Hydra islanders take them in stride and even join in—at least one local policeman is ardent poet himself. Only disharmony are American tourists who come on daily ferry from Athens to spend few hours gawking—but carefully keeping quay width distance from strange breed. Although surface atmosphere seems beat there are serious hardworking individuals in

> artist group. Leader of permanent colony is Australian novelist George Johnston with his writer wife Charmian Clift and three children own picturesque old island home and have lived there five years (unless you have another project for me in next couple of weeks eye would like give a try as a photographers story). Only spent few hours there the other day and not sure can bring off story but seems worth try if not doing anything else.

Burke's proposal did not immediately elicit the editorial permission he needed to proceed. Some four months later, on Saturday, September 10th, Burke again cabled Caturani announcing he was going to Hydra "until Monday" and then sent Caturani and senior editor Sam Welles another cable when he returned to Athens on September 12th. This time Burke expanded on the proposed story and its main characters, stressing the urgency of acting quickly before the summer slipped away and demonstrating astute insight into the island's social dynamics. Similar to Mingos, he also sounded a cautious note about the future of the island's foreign community.

> [H]ydra at its best right now and strongly recommend shooting it during next fortnight as antidote for political campaigns, cold war junkets and African chaos. Increasing number of artists and writers are getting away from it all on this sun drenched little Greek island which one day will probably become as jaded as Majorca or Costa Brava but which now still unspoiled enough to offer small house for seven dollars aye month—or you can buy it for twenty five hundred. Boat I went to Hydra on last Saturday brought Norwegian writer looking for house to rent and Canadian poet Leonard Cohen had just bought one the day before. Also watched architect James Speyer of Illinois Institute of Technology putting finishing touches to his new Hydra home. Another recent hydra arrival is Chuck Heckstal, American Negro paratrooper veteran on pension from Korean war wounds, whose writing play. Then theres bim and robbin Wallis, young New Zealand journalist couple trying write novels. Theres Jasper Ungood-Brown, oxford scholar, and David Goschen,

INTRODUCTION

another British intellectual whos just finished laying green tile on floor and walls of his bathroom. Theres rather mysterious American young woman who claims be writing paper on Chinese brain washing—why on hydra I do not yet know. Besides these permanent or semipermanent residents and others like Australian George Johnston and family (mentioned in my original research) theres daily and weekly influx and outflow of visitors ranging from Elizabeth Taylor, who arrived last week on yacht for one day visit to bearded German beatnik type who came on boat with me for one week stay. And there are ordinary tourist types who come to look at intellectual types. 'Why, he looks like Jesus Christ,' I overheard one tourist remark when he spotted bearded David Goschen.

There are several layers or epicentres in Hydriot intellectual colony. Theres lively waterfront group which revolves around australian Johnston and makes headquarters at grocery store-wine shop on busy quai. Then theres saroukis gika, famous Greek painter, who lives on Olympian heights above town and entertains his own flow of international guests like Osbert Sitwell and Cecil Beaton. Then there are couple of local grande dames who like to collect foreign groups for parties in their rococo mansions.

This time Caturani responded promptly, with a return cable on September 15th instructing Burke to be "aiming at subessay in black and white. Like get various layers of Hydra society new arrival perhaps househunting glamorous and ordinary tourists general look of place to show why people go there its color relaxed way of life charm". He concluded with "Wish we were there". Burke now had his brief and seems either to have responded immediately or, more likely, had already taken photographs in anticipation the previous weekend, as he dispatched one packet of film (consisting of four 35mm rolls and 147 images) to New York the following day, September 16th. This was followed by a larger second and final packet sent on October 1st, consisting of 40 rolls and approximately 1440 images. Burke also prepared an extensive list of notes and captions describing the contents of each roll of film and individual images. This was dated September 29th and presumably accompanied the second packet dispatched to New York two days later.

One witness to Burke's work on Hydra was his son Jim, who provided an evocative account of travelling to the island with his father and meeting Johnston and Clift.

> I did go to Hydra with dad once. I was 15 or 16 and, while I don't remember every minute of the trip, the image of the ferry arriving in that beautiful picture-postcard harbor with the whitewashed walls of the town swooping up the hill at about a 60-degree angle will never leave my mind. I remember George Johnston constantly smoking cigarettes guiding us from the harbor up a small cobblestoned street to his house. The street was lined with whitewashed one or two story sort of townhomes all joined together. George walked in front of our group as a constant cloud of smoke blew towards us. I remember thinking how thin he was.
>
> As I remember, his abode combined two townhomes and was sparsely furnished with a lot of mismatched furniture. He was not a slave to established rules of interior design. I was fascinated with Charmian. She was very relaxed, darkly beautiful, and had a deep, sexy voice. She was not like many of the women of her age I knew who looked like they recently visited a hair salon. I doubt Charmian had seen the inside of a hair salon in years. She was forceful and opinionated. George sounded educated and, to me, looked and acted like what I thought a writer should look and act like: outspoken, loud and a bit mad.

As the exchanges between Burke and his *LIFE* editors made clear, the social circumstances that Burke would visually document were seen at the time as outside the norm. His would be a piece on a bohemian artists' colony presumed to be unusual, if not radical, in the eyes of the magazine's middle-class readers. This readership was reminded with each issue, as Erika Doss described in her study of *LIFE*, of "the sure belief that the American way was the way of the world". Burke's Hydra photographs provided a glimpse of another way of being in the world.

INTRODUCTION

James Burke with Hydriot *grande dame*, Katerina Paouri.
(James Burke)

Burke's Hydra photographs do, in large part, adhere to what he had envisaged and pitched to *LIFE*. The photographs certainly move across and through the "several layers or epicentres in [the] Hydriot intellectual colony", including not only the expatriate community centred around the Johnstons but also several local Hydriot families and various types of tourists and travellers. Unsurprisingly, Burke also adheres to the photojournalistic practice of telling a story. On several occasions, it is apparent that he has followed a group of people over the course of several hours in the role of patient observer. He accompanies Johnston and Clift on social outings, as shown in photographs of the couple getting prepared at their house, travelling with friends, mixing in company and then leaving. On another occasion, he follows an excursion on donkeys away from the Hydra port. He depicts the party leaving the town; making the precipitous climb away from the coast in various stages; reaching two successive destinations, both monasteries; shopping for souvenirs inside one of the monasteries; walking in the surrounding grounds; and journeying homeward. At other times, he photographs occasional Hydra resident Nikos Hadjikyriakos-Ghika in his home and studio. This was only one of several sequences where Burke follows his artist-subjects to their homes just as he followed the 10th Street artists several years before. As a result, Burke recorded the other side of the artists' lives away from the sociability of the tables, taverns, *kafenia* and public spaces of the *agora* that were their usual meeting places.

Exactly why Burke's Hydra photos were not published by *LIFE* at the time is unclear. Caturani cabled Burke on March 26th, 1961, reporting that they had "Finally laid out four lively spreads" and asking a series of questions relating to the selected photographs. Burke responded, updating his editor with regard to the key people in the photographs, and in early May, he again contacted Caturani to report that Johnston's novel *Closer to the Sun* with its island setting was to be published in the US in June and had been selected by the Literary Guild as its "October selection". Clearly, however, there had been an editorial change of heart at *LIFE*. The "four lively spreads" never materialised, and Burke's images were relegated to the magazine's archive for half a century.

INTRODUCTION

Redmond 'Bim' Wallis and donkey, c.1960.
(Redmond Wallis)

The second archive to which *Half the Perfect World* is indebted comprises the diaries, correspondence and unpublished manuscripts of a hitherto little-known New Zealand writer, Redmond Frankton 'Bim' Wallis. (Wallis was known as either Frank or by the family nickname of 'Bim', but published under his given name of Redmond on the grounds that it was "a much more upmarket name for an author"). Wallis was the author of *Point of Origin,* a novel written on Hydra and published in 1962, and two later novels, *Starbloom* and *The Mills of Space*, both published in 1989 and aimed at a young-adult science fiction readership. The sum of his writing was, however, far more substantial than this modest published output suggests as he was an active writer of fiction and other forms throughout his life.

Wallis was born in Christchurch in September 1933 and developed an interest in student journalism while at the University of Canterbury. He commenced work at *The Press* in Christchurch in 1956 before transferring to *The Dominion* in Wellington the following year. Frustrated by the slow progress of his career, he decided to heed advice to obtain experience working on Fleet Street. Having married in 1958, Wallis and his wife, Robyn, immediately set about saving for their departure for London. The young couple was passionate about Greek culture and history and feared that once they settled into jobs in London, returning to Greece would be difficult. The plan, therefore, as described by Wallis, was that they would "get off in Naples, see Rome, travel down to Brindisi and across to Corfu, go to Athens, then to Crete, see one other Greek island and then run for London". Although Wallis's immediate concern was his career in journalism, his greater ambition was to write fiction, and in moving to London, he undoubtedly had an eye to his preferred career as a novelist.

The Wallises departed from Wellington on January 28th, 1960, and arrived in Athens on April 2nd. A week later they proceeded to Hydra for their experience of several days on "one other Greek island". Within twenty-four hours of arriving on the island, the couple had decided to extend their stay through until October. This rapid change of plans was the outcome of several factors, including a realisation of the island's cheap accommodation. Wallis noted in his diary that "We started all this when hearing about the rents people paid—200–300 drachma a month (200 dr = approximately £3/10/-)". It is also apparent from Wallis's diary that George Johnston, obviously seeing something of himself in the young journalist and would-be novelist, was instrumental in both helping Wallis find low-priced accommodation and urging him to stay and pursue his interest in writing fiction.

> It seemed like a scheme to do some writing that might not occur again and this was confirmed by a former very good Aussie journalist, George Johnston, who has been here four and a half years. So away we went. George mentioned causally to a Greek, Theodoros, that we were

INTRODUCTION

Robyn and Redmond Wallis on Hydra's *agora*.
(James Burke)

thinking of staying. He knew of a house. We looked at it and accepted @ 200 drachma a month. ... It has four rooms—kitchen with charcoal stove and bread oven—living room with view to port, bedrooms very big, with same view & view to hill behind Hydra, and the studio with the view of the same hill.

It is also likely that the Wallises were swayed by the presence of other artists and writers around their own age then living on Hydra. While Johnston and Clift were older (nearing fifty and forty, respectively), most of the island's expatriate writers and artists were of a similar age to the New Zealand couple. From Wallis's diary, we know that he almost immediately encountered some of those whom Mingos had met two years earlier, including Axel Jensen and Marianne Ihlen, and David and Angela Goschen. In addition, he met Lena Folke-Olsson, a Swedish woman staying with Clift and Johnston; American artists Patricia Amlin and Fidel Caliesch; Greek-American painter Demetri Gassoumis and his wife, Carolyn; Gordon Merrick and his partner, Charles Hulse; and Leonard Cohen, who arrived on Hydra several days after the Wallises. With the exception of Merrick and Caliesch, all were in their twenties, and, although many others would come and go in the coming months, this was the core group with whom the Wallises would socialise daily during their first summer on the island.

As it transpired, the Wallises didn't leave for London in October 1960, but, rather, in the late summer of 1961. After nearly two years in London, they returned to Hydra in August 1963, staying this time for a little over twelve months.

Although Wallis's brief entry in the *Oxford Companion to New Zealand Literature* makes no mention of his association with Hydra, the island had a central place in his imagination for the rest of his life. As he wrote to the Turnbull Library (National Library of New Zealand) when depositing his archive of unpublished material, by staying on Hydra he and Robyn embarked on a period whereby "many of the attitudes we had formed in New Zealand were greatly modified", and it seems that Wallis's island experiences continued to preoccupy him. He left to the Turnbull Library a trove of diaries, notebooks,

INTRODUCTION

personal correspondence and unpublished fiction, which offers a tantalising account of the day-to-day interactions between Hydra's expatriates, including the many personal dramas that played out amongst the group.

The documented account of the Wallises' second sojourn on Hydra differs from their first in that Redmond Wallis's diary for the later period, although deposited with the Turnbull Library, is inaccessible due to an embargo he requested on the grounds that "while there are some literary nuggets in it … there is material, particularly sexual, which probably needs to lie fallow for thirty or forty years". The key biographical elements from this period can, however, be pieced together from Wallis's correspondence and in particular the manuscript to his unfinished novel, *The Unyielding Memory*. (The title is gleaned from a quote from Friedrich Nietzsche's *Beyond Good and Evil* that serves as the novel's epigraph: "My memory says I have done this, my pride says I could not have done it. My memory yields"). The section of *The Unyielding Memory* dealing with Wallis's alter-ego character Nick Alwyn's first stay on the island includes sections transcribed almost exactly from Wallis's corresponding diary (altered to a third person point of view), and there are many indications in the manuscript that he employed the same method for the sections covering 1963 and 1964. Although the documents' claims can't entirely be taken at face value, they nevertheless provide a valuable first-hand account of contemporaneous origins, which can be confirmed and questioned by other evidence.

The Unyielding Memory is a rare document given Wallis's status as a key participant in the action described and its unvarnished account of numerous significant incidents and individuals who are only ever thinly disguised. The Wallises are recast as Nick and Sue Alwyn; Johnston and Clift appear as George and Catherine Grayson; Leonard Cohen is Saul Rubens; Marianne Ihlen is Margaretha; and the couple who would become close friends with the Wallises, Demetri and Carolyn Gassoumis, are Stephanos and Patricia Lamounis. Should there be any doubt as to 'who's who' of these or other characters, Wallis conveniently left with his manuscript a list headed 'Changes of names', which includes over sixty characters.

Wallis had long planned to write a novel based on his time on Hydra and seems to have worked on it at different periods in his life before eventually conceding that the task was beyond him. Certainly, a reading of the manuscript makes apparent his failure to extract a coherent narrative from its diary-bound origins, and although the archived draft (or, more accurately, drafts given that many chapters appear in variant forms) of *The Unyielding Memory* fails as fiction—or is, at best, a fiction that remains poorly realised and well short of completion—it nonetheless provides a rivetingly and, at times, witheringly personal account of life with Hydra's expatriates.

A privately-held archive of Wallis's photographs, some of which are included in *Half the Perfect World*, support the material found in the Turnbull Library. Wallis was a keen photographer who carried cameras that afforded high quality images. He also left notations and dates to accompany his photographs, which have been immensely helpful in identifying dates, locations and individuals.

A further photographic collection that has been important to *Half the Perfect World* is that associated with Johnston and Clift and which forms part of their shared archive in the National Library of Australia. This archive includes material from across the couple's lives, notably numerous photographs of them, their children, other Hydra expatriates and Hydriots. The photographs are largely uncredited and undated, although some include brief details mainly written on the reverse of developed images in Johnston's hand. We assume that most of the photographs were taken by Clift, Johnston and their children for use by the family and circulation among friends, but the collection also contains photographs that appear to have been provided to the Johnstons by others.

With its manifold attractions, it is little wonder that Johnston, Clift, Cohen, the Wallises, Burke and numerous others were drawn to Hydra. In the post-war years, the island offered an enticing balance between cheapness and chicness; a remoteness that was still sufficient to 'protect' against the worst ravages of modernity while within a daily commute of Athens; and an emerging

INTRODUCTION

Mediterranean stylishness crossed with a lingering 'authenticity', all of which more than compensated for the lack of modern conveniences and luxuries that were yet to reach this corner of the Mediterranean. Indeed, Hydra and other Greek islands attracted those looking for an island refuge such that Clift and Johnston were not the only Australians with writerly aspirations to find their way to the Aegean during this period. War hero Joice Loch lived with her husband, Sydney, in the region for many years, most notably in a coastal Byzantine tower on the Mount Athos peninsula as recalled in her 1968 memoir, *A Fringe of Blue*; novelist and historian (and Johnston's acquaintance) Alan Moorehead spent much of 1955 on the island of Spetses researching and writing his classic military history, *Gallipoli*; journalist Charles Sriber and his wife, Ruth, visited the Johnstons on Hydra on several occasions while living in Athens and then the island of Ikaria; writer and actor Kester Barwick lived on Lesbos and then Corfu for an extended period from 1960 (achieving belated 'fame' as the focus of Robert Dessaix's 2001 novel, *Corfu*); and playwright and novelist Betty Roland joined Berwick on Lesbos for some twelve months in 1960 and 1961, recording this period in her memoir *Lesbos: The Pagan Island* (1963).

As Mingos and Burke predicted, tourism to Hydra (and the wider Aegean) rapidly increased and broadened as the postwar Greek economy recovered and regional politics stabilised. As a result, this still poorly developed island, with its cast of struggling and impecunious artists, unexpectedly found itself a point of geographic desire for a rollcall of political and show business elites, minor celebrities, publicity-seeking bit players and island-hopping tourists. As Jorge Sotirios noted, "Hydra at its zenith photographed well" and served as a magnet for those who found benefit in associating with the glamour of newly 'discovered' Mediterranean destinations and being photographed on the island's spectacular dockside.

> Here was Jackie Kennedy alongside Aristotle Onassis, with just a small contingent of the yachting set: Melina Mercouri, Maria Callas, Audrey Hepburn too. In this natural amphitheatre they came as actors ready

to perform. Sentimental voyages, honeymoons, dirty weekends: Hydra seemed the place to pursue them.

Mass tourism led by cosmopolitan elites would be far from unique to Hydra among the Greek islands, but it took on a particular charge for Hydra's artist community, many of whom had been attracted to the island as a refuge from such blatant manifestations of commercialised modernity. And so it was that a particular moment in the island's life came and went, and the people who *made* that time moved on, leaving behind the images, words and memories shaped by their experiences.

For our purposes, the years of Hydra's artist colony are bookended by the near decade that Johnston and Clift were living on the island, a time that was crucial in their personal and creative lives as well as those of many others they encountered. What exactly the photographs and words left by Burke, Wallis and others 'tell' us about the period of Johnston and Clift's residency, is not absolutely clear-cut. In the case of Burke, the photojournalistic style he deployed over several weeks in the late summer of 1960 cannot be denied when those images are viewed, even after nearly sixty years. We can say, of course, "that *is* a picture of Johnston and Clift. That *is* a picture of Leonard Cohen. For that matter, that *is* a picture of a donkey." Yet the same pictures also reveal the truth of a claim made by Celia Lury, namely that "the photograph, more than merely representing, has taught us a way of seeing". What Burke's photographs teach us to see of Hydra and its international community of writers and artists is not Burke's unique vision alone. While Wilson Hicks, the former executive editor of *LIFE*, had left the magazine well before Burke was fleshing out his Hydra story, his ideas about photojournalism—"the photograph and the words that accompany it [should] constitute a single expressive statement or produce a unit of effect within the reader's consciousness"—shaped the style and ethos of the magazine, and indeed photojournalism, long after his departure. Yet Burke's photographs are not simply beholden to a house style. These images of and from the past can be read relatively independently of any known or preferred aesthetic intentions and the ostensible appearance of

INTRODUCTION

things at the same time that their history, verisimilitude and planned purpose are acknowledged and accounted for.

Half the Perfect World has shared interests with those that Burke proposed for his *LIFE* photo-essay, but it does not simply aim to finish the project Burke commenced any more than it can complete Wallis's manuscript of *The Unyielding Memory*. Rather, this book radiates out from Johnston and Clift to attend to both the "surface atmosphere [that] seems beat" and "the serious hardworking individuals in [the] artist group" and beyond to the broader social, political, technological and economic changes that were sweeping away the vestiges of postwar Europe. *Half the Perfect World* moves between the everyday and these wider historical contexts and borrows from the language of photography—'snapshots'—for its structuring principle. In doing so it seizes on moments, places and individuals and weaves observations and anecdotes around them that do not pretend or aim to tell the whole story of Hydra's expatriate community. Instead, the snapshots comprising the text, and those concluding each chapter—taken from Wallis's manuscript of *The Unyielding Memory*—are necessarily fragmentary like the photographs with which they share the page, focusing attention on things and people that might otherwise go unnoticed.

* * *

In two passages from *The Unyielding Memory*, Nick Alwyn (Redmond Wallis) recalls arriving on Hydra, encountering Australian writers George and Catherine Grayson, and setting out on his own literary—and personal —journey.

> *The Graysons were, in a way, responsible for the gamble Nick and Sue had taken; they had arrived on the island carrying packs, set to spend a couple of days before beginning the long trek back to London where their worldly goods and remaining money, sent on ahead, waited for them. They'd gotten off their boat at Naples, seen a bit of Italy, Corfu, Crete and*

Athens, and were seeing another Greek island, as they had promised themselves they would, before running for cover. George Grayson, supported by his wife, had suggested another possibility. The bottom line he had offered was simple: if you want to try, try now, while you can still afford to fail.

*

Someone perhaps less introverted than Nick, more aware of the environment in which he was living, for the first time and perhaps the only time, would have slowed down, arranged his day so that he could delve into what was going on, would even have worried less about completing his work, would have seen the loss of achievement more than balanced by the insights he was gaining, might even have seen what was going on as good copy, usable some time in the future; but Nick had always worked conscientiously, had never goofed off, had always been reliable and responsible, and was not about at this stage in his life to set himself a target—and announce it publicly—and then fail to reach it ... He was by now aware of the island's reputation. George had observed that it was a place that wrecked painters, but was good for writers, but that, he had discovered, had been short of the truth. It was a place, evidence and word of mouth suggested, where something happened to people when they decided to stay, a place where they lost the restraints of civilisation, where the foreign community was so small, so tightly knit, so thrown back on its own devices, that relationships broke up and reformed with new components, or split never to be put together, or split and came together again deeply scarred, but still working.

Chapter One

HYDRA: ISLAND AND TOWN

While Hydra has gained recent renown because of its association with the creative lives of mid-twentieth century expatriated writers and artists, it has a colourful history for other and arguably more important reasons, including playing a crucial part in shaping the modern, independent Greek nation. Due to a mix of geography and circumstance, the island's influence in the late-eighteenth and early-nineteenth centuries was massively greater than its modest size and rocky, barren demeanour would suggest. Indeed, although it boasts only one substantial town site, also known as Hydra or Hydra Port, the island has punched well above its weight in creating modern Greece.

The history of Hydra prior to the mid-twentieth century passed through several distinct periods. The first of these was the island's low-profile pre-history. While traces of occupation have been found reaching back to several centuries BC, the island made no impact during the period of Greek antiquity that was so influential in fashioning the political, legal, educational and cultural institutions of modern western societies. The island's shortage of tillable soil meant that early settlement was confined to the periphery, and, for many centuries, the small population fluctuated according to the incidence of disease, occurrence of regional wars and the movement of people through the Aegean. It is a testament to Hydra's inhospitable nature that it remained barely inhabited while being separated from the mainland of the Peloponnese peninsula by only a narrow stretch of easily navigable water. As a result, the island is entirely devoid of the classical ruins and antiquities that are a feature of other Greek islands and the nearby mainland.

From 1204 to 1566, Hydra was an outpost of the Venetian Republic before becoming part of the expanding Ottoman Empire. It was under Ottoman rule that the island entered a new period of its history with a rapid growth in population as Albanian refugees fled Turkish oppression during the late-sixteenth and seventeenth centuries. For reasons of security, these Albanian settlers occupied the high sites above the current port in an area now known as Kiaffa. Hydra gradually assumed greater importance during the course of the eighteenth century when use was made of its strategic location and the safety of several small harbours to create a centre for shipbuilding. As the Hydriots developed their skills and built ever-larger vessels, they were able to extend their influence beyond the Aegean. By the end of the eighteenth century, the island was a major regional centre for maritime trade, and, with some of the most advanced shipping available, Hydra's merchants traded as far afield as western Europe and the Americas. The island's economic power grew further as treaties between the Ottomans and Russia opened up new trade routes through the Bosphorus Strait and the Black Sea, and even greater wealth followed as the Hydriots used their maritime supremacy for blockade running in the Mediterranean during the Napoleonic Wars. By 1820 the island had acquired not only financial power but also significant political influence.

Things changed again for Hydra with the Greek War of Independence from 1821 to 1832. Hydra's navy, together with the navies of the nearby islands of Spetses and Psara to the east, was responsible for undertaking the maritime war against the Ottomans for control of the Aegean. At the outbreak of hostilities, Hydra's population had risen to approximately thirty thousand (by some estimates forty thousand) at a time when Athens was little more than a village with a population of around three thousand, and the war was largely underwritten by the manpower, shipping, and finances that the island provided. When victory was eventually secured, Hydra's admirals and patriots, such as Andreas Miaoulis, Iakovos Tombazi and Lazaros Coundouriotis, were among the first heroes of the newly independent Greek nation. The price paid for victory nearly bankrupted the island and its wealthiest families.

HYDRA: ISLAND AND TOWN

When Irish politician and diplomat James Emerson, a supporter of Greek independence, visited Hydra in 1825, he provided a detailed account of the activity and life in Hydra Port during the War of Independence. Alongside the record of the military activity and diplomatic wrangling that took place when the island was at the high point of its naval and political influence, Emerson also reports on the town's physical appearance, indicating that two centuries ago Hydra Port had acquired the distinctive visual appeal that endures into the twenty-first century.

> The town, on approaching it from the sea, presents an extremely beautiful prospect; its large white houses rise up suddenly from the sea, along the precipitous cliffs which form the harbour; every little crag displayed the white sails of an immense number of windmills, and every peak was bristling with a battery. In the background, the ragged and barren summits of the rock which formed the Island, with scarce a speck of cultivation or a single tree, are crowned with numerous monasteries.

Emerson was one of those who George Johnston would later refer to as "a select group of classically-educated Baedeker travellers who had revelled in [the island's] precipitous climbs and the magnificence of its views". English landscape artist William Linton was another of this "select group" who shared Emerson's love of Hydra's picturesque and romantic qualities that so appealed to the early nineteenth-century temperament. Linton toured Greece in both the 1830s and 1840s and recorded the spectacular vista of Hydra in 1856 when he published his engravings in *The Scenery of Greece and Its Islands*. Like Emerson, Linton was struck by the town's physical appearance, praising both the dramatically formed site and the imposing houses that scrambled for views as the town rose away from the harbour.

> It looks like a galaxy of marble palaces, rising from the recesses of two bays, tier above tier, to a great height; each roof seemingly a terrace to the dwelling above. A bold rocky promontory, crested with windmills

View of Hydra, c.1840. (James Linton)

Hydra windmill, c.1960. (Redmond Wallis)

> carrying numberless sails, projects into the sea from the midst, and ends in a precipitous bluff, with a ruined round tower on its summit.

Nearly two centuries later, the many windmills noted by Emerson and Linton have been greatly reduced in number, and the defensive batteries have either fallen into ruin or had their cannons reduced to decorative ornaments. But these nineteenth-century visitors would nonetheless immediately recognise modern Hydra as the town they knew. The second of the "two bays" referred to by Linton is Mandraki, which lies to the east of Hydra's harbour and was the centre of the island's boatbuilding in the nineteenth century. Today it remains a much-reduced outpost of Hydra Port that is serviced by a coastal pathway. To the west of Hydra Port, and almost as an extension of the main townsite, lies Kamini with its own attractive small fishing harbour. Kamini is reached by either a short coastal walk or a high road leading up from the south-western corner of the Hydra dock.

Not only would the cost of the war for independence take a substantial toll on Hydra, but prospects for economic recovery were dashed when postwar treaties created greater competition for shipping throughout the Mediterranean. As a result, the new Greek nation began to separate economically from the islands that had provided the financial muscle needed to defeat the Ottomans. In its weakened state, Hydra failed to keep pace with developments in shipbuilding, particularly in the use of steam and steel hulls, and the island and its population fell into economically hard times. In the absence of agriculture, the Hydriots again turned to the sea, and fishing for sponge off the North African coast became the mainstay of the island's economy from the second half of the nineteenth century. This also proved to have a limited life when Egypt substantially reduced the available sponge diving area in 1932 due to declining stock. Soon after, the introduction of synthetic sponge further diminished the struggling industry.

Hydra's illustrious past and the parlous state of its economy were both recounted by Henry Miller in his highly impressionistic travel memoir *The Colossus of Maroussi* in which he reported on his journeys through Greece on the eve of the Second World War. Miller was struck by Hydra's physical appearance, in particular the abundance of rock to which he attributed the island's unique existential appeal.

> The very rocks, and nowhere on earth has God been so lavish with them as in Greece, are symbols of life eternal. In Greece the rocks are eloquent: men may go dead but the rocks never. At a place like Hydra, for example, one knows that when a man dies he becomes part of his native rock. But this rock is a living rock, a divine wave of energy suspended in time and space, creating a pause of long or short duration in the endless melody. Hydra was entered as a pause in the musical score of creation by an expert calligrapher. It is one of those divine pauses which permit the musician when he resumes the melody, to go forth again in a totally new direction.

While Miller's idiosyncratic travelogue, with its effusive account of Greek lands and people as being close to the essence of a fulfilled life and an antidote to the relentless march of industrialisation and urbanisation, might not have been widely read when published in 1941, it was at least read by the 'right' audience. Miller's reputation ensured the book was picked up by intellectually ambitious and socially aware readers to whom the American writer represented a voice of resistance against the powerful engines of technological and commercial modernity that seemed destined to thrive in the aftermath of the Second World War. While Miller's time on Hydra was brief, his stirring account of the island and the region influenced many who were looking for more personally empowering and communally engaged alternatives in a postwar world. (Miller had acquired his awe-struck appreciation of Greece from his close friend English novelist Lawrence Durrell who moved to Corfu with his extended family in the 1930s. Miller preceded his travels through Greece by spending time with Durrell on Corfu. Durrell's 1945 memoir, *Prospero's Cell,* would further imprint for western readers a view of Greece as *the place* in which the over-stimulated urbanised mind could be cleansed of the clamour of modernity and reconnected to the abundant sensual and physical pleasures of *living*. Miller's and Durrell's books were landmarks in the development of a particular neo-romantic view of Greece that was quite uncritically imbibed by the west and that by the 1960s would be driving the Aegean tourism boom).

George Johnston had certainly read Henry Miller. In his island-based novel *Closer to the Sun*, he describes an argument between brothers David and Mark Meredith in which they disagree about the reasons for David's expatriation to an island modelled on Hydra, which is given the fictional name of Silenos. David argues the case for his expatriation in terms familiar to readers of *The Colossus of Maroussi*, proclaiming that he is "learning to know something about the light and shadow on rocks against the sky, the true taste of water, the rhythms of seasons, the values of simplicity". It is an argument that is immediately dismissed by Mark as "pseudo-poetic Henry Miller guff!"

Notwithstanding Miller's rhapsodic description, prospects for Hydra, and for Greece, continued to be bleak when the Second World War finally wound to a halt in the Mediterranean. Greece's desperate need for postwar economic and social recovery was thwarted by a period of civil war (1945–1949), which saw the government, backed by the UK and the US, fight a bitter war against the communist-supported Democratic Army of Greece. As the 1950s rolled into the 1960s, Greece remained not only politically riven but also left behind as western European economies prospered from massive international investment; infusions of new industrial and agricultural technology; and, in many cases, labour that drifted from Greece in search of opportunities. As historian Kostis Kornetis has described Greece during this the period:

> In structural terms, the country was still suffering from economic underdevelopment and social backwardness. Its socioeconomic outlook was comprised of a dominant peasantry, a relatively weak working class, a large petty bourgeoisie, an oligarchy of compradors, and a small-scale commodity-type production, coupled with delayed industrialization.

While economic prospects remained bleak, tourism offered hope for rebuilding island economies, and as a potential tourist destination, Hydra possessed several important advantages. The island's location in the Saronic

Hydra harbour, c.1960. (Redmond Wallis)

Gulf, only thirty-seven nautical miles from the port of Piraeus, made it very accessible from Athens. In the postwar period, the daily ferry would make the one-way journey in a little over three hours, and that time was halved in the 1970s with the addition of hydrofoil services. The island is also easily reached by smaller craft operating from the Peloponnese peninsula.

In terms of its touristic potential, Hydra was also singularly graced by its small harbour. It is difficult to overstate the impact of the harbour—frequently described as 'crescent' or 'horse-shoe' shaped—upon Hydra's history, development and tourist appeal. Not only did the harbour provide a spur to the island's earlier industry and prosperity, but its physical beauty has since underwritten Hydra's attraction as an island destination of choice. Despite its modest scale, the harbour is immediately appealing because it's both remarkably well formed and superbly matched to the contours of the surrounding town and the mountainous backdrop. Fringed by a broad dockside and a long line of cafés, taverns and shops, above which rise the town's boldly geometric houses and churches, the harbour provides an enticing setting for those wanting to live out fantasies of Greek island life.

Hydra's touristic credentials were also abetted by a largely 'unspoilt' atmosphere attractive to those looking to experience an 'authentic' Greek island. The island's lack of development since the first quarter of the nineteenth century meant that it retained the atmosphere of a traditional trading port within a naturally spectacular setting. In *Peel Me a Lotus*, Charmian Clift couldn't help but to draw upon the town's distinctive and 'untouched' visual appeal as a key element of its attractiveness:

> In appearance, the town today must be almost exactly what it was in the days of the merchant princes, for practically no houses have been built in the last one hundred and twenty years. It rises in tiers around a small, brilliant, horseshoe-shaped harbour—old stone mansions harmoniously apricot-coloured against the gold and bronze cliffs, or washed pure white and shuttered in palest grey: houses austere but exquisitely proportioned, whose great walls and heavy arched doors enclose tiled courtyards and terraced gardens. The irregular tiers are broken everywhere by steep, crooked flights of stone steps, and above the tilted rooftops of uniform red tiles rise the octagonal domes of the churches and the pierced and fretted verticals of marble spires that might have been designed by Wren. Above the town the mountains shoot up sheer, their gaunt surfaces unbroken except for an odd white mill or two, a field of grain standing on end, a dark patch of fir-trees, and three monasteries, the highest of them so close to heaven that at night its lights are looped among the stars.

Photographers, both professional and amateur, have found it easy to produce images that reflect the vista described by Clift, with James Burke and Redmond Wallis both recording the appealingly tiered houses rising from the harbour in a similar fashion.

Hydra. (James Burke)

Hydra, c.1960. (Redmond Wallis)

The wine boat approaching Hydra's dockside and mansions. (James Burke)

Clift's account goes on to note that Hydra's beauty had been effectively protected by the falling population and the resulting lack of modernising disturbance to the town's fabric. More recently, stringent planning laws have further stalled development or the altering of the town's essential characteristics that were firmly established during its 'golden age'. While new housing has been added since Clift and Johnston arrived in the mid-1950s, this has been confined to the town's existing footprint and in the form of sympathetically built new houses on sites that were left vacant as older houses fell into disrepair. Attempts at more intensive development, such as a 'Caribbean-style' resort proposed by entrepreneur Richard Branson, have been repelled in the recent past, and while discreet redevelopment transforms the lanes, modifies buildings and makes the old new again, Hydra Port's historic form remains hardly altered.

As Clift touched upon with her reference to the "old stone mansions", Hydra's housing stock is far from ordinary. The most obvious legacy of the island's period of maritime supremacy and wealth was a supply of spectacular houses almost unmatched in the Aegean. These were imposing, powerfully geometric, multi-storeyed mansions, which were built as family homes by the island's admirals and merchant princes. Designed and constructed by Venetian craftsmen, the houses displayed Italian more than Greek influences, and they boasted large internal spaces, impressive porticos, monumental doorways and internal fittings of the richest materials. Most were erected in the late eighteenth and early nineteenth centuries as Hydra went through its period of rapid growth that bequeathed to the island not only the impressive mansion-sized houses of the great mercantile families, but also the numerous very fine, if slightly smaller, houses of the well-remunerated sea captains and lesser merchants.

By the mid-twentieth century, Hydra's economic travails meant that a number of the mansions faced an uncertain future. While some remained in the hands of the families who built them, others had been abandoned and fallen into disrepair. And while the town's visual harmony was enhanced by the houses, streets and many stairways crafted from island stone, Clift noted that even large houses, unless well maintained, would soon return to the rubble from which they were constructed.

> What at first appear to be gaps of virgin mountain rock among the terraces usually reveal themselves—by a piece of carved marble, a Turkish inscription, a tarnished bronze door-knocker lying among the stones—as the foundations of great houses, tiers of houses, terraces of houses, hundreds of houses, long since sunk back to their elements.
>
> On winter nights when the wind whines I find myself listening for the last wild scream of the wrenched shutter, the last sad groan of the subsiding wall, as another house returns, stone to stone and dust to dust, from which it was first so proudly made.

But whether it was the mansions, the less-imposing 'captains' houses', or the modest abodes of the working Hydriots, mid-twentieth-century Hydra, by virtue of its diminished population, had an oversupply of housing. As a result, both purchase prices and rents were extraordinarily cheap and, by the 1950s, made the island a target for Athenians looking for substantial holiday homes, or 'weekenders', and for travellers or long-term visitors searching for houses or rooms to rent—many with astonishing vistas—at very affordable prices.

It is not surprising that Hydra Port's basic topographical layout of houses rising dramatically in semicircular tiers away from the harbour, and the flat expanse of the dockside, has frequently provoked comparison to the classical amphitheatres that dot the Greek islands and mainland. Miller reported that the town "clusters about the harbor in the form of an amphitheatre"; Aristomidos Sofianos noted in his mid-1960s book, *Hydra*, that the town is "Built all around the harbour like a great amphitheatre"; and Leonard Cohen's biographer Sylvie Simmons commented that "the island looked like a Greek amphitheatre, its houses like white-clad elders sitting upright in the tiers".

It is an amphitheatre adorned with a natural stage in the form of the wide flat space of the dockside *agora*, a remarkably intimate space fringed by the close ranks of harbour-side bars, taverns and shops, to which locals, expats, workers and tourists alike are irresistibly drawn by necessity or desire. Intimacy is something that Hydra does profoundly well. The town's only point of entry is by boat into the comforting welcome of the small harbour, with houses rising in a precipitous embrace above the dockside on all three sides and cosseted by the monastery-clad uplands. This sense of intimacy is completed by the view from the dockside out beyond the harbour, where the eye rests not on open water but on the reassuring presence of the not-too-distant hills of the Peloponnese.

In his nineteenth-century account, Emerson described "The quay, [which] for the entire sweep of the harbour, is lined with storehouses and shops", and this dockside stretch of buildings remains hardly changed nearly two centuries later. In the early nineteenth century, these harbour-side buildings were needed to serve a busy naval and mercantile port and, as a result, they were set well back from the dockside, creating a broad platform that catered to both the business of maritime trade and the shopping and recreational needs of the population. An intense array of dockside commerce is not uncommon in the Greek islands, but it reaches a particularly picturesque pitch in Hydra

Hydra dockside. (James Burke)

due to the distinctive shape and scale of the harbour; the broad and gently arcing dockside; the rugged and precipitous backdrop; and the resoundingly handsome presence of the dockside buildings. Many of those buildings have been adapted in the twentieth century to meet the demands made by tourists and leisure-seekers, but this has done little to alter the relationship between the harbour, the dock and the town, and the natural focus on the broad sweep of the *agora*.

The Hydra dockside, the *agora*, is a natural stage built for display, where the town breaks suddenly from its narrow, shadowed streets, high-walled courtyards and vine-clad trellises into the full splendour of the Aegean sunshine. It is where generations of locals and visitors alike have gravitated, certain of having both something to see and of being seen. Not surprisingly it is on the *agora* where Hydra's long-established social ritual, the evening *volta*, or promenade, takes place at day's end as the heat wains and locals and visitors move away from the indoors, courtyards and awnings to enjoy the evening passage around Hydra's stage. It was a ritual described by Clift in *Peel Me a Lotus*:

HYDRA: ISLAND AND TOWN

Shane and Jason Johnston (2&3-L) and friends enjoy the *volta*. (James Burke)

After supper, Friday and her friends make a formal promenade around the arc of the port, from the museum, past the shops and stalls and restaurants, as far as the cannon above the cave and then back again. The girls walk in twos and threes and fours, tenderly linked with soft arms clasped around flowery waists, and each cascade of shining hair caught with a white ribbon or a gilt butterfly. The gymnasium boys are out promenading too, but walking very slowly and lordly, swinging their key-chains and *kombollois*, each with a Cyprus badge in his lapel and his gold-braided cap set straight above his eyes …

All the more mature citizens are parading in groups, family groups almost as formal as the photographs on their walls. The matrons wear coats and skirts and high heels and carry patent leather purses which they clasp against their comfortable stomachs. The children are clean and well dressed and the little girls have huge starched bows perched on their heads.

Modern Hydra has also been distinctively blessed (from a tourist's point of view) by the complete absence of motorised transport. Of the populated Greek islands, Hydra alone maintains a carefully regulated resistance not only to cars but also motorbikes and bicycles. Donkeys, mules and hand-drawn carts remain the only means by which goods and people are transported to the town's upper reaches. The narrow streets and lanes of the town are constructed from small-scale cobblestone and were built to accommodate nothing wider than beasts of burden passing in opposite directions. This novelty of a town without cars has increasingly added to Hydra's romantic appeal as a 'real' Greek island experience.

Hydra's lack of vehicles is not only aesthetically pleasing, but it also helps the town achieve something else common to the best (amphi)theatres—great sound. In this regard, the natural shape of the landform is also important—something akin to a giant orchestra shell that holds sound in the air and sends it ricocheting off the hard surfaces of walls and rooftops and along the enclosed laneways. Without competition from vehicles and with little other mechanised noise, the clarity of sound further heightens the intimacy by bringing neighbours close and the dockside into every home. As poet Steve Sanfield reported in his diary when visiting his friend Leonard Cohen in 1963:

> The sounds of Hydra are all alive. They are the sounds of life—birds chirping, women screaming, children laughing, donkeys braying, cats fucking. Everything is sudden, spontaneous, & full of the reality of living. The sounds of the city, of 'civilization' are absent here. There is no traffic, no muffled grinding of machines, no all pervading music. The only intrusions are from the outside, specifically from the boat whistles, which seem to be constructed with intruding as their major objective.

Clift's account in *Peel Me a Lotus* is also constantly enlivened by the sounds of everyday living that rise with clarity and find their way into her house.

> Through the hot stillness sounds come distinctly—a splash of oars, the sharp yelp of the dog Max protesting against a bath, the children's voices calling away, and from the village the clear, bright sound of a single bell.

Good light is yet another expectation of great theatres, and again Hydra does not disappoint. American philosopher Daniel Klein recently described the theatrical quality of Hydra's light as he gazed into the backyards, kitchens and lives of his island neighbours, noting that "the celebrated trick of Hydra light" is that "it transforms daily life into intimate theatre".

> [H]ere on the island, even when the sky is as cloudy as it is today, every view is severe with detail. The shadow of a rock a mile off on the Peloponnesian shore appears as well defined as a lemon tree just outside my window. And because Hydra rises from the main port in a steep, horseshoe-shaped hill that is girded with houses, everyone is an innocent spectator to private scenes in remote courtyards and terraces.

As Klein observes, nearly every house in Hydra has a view—perhaps not the high perch and uninterrupted vista claimed by the island's mansions, but nonetheless views over rooftops and between walls, down to the houses and courtyards below, and beyond to the *agora* and to the harbour, the gulf and the Peloponnese. Redmond Wallis had found that, even when renting in 1960 for an exceedingly modest two hundred drachma a month, he could afford a house with views of the port from two rooms and views to hills behind—certainly not the broad sweep provided from the terraces of the great houses, but nonetheless tantalising glimpses of both the life-filled dockside and sun-drenched island.

While the town might be oriented to the water, Wallis found that views also take in the mountainside and hilltop, and the stern demeanour of rock rising above is as ever-present as the glittering promise of the Aegean below. (The island's high point, Mt Ere, rises directly above Hydra Port to just under two thousand feet). As Henry Miller had noted, the island's ruggedly mountainous interior is powerfully present, penetrating the town at many points with rocky outcrops thrusting alongside, between and even into houses, where they are often used as natural walls. Dense stands of prickly pear also wander down from the hillsides to take up unfilled plots, a further reminder of the inhospitable nature of the island that presses the town against its watery

View on a budget from the Wallises' rented house, 1960. (Redmond Wallis)

limit. And as Klein reported of his own view, even the structure of Hydra's windows seemed to be designed to highlight the competing attractions of the external spaces.

> In the whitewashed nineteenth-century house where I am staying, all the windows are screened with two crossed iron bars. 'To keep the Turks out,' some islanders say. 'To keep Albanian pirates out,' say others. Clearly these iron bars work: neither Turk nor Albanian has clambered into my room. The bars do not obscure the view from my desk window; rather they frame it into four discrete images: a Hill studded with houses in one frame, a grove of almond trees in another, the harbour, the sea.

Certainly Clift and Johnston, from their captain's house, enjoyed the benefit of a far reaching view from the upper rooms and a rooftop terrace where, reputedly, the captain's wife awaited the return of her seafaring husband and celebrated by firing a small cannon as he safely entered the harbour. Clift is drawn in *Peel Me A Lotus* to describe the intimacy of the household views, in this case as seen from the five windows of the upstairs room used by Johnston as his studio, and from where

> flights of neglected stone stairs leap up out of the lanes all about: from this strange room they might ascend to heaven. Mule-trains descend, bearing mountain brushwood, water tanks, planks of pale new wood; two children climb up slowly, hand in hand, and turn on the stair to look into the room; our Mrs. Silk appears, mumbling and prodding with her staff as she searches still for Sophia among the weeds exposed on a sunny wall. You feel that you have only to blink your eyes once and the hooves of the mules will be lifting delicately over the window-sill.

Clift also wrote of the view-enhancing quality of the Hydra light, seeing it as a welcome by-product of the abundant sunshine and clear air that had attracted her and Johnston to the Aegean as they waited out their tedious years in smog-bound London. To Clift, however, the clarity of light became more than simply an ambient novelty or sightseeing convenience but, rather, a talisman of the couple's quest for existential renewal.

> Sprawled inert under the great warm melting waves of light, I was glad that we had chosen to live in the sun. To live in the sun is reassuring. All is open, all revealed. Here are no deceptions, but the bare truth of things … It seems to me that we have become simplified too, living here, as though the sun has seared off the woolly fuzz of our separate confusions: the half desires irresolutely sought, the half-fears never more than half vanquished, the partial attainments half-rejected in perplexed dissatisfaction.

As Clift related, not only do the high views, clear light and close living make everyone a spectator, but they also make them players, where the other members of the cast also serve as the audience for the town's everyday dramas:

APRIL

House-proud Hydriots, *Peel Me a Lotus*. (Nancy Dignan)

One had not realized … that there were quite so many houses overlooking ours. Twenty windows round are private boxes filled with unabashed women and children, who jostle each other in their eagerness to see the curious spectacle of George at his typewriter. The terrace opening off the studio might as well be a public stage—and there go all my plans for nude sunbathing … If the neighbours' windows are the private boxes the school is the gallery, and the gallery is vociferous with enthusiasm.

All that was needed to complete this great theatre of Hydra were the actors, and by the 1950s and 1960s, the island had no shortage of players willing to take their part. As accounts from the time testify, the dramas (or melodramas) of the *agora* were enacted by a cast who thrived on public display for their talk, arguments, disagreements, romantic entanglements and disentanglements. In this they were led, and likely schooled, by the Johnstons.

Johnston and Clift were both carrying deep emotional scars by the time they reached Hydra. Johnston had a poorly resolved previous marriage and had not seen his daughter since she was a young child; had seemingly incurred long-term war trauma—what would now be called post-traumatic stress—and was doing battle with a longstanding personal unrest that bordered on self-loathing. Clift was troubled by dysfunctional relationships within her own family; the psychological aftermath of relinquishing her first born; and a complex desire for the admiration of men.

Johnston and Clift's relationship and marriage had been grounded not only in an immediate personal attraction but also in a mutual recognition of each other's emotional fragility. The couple instinctively knew how, and how easily, they could hurt and wound each other. They were both given to great passions and intense emotional responses, and with scant tolerance for indifference in themselves or others, there was little scope for compromise in their relationship. The London years had left that relationship in a vulnerable state—the result of their disenchantment with the grim postwar metropolis; an office affair conducted by Johnston; and Clift's frustration with being bound to motherhood at the expense of her writing. Moving to the Aegean and committing to their literary dreams temporarily relieved the interpersonal tensions, but living on Hydra also produced great dangers from the outset—particularly in what little opportunity the island provided for these two ardent and brittle personalities to get relief from each other, as their personal, working, and social lives played out repetitively within the intense confines of their house and the *agora*.

Johnston and Clift were nothing if not expressive about their emotional states. Fuelled by alcohol, their private dramas and battles constantly spilled over onto the public arena of the dockside taverns and *kafenia*. Irish writer Patrick Greer was witness to many of the couple's 'performances', reporting that "They needed the conjugal drama, preferably a public quayside enactment of it. Whether they were conscious of the desire, or drama occurred in spite of themselves, it was difficult to know." Johnston and Clift were entirely not alone in this regard—their arrival merely signalled the beginning of a time when public spectacle by Hydra's expatriates and visitors would become part of the island's intrigue.

HALF THE PERFECT WORLD

* * *

Redmond Wallis describes the physical appearance (and a little history) of Hydra Port.

> *The island lay long the eastern flank of the Peloponnisos like a shark, long, and grey. It had only one town, a semi-circle of tightly packed white blocks, interspersed with the brown of ruins, spilling up from its horseshoe harbour like the dried spume of a seventh wave. A long mole turned the horseshoe into an almost completed D. A century before the entrance had been closed each night by a giant chain; the tips of the semi-circle that protruded beyond the mole had ancient cannon mounted on them.*
>
> *The agora—the market place—was effectively the horseshoe, though near the harbour entrance it tailed off into administrative offices and a naval school and at the opposite end into the unpaved road that wound around the coast, high above the sea, and then descended to a cluster of houses called Kamini. Just before the road turned out of sight above the bathing rocks at Spelia, the town slaughter house fed blood and unwanted guts into the clear, blue sea.*
>
> *A monastery was placed centrally on the agora, its square bell tower containing four clock faces and topped by a flagpole from which flew the blue and white flag of Greece. Yachts moored at the mole, fishing boats and cargo caiques at the edge of the agora: the island ferry dropped its gangplank just inside the entrance below the naval school.*
>
> *The island had once been rich: now most of the great houses built by the blockade runners were closed and many of the whitewashed houses once occupied by their captains and crews were empty, even derelict. Sponge-fishing caiques still left each April, with the first north winds, for the beds at Benghazi and Derna, but the trade was a dying one. The island needed a new industry, new life.*

Chapter Two

TO SPITI TOU JOHNSTON: THE AUSTRALIAN HOUSE

It is fitting that Charmian Clift's opening words of *Peel Me a Lotus* report that "Today we bought the house by the well". If there was a single decision that determined the fate of herself and George Johnston for the next decade and shaped the lives of many others who drifted into the circle of the island's expatriates during this time, it was this seemingly commonplace decision to buy a house. By purchasing their own piece of island real estate, Clift and Johnston demonstrated that there was another way to experience the Aegean other than by joining the growing throng of short-term holiday-makers and island-hoppers. It was a declaration that they were here to stay.

In choosing to settle on Hydra, the Johnstons ensured that the house became a key element of both the practical and mythical aspects of their residency. Practical because, without *to spiti tou* Johnston, it is unlikely they could have sustained their expatriation. Lacking a regular income and depending on the occasional publisher's advance or royalties, the couple would have been unlikely to meet even the modest rents required on the island, with landlords being less generous than shopkeepers when it came to extending credit. It was the house—or, as it became known, the 'Australian House'—which centred their time on the island, providing the security they needed to ride out the maelstrom of a decade of frequent near-poverty, ill-health, interpersonal battles, disappointing sales and the insecurities that flowed from their unrealised creative ambitions. And mythical because the house came to symbolise Clift and Johnston's foothold in the Mediterranean dreamscape—the solid foundation that expressed their commitment to values other than the rapacious postwar modernity and conformity they had rejected in Sydney and London. It was the home they made for themselves and for their children and the house to which so many of the island's visitors found their way by invitation, strategy or chance. It was the place where wandering artists, writers and itinerants would find a meal, a bed and a helping hand; solicit introductions to local landlords, shopkeepers, tavern owners and enablers; and leave knowing they had made it to the inner circle of Hydra's expatriate colony.

It was also within the house where the practical and the mythical became enmeshed through the couple's creativity—where they wrote the thirteen books that allowed them to retain a tenuous grip on their island lifestyle and the fourteenth book that permitted, indeed induced, them to repatriate to Australia. In turn, it is a house to which Australians have long gravitated—both while Clift and Johnston were in residence, in the hope of 'dropping in' on these celebrated runaways; and in steady numbers in the half-century and more since, in the search for a glimpse or remnant of what is increasingly seen as a bold and romantic commitment to freedom, beauty and creativity.

The renown of the Australian House was sealed when Clift wrote about it at length in *Peel Me a Lotus*, wherein its discovery, purchase and tentative renovation become a talisman of the general good fortune that befalls the family in their first year on Hydra. *Peel Me a Lotus* might be rife with intimations of trouble ahead, but it is also buoyant with the optimism of a new home, new baby and new friends—indeed, the promise of a new way of life, and for Clift, this sense of a re-*naissance* was intimately connected to the house.

The Johnstons started looking for a permanent house on Hydra in late 1955 under the pressure of Clift's advancing pregnancy. Clift recalled that the search took some "three months of panting up and down steps, through lanes and arches and alleys, into courtyards and out". The length of time it took to find the right house did not reflect a shortage of houses for sale. By the mid-twentieth century, insofar as Hydra had any reputation, it was for the signature mansions that were the foremost reminder of the island's illustrious past.

TO SPITI TOU JOHNSTON: THE AUSTRALIAN HOUSE

Martin Johnston and James Barclay (obscured) play at the well in front of the Australian House. (James Burke)

However, as Clift noted, although the house they eventually purchased was substantial, it was also of a lesser scale than the great mansions.

> The house we have bought is not one of the grand houses of the island. Would that it were … Ours is in the second category of houses; that is to say, not the house of a merchant prince or renowned admiral, but of a prosperous sea-captain. It lies in the village behind the waterfront, beyond the little church of St Constantine, and below the crag where the Down School is perched so impossibly Up. It occupies one side of a small cobbled square, in the centre of which is a well of rather brackish water, reputed to never run dry.

As with many of the town wells, the water was unsuitable for drinking. Hydra's only reliable supply of drinking water at the time came from *Kala Pigadia*, the good wells (or "sweet wells" as Clift called them) much higher above the dockside. In times of need, the island's water supplies were supplemented by shipments from the mainland, but, either way, obtaining water meant the inconvenience of either carrying it down from the wells or taking delivery from the water carrier working with his mule.

As Clift noted, the house stood close to the school and this proximity may have been another attraction—Clift later recalled she was close enough to hear the children reciting their lessons as she went about her housework. Johnston was also apparently much pleased to learn that the house had been built in 1788, the year the British first 'settled' in Australia, and a coincidence that made its designation as the 'Australian House' all that more apposite.

The house had been unoccupied for sixteen years when Clift and Johnston came upon it, with Clift writing that they found it "still, dark, secret, odorous, waiting". The purchase was not made without considerable anguish about both the commitment and the cost. This was the first property that either Clift or Johnston would own, and the common sense (or otherwise) of making this decision so soon after arriving on the island troubled them. The asking price was one hundred and twenty gold pounds, or, as Clift noted, "six hundred and twenty Australian pounds, or about thirteen hundred [US] dollars". For the price, they acquired a substantial house spread over three floors with views of the harbour from several of its nine sunny rooms, plus a spacious rooftop terrace. It also had, by Hydra standards, a large courtyard garden. Despite these attractions, Clift conceded that "the purchase was lunacy in any currency" given their generally impecunious circumstances; the possibility that they may find themselves to be the only English speakers on the island; the lack of health care important to a young family; and their isolation from the great cities of Europe to which they remained attracted.

Why then did they go ahead? Firstly, as Clift noted, although exorbitant given the couple's uncertain income, the price nonetheless represented a

Shane Johnston (back left) with classmates taking part in a flag ceremony at school.
(James Burke)

bargain when for the same sum in England or Australia, they "would scarcely buy an outhouse". It is also likely that the motivation was no more complex than the atavistic desire to own a slice of their newly found paradise. Not only had the couple discovered Hydra to be immediately appealing, but they were also drawn to the physical appearance of the house itself and its undeniably attractive setting on the small square. In Johnston's novel *Closer to the Sun*, David Meredith expresses obvious pride in "his house by the well above the Church of the Virgin", describing it as "square and white and uncompromising", and how "an accident of placement and proportion made it beautiful". The house's position is certainly important to both its visual and practical appeal in a town where streets are narrow and many houses adjoin their neighbours. In contrast, the Australian House stands proudly independent and with sufficient space in which to convey its solidly handsome presence. Unusual for Hydra, it is possible to walk around the house, and high walls define the property, making it an 'island' within the island. It is also conveniently close to the commercial and social attractions of the harbour, and, sitting on the least precipitous of the routes away from the dockside, it is reached by a gentle incline rather than the steep stairways required elsewhere.

The purchase of the house was also a decision that could be justified in terms of the couple's shared narrative built on the grand gesture of giving up the financial security they had in Sydney and London and relocating for beauty and art. It was a way of declaring (to the naysayers in London and Australia; to the Hydriots; and perhaps, most importantly, to each other) their commitment to the island, to their artistic lives, and to making this 'experiment' work. As Clift wrote, "When one has had a lifetime's conditioning in terms of building societies, insurance policies, and second mortgages it *does* seem to be a reckless romantic thing that the first piece of earth one has ever owned in all the world should be Greek earth". The house was therefore both a symbolic and practical commitment to themselves and their future together. The Johnstons' eight months on Kalymnos had gone some way to rekindling their personal wellbeing, their marriage, and their writing, and, with Clift

TO SPITI TOU JOHNSTON: THE AUSTRALIAN HOUSE

Charmian Clift and George Johnston at the entry to their courtyard.
(James Burke)

Happy days on Hydra.
Martin Johnston, George Johnston and Charmian Clift, c.1955.
(Johnston and Clift Collection)

now pregnant, the move to Hydra must have left them feeling that the purchase of the house culminated their rebirth as a couple. Clift in particular took to the house as a means by which she and Johnston could extend their creativity in new ways, by shaping a crucible for their family, their writing and their future. As she wrote:

> What pleasure one had in thinking, here I will make something very beautiful, here will be cleanliness and order and warmth and comfort, here where there is only an old dilapidated house there will be a home, a refuge, and my own light will shine on my own bit of creation.

TO SPITI TOU JOHNSTON: THE AUSTRALIAN HOUSE

The Australian House became a fixture of Clift and Johnston's Hydra story from soon after it was acquired. While details about their island life would trickle into the Australian media over the coming years, the first account appeared in the May 14th, 1958 issue of *People* and emphasised the purchase of the house. The article, by Johnston's Athens-based journalist friend Charles Sriber, opened with a distillation of the couple's myth so concise that it was almost certainly narrated by Johnston himself.

> Three years ago an Australian journalist living in London threw in a brilliant career and went with his wife and two children to live on a rocky Greek island.
>
> The family had little money and no promise of getting any. But both husband and wife had a great deal of hope. They wanted to make their living as writers and to pass their days in a community free of most of the strains and fears of modern civilisation.
>
> The husband is George Johnston formerly of Melbourne and Sydney, and his wife is Charmian Clift of Kiama … The story of their struggle and success is a modern romance.

Sriber then relates the story of Clift and Johnston's success, including the sale of the story that provided the money for the house; the purchase of the house; and the birth of Jason. The decision to buy the house is described as "symbolic", and Sriber notes its transformation from an empty building where the "roof leaked and there was no glass in the windows" to a place with "good home fittings" and a renovated kitchen where the family "can afford to relax and enjoy the island paradise". The article was accompanied by a photograph of Clift standing nonchalantly, and perhaps a little proudly, in front of her kitchen range.

As Sriber noted, when Clift and Johnston moved into the house, it required considerable repair and modernisation. The family found it difficult to adapt to the lack of running water or reliable sanitation, a situation that was the norm for Hydra in the mid-1950s. An ongoing subplot of *Peel Me a Lotus* is the battle to upgrade the house's water supply—particularly in order to create a more commodious and sanitary latrine—along with various other tasks required to improve, furnish and decorate the house. In an important statement of purpose, they also set about converting two rooms into one on the upper part of the house in order to create a generous 'studio' where Johnston could dedicate himself to his writing. As Clift reported, "Even in its nakedness it is a lovely room, long and low-ceilinged, which because of its five arched windows seems to be mostly air".

What the couple eventually created with their island home was a living environment unlike either the suburban houses of Australia or the terraced apartments of London. Perhaps taking inspiration from the seaside styles she had known in Kiama, Clift led the way in creating a house that referenced the history and location of their Aegean idyll. When Australian Colin Simpson, a journalistic acquaintance of Johnston's, visited unannounced in 1962, he found the family absent on a day trip to Athens, but he was escorted to the house by a local and given entrance to the unlocked rooms. Here he found a living room that was decorated "in Greek-islands style, stone floor with hand-woven rugs, a couple of smaller bright rugs on the whitest of walls, with a Sidney Nolan drawing from the Leda series. It was their place all right, even if there hadn't been the bookcase with the books they'd written … It was a house so attractive that I should have wagered against them ever leaving it".

Redmond Wallis, describing the house in *The Unyielding Memory*, also noted the Nolan paintings, plus many other decorative touches and artefacts representing the various travels of George and Catherine Grayson.

> There were Nolan paintings on the walls of his study, and hung downstairs in the main living room. The bookcases were full of travel books, histories, novels. There were artefacts collected by George, and perhaps Catherine, on his or their travels: figurines, vases, ornaments, pieces of pottery. At the head of the stairs, just outside George's study, was a wooden carving of an anthropomorphic sun, a dramatic greeting to the first floor. The house was comfortable, organised, cool. The walled garden

was shaded by a rambling grape vine woven into a mesh canopy and a clump of ancient olive trees, so close together they also made part of the canopy. From the terrace outside George's study there was a view over the top of nearby houses to the port and beyond to the Peloponnisos. This was where the captain's wife had stood, looking for a sail.

The centrepiece of the house's living spaces was a large ground floor kitchen boasting a generous table that was a frequent site of meals and hospitality for family and visitors alike. Nadia Wheatley described the kitchen in detail, pointing out how Clift's use of the room facilitated the social gatherings for which the couple and the house were to become so well known.

> White-washed walls, dark ceiling beams, cool flagstones … This was the area that Charmian would transform into the kind of Mediterranean kitchen found in lifestyle magazines—except that this was twenty years or more before the peasant vogue began. Here, strings of garlic and huge earthenware pitchers were set off by glowing Arachova rugs, comfortably sagging chairs, and Greek *objets trouves* ranging from a two thousand year old amphora to a crazily ornate birdcage. On the walls were old lithographs of the Heroes of the War of Independence, a set of antique pistols, and paintings by visiting artists—including the little Icarus sketch [by Sidney Nolan]. At a time when Australian domestic architecture enforced an apartheid system between the kitchen and the living area, this was a woman's workplace which allowed the cook to be at the centre of the party.

In keeping with the spirit of domestic sociability noted by Wheatley, Clift would later dedicate the essay 'Living in the kitchen' to the subject of kitchens. The essay decried the miserable proportion of 1960s Australian kitchens and extolled the importance of large, generously proportioned spaces where whole families gather, and where the cook remains a part of the conversations, "a high priestess, presiding over rituals and ceremonies, repository of hoarded culinary lore".

Johnston was also enamoured of the kitchen. In the early pages of *Closer to the Sun*, it is described as the centre of the house and also the space in which the marriage of David and Kate Meredith is centred. The kitchen is a reminder of the domesticity and commitment to a shared purpose that has brought order to Kate's life and which might yet enable their marriage to survive the stresses that have brought them from London to the island.

> He went across and lifted himself on to the big, eight-feet slab of marble, and reached across and fingered out some chopped lettuce. 'Kate?' he said.
>
> 'Yes?'
>
> 'This is a very fine kitchen.'
>
> 'This is a wonderful kitchen,' she said. 'I adore this kitchen. Do you know, it's exactly the sort my mother always dreamed of having and never did.'
>
> He looked carefully about him. From the varnished beams which were almost the whole trunks of trees dangled the pale strings of garlic and the purple onions, a bunch of bay-leaves, rosemary and mint and basil, and tufts of wild thyme and *rigoni* from the mountains. A wreath of early vine-leaves hung green as youth over the great stone water-jar in the corner by the well. The flagged floor was damp and cool. He watched his wife as she moved across to the arched stove with its ledge of scarlet tiles. She looked slim and cool and very beautiful. She looked as if she belonged. Eleven years ago, they had said the marriage would never last six months. She had been wild then, and unpredictable.
>
> 'It's got a nice feel about it, this house,' he said, munching on the salad. 'A sort of lucky feel. I think we'll be very happy here.'
>
> 'I am happy here,' she said simply. 'Happier than I have ever been in my life darling.' She turned with a smile.

It would seem that Johnston's island friends were familiar with his faith in the kitchen as the focus of the household and a marker of domestic stability. In Gordon Merrick's novel *Forth Into Light*, a memorable opening sequence describes novelist George Leighton awakening dishevelled and hungover after a night of drinking and arguing with his wife, and with a large sum of money missing. As Leighton frantically searches the house, it is the kitchen that offers the only steadying space in his crumbling life.

> Here, sustained by the vivid picture of stability and order evoked by the kitchen—dark hand-hewn beams, rosy time-smooth stone floor, glow of copper, bunches of wild herbs hanging from the ceiling, loops of garlic and onions, rustic baskets overflowing with fruit and vegetables—he was almost lulled into feeling the money didn't matter.

But perhaps the dreams and memories associated with the house and the kitchen were not always so reassuring for Johnston, despite what he hoped they might nurture within his marriage. In *Clean Straw for Nothing*, it is the kitchen that is the scene for one of David Meredith's most mortifying moments in his unravelling marriage after he leaves his wife, Cressida, at a party hosted by his rival Galloway and returns to the house. Here he wanders through empty rooms that "[seem] swollen by the presence of Cressida and his own absences, and in the awful hollow of these absences another figure move[s], a tall strong figure, bearded and brown, with a flash of white teeth, roaring with laughter". With his suspicions about his wife's affair confirmed, Meredith retreats to the "cool dark kitchen" where, with Cressida absent with her lover, he must self-administer a needle to treat his consumption. Meredith's torment builds when, with trousers around his ankles, he strikes the needle to his buttock only to find that it "click[s] on a bone and [breaks] off; he jump[s] back with a sharp cry and his clenching fingers [snap] the thin glass of the syringe ... It [takes] him some time to extract the length of broken needle and to staunch the blood and clean the broken glass and mess from his body and the floor." Meredith's abjection is complete when he has to make his way back to Galloway's house to seek his wife's help amid "torments of pain and anger, shame, self-pity, humiliation, and a hopeless desperate wish to find some conclusion to his trials".

The truth of this sad incident was confirmed by Redmond Wallis in *The Unyielding Memory*, where it is recounted to Nick Alwyn by Stephanos Lamounis.

> Certainly Stephanos had a few stories to tell about the Graysons. ... There had been, he told Nick, a party at the art school, a building which during the summer offered working holidays for those prepared to pay. At the time George was in the grip of Tb and having injections every few hours, administered by Catherine. Bed-ridden, he sent Catherine off to the party where she was able to meet her lover, Chip Wilson. She forgot about George. Came the time for George to have his injection and he decided to administer it himself. Something was wrong: he succeeded in breaking the needle off in his thigh. Seeking aid he managed to get himself to the party, clad in his dressing gown, to discover Catherine in a back room with Chip. There was a considerable scene, Catherine crying and shouting 'I love him! I love him!' as poor George tried to get her—anyone—to deal with the needle. The upshot was that the following morning Chip packed his bags and left; Catherine, a picture of misery, stood on the agora watching him being rowed out through the breakwater to the ferry. George was back in bed.

James Burke took numerous photos both outside and inside the house that tell other stories about Clift and Johnston. In these photos it is the people within, both family and visitors, that are the primary focus for his lens, but the images also convey a vivid impression of the house as it was in 1960, including the kitchen area. In one extended sequence of photographs, we see Clift, Johnston and their children sharing a meal with Demetri Gassoumis, his wife Carolyn, and their daughter Athena. Also seen seated at the table is the family's Hydriot maid, Zoe Skordoras, who was an integral part of the household for the duration of their time on the island, helping with both the household chores and the care of the children, Jason in particular. Burke's photographs capture Clift cooking and distributing the food while Johnston dispenses drinks and the adults and children all find ample space at the generous table.

TO SPITI TOU JOHNSTON: THE AUSTRALIAN HOUSE

Kitchen of the Australian House. L-R: Martin Johnston, Charmian Clift, Shane Johnston, George Johnston, Demetri Gassoumis. (James Burke)

Sharing a meal. L-R: Charmian Clift and Jason Johnston, George Johnston, Zoe Skordoras, Athena and Carolyn Gassoumis, Shane Johnston and James Barclay (both obscured), Martin Johnston, Demetri Gassoumis. (James Burke)

Being entertained at the Johnstons' table was something of a rite of passage for many who came to the island—an indication of acceptance by the couple in their self-appointed role as the arbiters of admission into the inner-circle of the island's artists and writers. As Nadia Wheatley noted, "Charmian's need to 'own' the Hydra scene would become more and more evident. In her eyes, it was she who gave the thumbs up—or down—to new arrivals", and there could not be a more emphatic declaration of acceptance than being invited inside the Australian House. Although, as Clift would later recall, perhaps the choice of those who made it as far as the kitchen might have been made more carefully.

> There were two young ladies of Notting Hill Gate with five children between them and libidos as loose as their dirty and travel-stained shifts. There was—and I shudder still—a Dane who played a trumpet and had genetic theories. There was an American poet of some beat renown who drugged himself into somnolence at our kitchen table and wouldn't waken up properly for two whole days. There was another American poet who got into the kitchen and talked for a week and made a play about it which went like a bomb off-Broadway.

Australian novelist Rodney Hall was another island visitor who came to know the kitchen well. Hall and his wife, Bet, arrived on Hydra with their baby daughter just after Christmas in 1963. They met the Johnstons almost immediately and soon found themselves spending a large amount of time in the house, particularly at the kitchen table. It was, Hall recalls, "A lovely, stone-flagged kitchen, beautiful kitchen", which he later attempted to re-create in a home he built in Australia. Johnston, at the time, was anxiously awaiting the publication of *My Brother Jack*, and the Halls found him and Clift in "a combination of shellshock and euphoria after getting *My Brother Jack* finished". Johnston was anxious for an Australian reader's response to the novel, and Hall was called upon to read a manuscript copy in the kitchen while Johnston eyed his reaction.

George said 'I've finished this book, would you like to read it?' This is when we had known them for five or six days, and he said 'You will have to come over to our place because I have only got two carbon copies and I can't let either of them out of the house.' So I went over there every morning and left Bet with the baby, and I went over for a period of sitting at Charmian's table, a big long wooden table running along one wall with a bench on one side and ladder back chairs. And I would read *My Brother Jack*, and sometimes George would come down to watch, and it was a bit intimidating and he would sit at the end of the table and smoke. The table would seat sixteen or maybe eighteen people, and he would sit at the far end of the table, pretending to read a book, but really checking on what my response was. And it was very exciting because certainly the opening of that book is marvellous, the first third is truly wonderful, and I was able to be highly demonstrative about it and that went down the right way.

Another Australian guest of the Johnstons during this period was Mungo MacCallum (his father, Mungo Snr, had been a colleague of Johnston's in Sydney) who arrived before the Halls in April 1963 and also found Johnston and Clift anxiously awaiting the publication of *My Brother Jack*. Unlike the Halls, MacCallum arrived without a baby, but he soon acquired one. MacCallum had finished at Sydney University and just turned twenty-one when he set out with several university friends to drive through the Indian subcontinent and Eastern Europe. On reaching Delhi, he received a phone call from his father informing him that his girlfriend Sue McGowan was pregnant. It was arranged that Sue would be put on the next available boat, and the suddenly engaged couple would meet in Athens. MacCallum spent the weeks waiting for Sue's arrival on Hydra with the Johnstons and recalled that "George and Charmian made me feel welcome immediately, and I fell in love with them". MacCallum returned to Athens to greet Sue and to travel with her to Hydra. They then returned to Athens for both their wedding and the birth of their daughter, Diana, in early September. In addition, MacCallum's

The MacCallums return with their new baby. George Johnston, Shane Johnston, Diana Wentworth MacCallum, Sue MacCallum, Mungo MacCallum, Diana MacCallum (in basket), 1963. (Johnston and Clift Collection)

mother arrived in the Greek capital for the birth of her grandchild, accompanying the newlyweds back to Hydra with the newborn Diana, who soon after acquired Clift and Leonard Cohen as godparents. MacCallum reported his mother's arrival as "well-meaning of her but a bit of a mixed blessing: she tried to hide it but she was clearly appalled at our casualness and ineptitude".

As with Hall, MacCallum was encouraged to read *My Brother Jack* in manuscript and found that he "enthusiastically agreed" with Clift's assessment that this was the "Great Australian Novel".

This ready hospitality wasn't extended only to newly arrived Australians, such as the Halls and MacCallums. As Clift herself later noted, the visitors were constant and likely to come from any point of the compass, and the couple were driven by a need "to preserve a reputation for hospitality of which we were proud".

> French, Italian, Swedish, Norwegian, Italian. Poets and painters and potters and novelists. I remember these better, because I connote them with long early-morning sessions over the kitchen table, cups of coffee, making up spare beds, the lonely, the lost, the desperate, the raging dreamers, the sick and the desolate, the stifled, the suffocating. Did we give *them* anything, I wonder, except momentary comfort?

While Clift and Johnston ensured the Australian House was an undeniably welcoming and social space, it was also, of course, the site for the normal intimacies of personal, family life—including, most significantly, the birth of Jason. It is, therefore, appropriate that Burke's photographs include images of the couple, both alone and together, to remind us that this was the scene for the life of a family and a sometimes strained marriage. There are three series of portraits of Johnston alone in the living spaces of the house. These photographs depict their subject smoking and drinking intensely, communicating to the camera the stress that emerged soon after he arrived on the island and found himself battling poverty, ill-health and his own unrealised literary ambitions in order to keep his family fed and his dreams alive.

Burke's portraits of Johnston recall Wallis's description of George Grayson in *The Unyielding Memory*:

> He had a lived-in, uncared-for face, all crannies and wrinkles, his nose was like a curved flight deck of a carrier, a lank of blank hair fell across his forehead and was constantly being brushed back, and his teeth were none too good. It was a Cockney face and a cocky face, but a throw back to when Cockneys would have been almost all of London. He was thin, painfully thin. Had his hair been grey he would have looked seventy; he was, in fact, forty-eight.

There are fewer house-based portraits of Clift, but one striking set of five captures her in the kitchen preparing a meal and bringing to mind her words from *Peel Me a Lotus* that "A housewife is a housewife wherever she is—in the biggest city of the world or on a small Greek island. There is no escape. She

George Johnston drinks. (James Burke)

must move always to the dreary recurring decimal of her rites" and that "to keep even a semblance of order, in such a big house is an all day job".

Such protestations by Clift were a little disingenuous. The household was supported by Zoe, and it was only the maid's presence that allowed Clift the freedom to join the daily dockside gatherings and to frequently drink and talk away her afternoons without immediate concern for her house or children. Nevertheless, it was, as Clift indicated, a large and busy household that had to be managed, all while she was trying to write.

It is, however, the images of the couple together, observed only by Burke and his camera, which are powerfully suggestive of aspects of their intimate relationship. In several, we catch Clift apparently in the final stages of dressing, likely in preparation for an outing, as she pulls herself into her 'ready for the world' garb. In these images, there is a palpable tension as Clift performs these personal rites under her husband's watchful eye.

TO SPITI TOU JOHNSTON: THE AUSTRALIAN HOUSE

Charmian Clift cooks. (James Burke)

Burke's most intimate images return us to the kitchen. In a series of startling late-night shots, Johnston is pictured sprawled on the communal table, deep in conversation with the seated Clift as they share a drink, a cigarette and likely an end-of-day reckoning. The kitchen range is a brightly lit and attractive workspace, but, in these photographs, it is merely background detail. The eye is irresistibly drawn to the two figures cast in near silhouette, their deeply engaged poses and barely visible expressions suggestive of the sort of domestic intimacy that might only take place in a kitchen or a bedroom, which brings to mind Clift's declaration that a kitchen is the place for "confidences and confessions". While it is sensible to not overly determine these images—given that the subjects were to some extent complicit in their creation—they nonetheless remind the viewer of the everyday realities of the complexly intertwined lives that were played out within, and shaped by, the house in which they unfolded.

George Johnston and Charmian Clift. (James Burke)

Domestic intimacy. Wife and husband take time out in the kitchen. (James Burke)

Although, as Johnston told Colin Simpson in 1962, both he and Clift loved the house, it was not an unproblematic part of their lives on Hydra. The upkeep and ongoing modernisation demanded time and money, and there was also the physical and psychological effort needed to sustain a house in which they took great pride but that, as Clift declared as she returned to Australia, had "become a show-piece".

> For what I had not realised was that this so-desirable house would begin owning us. We were lured into a sort of perpetual treasure hunt for the precise copper pot for the kitchen shelf, the genuine sea-chest, the inlaid commode that somebody said an old lady up on the mountain wanted to sell, a carved island sofa hidden among a mess of junk in an old sponge warehouse, a shipbuilder's model of a diving caique, an oriental birdcage, useless but beautiful.

The attempt to simplify their lives by consciously escaping one form of modernity and acquisitiveness had instead left them relentlessly accruing, and increasingly tied to, another set of possessions. Not only had the house become something of a chore, but it made Clift aware that the decision she and Johnston took to make their expatriation 'permanent' was also implicated in the less desirable changes impacting their island haven.

> [W]e had unwittingly started a sort of cult, since other foreigners followed our example and bought houses, too, and our quiet, cheap, remote little island became very fashionable and not really cheap or even quiet any more.

Little has been recorded about the sale of the house. Clift remained there until she and the children followed Johnston back to Australia in late July 1964. Garry Kinnane reported that she had "neither the time nor the will" to sell the house and left her then lover Anthony Kingsmill to manage the sale. The Australian House was last for sale in 1977, and it had by then achieved such notoriety in Australia that the occasion was reported in the national press. In a lengthy article in the *Age* bearing the headline 'Island legend for sale', Tom Rothfield retold the story of the couple's island lifestyle by focusing on what he called the "raffish life of the writers". But if Clift and Johnston are recalled by Rothfield as drunken, argumentative and adulterous, then the home they created is described as having a very different temperament—something solid, comfortable and stylish. As Rothfield reported, "The elegant and lovely house … is almost exactly as it was then, a decade ago. Sparkling, airy rooms, heavy wooden ceiling beams, and a cool, sheltered garden of lemon trees and trailing vines." It is, he notes, a place where "the anguish of the writers' last years seem far away". Rothfield also reports that the house has become a draw card for Australian travellers, a place they seek out in order to catch a glimpse of this celebrated episode in the history of Australian bohemianism and expatriation, and closes his article with the hint that the house might yet be purchased by "some literary foundation in Australia".

Such a purchase did not eventuate. The house was instead acquired by the father of the present owner and, subsequently, changes were made. Several rooms in the interior were redesigned, and additional modernisation was undertaken. An upper-storey addition to a house on the opposite side of the square robbed the upper rooms and terrace of much of their harbour view, and, at some point, the Australian House even lost its 'whiteness', with the painted render of the exterior walls scraped away to reveal the rock beneath.

It hasn't been as easy to erase other features of the house. In *Clean Straw for Nothing*, David Meredith ponders on the fate of this house, deciding that

> In the fashion of island nomenclature it would probably go on for a very long time being referred to as 'the Australian House,' just as, until the novelty of us having bought it, it had always been called 'the House of the Cannons,' because Pavlos Zaraphonitis, the brig captain who had built it way back in 1788—the very year, oddly enough, when my country was first settled—had mounted two brass cannons on the roof terrace.

As Johnston predicted it goes on being the 'Australian House', or perhaps to some 'the Johnston-Clift House'. Either way, it remains the most recognisable, evocative and poignant reminder of the couple's island years.

TO SPITI TOU JOHNSTON: THE AUSTRALIAN HOUSE

* * *

Together with the Australian House, the house owned by Leonard Cohen is the one most identified with the Hydra expatriates. In this passage from *The Unyielding Memory*, Redmond Wallis describes Saul Ruben's (Cohen) house when Nick Alwyn moves in for a period in 1963.

> *Saul's house was set almost on the crest of the hill behind the port, on the road that led inland to Kamini. The house was L-shaped, built around the south and west side of a raised terrace. It had three floors, with a lavatory underneath the terrace, just inside the main gate. The ground floor was unusable: the remaining two floors had seven rooms and a kitchen with a charcoal oven and a trap to the* sterna *below. Off the kitchen in one wing of the L was a bedroom: off in the other wing lay a small living room and another bedroom, which Saul had used as a studio. The Alwyns set up their bedroom in the room above this.*
>
> *The house was more difficult than any in which they had previously lived. It was a long haul up Donkey Shit Lane and the only local amenities were a tiny bakery and a small general store, run by a woman called Evyenia, that sold bare necessities. There was no fireplace—it was heated by charcoal braziers—and, in common with most of the houses on the island, no bathroom and no running water. There were, it turned out, red worms in the* sterna, *which meant the water could not be drunk. Nick thought he might write a book: From bed bugs to red worms and how I coped.*
>
> *From the terrace it was possible to see straight across the valley to the house owned by Paul and Lee and, further to the north-west, to that now owned by Margaretha, the house that had been Lars Pinten's and in which he had lived with her before he had left with Carol. It was not possible to see the harbour and in consequence the Alwyns lost some of the sense of living on an island. This was perhaps more important to Sue than to Nick: Sue believed that people who lived on islands were in some way special.*

Chapter Three

ISLANDS: DREAMING AND LIVING

Islands occupy a complex space within the human imagination. They can mean many things that stand in stark opposition—islands as paradise or hell; islands as sanctuaries or prisons; islands as free and autonomous spaces, or dependencies; islands as a world complete unto themselves, or remote from the mainstream of life. The various ways in which islands are understood reflects their diversity in scale, climate, topography, proximity to other islands or a mainland as well as their individual histories and state of development. The perception of islands also reflects the experience of individuals and their personal imaginative response to confined and bounded spaces.

Perhaps the most persistent notion is that islands are somewhere 'other'. Comparatively few people live on islands, and most of those who do live on larger islands, a de facto mainland that is frequently in touch with a constellation of smaller and remoter islands. Islands are therefore situated at the fringes of most lives, places we go to in order to experience something outside our day-to-day reality and the relentless grip of time, space and urban experience that govern modern perceptions of the world. As such, islands are both romanticised and commodified as fodder for tourist brochures pushing bucket-list boat cruises and escapist fantasies, ensuring the powerful engines of modern tourism constantly rub up against these persistently premodern spaces.

As the world assumed its mid-twentieth century postwar shape, the future relationship between mainlands and islands was being formed in the eastern

Mediterranean. The Aegean islands, sitting within the orbit of three continents and at the crucible of several civilisations and empires, had been at the centre of trade and migratory routes for millennia. While they enjoyed some of the planet's most enticing climates and natural attractions, they were also generally poor, underdeveloped and struggling for relevance after several centuries of economic and social development had driven western populations to mainland cities. But what modernity had taken it could yet give back, as postwar Europe looked to make the most of economic growth and expanding opportunities for leisure and travel.

There were several reasons for George Johnston and Charmian Clift to move to the Greek islands, but the one the couple aired publicly was their desire for time and space away from the daily grind of metropolitan living and waged work in order to fulfil their literary aspirations. For the Johnstons, an island was a place of escape and, as Clift explained, although their London departure was seen as sudden, it was certainly not a decision made without thought—islands had been on their minds for some time.

> For many years George, like other journalists, had grizzled fairly constantly about the nature of his work and sworn in his cups, like other journalists, that one bloody day he would just go off and live on an island and write books.

Greece and its islands had increasingly interested the Johnstons as they began to consider places to live in Europe that were both cheaper and had a more amenable climate than London. Johnston knew something of the country from a brief wartime visit, and by mid-1953 the couple was planning to travel there on one of their occasional continental breaks. In preparation they undertook extensive reading, including both classical Greek literature and myth and contemporary travel guides. A London encounter with Australian woman Clarisse Zander (a friend of Johnston's friend Sidney Nolan) made an impression. After hearing of the couple's mounting frustration with London, Zander enticed Johnston and Clift with the possibility of living cheaply and writing on the Greek islands—and one island in particular. Johnston later gave a version of this conversation in *Clean Straw for Nothing*:

> 'It is sad about Italy. Now one must go further afield, I am afraid. Greece is the place I think. Yes, Greece is still possible, I feel. You know Greece, Mr Meredith?'
>
> 'Not really,' he said. 'I was there twice during the war, but not for very long. Cress has never been there.'...
>
> 'I was back there only six months ago,' she said, and went on to tell them of her discovery of an unfrequented little island in the Aegean, crumbling into picturesque ruin, where the most wonderful old houses could be brought for twenty or thirty pounds and stately mansions for a hundred, where life was sublimely leisurely and peaceful, and living very cheap.
>
> 'You should find a place like that, Mr Meredith,' she advised, out of an old and kindly wisdom. 'You should find a place like that where you can get away from all this and try to write something worthwhile.'

The island of which Zander was speaking was Hydra.

Johnston and Clift's exploratory trip to Greece followed in April and May of 1954. Unaccompanied by their children, they travelled quickly and widely, taking in a number of the country's important classical sites (Epidaurus, Sparta, Delphi) while collecting background details for Johnston's next novel, *The Cyprian Woman*. They also made their way to a number of islands (Crete, Rhodes, Delos and Paros), and, recalling Zander's advice, they included an overnight stay on Hydra. Although they came away with no particular sense that this was *the* place, Johnston later recorded his favourable, if fleeting, first impression, whereby from their window of the dockside Poseidon Hotel, the couple "looked below to a vivid rocking tangle of fat-bellied *caiques* unloading lemons and loquats and quinces and goats and earthenware water-jars". In other words, Hydra was remembered as being sufficiently exotic, picturesque and authentic.

ISLANDS: DREAMING AND LIVING

George Johnston seated at centre with Charles Heckstall outside Katsikas *kafenio*. The Poseidon Hotel, where Johnston and Charmian Clift stayed overnight in 1954, is to the right, above Tassos *kafenio*. (James Burke)

Returning to London, Johnston put his newly gathered knowledge of Greece to use by commencing *The Cyprian Woman* while the couple continued to find the city conditions bleak and their circumstances unchanging. They also suffered a disappointment when the considerable energy they had invested in their previous novel, *The Big Chariot*, resulted in little benefit. The couple believed the novel's anticipated success would provide the financial security necessary for Johnston to throw in his Fleet Street career, but positive reviews failed to translate into sales, and pre-publication talk of a film adaptation was quickly dropped. It therefore became ever more apparent that if they were to absorb this setback and commit themselves to writing full time, it could only happen if they decamped to somewhere far cheaper than London to live and raise a family.

The spur to initially choosing Kalymnos, an island close to the Turkish coast in the south-east Dodecanese, came when Clift heard a BBC radio program about the miserably difficult and dangerous lives of the island's sponge-divers who endured long periods fishing the once lucrative sea beds of North Africa while facing the constant dangers of drowning or being crippled by the bends. The program also discussed plans that were afoot to have divers and their families move to Australia to work in the pearling industry. Clift and Johnston decided there was a book in the subject, the research for which could be married to their dream of escaping from London and finding their island in the sunshine. With little time for detailed preparation, but faith in their own capacity, they simply decided to go. As Clift recalled:

> It burst like a star, so simple and brilliant and beautiful that for the moment we could only stare at each other in wonder. Why the devil shouldn't we just *go*?
>
> So we did.
>
> We had no means of communication other than sign language, and we had a bank account that didn't bear thinking about. Still, we thought we might be able to last for a year if we managed very carefully and stayed healthy. We had for some years published a novel every year or so, not very successfully, but we thought it might be just possible to live by our writing.

Arriving in early December 1954, Kalymnos sparked a renewal in the Johnstons' marriage. While island life, in some ways, was initially hard on the children in particular, it had the immediate effect of restabilising the couple's relationship while redirecting their energy to their writing. When Australian friends Cedric and Pat Flower joined them in July 1955, they found Johnston and Clift happy, consumed by their work and determined to extend their stay in the Aegean. Island living, it seemed, was good for them. The Flowers convinced Johnston and Clift that if they were to remain in the Aegean, then the extremely remote and poorly serviced Kalymnos was no place for a young family. The Johnstons used the presence of the Flowers as an opportunity to leave the children in their care, and in early August, they set out to explore islands closer to Athens. Their absence was short. Having returned to Hydra only fifteen months after their first brief visit, they rapidly determined that it was the ideal destination. With the decision made, they went back to Kalymnos to collect the children, some furniture and the Flowers, and, by the end of August, they were in rented accommodation on Hydra. The second phase of their Aegean expatriation had begun.

For all its differences, Hydra would have initially seemed welcoming, or at least familiar, to Johnston and Clift. Since his mid-teens, Johnston had been fascinated by ships and shipping and had started spending lunchtimes away from the city (where he was apprenticed as a commercial artist) and down at the Melbourne docks. While Johnston's particular interest was in classic sailing ships (according to Garry Kinnane, this passion became "all-consuming in his mid-teens"), he was irresistibly drawn to shipping in all forms and to the busyness and clamour of dockside activity. Writing on Hydra, and narrating *My Brother Jack* in the guise of David Meredith, Johnston vividly described the "beauty" he found in Melbourne's docklands:

> I could go wandering around the waking wharves, and for the first time in my life I came to be aware of the existence of true beauty, of an opalescent world of infinite promise that had nothing to do with the shabby suburbs that had engulfed me since my birth. The fine floating calligraphy of a tug's wake black on a mother-of-pearl stream in the first glow of a river dawn, the majesty of smoke in still air, the pale and tranquil breath of river mist and morning steam, the rising sun picking golden turrets out of derricks and Samson-posts and cranes and davits, the coloured smoke-stacks and the slender gilt pencillings of masts declaring themselves little by little against the dark haze-banks that always in the waking time veiled the river flats, the faint images of ships far down the stream, coming in from Gellibrand, looming out of dew and light and sea mist, and then, at every bend and twist of the river, changing the shapes of beauty like a rare vase turned in the fingers of a connoisseur.
>
> It filled me with an excitement, almost an exultation, that I could tell nobody about.

Charmian Clift, n.d. (Johnston and Clift Collection)

Johnston would have been thrilled in the mix of Hydra's shipping, serving not only the sponge and fishing industries but also the naval training college, the daily ferries with their cargo of tourists, and the increasingly glamorous tall-masted yachts and luxury vessels catering for well-heeled travellers. In London, Johnston had, on several occasions, photographed Clift amongst the riverside docks and ships, and on Hydra the family albums collected numerous images of her posing amongst or on-board the *caiques* and other small craft that dotted the dockside.

Dockside activity was also familiar to Clift, whose childhood in Kiama had meant exposure to the port servicing the region's timber industry, quarries and dairy farms. However, for Clift her main connection was to the recreational possibilities of the beachside location. From an early age, she was a strong and keen swimmer who was trusted to swim alone amongst the area's notoriously dangerous rips. The beach was her playground during her childhood and teenage years, and she was equally at home on the sandy expanse of the crescent shaped Bombo Beach to Kiama's north as she was at the granite-sided pools that were shaped from the rocky headland jutting from the town centre. She later described these beaches as part of the town of 'Lebanon Bay' in *Walk to the Paradise Gardens*, a novel that is as imbued, as any in Australian fiction, with the salt tang of ocean swimming and seaside breezes.

> Each day they swam, either at the main town beach—a pretty yellow half-moon of sand crowded with spreadeagled bodies in every shade of suntan from blush-pink to mahogany—or in the pool that had lately been carved out of the rock shelf on the ocean side of the headland.

Clift was therefore completely 'at home' at Spilia, Hydra's rocky swimming spot just outside the western entrance to the harbour and an important summer gathering place for Hydra's expatriates. With the Hydriots unaccustomed to the practice of swimming due to over-familiarity with the dangers of the sea and customs of modesty regarding public dress, gathering at Spilia at the bottom of "twenty descending stairs, [with] rock platforms cemented over to make sun-bathing levels" was marked out as a social and leisure activity for the island's foreigners. It is little surprise that Clift found her way there regularly, as did James Burke with his camera. Burke recorded Clift and Johnston, and Leonard Cohen and his partner Marianne Ihlen, in numerous shots relaxing on the concrete steps and swimming, surrounded by other island visitors.

This unlikely swimming spot, crafted from rock and occasionally troubled by the blood and offal disgorged from a nearby abattoir that brought with it the fear of sharks, enabled Clift to keep in touch with her Australian childhood. If expatriation is, according to one understanding, a form of 'flight', then it was in the performance of taking flight while diving that Clift could momentarily leave her adopted island home both physically and imaginatively.

Charmian Clift (back to camera), Marianne Ihlen and Leonard Cohen, Spilia.
(James Burke)

ISLANDS: DREAMING AND LIVING

Charmian Clift, Spilia. (James Burke)

> [H]ow good it was to be alive and sprawled in the sun; how fine and free to dive from the highest rock above the cave-lip, willing one's spread arms to hold one arched in air. It was a day to attempt the unreasonable, so close it seemed, so almost within one's power to defy the laws of gravity. Launched in an arc above the waiting sea it seemed possible that one might hang there for a moment before the downward plunge … or even soar on, on and on like a bird soaring across the brilliant gulf.

It is not too fanciful to believe that in such moments Clift supposed herself soaring across the "brilliant gulf" and eventually alighting on those other beaches and swimming places she had known and loved on the Australian coast.

Burke's Spilia images evoke passages in *Peel Me a Lotus* wherein Clift extols her love of swimming, associating it with her existential desire to live an 'exposed' life in the sun. But she was also a night-swimmer—as indeed were a number of Hydra's expatriates, finding it companionable to "share crab sandwiches and a flask of red wine" at a time when the rocks were largely deserted. As it seems to have done for Clift all her life, the act of moving through water had the power to bring her nearest to herself and was another reminder of why she was living on this island and not in London.

> At night the water slides over your body warm and silky, a mysterious element, unresistant, flowing, yet incredibly buoyant. In the dark you slip through it, unquestionably accepting the night's mood of grace and silence, a little drugged with wine, a little spellbound with the night, your body mysterious and pale and silent in the mysterious water, and at your slowly moving feet and hands streaming trails of phosphorescence, like streaming trails of stars. Still streaming stars you climb the dark ladder to the dark rock, shaking showers of stars from your very fingertips, most marvellously and mysteriously renewed and whole again.

Yet not everyone on Hydra shared such moments of rapture, or, indeed, came to Hydra with the same unresolved web of personal and artistic aspirations as Clift and Johnston. Those who made their way to the island in the couple's wake had their own sometimes complex reasons for being there. Along with their typewriters, easels and cameras (and later, drugs), they carried varying ideas about islands that would be tested by Hydra.

Among those who drifted to Hydra was poet and folklorist Steve Sanfield. Sanfield first turned up on impulse from Athens in the early 1960s, and once on the island, he encountered Leonard Cohen who would become his lifelong friend. In *The Unyielding Memory*, Redmond Wallis has Sue Alwyn describe "Sunfield" as "Jewish, beat, Californian, black jeans, black shirt and black shades. And he's got a great drooping black moustache, like a Mexican bandit"—apparently someone who would have been a great addition to Burke's photo-essay on Hydra's Beat-culture. Not only did Sanfield physically stand out from the other expatriates with that distinctive moustache, but he also signalled the flourishing of one aspect of 1960s youth culture on Hydra—drugs. Sunfield is presented in Wallis's manuscript as someone who encourages and facilitates the island's drug culture (hash being his drug of choice), a development noted by Nick Alwyn on his return to Hydra from London in August 1963. (Sanfield's correspondence confirms that he was on Hydra for the early months and summer of 1963, with his available diary covering five weeks from May 6th to June 10th). Sanfield's writings and remembrances from this period offer an important perspective on Hydra at a time when the island was undergoing noticeable change and various cracks were becoming evident in the expatriate community. As a friend of Cohen's and a periodic Hydra visitor who stayed for more than a few days each time, Sanfield offers a viewpoint distanced from the close-knit group that framed Wallis's impressions, providing insights into island living that complement and challenge other accounts.

Sanfield's later recollections of his time on Hydra are generally rhapsodic. He told Cohen's biographer Sylvie Simmons of a time "of light, sun, camaraderie, the voluptuous simplicity of life, and the special energy that emanated from its community of artists and seekers". It is an account of island living given by Sanfield in the knowledge of the mythical stories surrounding his friend's years on the island, but which is unlike the version recorded in his diary, which registers with more immediacy his emotional state and response to fellow island visitors. He wrote on May 21st, 1963:

> Most of the foreigners here claim they have come to this island to get away from certain aspects of western society—specifically things like social status, morality codes, & other people's opinions. But it is these very things they have brought with them. They have set up a status structure with all its inherent pressures that is dangerous to live in as anywhere in America or Eng.—only here it's much more obvious, since everything seems to be magnified on the island. And the most absurd aspect of the whole thing is that these people continue to pat themselves on the back for having the courage to leave all that behind.

It is probable that Johnston and Clift were among the self-congratulatory group at whom Sanfield was taking aim. The status structure he writes of certainly accords with the image the Johnstons had of themselves, as did others, as the leaders of the island's expatriates. In turn, while Sanfield arrived on Hydra several years after Clift wrote derisively of the island's summer visitors in *Peel Me a Lotus*, he no doubt embodied for her that undesirable peripatetic impulse that she saw as common to the many young men who found themselves on Hydra as part of the "nomadic trail" through Europe. It would be surprising if the relationship on both sides did not carry some tension.

At the time, Sanfield was twenty-five years old and down in the dumps. He was suffering the emotional aftershocks of a relationship breakup that propelled him to seek out Cohen, whose friendship and house were a welcome sanctuary. Sanfield notes in a diary entry for May 15th that "I was too empty & afraid to be alone, with myself for too long, so I spent the night there [at Cohen's house]. If it wasn't for L[eonard] & M[arianne], I'd hate to speculate on what yesterday would have been like." Despite Sanfield's personal dramas, his diary demonstrates a canny awareness of the island's wider intrigues, and he suggests that because of its confined space, Hydra draws its inhabitants into the sort of intimacy that makes obvious otherwise covert or subtle exercises of authority. Yet he does so in a state of heightened annoyance—not only was he suffering a broken heart, but island events and people exacerbated his depressive mindset. In the diary entry for May 19th, Sanfield relates, with anger, an unwelcome encounter at the island's only cinema, The Gardenia, with Australians Mungo and Sue MacCallum:

> Last night I took Leonard & Marianna out to the movies & dinner to celebrate her birthday. We looked forward to a pleasant & personal evening, but we were only fooling ourselves. Mungo & Sue came into the theater just before the movie started & despite a half-empty theater asked us to move over. When we didn't they sat directly behind us & imposed their inane conversation upon us. Damn these fuckin' people! Don't they have any respect for privacy?

Sanfield liked both Cohen and Ihlen greatly, writing in his diary that "[I may] be in love with her. As a matter of fact I may be in love with both of them." Sanfield clearly saw himself as having a special friendship with the couple, which is why the intrusion of the MacCallums was such an affront. However, Sanfield does not lay the blame for this trespass entirely with the Australians' lack of social graces—the island itself, it seems, must also shoulder some responsibility:

> This is probably the greatest drawback of living on Hydra—the lack of anonymity. Here you recognize everyone & they recognize you. There is no chance to escape into strange faces; no chance of seeing hundreds of new people; no chance of those unexpected & exciting meetings of someone you haven't seen for a while. You're even forced to recognize people you wouldn't even be conscious of in a bigger place. And then too they recognize you & usually impose themselves. The loss of anonymity can be a crippling thing.

The privacy and anonymity that Sanfield yearns for is something that Hydra cannot provide. He notes ruefully that "To be alone on the port has become a major problem. If you sit alone, someone inevitably joins you or tries to. … If you say that you would rather be alone most people think you're joking. They're so goddam insecure they can't imagine anyone wanting to be alone." In *Peel Me a Lotus*, Clift made a similar observation about Hydra's enforced sociability, although her attitude towards this aspect of island life is more ambivalent. Whereas Sanfield *wants* to be left alone, Clift gives the impression of seeking out company, of revelling in the opportunity to pull up a chair and start (or interrupt) a conversation.

> Here on the waterfront there is always company. It is easy to join a group around a plastic tablecloth and a flask of wine, and to sit for hours, gossiping, watching the evening promenade go by, conscious that one's skin is still salty and one's hair still damp from swimming, that one's limbs are relaxed, that one is not really attentive at all. Chitter, chitter, chitter, the conversation spurts and falls and chitters on again, idle, derisive, malicious—summer talk. Feodor is to be run off the island … Hippolyte has found an adelphic friend and my God you should see the little monster

> ... do you know what Mitzo sells in those cigarette tins he keeps on the top shelf?

But Clift is also well aware of the tedium that went hand-in-hand with the repeated conversations, entrenched social rituals and overfamiliarity that hallmarked expatriate life on the *agora*. Even in her first Hydra summer, she is cautious of the danger posed by such an intense social space.

> Inevitably we all meet again, and yet again. We are endlessly meeting … the same people over and over again, endlessly meeting … Always the same conversation, yesterday, today, tomorrow, the same smart verbal catch-ball with obscure poets and philosophers, the same Freudian terms, the same 'frank' piggery, the same shafts of malice and spite, the same derisive laughter.

Clift herself was therefore not without her own ideas regarding islands and the risks involved to those who stayed. Witnessing the influx of summer tourists, she writes that "There begin to arrive the people who have dreamed of islands". Clift understands that it is a dream of an island as an escape, a paradise, or an adventure—perhaps similar to those that also enticed her and Johnston—and not Hydra and its everyday realities of confinement, forced intimacy, and social tedium. Whereas the visitors depart on the next ferry with hazy fantasies intact, the residents face, without respite, the same cossetted intensity and lack of big-city anonymity that feed the touristic illusion of 'escape'.

Peel Me a Lotus can be read as a patchwork of various dreams about islands that Clift herself still carries and that gives shape to her understandings of her own experience and purpose on Hydra. This includes moments of wonderment in which Clift catches the soaring existential possibilities life offers on her chosen island.

> Living simply in the sun, we are at least in touch again with reality; we have bridged that chasm that separates modern life from life's beginnings and come back to magic, and wonder of such sensible mysteries

as fire, water, earth, and air. And more than this, we have no masters but ourselves.

Clift is also aware, however, that this Miller-esque dream of "living simply" on this small, austere and undeveloped island can also mean living without. Her rejection of urbanised modernity is not so romantically blinkered that she is not also quick to point to the drudgery of house work and mothering in the absence of the labour-saving technologies and services to which she had grown accustomed in London.

> All is to be done again, and yet again. And was it for this, I think, examining my grimed hands ruefully, that I renounced so gladly the material comforts of civilization? The gadgets? The labour-saving devices? The advantages of technological progress? The hot-water supply? The telephoned shopping-list? The Mister Stork Nappy-Wash?

Not only is the lack of such gadgetry an inconvenience, but, as Clift pointedly asks, "What creativeness is this?" when she is so bemired in day-to-day domestic work that she is unable to find the time for her writing. Clift was not alone in realising there was nothing remarkable about a woman on Hydra being tethered by domestic labour. Despite Wallis noting in *The Unyielding Memory* that "the thing that struck Nick most forcibly was that island society was a matriarchy", the novelty of a photograph he took of his wife, Robyn, doing the washing on her knees surely rests on the outdoor tub and the lengths that she must have been gone to in order to fill and transport a pail of water for the task.

Greek islands in the early 1960s remained conservative, and it was often women who bore the brunt of the delayed arrival of not only modern domestic appliances but also convenient birth control. A running concern in Wallis's diary is the prospect of an unwanted pregnancy for Robyn, and the arrival of a contraband tube of contraceptive jelly smuggled from the UK in a wad of newspapers warrants a lengthy entry. He also writes of the women travelling to Athens for abortions where they were fortunate enough to have the services

Robyn Wallis, 1960. (Redmond Wallis)

of an understanding doctor—described in a diary entry as "very nice, speaks English, attends to Hydra foreign colony". In contrast, it is to Athens, and particularly to the *troumba* (a red-light district in Piraeus), that Wallis has Californian Stephanos travel in *The Unyielding Memory* to satiate "the nostalgia he felt for the life he left behind, a life of fast cars, freeways, burlesque houses, swishy bars, women in fine clothes, waste disposals and bathrooms that worked". Everything it seems that a heterosexual American man would find conspicuously lacking on Hydra.

Australia's housewives were given a woman's perspective on Greek island life when an article by the Johnstons' friend Ruth Sriber appeared in *The Australian Women's Weekly* in July 1960. Ruth and Charles Sriber had recently moved from Athens to Ikaria, in the eastern Aegean, and the pretext for Sriber's article is a trip to the "isle of Hydra to spend a weekend with Kiama-born writer Charmian Clift" in order to get some woman-to-woman tips on island living. The article describes the many attractions of Aegean islands—they are wonderful places for raising a family; cheap, with affordable household help; blessed with wonderful seasonal produce, beautiful summer weather, and no need to ever "dress up"—and the challenges, including the standard of education, the absence of some luxuries and domestic conveniences, and the isolation during winter storms. There is a record of food prices (seafood includes "tiny whiting at 9d a pound to red snapper at 3/-", and meats "range in price from 3/- to 5/- a pound") and descriptions of dishes foreign to the Australian table, including "octopus stew with rice or spaghetti, fried squid in breadcrumbs, or dolmades". The exotic touches stretch to daily alcohol consumption by the locals, with Sriber declaring that:

> We like to follow these same drinking habits and to pause for a midday glass of wine or ouzo beneath a pine-scented awning on the quay. This is served with pickled octopus, anchovies, olives, or fetta cheese—fourpence a glass with the snack thrown in.

While Sriber accounts for both the pros and cons of island life, the balance sheet is firmly resolved on the side of the exotic simplicity of the Aegean, far removed as it is from the stress of city living. Sriber concludes by noting that "Charmian and I agree that the experience has been wonderful, and we have acquired an appreciation of calm ways and basic values".

It is uncertain what the *Women's Weekly*'s readers, in the suburbs and towns of Australia, made of this account. Sriber's article leans toward the self-congratulatory tone that is common to travel notes from 'paradise', but at a time when the genre of Mediterranean escapism was in its infancy, it is easy to believe how potently her portrait of remote, low-stress Aegean living would have fed the suburban fantasies of those who dreamed of islands.

Clift's own account of island life in *Peel Me a Lotus* is sufficiently honest to acknowledge the extent to which she misses advantages of the urban life she has rejected. It is a symptom of lingering ambivalence that while she happily points to the pleasures of shopping amongst "the abundance, the variety, the

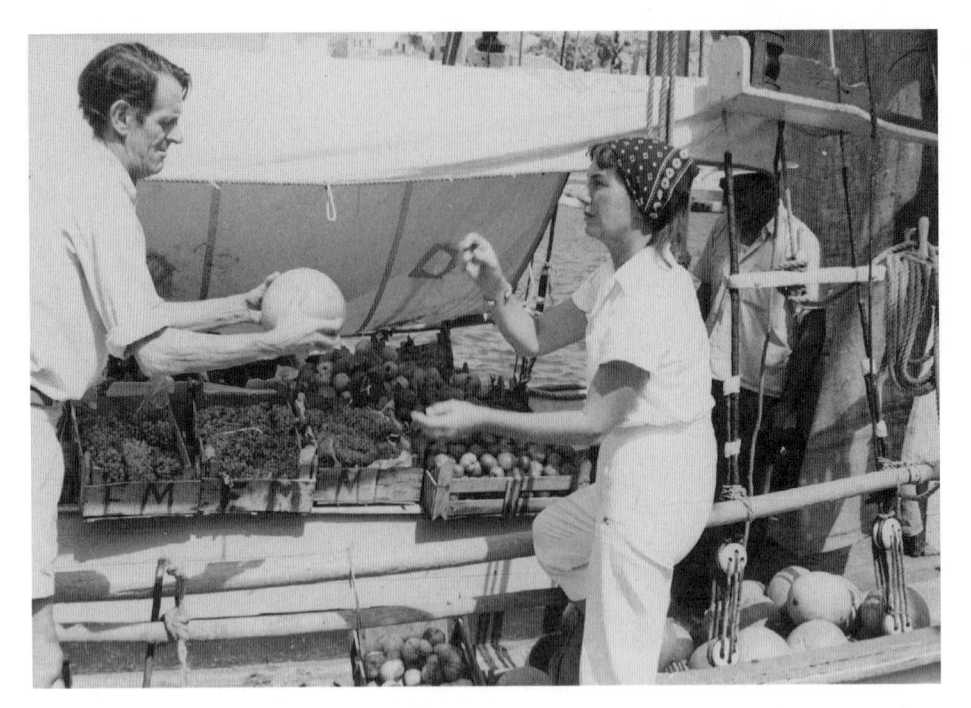

George Johnston and Charmian Clift shopping dockside, 1962. (Colin Simpson)

cheapness of the summer foods heaped and spilling from every store along the cobbled waterfront", she also pauses to ask, "Then what imp of perversity is it that makes me long for asparagus, for mushrooms, for tender-loin steaks, and chateau-bottled claret?" Of course, this imp of perversity is no more than the desire for the familiar that most people feel in changed circumstances. However, in the case of the Johnstons, it was exacerbated by the realisation that this may not be a temporary state—that being "castaways on a little rock" was their fate for the foreseeable future, so that no matter how perfect Hydra may be in itself, Clift found herself longing for not only familiar foodstuffs but for the grittier realities of a modern metropolis, "for the asphalt crust of city streets, for cinemas, taxi-cabs, neon-lights, meaningless clamour, or even just a box of good expensive make-up".

In *Peel Me a Lotus*, Clift constantly negotiates the narrow space between Hydra as a neo-romantic dreamscape of premodern wonderment infusing her life with beauty and radiance; and the relentless need to keep her dreams afloat in the face of the struggle for money, the petty annoyances of tourists, the battles against bureaucratic authority, the sometimes dispirited mood of her husband, and the occasional desire to throw in the bucolic isolation in favour of somewhere comfortable and familiar. So that one chapter concludes with Clift describing her exhilaration as she walks the dockside ("I almost have to pinch myself to believe in my own existence … floating just above the cobbles through a myriad small radiant explosions of sunlight and the intoxicating geometry of café tables, ship's prows, doors, windows, houses, roof-tops, rigging, that sing their coloured scraps of arcs and cubes and angles so piercingly as to almost burst my heart"), while the following chapter immediately commences with George fighting the police bureaucracy in order to establish his right to stay. The bewildered police captain wonders why anyone would leave Australia to live on Hydra—"Just look out the window. Rocks and ruins, that's all this place is".

Clift also understands the distorting fantasies of island living that other expatriates bring to the island as part of their ontological luggage. Toby and Katharine Nichols, an American couple, are among the romantic dreamers Clift includes in *Peel Me a Lotus*, and they are determined to "get the knack of living as *Greekly* as possible". Clift describes how the couple aspires to live a fully authentic island life, which includes mistaking as tea the mountain herbs the locals drink to relieve constipation and declining to make use of a cooking range coveted by Clift, choosing instead to prepare food over a charcoal grate. The impression is that Clift has little time for such fantasists, and her sceptical response to Toby and Katharine's desire to live "*Greekly*" is shared by Katharine's mother, the overbearing Mrs Knip, who arrives for an island visit and constantly voices her disapproval at her daughter's reduced circumstances.

> You must not think that I don't admire the way you all manage in these terrible circumstances. Gracious me, every one of you deserves a medal, and it is only surprising to me that poor Katharine has put up with it all for as long as she has. Toby, you know, could command a very important

position in one of our universities, and I am sure he will do so once the two of them have come to their senses.

Eventually, Mrs Knip asks the same question that has troubled Clift about her own decision to live an island life: "But what I want to know is what are you doing it all *for*?"

One response to that question, and one that presents a very different view of Hydra in the 1960s, is found in Welsh artist and writer Brenda Chamberlain's 1965 memoir, *A Rope of Vines*. Chamberlain first went to Hydra in May 1963 and then lived on the island for extended periods until the impact of the military coup in April 1967 became obvious. She stayed initially in the recently acquired house of English couple Peter and Didi Cameron. The Cameron House stood alongside the *Kala Pigadia* wells, where the town gave way to what Chamberlain referred to as the "desert" and well away from the *agora* where "international travellers throw an unreal glamour".

In *A Rope of Vines*, Chamberlain records her first summer on Hydra, and her response is almost entirely conditioned by her internalisation of the harsh, dry, heat-struck season and an environment where she is exposed to the rawness of island life. Chamberlain announces at the outset that "A powerful dual reality exists on the island", and it is immediately apparent on which side of that duality her interests lie—not for her the bustling *agora*, the bobbing *caiques*, and the boisterous taverns. Chamberlain's Hydra is an "ironbound savage island", imaginatively constructed from the bones and skeleton of the rocky uplands. It is a place of rampant prickly pear and treacherous bougainvillea; of suffering donkeys and diseased kittens; of scorpions and wasps and vipers; poverty stricken and drunken neighbours; violent storms and earthquake; and unspecified ghosts that wander through all her imaginings. Chamberlain's is a confronting existential response to the island, shaped not by long afternoons of dockside conviviality and talk—"The port and the people in it do not interest me" she declares—but rather by a retreat into a cell of the monastery of Agia Efpraxia, high above the port, the one place "where the mind can clear itself".

Chamberlain went to Hydra to give herself time and space to work and encountered a place that made particular demands of its artists—at least of those who are prepared to leave behind the "tender elite" of the dockside and test their mettle against the island's austere spirit. She recounts a conversation with her Greek friend Leonidas:

> He told me once of his belief that there is something in the air of the island that causes tension, gives a sense of nightmare unreality. 'It is just the island,' he said.
>
> His heart was broken when he had to leave it though he had often felt imprisoned by it, and longed for somewhere less powerful in which to live, for example, the next island, elegiac Poros. Everything comes back to love, or hate, to not being able to decide, once and for all, this I want, that I reject.
>
> He used to say, it is because we are cooped up here between the sea and the mountains, trying to be artists, or pretending to be artists, exiles in a strong context, in an island too strong for most of us to fight against.

Chamberlain's is a singular description of Hydra life, well removed from that given by Clift in *Peel Me a Lotus*, and later by Johnston in his novel *Closer to the Sun*. Although dig deeply into almost any Hydra narrative, and there are intimations of the island's forbidding presence once away from the port.

Despite these dissimilarities, however, Clift and Johnston would have said that, like Chamberlain, they were on Hydra to work. Early in their stay, they declared as much to John Laffin, an Australian military historian who took time out from his schedule retracing Middle Eastern battlegrounds to visit the couple in 1957. Laffin later published an account of his visit in *Middle East Journey*, and, between casual observations about Hydra and its inhabitants, he noted with scepticism the Johnstons' claim that they "find life on Ydra intellectually invigorating". After sharing a dockside lunch with the couple, Laffin reported, "I, too, could believe that I had found a paradise, but one in which to sleep, not to work". For this visitor, Johnston and Clift's decision to stay on Hydra was at first baffling as it "seemed to me that they had buried themselves". Finally, however, on his ferry returning to Piraeus and with time for reflection, Laffin realised that it is the very tedium and immunity to distractions that feeds a writer's creativity.

> [T]he secret lay not so much in the island's ability to stimulate, but in its inability to dissipate. It has none of the civilized distractions. Newspapers, telephones, traffic, and crime are unknown; there are few radios. The only films shown are documentaries for the school children. There are no frustrations or upsetting interruptions, no social obligations demanding attention. Hence a writer's creative energy has nothing to sap it. His whole time and being is devoted to his craft or to discussion and thought—both part of his craft, anyway.

Laffin concludes by conceding that "Perhaps this is why writers and artists of many nationalities live and work in the Greek islands of the Aegean Sea. All the islands are enchanting", before declaring, in a down-to-earth fashion, that for a military historian, Crete is "the most interesting".

Despite the quasi-romantic portrait Laffin leaves of Clift and Johnston, with island living sustaining their creative vigour, Johnston in particular was beset with concerns about his accomplishments as a writer and as a writer on an island. It was a theme that would be central to *Closer to the Sun*, a novel Johnston wrote on Hydra with the working title of 'The Islanders', and which he declared on the cover blurb of the US Book Club edition to be "naturally the fruit of the experience of some six years of living on Greek islands as an expatriate free-lance". Within the novel's pages, Johnston debates at length the merits of living and writing on islands, exposing, in the process, some of the differences he and Clift felt on the subject. While the title *Closer to the Sun* might seemingly promise readers a sun-lashed Mediterranean haven, the title's evocation of the Icarus myth amounts to Johnston's admission to hubris in believing that he could avoid the harsher realities of island living and find the freedom to live and write on his own terms.

As Johnston wrote *Closer to the Sun*, he was at a low ebb both mentally and physically. His relationship with Clift was increasingly acrimonious and beset by jealousy and suspicion; his writing was entangled in bill-paying genre fiction; meagre royalties left him living on credit from Hydra's shopkeepers; and, despite recently escaping a cancer diagnosis, his health problems were entrenched. The novel that results is deeply ambivalent and even bitter in its scathing portrayal not only of the protagonist's marriage and writing career but also of island life and the expatriate 'scene'. Although *Closer to the Sun* may leave an impression of inconsequentiality, it is redeemed by its precise expression of David Meredith's fraught state as he struggles to keep his exotic expatriate lifestyle in balance with his ambition to produce quality fiction while sustaining his family's finances.

Meredith's continued presence on Silenos (as the island is called) is questioned when he is visited by his brother Mark, who hopes to talk his sibling into returning to London. Mark is a successful playwright who arrives on the island by yacht with a retinue of wealthy friends. Little time passes before Mark challenges his brother on his decision to continue living on the island, thereby condemning his family to poverty while he produces mediocre fiction with little commercial success.

In a protracted early scene, Mark argues why this far-from-London island is no place for either a writer or a family, a charge David defends in terms of the quality of life he has gained for himself, Kate and their children. Mark's arguments circle around the meagre returns from a few poorly selling novels and, more particularly, what *hasn't* been achieved.

> 'David, as a journalist you were a considerable success,' said Mark, unperturbed. 'And now?' Again he examined his fingertips. 'As an author?' he said meaningly.
>
> 'I'm learning.'
>
> 'Of course you're learning. All of us are always learning. That's not the point is it?'

Although David Meredith defends his island lifestyle to his brother, he too is concerned by his lack of achievement, as he finds his time swallowed up by both the responsibilities that come with his position as the senior permanent resident amid a transient international community and by the growing pressure to actually write something of lasting value. In response to his wife's question about how he has spent his day, Meredith explodes in frustration.

> 'Work!' He repeated the word sourly. 'I didn't write, if that's what you mean. I don't think I do that sort of work any more. I have a new job. House-agent for the important people, general rouseabout errand boy. The village Figaro, that's me.' ... Behind the bitterness of his words lay the arid hours of the wasted afternoon, the maddening frustration of staring at a blank sheet of paper in an unresponsive typewriter, the leaden despondency of seeing all that he had written before as something contrived, artificial worthless, unpublishable ...

As is the case with George in *Peel Me a Lotus*, David Meredith in *Closer to the Sun* reaches the point where he, at least, appears ready to draw a line under his stumbling personal and professional circumstances and return to London. While this might seem the logical conclusion to the storyline, it is not ultimately the narrative solution Johnston offers any more than he chose it for himself. When David momentarily appears to accept that he must leave, he is again confronted by Mark who now convinces him that he should stay, based not on his concern for David's future but rather on what he has learnt of Kate and the way in which the island has met *her* needs. Kate has dismissed Mark's idea that the island is a producer of isolation, arguing instead that it represents a chance for the couple to build intimacy, introspection and the possibility for self-fulfilment, something she whimsically attributes, Clift-like, to the island's light: "You see people all the way through, as if they are transparent almost. And you see yourself just the same way". Above all else, Kate claims that, for her, living on the island marks "*permanence* ... a sense of belonging, of family, of home, of children", a position strikingly close to the idea that Clift expresses in *Peel Me a Lotus*.

The final argument on the subject between the brothers produces a somewhat contrived resolution to David Meredith's dilemma and conveniently shifts the responsibility for the decision from David to Kate—an acknowledgement that, at this point, it was Clift rather than Johnston who was driven to persevere on Hydra. It is also, however, a conclusion that can be read as a statement of purpose by Johnston and a final commitment to making a go of his marriage, his writing, and his island life, albeit with some misgivings. David concedes that the ideals and dreams that drove him and Kate to the island, including romantic fantasies about islands generally, are beyond their grasp, while accepting that the independence they have gained is sufficient justification.

> He and Kate had built something. He could see that now. They had built something that was better than either of them realised, and they had built it with the things that were to hand, here, now … with the materials available. All right, the talent of David Meredith might not be as great as he might wish it to be, nor his marriage as romantic, nor his island as idyllic … but he had brought off his own stand for the right to hold the tiller in his own hand, and, by God! This was something.

"Something" it might be, but *Closer to the Sun* also speaks to the quotidian realities of island life that bump up against idyllic notions that the Merediths are truly free to follow their passion. Several passages focus on Silenos' resident policeman with whom David Meredith engages in imagined conversation that returns the protagonist to a subject that was ever-present in Johnston's mind: money. When questioned by the figure of state authority as to why he remains on Silenos, Meredith replies: "I have no alternative, Commandant. Mr. Vilkos, the banker, will explain that our account will not stand the fare out—not for all of us. And I must finish my book." Meredith doesn't finish the book—there is scant evidence that he is actually writing one—but his humorous two-page 'interview' with a representative of the Greek state is illuminating.

The need for expatriates to annually renew residency permits authorising their presence on Hydra was a constant reminder of their status as 'foreigners' in the eyes of the law and almost certainly to Hydriots. This possibility is half-acknowledged by Clift's admission in *Peel Me a Lotus* that "Someone has chalked EOKA on our front door". EOKA, or *Ethniki Organosis Kyprion*

Agoniston (National Organisation of Cypriot Fighters), was the guerrilla movement fighting British colonial rule in the mid-1950s and pushing for the political union of Greece and Cyprus. Clift suspects seven-year-old Shane of being the graffiti culprit, and the incident is used to confirm the Hydriots' loyalty to the Australian family "when the women [gather] around the well … Kyria Heleni dip[s] the end of her apron in the bucket of well water and carefully washe[s] the sign away". While Shane is made the playful scapegoat for this incident, what lingers is the unsaid possibility that not everyone on the island shares *Kyria* Heleni's affection for the Johnston family, and that, for some, their presence has an unwelcome political dimension.

The renewal of permits was an administrative necessity that is represented in *Closer to the Sun* by the character of Lieutenant Fotis, who is sharply differentiated from the artist-workers on the island. The spectre of Fotis is raised at the thought of Meredith undertaking the task of permit renewal: "Aggravating. A Nuisance. But this was the way you had to kowtow for time to live, for slices of your own life … the dry voice of bureaucracy that was the deafening sound of the spinning twentieth-century globe." The notion that the island is a place over which government control is vulgarly exercised in this scene sits alongside another vision of islands as a blank canvas for artistic self-deprecation and self-doubt that Meredith admits to when interrogated by Fotis. His motives for staying another year on Silenos are that "My wife and family are here. My brother is here. Freedom is here. Freedom of course is everywhere. One reads about it all the time. It is fashionable now to find freedom of a special sort on a distant island. Freedom to fail even." According to Meredith, postwar freedom transcends the boundaries of nation states that produce categories such as the expatriate, which Johnston and Clift's commitment to art and Hydra sought to overcome. As Clift wrote in *Peel Me a Lotus*, "Damn all flags, damn all slogans, damn passports and permits and visas and dossiers". Yet it was another dream of islands that so often fell short.

One expatriate to fall foul of the island authorities was Magda Tilche. In Tilche's case, her residency became tenuous when her marriage to Paolo

Tilche broke down, and she established a relationship with Theodoros Anargirou, a married islander. In early 1961 Tilche's permit to remain in Greece was revoked, suggesting that bureaucratic intervention could be used to regulate integration between Hydriots and foreigners. Soon after, she wrote from Milan to Leonard Cohen in Montreal, revealing her fraught response as her residency was terminated, and she was forced to leave the island.

> The Sword of Damocles during all this time has oscillated above my head. Would I be able to stay or would I have to leave? And as I waited for the coming day and the thumb turned down I could not hope for any more grace. The decision of the xenophobic civil servant condemned me to exile, and I did not even try to be heard. He would never have understood. It was bewildering to realize the pit that existed between me and him.

Tilche's letter registers the shock of her expulsion, which recalled her postwar flight from Czechoslovakia, finding that "Once again I am uprooted and brutally deprived of all that was familiar to me and that I loved". (In Tilche's case, a reversal of the decision seems to have been possible, as she was back on Hydra by late summer in the same year).

Clift and Johnston's experience of islands had been shaped on Kalymnos, where prospects were so poor that the couple was seen by the locals as a possible conduit for escape—an exit strategy to reach Australia. The situation was similar on Hydra, for although tourist numbers were increasing, the island's economy remained uncertain and many Hydriots looked for opportunities to move to continental cities. As it happens, Burke photographed one such Hydriot, policeman Emmanuel Androlakis.

At first glance, Androlakis might seem to be fulfilling the same paper-shuffling role assigned to the unnamed captain in *Peel Me a Lotus* or Fotis in *Closer to the Sun*. He sits stationed at a table with papers in hand, his uniform evoking a formality that contrasts with Demetri Gassoumis's casual pose and Wallis's sandaled feet. This, the photograph might say, is the smiling face of bureaucratic authority. Yet Burke's image of this island

Emmanuel Androlakis, Robyn Wallis, Redmond Wallis and Demetri Gassoumis.
(James Burke)

policeman is not what it might seem. Burke was seemingly fascinated with this man, having referred to him in his cable to *LIFE* when he pitched his Hydra photo-story, noting that "at least one local policeman is ardent poet himself". In a subsequent cable, Burke wrote: "Another good reason for shooting story now is that by next summer we will lose local policeman poet. Hes going Chicago soon to take job as bouncer in his uncles bar." Obviously this Hydriot policeman-poet was dreaming of a place and a job that offered the sorts of opportunities that others were seeking on Hydra. In his caption notes, Burke recorded that Androlakis wrote romantic poetry, and that he would "take a break from his waterfront beat anytime to read one of his poems to anyone inclined to hear it". Burke took over three dozen photographs of Androlakis doing just that—reading his Greek-language poems to the Wallises outside Katsikas *kafenio*, with Demetri Gassoumis translating.

Steve Sanfield also eventually realised he couldn't stay on Hydra either. In his diary, he projected this "Possible future conversation":

>—How did you like living on Hydra?
>—It was magnificent.
>—Why didn't you stay?
>—I missed the city.
>—I thought you dug Hydra.
>—I did. It was an important & valuable experience but it was useful for only so long.

For Sanfield in this imaginary scenario, island living represents a temporary escape from the metropolitan scene where real living takes place. These are ideas Sanfield returns to in a letter to Cohen and Ihlen written from Granada, Spain, on August 8th:

> Leaving Hydra was more difficult & bewildering than I thought it could be. There was much I wanted to say to you both before I left, much I wanted to thank you for. But how the hell do you say thank you for

emotions & experiences exchanged, for empathy & understanding? The Hydra experience taught me much about many things including myself. You were an important part of it, and although I'm still not able to separate the people from the place, all would be a lie if I did not tell that I loved you. Once on the boat I found myself crying openly—crying for myself and for all the others who were somewhere without wanting to be there, without even knowing how they got there … But the sadness and bewilderment remained … until two hours later when I discovered I had lost my hash. Anger, frustration & fear (Could I get along without any at all? Answer is yes.) suddenly set in, and perhaps it was a good thing. To go on feeling as I did … would have been an indulgence that could have become a dangerous habit.

Reflecting ambivalently on his departure, Sanfield offers the impression that, while his experiences will be lasting and are deeply felt, he is also relieved to be leaving. Hydra is not a place to stay but rather a stop on his physical and emotional journey. Just as Sanfield was leaving, the Wallises were returning overland to Hydra from the UK where they had spent almost two years. Wallis planned to write another novel and thought Hydra was the place to do it, but in recording in his diary entry of August 22nd, 1963 that he was back on the island, he also noted, "Hydra the same, but for about three new bars, but full of people … George, Charm etc. exactly the same—couldn't take it the first night and only rarely since then".

Whereas Sanfield might have reflected from Granada on the existential education the island provided, for the returning Wallis, Hydra, and those who had previously rattled his nerves, remained unchanged. For Wallis, the idea of Hydra as a place to escape to in order to write was an abiding one, at least until Johnston's departure for Australia in February the following year, which Wallis marked out as a defining moment for the island and its expatriate colony. From his own final departure six months later until his death, Hydra was cast in Wallis's mind as a place to return to in his writing, but not a place to live physically.

While Sanfield, Wallis, Cohen and most others could presume to leave Hydra as they wished, and a few, such as the Johnstons, found themselves tethered to the island by their sorry finances, the region was nonetheless peppered with histories of islands being used for forced detention and worse. Within weeks of completing his work on Hydra in September 1960, James Burke found himself on a very different island and recorded a much darker island experience. In October he was dispatched by *LIFE* to the tiny Turkish island of Yassıada in the Sea of Marmara to photograph the political trials of key figures in Turkey's elected government, which had been overthrown by a military coup earlier in the year. Yassıada had been converted to a prison island for this purpose, and those on trial included deposed Premier Adnan Menderes and President Celâl Bayar. As a result, Menderes and others were incarcerated and executed the following year on the nearby island of İmralı. It was a harsh reminder of the political instability of the Aegean region and of how dictatorial regimes could easily transform islands from places of leisured escapism into sites of state oppression.

Later in the decade, following the April 1967 military coup d'état, many Greek islands became prisons for citizens the colonels decreed to be 'undesirables'. Initiated in 1965 by the court-sanctioned ousting of the elected government of Georgios Papandreou, the upheaval of 1967 saw tanks rolling through Syntagma Square in Athens and surrounding the Parliament. Led by Colonel Georgios Papadopoulos, the regime took control of Greek life, advocating for the most conservative values of the Orthodox Church and attempting to wind back the 1960s by introducing a short-lived ban on miniskirts, beards and the music of The Beatles.

More profoundly, a suspension of press freedoms came into effect, and people singled out as leftists, communists or broadly opposed to the regime were rounded up and arrested. Surveillance networks were ruthlessly deployed with at least one informant stationed on Hydra before the waterfront was increasingly occupied by military agents. Thousands of Greek citizens were transported to detention centres on islands including Léros, Markonisos,

Syros and Yaros—the latter in particular had a dark recent history when, following the Civil War, it had been used to incarcerate left-wing dissenters who were forced to build their own prisons and torture cells. The colonels now revived the prisons on Yaros to detain leading dissidents, including poet Yiannis Ritsos and the founder of the Democratic National Resistance Movement, Ioannis Charalambopoulos.

At the same time that the regime was treating some islands as prisons (while denying their existence), other islands were pushed to accept other, new roles. The Junta planned a tourist route for favoured visitors that would take them to Athens and then to Rhodes and Corfu, which were being transformed into "island vacations centres" to showcase a carefully managed version of the Greek island experience. Despite these efforts, it was islands such as Crete, Ios, Paros, Santorini, Mykonos and Antiparos of which the hippies were dreaming. As a result, the style of postwar tourism that had been pioneered on Hydra and then flourished throughout the Aegean was exactly the form of independent tourism the colonels sought to deter. However, the Junta's denial of the penitentiary islands wouldn't last, and Yaros became the rallying point for Greek political and physical freedoms when aerial photographs taken by German journalists forced the Junta to acknowledge the prison camps and the Council of Europe to expel Greece for violating human rights. The colonels were largely unmoved and would remain in power until 1974, when the island prisons were finally closed.

* * *

As a New Zealander, Redmond Wallis was accustomed to island life, but he found many new experiences on Hydra.

> *Island firsts: bed bugs; queers; writers who made money from it; mules; eating squid and octopus; rabid infidelity; poverty; siestas; total lack of inhibition. White walls, blue sea, grey rock, brown mules, red roofs. Fishing boats with eyes painted on the prows ... People who gestured constantly as they spoke.*

ISLANDS: DREAMING AND LIVING

And sounds: the braying of donkeys, the hoot of the owl (delightfully called a 'koukouviya' in Greek); the thump-thump of the diesel engines of the fishing caiques; wives telling their husbands to get their idle arses back up to the house, the message being passed from wife to wife across the amphitheatre of the island's dwelling and thence down to the agora where Yanni was shame-facedly obliged to leave his game of backgammon and his glass of cognac and march back up the hill to see why he was needed; thunder rumbling away over on the Peleponnisos; the sound of fresh rainwater cascading from the roofs across the terraces and into the deep sternas, carved out of the rock.

Smells and tastes: fresh bread; shit, in toilets and up what the foreigners called Donkey-Shit Lane, the inland route to the next village; meat being cooked over charcoal; charcoal braziers, smoking outside the house before they were settled beneath the voluminous black skirts of the housewives and mothers; ouzo; unwashed armpits; sickly perfume and hair oil; heat; cooked vine leaves; fresh yoghurts delivered over the mountains by a man who called "Yaoutass!" as he move[s] sure-footedly across the rocks; retsina, which could be very good or very bad; smells and tastes inherited from the Turks and from the Albanians, because the island had been populated by Albanians, not the Greeks.

Chapter Four

COMINGS AND GOINGS

Accounts of Hydra's postwar revitalisation frequently recognise the island's long association with the arts. The period of the late 1950s and early 1960s is singled out as being particularly vibrant following the arrival of George Johnston and Charmian Clift and the permanent foreign presence that flourished in their wake. So rapidly did the number of island visitors grow that Johnston himself soon recorded his displeasure. In the short story 'Vale, Pollini!', written in the early 1960s, he has the writer-protagonist vying for space and credibility on Hydra with the ever-increasing number of artists and intellectuals, and irritably declaring, "Now those sons of bitches have taken over the sea ... They're littered all over the rocks by the cave. We can't work. We can't talk. Now we can't swim, either". Johnston was not alone in voicing disapproval, although other judgements were more about morals than contested living conditions—in October 1961 the weekly magazine *Eikones* described the island's artist community as a modern-day "Sodom and Gomorrah". Such were the perceived excesses of the island's foreign colony that it became associated not only with the arts but also with the 'degeneracy' that at the time was loosely linked with Beat culture and bohemianism. However, insofar as the Beats (and the Beat generation) had a spiritual home in the Mediterranean, it was well to the west, in Tangiers, where Paul and Jane Bowles played a similar role to that of the Johnstons on Hydra. Furthermore, any excesses on the Greek island were as likely to have reflected the activities of transient tourists as much as those of the longer-term expatriates.

Most accounts of Hydra in the 1950s and 1960s provide a rollcall of names associated with the expatriate group. Leonard Cohen is universally highlighted, and Johnston and Clift are frequently mentioned. Others include poets Gregory Corso, Allen Ginsberg, Irving Layton and Kenneth Koch; writers Axel Jensen, William J. Lederer, Rodney Hall and Göran Tunström; artists Sidney Nolan, Anthony Kingsmill, John Craxton, and Norris Embry; actors Sophia Loren, Melina Mercouri, Peter Finch and Anthony Perkins. The names vary, likely according to the nationality of the compiler and the interests they are trying to foreground, but such lists do not completely explain conclusions such as that reached by Anthony Reynolds in his biography of Cohen.

> [By] 'fleeing' to Hydra, Cohen had placed himself within the heart of an almost inexhaustibly rich and catholic social scene, one that compared with almost any capital city on the planet, albeit in microcosm. By putting himself into a kind of exile upon a relatively tiny and obscure Greek Island, Cohen had somehow found himself at the centre of the world itself.

Nor do such lists explain the nature of each individual's circulation through Hydra—some were tourists and some were travellers while others were there to work and a few were genuinely expatriated. The term 'expatriate' is somewhat unstable in the context of Hydra at that time, given that it implies a long-term commitment or permanence, which was never likely for most international visitors who found themselves on the island. The number of foreigners who remained over the long term was small compared to those who stayed for days, weeks or perhaps months.

Indeed coming and going from Hydra was the norm for even those who settled to the extent of buying property. For most artists and writers, there was the need to remain connected with the world's intellectual and cultural centres, and the island was simply too small and too removed for them to live there permanently given the excitement of a continent and a world re-emerging from the protracted postwar era. As seductive as Hydra's bucolic lifestyle might have been, the insularity and isolation meant that the very things that made the island enticing also made it a place from which most of the international colony eventually needed to escape.

For Clift and Johnston, travel was in their blood and in their plans when they moved to the Aegean, and they thought the island would be an ideal base from which to explore the region. In 1958 Charles Sriber reported in *People* that "The Johnstons' ambition is to become sufficiently successful at writing to allow them to tour the eastern Mediterranean for six months each year". This did not turn out to be the case—Johnston's fragile health, financial shortfalls and need to care for a young family meant that opportunities for travel were limited. Short breaks in Athens, usually for medical matters, or infrequent day trips to the Peloponnese or nearby islands were as much as they could hope for.

Although Clift's memoir *Peel Me a Lotus* encompassed only the first year she and Johnston were on Hydra, it is possible to read her acerbic commentary on those who drifted on to the island over summer as a reflection on her own situation, as she found herself "marooned" on this barren rock. A bitter edge emerges over the course of the book, as Clift realises that she and Johnston are tied to the island in unforeseen ways. In particular, she resents the young itinerant and aspiring writers and artists who, devoid of the responsibilities of families and houses, are free to come and go as they wish. Clift carefully differentiates herself and Johnston from this "war generation who grew up to horror and inherited despair and disillusion", and who now brandish a desultory set of values and a spiritual lassitude that derail their artistic ambitions.

> It is even difficult to think of them as individual. The boys. The *poste-restante*, interchangeable, culture addicted, Europe-sick boys, with grey sprinkled through their crew cuts and little pads of drink-fat around their middles, who yearn for the Europe of Gertrude Stein and Scott Fitzgerald and the 'lost generation' of a generation who were losing themselves while they were being born.

Clift registers revulsion in describing these nameless young men (and it is men of whom she writes) with their faces of "expatriate anonymity"; their accents distinguished by a "sedulously acquired stammer added for interest"; and their eyes with a "dreadful centre of purposelessness". To Clift they are caricatures of the expatriated artist, aimless wanderers empowered by economic advantage but conflicted by a postwar deracination that strips them of the wherewithal and purpose that would bring reward from their talents.

> They were to be poets, to be painters, to be writers, come to drink in their culture at its source, the old mystic fountainhead. Perhaps their stomachs weren't strong enough, perhaps their gifts were weighed and found wanting, or perhaps that little private income, the remittance, made it all too easy to put off until tomorrow the actual hard work that might be involved in being the new young prophet.
>
> And now, when they are no longer really young, and Europe is stale old ground, it is too late for them to begin and too late for them to go back. So they go round and round and round, treading the same old beaten track, the clever young men, the witty young men, the careless young men, the oh-so-European young men, the sad young men, who are looking for Gertrude Stein.

By sympathetically evoking Stein, Fitzgerald and the lost generation of the interwar years, and in distancing herself from the Beat generation who were now flocking to Hydra, Clift exposes the uncertain place she and Johnston shared within the chronology of twentieth century literary expatriation. In generational terms, the Johnstons fell between these two groups, and it is not surprising that they were intellectually out of step with Hydra's younger visitors. To the extent that Clift and Johnston had a like-minded cohort, it was the Australians who flooded London in the postwar years, so that when Clift and Johnson chose to leave London, they not only left behind the literary capital but also the type of supportive intellectual community on which they thrived. This generational mismatch was a problem the couple would find increasingly troubling as their years on Hydra progressed.

In the meantime, by taking the island's younger visitors to task for their failed work ethic, Clift arguably reveals much about her fears around her own circumstances. After all, she and Johnston put everything on the line to settle on Hydra and pursue their literary ambitions, and now she finds they are enmeshed in an existential battle that threatens to undo their dreams. *Peel Me a Lotus* is laced with passages of self-doubt—Clift is too self-aware and engrossed in the drama of her own circumstances (and arguably too enmeshed in her own narrative) to pretend otherwise—and there is genuine poignancy when she concedes:

> Well, thank God we *are* marooned, that there is no question of going back. If there was a chance to escape I suspect that George might take it. … It's hard for him to be caught like this. I watch him sometimes hating the mountains. He looks baffled, uneasy, and afraid.

The troubling cleft in which Clift and Johnston found themselves was that the summer visitors might have been an irritant and distraction, but, as long as Clift and Johnston themselves remained fixed on Hydra, this annual influx was also a much-needed conduit to the familiar world of Anglophone cultures.

> We all talk the same language, have more or less the same culture patter, the same frame of reference. We laugh at the same jokes, understand the same implications in events, and are equally perturbed at the trend of modern civilization. We are all here, all together, on the same small island, living more or less the same way, and looking—alas!—most definitely A Foreign Group, variations on a theme of escapism.

It is therefore not surprising that watching for the arrival of interesting visitors was part of the Johnstons' routine. When they first arrived on Hydra, new arrivals were disembarked from ferries at the harbour mouth and transported in smaller boats, but, by 1960, alterations to the harbour allowed ferries to fully dock, making the greetings more intense as incoming passengers spilled on to the dockside. James Burke described greeting ferries as "one of [the] main pastimes of Hydriots, foreign and native", and, while for some Hydriots it was a way of doing business—touting for hotels, *domatia*, donkey rides or restaurants—for expatriates it was a means of remaining abreast of the island's revolving population.

COMINGS AND GOINGS

George Johnston and Charmian Clift greeting the *Saronis*. (James Burke)

Twice Burke photographed Johnston and Clift meeting incoming ferries, apparently not welcoming anyone in particular but indulging in both a diversion and a form of information gathering as they observed passengers arriving and departing. The couple is shown standing back from the dockside, away from the hurly-burly of personal greetings, as they hope to spot a familiar face or overhear a familiar accent or find someone who looks sufficiently interesting.

A number of those reaching Hydra went on to be more than casual island visitors—they became house guests of the Johnstons. One of the earliest arrivals was Ramblin' Jack Elliott (born Elliott Adnopoz) and his wife, aspiring actress June Hammerstein (later June Shelley), who spent late 1957 with the Johnstons and brought with them the kind of exposure to the world's cultural and literary centres the Johnstons found irresistible. Elliott was a friend and protégé of Woody Guthrie, a sometime resident of New York's Greenwich Village where he befriended Jack Kerouac, Allen Ginsberg and Gregory Corso, and would be a crucial influence on a young Bob Dylan, who was billed for his first New York gig as 'Son of Jack Elliott'. A folk singer born with the soul of a Beat, Elliott's career eventually intersected with most major strands of twentieth century American music and its foremost practitioners, including collaborations with everyone from Dylan to Johnny Cash, the Grateful Dead and Red Hot Chilli Peppers.

For several years in the late 1950s, Elliott busked around Europe while Dylan was looking for him in New York, and when he and Hammerstein travelled south on a Vespa in October 1957 in search of winter sunshine, they eventually made their way to Hydra. As Hammerstein later recalled, "One day, in a café on the port, we met an Australian couple, George Johnston and Charmain [sic] Clift". The Elliotts soon found themselves staying with the Johnstons, who were no doubt enamoured by the talkative young troubadour with literary affiliations and his Hollywood-connected wife. And the attraction was mutual—in Hammerstein's words, "There was a glow to being with this family".

June Hammerstein and Ramblin' Jack Elliott, 1957. (Johnston and Clift Collection)

The Elliotts' stay extended until Christmas of 1957, with Hammerstein recalling that the two couples decided to celebrate the season by preparing a roast turkey to share with the townsfolk, with the sacrificial bird being delivered from Athens.

> When the Athens ferry was due to dock the four of us went down to the portside grocery store and café where we had first met and waited, as it had been arranged that the turkey was to be delivered to her [Clift] there. As we sat drinking coffee and talking, the door opened and a man

came in followed by a huge, live turkey. We were dumbstruck. We had all these people to feed the next day and the turkey was still walking around! Everyone was shouting at everyone else to 'kill the turkey,' passing the knife around like we were in a Marx Brothers movie. Eventually the mayor agreed to do the deed, but we still had the problem that there wasn't enough time to 'hang' the bird, and there were dire predictions that it would be inedible—or at the very least, tough. By now the whole village was involved in the discussions. In the end we just went ahead as planned. The turkey was tender and delicious and villagers kept dropping in all day at their house to try a little bit. It was a truly wonderful Christmas.

At the time, the Elliotts were living in an open marriage and "skirted around the issue" with Johnston and Clift. Despite the track record for infidelity building in the Johnston marriage, on this occasion both couples let the opportunity pass, with Hammerstein simply reporting that "George and I kissed once but I felt a little embarrassed that we [herself and Elliott] always seemed to be the aggressors".

Eventually Elliott and Hammerstein moved on, but not before Hammerstein had received advice from Johnston that, four decades later, served as an epigraph to her autobiography: "Eat the world". It was something conspicuously difficult for Johnston to do from his remote island outpost. In the short term, Ramblin' Jack's wandering ways and connections to New York's literary circles would have been a sharp reminder to the Australian couple as to exactly what they were missing by living on Hydra. Elliott would not be Hydra's last visitor from Greenwich Village, nor would he be the last guitar-playing Jewish folk singer to reach the island. Several years later, another visitor with musical interests came expressly to Hydra to see Clift and Johnston. Don McGill, a Canadian broadcaster and theatre director who visited the island in 1960, returned in 1963 with a musical based on *Peel Me a Lotus*. An unimpressed Redmond Wallis wrote in *The Unyielding Memory* that "The Graysons are reported to be 'wildly enthusiastic' about the concept [and] its principal song—'Peel me a lotus, pour me some wine, I hope you've noticed I'm feeling fine'". Unsurprisingly, performances of *Peel Me a Lotus* the musical seem to have remained confined to Hydra.

James Burke's 1960 photographs provide a tantalising insight into the passage of ambitious young literary and artistic travellers through Hydra. Burke's images and the people they include—a mix of earnest artists, casually inclined bohemians, and tourists catching a glimpse of their island dream—help describe the 'categories' of Hydra's visitors and what it was, intention or chance, that brought them there. The varied cast Burke photographed provides a retrospective index of Hydra's metamorphosis from a forgotten dot in the Aegean; to a sleepy and remote backwater for the creative poor; and finally to a point of geographic desire for the shiftless Beats, the day-trippers from Athens and the leisured rich.

With hindsight, it can also be appreciated that Burke's photographs captured a tipping point for the Hydra expatriate community, which, until that time, remained comparatively small. In addition to the Johnston family, the established foreigners on the island at the beginning of 1960 consisted of only Christian Heidsieck and Lily Mack; Axel Jensen and Marianne Ihlen; David and Angela Goschen and their children; Magda Tilche and her son Sandro; and novelist Gordon Merrick and his partner Charles Hulse—but numbers were about to grow.

The year had begun propitiously for the small colony, when Ihlen, having travelled back to Oslo, gave birth to a son on January 21st. Jensen had also travelled to Oslo for the birth but returned to Hydra in late January ahead of his wife and eager to recommence a relationship with American artist Patricia Amlin. On April 9th, Redmond and Robyn Wallis arrived and quickly decided to stay, and in the same week, Leonard Cohen also arrived. He too determined to extend his stay, but not before spending a short time with Johnston and Clift. The Johnstons already had a house guest at this time, Lena Folke-Olsson, and, according to some sources, she and Cohen soon commenced a brief relationship.

In late April the Wallises moved into the Johnstons' house for several days in order to look after their children while the couple travelled briefly to Athens. According to Wallis's diary, Clift had an abortion while in the city. If this is the case, it must have been a fraught time for her, not least because Ihlen arrived back on the island with her baby in late April. It was also a difficult time for Ihlen as she immediately realised that her husband was in a relationship with Amlin and that her marriage was in danger.

In the first week in May, Merrick and Hulse returned to the island—they had purchased a house the previous year—after spending some months in the US and Paris, where they also had an apartment. As Wallis recorded in his diary, the two men were soon at the centre of an upheaval amongst the expatriate community when a physical fight broke out at Katsikas *kafenio* after they were the target of homophobic abuse from David Goschen.

> Patricia, 24, US apparently has had an affair with Axel 27 Norw. Axel's wife, Marianne 23? Also, before marriage, played around a lot and with Sam who runs the Stormie Seas for charter. Sam in love with Marianne. She marries Axel. Few weeks ago—2, about—comes back from Oslo with baby. Axel back in with Patricia. One night, week before last, two US pansies arrive. George, Charm, Axel, Patricia, Marianne, David, Sam and his new mistress, Anna, all sitting talking. David starts in on queers 'Thank God Angela and I always say our little prayer in the morning, "God preserve us from all pansies."' Fight develops during which Axel takes Patricia home. Marianne breaks down on George's knee, Anna has hysterics, George finally breaks it up. Charm walks into wall or something and gets black eye.
>
> Axel goes home the following night and wrecks the house, breaking a lot of the windows and throwing a lot of stuff out the window. Marianne, with baby, arrives at 3am at Georges. … Things simmer for a day or so. There are more fracas and drama in public.

Wallis later retold the story of this fight in more detail in *The Unyielding Memory*, this time concluding the scene as Adrian Gosling (Goschen) storms off while shouting, "At least I don't shove my prick up other men's arseholes!" Such scenes underscored a chauvinism that would have been all-too-familiar and insulting to Merrick and Hulse even though, as Kostas Yannakopoulos has argued, Greek men might not have been broadly understood within their national culture during the mid-twentieth century as 'heterosexual', 'homosexual' or 'queer' but rather as 'masculine' and 'feminine'. These identities and 'imported' ideas about sexuality were played out on Hydra in various and complex ways. In contrast to Goschen's reported prejudice, Wallis noted casually in a diary entry from 1963 that there were "Lots of queers, kissing on the rocks", and, likewise, Colin Simpson, who was on the island twice during the 1960s, observed without judgement the presence of "young men in tight pants who were clearly not interested in girls but in each other". Hydra's growing reliance on tourism meant that many gay men during these years found it was a place where they were recognised as part of the island's bohemian diversity.

The most immediate outcome of the upheaval on the *agora* was a permanent break in the Jensen and Ihlen marriage. Jensen departed Hydra on his own yacht for Athens on May 12th, and Amlin left the following day by ferry, with the two rendezvousing on nearby Poros in a ruse designed to spare Ihlen the humiliation of seeing them depart as a couple. The *agora* fight and its aftermath are also recounted in Ihlen's biography, including a letter from Jensen written shortly afterwards from his yacht in Piraeus.

> I'm sitting here frying in my own fat and writing on your rival's typewriter. Everything I undertake (even with the most effective camouflage and emotional lubrication) will (in the eyes of the world, perhaps also in your eyes) have the unmistakable character of brutal insensitivity. And not only that. The unpleasant taste of overblown egotism. I am therefore not going to beg for forgiveness. Or even plead for understanding. What I have done, what I am doing, is far beyond the common morality as is possible to be, but it is not without consequences. And not without desperation.

It was also in mid-May that Ihlen and Cohen met for the first time, when he invited her to join him and others for a dockside lunch. Their relationship developed quickly over the early summer months as Ihlen came to terms with the end of her marriage.

Whatever plans Jensen and Amlin had for their immediate future were disrupted when Amlin was involved in a car accident less than a fortnight after they left Hydra. Wallis recorded the incident in his diary when the news of Amlin's misfortune reached the island.

> May 25 (Wednesday) Last Saturday night, half way between Piraeus and Athens, Patricia, alone in Axel's sports car, swerved to avoid a horse, skidded, hit a bridge and was thrown through the windscreen and down 30' into a dry, concreted river bed. Fractured skull, broken collar bone, arm broken in two places, crushed right hand, probably have 2–3 fingers if not amputated, leg broken in two places and foot so badly crushed hardly a bone left in it. God knows about internal or superficial injuries. In fact, she may now be dead.

Amlin was not, in fact, dead but hospitalised, and Ihlen responded to a plea from Jensen and left for Athens to support her wayward husband—or, in Wallis's assessment, "to extract drama at Patricia's bedside". Such were the conditions of the Athens hospital that Ihlen was called upon to provide basic medical care for her husband's lover. According to Wallis's diary, Cohen travelled with Ihlen on this 'mercy dash' to Athens. Wallis also recorded other news in the same diary entry, which seemed only likely to further ratchet up the personal dramas, reporting that "On top of this, Charmian tells us last night that Lena Folke-Olsson, the Swedish girl staying with them, is pregnant by Leonard who doesn't know but will be told by George when he comes back". (Wallis later amended his diary to indicate that "Leonard didn't do it" and cast doubt as to whether Folke-Olsson had indeed been pregnant).

It was into this atmosphere, with Hydra's foreign colony engulfed by (melo)drama, tension and rumour, that James Burke stepped when he arrived for a fleeting visit on the weekend of May 22nd and 23rd. It is little wonder that amid the carryings-on and the various couplings and un-couplings—presumably recounted to him in detail by his friend Johnston—together with the natural beauty of the island and town, and the wider relationships between the international artists and writers, summer tourists, and the Hydriots, that it occurred to Burke that here was a story he could tell through photographs.

When Burke eventually returned with his camera in September, the personal relationships and other comings and goings from the island had progressed. By mid-July Amlin had recovered sufficiently from her injuries to return to the US. Jensen accompanied her before he moved on to Mexico to spend time sharpening his sixties consciousness with John Starr Cooke—a mystic, and advocate of Ouija boards, tarot and drugs. Jensen returned to Hydra during August, and Amlin would join him the following year. When Jensen arrived back on the island he found that Ihlen had established her relationship with Cohen, and the couple were soon to settle in Cohen's newly purchased island house. Lena Folke-Olsson left the island in early August, after a fleeting, quasi-romantic entanglement with Redmond Wallis; she would return several years later and have a lengthy relationship, and two children, with Jensen.

As Hydra's foreign colony departed at the end of the summer of 1960, they had plenty of wounds to lick, but it was a year that had delivered not only its share of drama but also some new 'members' of a group that was both growing and fracturing. Certainly Leonard Cohen's decision to buy on the island that summer would have a lasting impact on the expatriate colony as well as on Hydra's future reputation and profile. Cohen had arrived on the island on April 14th and, as with so many others, met Johnston and Clift almost immediately. There was an instantaneous rapport, with the young Canadian taken by the charismatic, helpful and determinedly non-bourgeois older Australian couple, and the Johnstons impressed by Cohen's quiet charm and his already established credentials as a poet.

Cohen stayed briefly with the Johnstons—probably just several days—before they assisted him in finding rooms to rent and helped him on his way with a bed and other furnishings. Although Cohen's intention had been to stay on Hydra for a short while only, the island's conviviality and beauty, coupled with the opportunity it provided him to work, soon convinced him to remain longer—as no doubt did his blossoming relationship with Ihlen. When he later recalled his island arrival, Cohen spoke of the comfort and familiarity of being both on the island and amongst the people he encountered.

> I felt that everywhere else I'd been was culture shock, and this was home. I felt very, very much at ease in Hydra. … [W]hatever you saw, whatever you felt, whatever you held was beautiful, and you didn't have to say those words to yourself, it was just when you picked up a cup you knew by the way that it fitted into your hand that it was the cup that you always had been looking for. And the table that you sat at, that was the table that you wanted to lean on, and the wine, that was ten cents a gallon, was the wine that you wanted to drink, the price you wanted to pay.
>
> And then I started to bump into these wonderful people, like Marianne and her husband at the time Axel Jensen, and many other people, who also felt not at all like foreigners. The people that I bumped into, both the Greek and the foreigner, had the feeling of the people that I was meant to be with. It was a great sense of inevitability and hospitality, although it never really occurred to me, just, this is the place where I was meant to be.

Cohen staked a more permanent claim to Hydra in September when he received a $1500 inheritance and immediately used it to buy a house. For this he acquired a considerable dwelling in poor repair, which he described as "a big house full of little rooms". Despite being on the high part of the town, on the ridge that runs to the west of Hydra Port and separates it from the valley and harbour of Kamini, the house is unusual in that it does not provide a view of the harbour or sea.

Cohen purchased the house on the eve of his twenty-sixth birthday. It was a considerable commitment for a young man of uncertain prospects to

Leonard Cohen brandishing the key on the terrace of his new house.
(James Burke)

buy his first piece of real estate on an island so far from his homeland, and Cohen found himself justifying the decision to his family. As he wrote to his mother:

> It has a huge terrace with a view of dramatic mountains and shining white houses. The rooms are large and cool with deep windows set in thick walls. I suppose it's about 200 years old and many generations of sea-men must have lived here. I will do a little work on it every year and in a few years it will be a mansion … I live on a hill and life has been going on here exactly the same for hundreds of years. All through the

Leonard Cohen, Maryann Davis and Fidel Caliesch at the front door of Cohen's house. (James Burke)

day you hear the calls of the street vendors and they are really rather musical ... I get up around 7 generally and work till about noon. Early morning is coolest and therefore best, but I love the heat anyhow, especially when the Aegean Sea is 10 minutes from my door.

What he didn't mention was that the house required considerable repair and modernisation as it lacked even rudimentary plumbing or electricity. As Burke wrote at the time, "It has two floor(s) and a fine upper terrace and when fixed up (for probably another $1,500) will be equal to anything 10 times the price most anywhere else in the world".

Maryann Davis and Leonard Cohen at the rear door of Cohen's house. They are among the ruins of another house that once stood on the adjacent site.
(James Burke)

However, as much as Cohen loved his new house, he was not to enjoy it for long on his first island visit. By late October, a month after making his purchase, he and Ihlen would set out to drive to Oslo. Cohen would be back in Canada by Christmas and would not return to Hydra until August of the following year. As an ambitious young writer and a constant traveller, he could not have countenanced spending a full year on Hydra, and, at that time, his island home was inadequate for the harsh winters. When he departed from Hydra, Cohen left his house in the care of Magda Tilche, giving it to her free of rent and apparently with permission to commence renovations. As Tilche would write (in French) to the absent Cohen:

> I have wanted to write to you about how much I loved your house. I called it the House of Happiness. [I] painted it white, windows, doors, inside, out, and it seemed to me that the days were very short. Every

stroke of the brush resulted in a metamorphoses, the little black duck became from day to day a wonderful white swan, and in my joy I had the impulse to write to you and share the joy. ... I covered everything madly in lime and white paint, until everything was white, and it seemed to me that this whiteness could chase the shadows from my horizon.

Another North American photographed by Burke who would acquire property (not his first) and undertake renovations on Hydra that year was Chicago-based modernist architect James Speyer. From 1957 to 1960, Speyer worked at the National University of Greece in Athens as part of a Fulbright exchange program, and after returning to live in the US in 1961, he was appointed as the curator of Twentieth Century Painting and Sculpture at The Art Institute of Chicago. It was a position he held until his death in 1986, by which time he was considered one of North America's foremost curators and an authority on contemporary American and European art. While he was based in Athens, and for many years following, Speyer was also a regular Hydra visitor.

Speyer purchased his first house on Hydra (up the hill to the south of the harbour) in 1958, and over subsequent years, he acquired several adjoining properties. Although Burke had stated in his letter to *LIFE* that Speyer was "putting finishing touches to his new Hydra home", the task would continue for nearly another decade. Working with his sister Darthea—a leading figure in rebuilding Parisian art galleries after the Second World War—and local craftsman and contractor *Kyrio* Pinotsis, he would spend much of his spare time throughout the 1960s renovating the interconnected properties into a substantial complex.

Burke photographed Speyer on two occasions, and both depict him in the process of departing. The first is a series of photos in which Speyer is shown overseeing his housekeeper and her family as they remove suitcases from his house, and in the second he is shown at the port about to board a departing ferry. According to Burke, in this photograph Speyer is "dressed up for civilization again" as he "looks rather longingly back at Hydra town".

James Speyer supervises the removal of his luggage.
(James Burke)

James Speyer takes his leave.
(James Burke)

There is little to indicate that Speyer was ever deeply connected with Hydra's wider expatriate group. In his late forties, he was older than most and was likely too scholarly by nature and reserved in temperament to feel comfortable with boisterous afternoons on the *agora*. But unlike Speyer, another US academic who visited Hydra in the summer of 1960 did bond with the expatriate group as evidenced by a number of Burke's photographs. This was Inge Schneier. Burke met Schneier on his first September trip to the island, with his cable to *LIFE* on September 12th noting the presence of a "rather mysterious American young woman who claims be writing paper on Chinese brain washing—why on hydra I do not yet know". Schneier was this mysterious young woman, about whom Burke would learn more when he returned to complete his assignment.

As it transpired, Burke's description of Schneier was a reference to her professional role as a psychologist, and, at the time, she was co-authoring the book *Coercive Persuasion: A socio-psychological analysis of the "brainwashing" of American civilian prisoners by the Chinese communists*, which was published the following year. For Burke, who was detained with his family in Beijing for several months after Mao Tse Tung's communist forces occupied the city in January 1949, Schneier's presence must have made for a very unlikely encounter in a most unexpected location.

Schneier had come to Hydra in late August or early September in order to write and spend time in the company of her former teacher, influential literary scholar and Victorianist Dorothy Van Ghent. Schneier recalls of Van Ghent:

> [She] was enthusiastic about Hydra for its beauty and atmosphere enabling creative work. I was to join her for two weeks but I fell in love with the lively community which attracted a march of constantly arriving interesting artists and intellectuals. Conversation was intense and intellectual and FUN!

Schneier stayed on after Van Ghent departed, and her intended two-week stay became two months as she soaked up the "glorious morning, sunset, and

Inge Schneier and Leonard Cohen outside Katsikas *kafenio*.
(James Burke)

midnight swims punctuated with quiet periods of writing in the cool whitewashed room I rented in a friendly nurturing atmosphere".

Among the other intellectuals who Schneier spent time with during these two months were French resistance fighter, communist, academic and writer Dominique Desanti, and French historian Jacques Lacarriere. (French visitors were plentiful in 1960—Burke also photographed artist Jean Marie Courchinoux sketching his wife, Christiane, on the waterfront). Schneier forged a friendship with Leonard Cohen in particular, and she is in his company in most of Burke's photographs in which she appears (lunching dockside with Cohen, Ihlen, Johnston and Clift; riding donkeys to the island's monasteries; singing around the guitar at Douskos Taverna). As Schneier remembers:

> I was absorbed at the time in a study at MIT based on my interviews with American intellectuals who were subjected to brainwashing in Chinese thought reform prisons. Leonard was my main sounding board. We had a daily routine: to go swimming very early morning and many evenings to withdraw to his place and sing into the night, just the two of us. Often we ate together with Marianne.

Burke captured the intellectual engagement between Schneier and Cohen in a series of late evening photos taken outside Katsikas *kafenio*. The photographer reported this encounter in his notes as a meeting of "two intense intellectuals" in which "Inge is shown here getting Leonard to read and criticize part of her manuscript".

Schneier, Van Ghent and Speyer weren't the only Anglophone intellectuals visiting Hydra in 1960. Others included a group of Oxford University students, led by young mediaevalist V.A. (Del) Kolve. A Rhodes Scholar from the University of Wisconsin, Kolve was completing his DPhil. at the time and would spend seven years at Oxford including a period as a Research Fellow of St. Edmund Hall. Upon returning to the US in 1962, he took positions at Stanford University and the Universities of Virginia and California (UCLA), writing major texts on Chaucer and medieval iconography.

Among those travelling with Kolve were Peter Hughes, a polymath Canadian, who, after taking his B.A. at Oxford, completed a Doctorate at Yale and later taught comparative literature at the Universities of Toronto and Zurich; and Donald Moyer, an American from Cornell, who stayed to work in London before becoming a disciple of yoga master B.K.S. Iyengar. Moyer eventually returned to the US, working as a yoga instructor in Berkeley, California and writing several books based on the Iyengar method.

Whereas others had arrived on Hydra with a purpose, these young Oxonians were typical of those who found themselves on the island by chance. Kolve and Moyer preceded the rest of their group in June, with Kolve recalling that they knew nothing of Hydra but had decided they would spend the summer somewhere in the Greek islands.

> Don and I were charged with looking for a beautiful, happy place, where the culture would be different, rewarding and inexpensive. The boat we took from Piraeus made its second stop at Hydra, and we were blown away by the beauty, the scale, the welcoming aspect of that island, with its small horseshoe bay, steeply rising hills, and its largely neglected but once grand houses stacked upon each other. It was, from first sight, a place where we knew we wanted to stay.

After staying in a room for several days, they set about looking for a longer-term rental with the services of a "self-appointed real estate agent"

> who showed us a large-ish empty house halfway up one of the steeply ascending streets, and promised to enquire into its cost and availability. We waited three days, meeting him each morning for a benevolent greeting and a reassurance that these things "take time". Finally a deal was proposed—$34 a month—which, split five ways, we knew we could afford. All we needed were some (used) mattresses for the floor, a few pans for the kitchen, and some ancient passed-along folding chairs.

Kolve and Moyer then informed their Oxford friends of where to find them, and so "began a magical four months on that beautiful, exhilarating, but challenging island". During their stay they were also joined by other friends from Oxford and America who would visit for several days and sleep on the floor. This was not wholly a summer break for these students; it was also a place of work, where Kolve's mornings were committed to his doctoral thesis before an afternoon swim and evening meals in the tavernas. These young travellers were, Kolve recalls, engrossed in their own Greek island summer and "interested witnesses at best to the 'older' bohemians on the island".

The very first subject Burke chose for his camera in mid-September 1960 was an incoming island visitor seeking a touch of that bohemian life, Norwegian artist Tore Pedersen. Burke's photographs of firstly Pedersen, and then later his family, provide an insight into his photojournalistic mode and his desire to tell a story of a young artist looking to join Hydra's expatriate colony. Pedersen was a commercial artist working in Oslo with dreams of pursuing his own art in a more liberal environment. When he won a commission to illustrate a biography of Henrik Ibsen's time in Rome, he conceived the idea of completing the work on Hydra after learning that fellow Norwegian Axel Jensen was living there. Jensen had enjoyed immediate success in Oslo in 1955 with his debut novel, *Dyretemmerens kors*, and had subsequently published two further novels: *Ung Mann i Sahara* (*Icarus: A Young Man in the Sahara*) in 1957 and *Line* in 1959. (*Line* was largely rewritten for and in the English language and published in 1962 as *A Girl I Knew*, prefaced by a Leonard Cohen poem, 'One Night I Burned the House I Loved').

In 1960 Jensen was the most internationally visible of Hydra's foreign residents, with Burke's notes recording that "Last year he made $26,000 from his book sales, practically all of it in Norway, where he has considerable fame as a writer of soul-searching travelogues in sort of an angry-young-man style. He might be called Norway's Henry Miller." The earlier chronicler of Jensen's island presence, Vasso Mingos, noted in his 1958 *Pictures from Greece* article the success of Jensen's first novel, reporting that its author was working "18 hours a day, putting the finishing touches to his second book, *Line*". Mingos also reported Jensen's motivations for writing: "I felt that someone *had* to write about my generation and their problems from their own viewpoint and try to understand them. It has of course been done before, but not penetratingly enough." While Jensen wrestled with the existential problems of his generation, Mingos photographed Ihlen twice in the role of a decorative helpmate, once with Jensen draped over a wall, seeing her off on a shopping expedition as she descends the stairs of their whitewashed house, and again as one of "Two model housewives" as she and Loetitia Schwartz, baskets on hip, make their way to the *agora*.

While Mingos's vision of the couple (and Ihlen's role in the relationship) suggests a familiar middle-class outlook, Jensen's novels resonated with Beat sensibilities, as their young, swinging male Scandinavian protagonists seek the meaning of life (in the desert in *Icarus*, and the fjords in *A Girl I Knew*)

COMINGS AND GOINGS

Marianne Ihlen and Axel Jensen, 1958. (Vasso Mingos)

Loetetia Schwartz and Marianne Ihlen go shopping, 1958. (Vasso Mingos)

but discover few answers. Pedersen would not be the only creatively ambitious young Scandinavian attracted to Hydra by Jensen's depictions of youthful angst. Swedish poet and budding novelist Göran Tunström also travelled to Hydra to meet Jensen who would in turn use Tunström as the model for the protagonist of his 1961 novel *Joachim* although, in some accounts, Cohen is said to have played that role. Cohen himself recalled some fifty years later from a concert stage in Gothenburg that he and Tunström "began our first novels around the same table" while living on Hydra—Tunström published *Karantän* in 1961 and Cohen's *The Favorite Game* appeared in 1963. Tunström's friendship with Swedish writer and translator Sun Axelsson also saw her join him in the early 1960s on Hydra, where she met English sculptor Michael Piper. Piper had found his way to Greece in the mid-1950s on a Royal College of Art Scholarship, leaving behind a young family and his mathematician wife. Axelsson and Piper later settled more permanently on the Dodecanese island of Leros.

Pedersen had travelled to Hydra alone in order to contact Jensen and find a house before bringing his wife, Dinnie, and their young son to the island. Burke photographed Pedersen disembarking from the ferry *Nereida*, suitcase in hand, not knowing anyone but determined to make a go of this opportunity to work in the sunshine alongside like-minded artists and writers. Pedersen apparently succeeded in making a connection to Jensen almost immediately, as, later on the day of his arrival, Burke photographed him talking with Jensen's estranged wife, Marianne Ihlen, as she lunched with Cohen, Johnston and Clift on the Hydra dockside. Burke recorded that Pedersen was enquiring about the availability of a house to rent and that "Marianne didn't happen to know of any houses for rent, but she passed him on to someone who did, and within a week Tore was all settled in and ready for his wife and baby". Burke remained on hand to record Pedersen as he settled in, creating a series of photographs in which he is seen borrowing a cot bed from Jensen in order to prepare for the arrival of his baby. This cot already had some history, having been used by Clift and Johnston for their son Jason and then by the Jensens

Axel Jensen, wearing his favourite working costume—an Egyptian fellahin's robe—passing on the Johnstons' cot to Tore Pedersen. (James Burke)

Tore Pedersen carries the cot. (James Burke)

when they returned from Oslo with their baby earlier in the year. With Ihlen now living with Cohen, the cot was being handed on once more.

Burke also photographed Pedersen carrying the cot back to his new home, high above Hydra Port, and stayed long enough to take another two dozen photographs as he checked out the features of the new house, took in the expansive view from the terrace and tested the *sterna* that opened into the kitchen.

Burke's engagement with Pedersen was not yet ended, as he returned to photograph the arrival of Dinnie Pedersen (later Blair) and son, Simen, capturing the family as they reunited at the dockside and proceeded through the lanes from the ferry to the front door of the house and, presumably, the waiting cot. The friendship between Pedersen and Jensen produced much more than a second-hand cot. The pair later teamed up to create the short-lived but influential cartoon series *Doktor Fantastisk* (published in Oslo in weekly instalments in 1972), an artistic interest that might explain the dedication of Jensen's *A Girl I Knew* to American cartoonist, musician and author Shel Silverstein.

Despite their cheap rent and the spectacular location above the port, things did not go well for the Pedersens. Money remained short, life on the island over winter was difficult, and their marriage struck trouble. As Blair has recalled, the cheap rent was in part explained by the "hole in the ground outside the house for a toilet", and for a young mother, the house and island life were challenging.

> For the whole winter I used a primus in the kitchen and tore up towels as diapers for the baby. To feed my son I dove down to 7m depth on the way to Mandraki to gather female urchins, get the roe out, drench it in lemon juice and retzina and feed the child. There were eight foreigners on the island plus the 2000 Hydriots living off a case of fish for winter, when the storms were so bad that the ferry could not make it into port. The electricity was snuffed every night at 10PM and there was no postal service for weeks.

COMINGS AND GOINGS

Dinnie and Simen Pedersen, Tore Pedersen (rear) and Klaus Merkel (foreground), Hydra Port. (James Burke)

Despite the hardships and her floundering marriage, Blair's experience on Hydra delivered the sort of liberal and inclusive social life she had hoped for in leaving Oslo, and, unlike Pedersen, she would go on to spend much of the next two decades on the island.

> I pat myself on the shoulder for having had the guts to leave my conservative upbringing and search for a more bohemian touch of life. I suppose that's what life is all about, to find out who you are and what you can do with this gift of being alive. But do I miss those times in Greece? You bet. I'd do it all over again if I had the chance!

A young German, Klaus Merkel, is pictured helping the Pedersens carry their luggage. Merkel is almost certainly the man Burke described in his cable to *LIFE* on September 12th as a "bearded German beatnik type who came on boat with me for one week stay". As it transpired, Merkel (like many others) extended his stay for some months, and he features in many of Burke's photographs—socialising with the established expatriates; relaxing on the rocks at Spilia; taking classes at the Art School; and lingering on the waterfront while watching the annual arrival of the new wine. As Merkel is pictured observing, the season's wine was delivered by *caique*, unloaded and transferred from barrels to goatskin or sheepskin 'bags', which were then transported by donkeys to the island's taverns. Del Kolve was another visitor who witnessed the arrival of the wine that year, recalling:

> It came in the skins of sheep, scraped clean and supple, leaving just enough of each foot to be securely tied, and enough of the neck to be closed off after the body was filled with wine. These plump bundles were rhythmically passed from one man to the next, loaded onto donkeys and taken off to be emptied into wooden barrels elsewhere. It was solemn, beautiful and joyous, a custom not much changed since Homeric times.

Merkel found himself travelling through Greece by intention but on Hydra by accident. After studying classical Greek during six years of schooling, he was driven to see the land from where the language sprang, "and so I went

Klaus Merkel watches the unloading of wine. (James Burke)

to Greece to see the places Homer, Herodotus, Plato, Thucydides and others mentioned". Touring the sites of ancient Greece was unlikely to lead to Hydra, however, and Merkel simply recalls, "I came to Hydra because somebody offered me a place. I didn't know anything about the island nor the people before."

Burke's apparent fondness for photographing Merkel (or including him in photographs) might be explained by his subject's visual representation of the Beat culture Burke had described to *LIFE* as characteristic of the island. Merkel's habitually bare feet, slight beard and casual dress marked him out as pictorially 'different' and more obviously Beat than the ineradicable middle-class appearance of Cohen, Jensen, Wallis and others.

Among Burke's photographs of Merkel, a number of them depict the solitary German reading amongst the rocks of Spilia while other international visitors swim and sunbake around him. It is almost certainly coincidence rather than influence, but Merkel would go on to a future as a black-and-white art photographer, producing a series of large scale volumes focusing on rocks and trees.

David Goschen painting cabinet doors in the house he was renovating.
Goschen designed and built the table. (James Burke)

If Burke was drawn to Merkel by his Beat aesthetic, then this attraction also explains his keenness to photograph David Goschen. As Merkel has recalled, "I remember Lord Goschen who like me walked shoeless, but well dressed in a suit". Merkel's reference to "Lord Goschen" was not incidental; he was accurately remembering the English, upper-class antecedents of his habitually under-shod Hydra acquaintance. Burke also spotted Goschen's distinctive visual appeal, reporting to *LIFE* that he had overheard a tourist exclaiming how much the bearded Goschen resembled Jesus Christ. Coupled with the bare feet—an odd choice for someone frequenting Donkey Shit Lane—this was a 'look' that Burke found well-suited to illustrating the island's beat credentials.

COMINGS AND GOINGS

David Goschen overseeing the renovation of his new studio. (James Burke)

At the time of Burke's photographs, Goschen and his sculptor wife, Angela, had been living on Hydra for several years, where their presence had already been reported by Vasso Mingos. Goschen's landed family included his grandfather, Sir William Edward Goschen, the British Ambassador in Berlin who declared war on Germany in 1914; and his mother, renowned adventurer and travel writer Vivienne de Watteville, who hunted big game in Africa in the 1920s where she nursed her father as he died after being mauled by a lion. After borrowing twenty-five pounds from his family, Goschen set out for Greece in the early 1950s, thereby avoiding a life where he might be expected to declare war, hunt lions or manage an English estate. After a year spent living in a tent on Mykonos, he moved to Athens where he went into business as a self-taught carpenter and cabinet maker. This business was successful, but Goschen moved on again in search of a simpler life, a journey that brought him and Angela to Hydra in 1957. When Mingos visited the island in May 1958, he found a recent inheritance had come Goschen's reluctant way, allowing him to spend his time playing a newly acquired clavichord and writing poetry. With the birth of the Goschen's second daughter, Mariora, in October 1957, Clift and Johnston could no longer claim that Jason was the only 'foreigner' born on the island.

At the time Burke was taking his photographs, Angela Goschen had returned to the UK to have a third child, while Goschen appeared well-settled on Hydra and intent on improving the family home. Burke captured a number of images of Goschen at work renovating the substantial house he had purchased, which sat high above the south-western corner of the harbour, close behind the current-day Coundouriotis Museum.

Despite giving every indication of being permanently settled on the island, Goschen was to leave unexpectedly before the year's end. This sudden departure resulted from his expulsion after he offended island authorities in a series of incidents that culminated in a calculated insult directed at the visiting Governor of the Dodecanese. Hydra's police, who had been waiting for their chance, moved quickly.

Not surprisingly some (or perhaps many) of those who made it to Hydra with ambitions to forge their way as writers or artists went away disappointed—some wandered off into obscurity, their presence on the island registered nearly sixty years later only by Burke's images; in other cases, they surfaced elsewhere in notable careers. Among the latter is Eugene (Gene) Case, who arrived on the island with his wife, Mary Jane, and young son, Christopher.

Gene Case was from Tennessee and Mary Jane from New York State, and the couple had met at Cornell University. While Gene majored in architecture, his immediate ambition was to write fiction, and, for this, he and Mary Jane decamped to Vienna where Christopher was born. Like many others, the Cases soon felt the need for somewhere cheaper and sunnier, and they moved on, a decision that brought them to Hydra for several months before they returned to the US.

Burke took some four dozen photos of the Cases—they too seemed to meet his need for young Beat types with literary ambitions. As with Merkel and

Mary Jane Case shopping on the *agora*. (James Burke)

Goschen, they were photographed walking Hydra's backstreets barefooted, and in another engaging set of images, Burke depicts Mary Jane shopping for fruit and crabs on the *agora*.

Mary Jane Case (Pease) recalled the 'negotiations' that enabled this financially stretched young family to remain on the island, beyond bartering with grocers.

> We had a landlady, who knew little English, and we had only a few words of Greek. At one point we realized that we didn't have enough money to pay the rent. With trepidation I told the landlady that we would have to leave. When she asked why, I said it was because we couldn't afford the rent and had to move somewhere cheaper. The landlady was outraged. She asked what we could pay, and I told her—we had figured it out to the penny. She insisted on a higher amount, but I kept saying, with many apologies, that we couldn't afford it. The landlady was sorry, but we would have to leave. I felt terrible, that we were making an enemy out of this woman who had been so kind. Finally she threw up her hands and said all right, we could stay for the amount I offered. I was astonished, and happily agreed. I was even more astonished that as soon as the matter was settled she became effusively kind, pulling out liquor to celebrate and inviting in a neighbour—things she had never done before. Apparently, what I had thought was a humiliating confession of poverty was to her a sterling example of professional haggling, and her respect for us rose accordingly.

In a number of Burke's images, the Cases are shown sharing a meal in the house for which they were paying fifteen dollars a month, presumably the amount to which the landlady finally agreed. At the desk in front of Gene sits his typewriter, a momentarily silent reminder of his reason for being on the island, while the presence of his wife and child flag the responsibilities faced by middle-class young men who mix literary dreams with a touch of bohemianism.

Christopher, Mary Jane and Gene Case. (James Burke)

Burke reported that Case hoped to have his novel completed within a month before returning to New York to look for a job. The novel seems to have disappeared without a trace. By 1961 Case had a position in advertising, and in 1964 he wrote some of the crucial ads for Lyndon Johnson's presidential campaign. He continued to work intermittently on political campaigns (for both Democratic and Republican candidates), all the while building a successful marketing agency, and in the final stages of his career, founding a left-leaning advertising firm supporting liberal causes.

Two other recent arrivals on Hydra featured in Burke's photos, Charles Heckstall and Robert (Bob) Maxwell, were also aspiring writers. Heckstall in particular is included in a number of photographs depicting gatherings of the expatriate community. He was described by Burke as "a member of an American negro paratrooper outfit in the Korean War and was seriously wounded by shrapnel". After his discharge, Heckstall travelled to Germany where he settled in Munich and married a German artist early in 1960. The

Charles Heckstall living in a "dilapidated state". (James Burke)

couple then travelled to Hydra, although at the time of Burke's photographs, Heckstall's wife had returned to Germany, leaving her husband to share a house with her cats and Klaus Merkel.

Heckstall was working on two projects—one of which was autobiographical and the other, a series of essays on the contribution of African-Americans to American society. The house in which he was staying was provided by a friend from Athens and had been purchased four years previously for just one hundred dollars. Burke took a number of photos of Heckstall amid the ruins of an adjoining house—one of the island's decayed mansions—and he described the house Heckstall and Merkel shared as being in a "dilapidated state". While Burke's photographs of the house show only one room, they seemingly reveal something other than dilapidation, with Heckstall busy at the typewriter in a setting that looks to be the essence of Aegean refinement—whitewashed walls; paneled ceiling; scattered rugs; and sparse wall adornments. And, of course, glorious sunshine.

COMINGS AND GOINGS

Charles Heckstall, Robert Maxwell and Rosemary Whitman. (James Burke)

Bob Maxwell shared a service background with Heckstall, having been stationed with the US Air Force in Athens before moving to Hydra in order to write a novel. If Heckstall was said to be roughing it, then Maxwell, by comparison, was enjoying the Hydra good life. His rental was high by island standards at twenty-five dollars per month, and for this, he enjoyed a house close to the eastern entrance to the harbour with a terrace providing a superb view across to the *agora*. Burke wrote of the view that "other members of the island's foreign colony often drop in at coffee time (which is most anytime on Hydra) to share it with him". Burke's photographs depict one such occasion as he is joined on the terrace by Heckstall and a sunbaking Rosemary Whitman, a student from the University of London who was visiting for the summer.

Not everyone who came within the orbit of the Hydra expatriate community was trying to write or paint—there were some who were on the island simply to visit those who were there for those reasons. In late January of 1960, Sue Davis was on the wharf in Wellington to see friends Robyn and Redmond

Wallis depart on their great London adventure, and by August, they were reunited—but on Hydra rather than in the UK. Sue Davis and her sister Maryann moved in with the Wallises in the house they were renting on the eastern side of the harbour for seven dollars a month. As often was the case on Hydra, there were problems with the plumbing—as Wallis reported candidly in his diary.

> The pot, al fresco, is the worst I've ever experienced because the hole is cut hard against a brick wall & you have to train your cock round to your arse to piss into it. It also produces cramp in the calves. We're working on the problem.

Burke chose to photograph the Wallises and the Davis sisters in a more becoming part of the house—at the base of the steep whitewashed stairs leading to the upper level. This was an unusual set of photos for Burke in that he shifted away from his photojournalistic method in favour of a contrived group portrait, with his subjects arranged unnaturally on the sharply rising stairs. However, as with Heckstall's house, the striking simplicity of the interior is highlighted, with the human forms softening and adding scale to the hard and angular surfaces of the tile, wall, stairs and timber ceiling.

Sue and Maryann Davis spent August and September with the Wallises, after which they completed the journey on which their friends had embarked by moving on to the UK where Sue, an archaeologist, found work at a museum in Saffron Walden in Essex. When the Wallises finally made it to the UK some twelve months later (with financial help from another New Zealand visitor, Wallis's worldly Aunt Ruve, who—as Wallis noted—"observed the extravagances of the foreign colony without expressing any judgements"), they received some return on their hospitality by staying for several weeks with Davis in Saffron Walden. To get there, they drove overland with Ruve from Athens to the UK, passing through Paris where they spent time with Gordon Merrick and Charles Hulse.

Of Hydra's long-term international residents from the period who failed to make it into Burke's photographs, Merrick and Hulse are the most obvious.

COMINGS AND GOINGS

Maryann Davis, Sue Davis, Redmond Wallis and Robyn Wallis.
(James Burke)

They were on the island when Burke first visited in May but were back in Paris when the photographer returned with his camera in September. There were also many other visitors from that summer who eluded Burke's lens, among them Gregory Corso, painter Norris Embry, and American poet Kenneth Koch, his wife, Janice, and their daughter, Katherine. Five-year-old Katherine, having befriended Leonard Cohen, came away infused "with dreamy ideas about what a poet's or an artist's life could look like: living in some sort of inspired state of mind, in a beautiful place which would spread out in front of you when you walked outside your studio. You would have friends who loved making their work—the same way you were thrilled by what you were doing and thinking."

Others were left with different impressions. In a short story published in the Australian journal *The Bulletin* in October 1962, Charles Sriber—Johnston's Sydney friend who, with his wife Ruth, had previously sent several flattering accounts of the Johnstons' island lifestyle back to the Australian press—provided a fictionalised and by no means kindly portrait of Australian writers "Norm" and "Julie" who live on an unnamed Greek island. There were obvious parallels between this fictional couple and the lives of the Johnstons. The story's narrator, Phil Stanton, focuses on Norm and Julie's unwavering commitment to the island, including Julie's oft-repeated refrain that provides the story's title, 'We'll Never Go Back'. For Julie, this claim is a badge of expatriate pride: "So many people come here and remain intrinsically foreign. We've assimilated … Damned few letters with an Australian stamp we get these days." Stanton sees things otherwise, witnessing Norm crash drunkenly into the performance of a Greek dance, and Julie's myopic refusal to acknowledge anything other than this is a "Wonderful place, wonderful people". 'We'll Never Go Back' portrays the couple eking out a meagre existence and relying on alcohol to sustain their delusion of being integrated into the community, whereas in reality their presence is resented by the locals at the same time as their ties with their homeland are diminishing.

Someone in Australia recognised that the story was based on Hydra and sent Johnston a copy. He responded explosively, treating the story as an act

George Johnston and friends. The caption to this photograph in *Pictures from Greece* reads, "A party at the Johnstons. 'Retsina' (community's favourite drink) flows freely and host gives own interpretation of Greek dance", 1958.
(Vasso Mingos)

of betrayal. When interviewed by Garry Kinnane about this incident some years later, Sriber responded not unreasonably that "it is all right for George to write about others, but not for anyone to do it to *him*".

Sriber's story also hints at the numerous comings and goings that swirled around Clift and Johnston. While Stanton packs up and returns to Sydney, Norm and Julie do not—perhaps as a matter of pride or because they have cut themselves off from their Australian past, but also because the slender income from their writing means they have lost the capacity to leave. Julie tells Stanton that the island's more avant-garde writers call her and her husband "hacks", an appellation she turns to her advantage: "we're making enough money to stay on here". But the twist to this claim is that while they are making enough to stay on, they are not making enough to leave, as others can, and do.

It was at the end of October 1960, a month after Burke had taken his photographs, that the Johnstons found their one opportunity to take an extended break from the island. Certainly at the end of this summer, during which they had welcomed many new arrivals and were now watching them slip away to places where social and intellectual life did not wax and wane with the seasons, they were ready to go with them. They had been on Hydra for over five years with little respite from the isolation, and the prospect of another winter could hardly have been welcome. In addition, their finances were at a particularly low ebb. The occasional advances and royalties were no longer meeting their needs, and what money they did receive was lost in the repayment of debts and Johnston's acts of spontaneous generosity. Even today Johnston is remembered on the island for giving—probably literally—his last drachma to the husband of the family's maid, Zoe Skordoras, for an eye operation in Athens.

The opportunity to leave was unexpected, arising when a wealthy English couple—Didi (or Didy) and Peter Cameron—proposed a house swap. The Camerons, who were holidaying on Hydra, had contacted Johnston and Clift on the recommendation of English novelist Elizabeth Jane Howard who had befriended them while spending several weeks on the island in 1957. (Part of Howard's 1959 novel *The Sea Change* would be set on Hydra). While the Camerons took the Johnstons' Hydra house as a holiday base when not in their London home, the Johnstons moved into the Camerons' country house, Charity Farm (a name Clift described as "thought provoking at times"), near Broadway in the Cotswolds. The Camerons made the offer after witnessing what they considered to be the near-poverty conditions in which the Johnstons were living, with Didi Cameron telling Garry Kinnane that "a tin of corned beef was a rare treat, and Charmian ran anxiously to the vegetable boat when it came into port to get fresh, cheap vegetables, with cabbage forming

Charmian Clift shopping. (James Burke)

a large part of their diet". Both Johnston and Clift were adept at putting a positive spin on their island existence, and certainly the hardships referred to by Cameron are difficult to discern in Burke's photographs. With images of Clift shopping extravagantly on the *agora*; of the family table surrounded by guests and weighted with food as Johnston pours the wine; and of the couple passing their days in the taverns, *kafenia* and homes of the island's wealthy, Burke's photographs leave an impression of abundance and comfort. This was, however, far from the case, with the generous credit provided by island shopkeepers being essential to their survival.

Johnston and Clift left Hydra for Charity Farm at the end of October on an open-ended arrangement. Unfortunately, the six months they were in England were a financial, personal and professional disaster. At first they enjoyed playing the role of country squires, surrounded by an England they loved—Clift affectionately recalled "men wearing either tweeds and caps and driving utilities or dinner jackets and driving Bentleys, mucking in with the pigs or serving champagne by candlelight". However, as tantalising as these circumstances were, they soon found themselves back in the situation that had contributed to their previously leaving England—it was expensive, and the weather was foul. If they had hitherto kept their financial woes from Burke, this was no longer possible, and, in early February, Johnston wrote to his friend revealing his dire circumstances (although, as usual, sprinkling his problems with the gold dust of optimism):

> The problem, and perhaps the reason why you haven't heard from us, has been basically an economic one. In other words, we've got ourselves into a bit of a spot and the problem now is to get out of it. Charmian and I are pretty sure, anyway, that we can no longer afford the luxury of being free-lance authors. Somehow, what with increasing costs of living and the ever-greater expense of ever-larger kids, to say nothing of the costs incurred in getting over here, ends no longer seem to meet. My novel [*Closer to the Sun*] was a flop in London (it might do better when it's published in New York in June) and Charm, what with the anxiety, hasn't been able to make headway on hers at all.

The point of the letter is reached when Johnston asks Burke not to cash a cheque he is holding "until I get this temporary mess straightened out".

Johnston's plan was to look for work in London, but he soon found that much had changed on Fleet Street during his years away, and, although old colleagues were pleased to see him, they were not about to offer employment. He was not only considered out of touch, but the ravages of his tuberculosis were all too obvious. With this experience confirming the hopelessness of their situation, and with the whole family pining for their island home, Johnston and Clift again found themselves in need of the very thing that had taken them to the Aegean initially—somewhere cheap to live in the sun.

But while the sunshine remained, Hydra's days as an economical haven were coming to an end. When Burke returned to the island in March 1961 to update information for his still-hoped-for photo-essay, he reported to *LIFE* that while the island still offered opportunities for the "creative poor", the real story was the sudden surge in housing prices.

> Real rumblings of coming hydra boom however are evident in soaring real estate values. A wealthy Greek ship owner last month rented an hydra house for one hundred dollars monthly with option to buy it for fifteen thousand dollars. Everyone on Hydra is talking about this deal and all house values are being reassessed. The Johnston house which cost less than one thousand dollars six years ago is now valued at ten thousand and Bob Maxwell's landlord has announced his rent will double this summer from twenty five to fifty dollars, which is more than Bob is prepared to pay. An English lady recently bought an hydra house which she is advertising in London papers for summer rental to highest bidder and she received dozens of offers of up to fifty pounds monthly.

The Johnstons managed to paper over their immediate financial problems when Sidney Nolan, sensing his friends' despair, provided them with much-needed cash to enable them to return to Hydra—his gift came in the form of a lavish book with the pages interspersed with five pound notes. Johnston and Clift immediately grasped the opportunity, with Johnston writing to Burke in early April announcing they would be arriving in Piraeus on April 17th and asking for an overnight bed before they returned to Hydra the next day.

The Johnstons' Hydra homecoming was something the couple would frequently recall in the coming years, as it apparently instigated an outpouring of affection from the expatriates who were assembling for another summer. Clift recounted the splendid occasion, organised by the Camerons, days later in a letter to James Burke's wife, Josephine:

> I am just coming out of confusion and emptied suitcases. George and I were so touched by your kindness and hope that we can repay it someday … George was still panting when we tumbled off the Nereida into a madness of foreigners carrying banners saying 'They Never Left' and 'Johnstons Welcome Home' and so on: the other Nereida passengers

> were bewildered and we were overwhelmed. They should have had one saying 'This Way to the Restored Villa' because they'd all been in the house for a week before, painting the walls and floors and slapping gallons of whitewash about: a lot of hard work as well as emotion had gone into our welcoming party, which moved me deeply, having expected The Worst as far as the house was concerned.

While the Johnstons were comforted by their reception, it seems that at least some expatriates took quiet pleasure from their failure to make good in the UK. Wallis's biting but no doubt accurate account in *The Unyielding Memory*— it tallies with the version Johnston himself gave to Colin Simpson—conveys the difficult situation in which the couple had found themselves.

> The Graysons were back from a prolonged stay in England, George embittered by the reception he had got from old friends in Fleet Street. They lived on charity in England … George, perhaps humiliated by this, certainly aware that his finances were in terrible shape, perhaps even had to admit that the experiment of living on an island and raising a family had failed, had decided he would have to find a job; to his astonishment and disgust his old friends, now in position of power, had told him he was too old, too ill and too out of touch to be employable.

When Clift wrote of this house exchange in a later essay, she recalled the sense of unmitigated failure. The family's sad finances that blighted the experience are duly noted but given secondary place to the personal failure to embrace someone else's house and the life that went with it. For while they were delivered to a privileged position with the keys to the 'big house', the sad truth was that the family was broke and homesick and little good was likely to come of being in England, other than Jason finally learning to speak English. Clift recalled of the experience that "It all ended badly".

> In both cases personal possessions were damaged, things were lost or mislaid, books were missing, and some sadly querulous correspondence

ensued in which a very real friendship suffered traumatically never really to recover.

So in less than six months, Clift and Johnston found themselves back where they had been and in much the same circumstances. After wanting to create some distance from Hydra, they found the island was, for the time being, the only place they belonged. It seems the Camerons also decided something similar, as soon after they purchased an island home of their own, a large house overlooking the wells of *Kala Pigadia*.

* * *

In *The Unyielding Memory*, Redmond Wallis fictionalises correspondence originally exchanged between himself (Alwyn) on Hydra and Leonard Cohen (Saul Rubens) in Montreal. The exchange serves as a reminder that intellectual and literary life was happening elsewhere for those with the means to travel, while for those left behind, Hydra could seem like the whole world.

> *'Autumn here, the one I've always remembered, red trees and sunlight, a bright wind swirling the leaves and skirts, the building more solid for all the fragile movement of the trees and walkers,' wrote Saul from Montreal.*
>
> *'Book on the best-seller list here, no thanks to publishers or critics, the first negligent, the second unnecessarily vicious.'*
>
> *'The synagogue has rejected the cornerstone, many people who always bored me now refuse to talk to me, my mother is sick—a white uniform roams over the house—everything is the same. Love to my friends.'*
>
> *Alwyn replied: '… I'm sorry the critics have been unpleasant to you, but I suppose you are crying all the way to the bank and I always say all's well that ends well. I'm surprised at you, Rubens, I thought you were above being thrown by reviews and sales and all that sort of crap. Where is Montreal, anyway? They've reprinted another thousand of the book, so we might make fifty quid or so and my mother tells me the largest bookshop in Christchurch has displayed it satisfactorily. Where's Christchurch?'*

'Sue says to tell you that you may not be able to come back to the island, ever, because there is some doubt whether there are going to be any more movies, ever. Mitsou has got tired of not understanding what he's projecting and we are movie-less. This is sad. We are thrown back on having to entertain each other. This is awful...'

Chapter Five

ARCHONTIKÁ

The Hydriot families who made their fortunes during the eighteenth and early-nineteenth centuries and in turn dominated the island's commercial, civic and political life—Coundouriotis, Kokovilas, Voulgari, Boudoris, Tsamados and others—also left behind the *archontiká*, the island's renowned grand mansions. Unlike the wealthy elsewhere, who often cluster in particularly desirable areas or suburbs, the siting of Hydra's great houses was determined by a topography whereby even those of modest means might expect to have a view, and the benefit of a site high above the harbour was balanced against the desirability of having easier access to the port. As a result, the mansions stand scattered on both sides of the harbour and at high points above the town from where they command the most prominent sites and far-reaching views. Built by Italian craftsmen in a style that owed more to Venice than an Aegean vernacular, their imposing geometric exteriors were originally matched by the quality of the furnishings within. Charmian Clift wrote of Hydra's *archontiká* that they constitute a "rare example of a *nouveau-riche* community spending its wealth with faultless good taste; and also, I suppose, an instance of war profiteering which one cannot really condemn".

If family fortunes on Hydra were built on the back of naval power during the Napoleonic Wars, then it was the Greek War of Independence that brought many of them undone. Such was the decline in the island's wealth during these years that a number of the mansions fell upon hard times. In addition to the houses that eventually collapsed into ruin and were permanently lost, others were pressed into non-domestic use. The harbour-side mansion of the Tsamados family became the base for the School of the Merchant Marines in

1930, and the mansion of Emmanuel Tombazi, hovering above the western side of the harbour, has, since the mid-1930s, housed an annex of the School of Fine Arts of the Athens Polytechnic. Others still were transformed into small museums and opened to the public, most notably the Coundouriotis mansion, prominent today with its deep mustard exterior and its dominant position above the south-west corner of the harbour. Aristomidos Sofianos estimated that in the mid-1960s some twenty of these great houses were left standing, some of which were still in the hands of the families that built them.

One might expect that Hydra's mansions and the renowned families that remained were outside the social sphere of the island's poverty-stricken expatriates, but this was not necessarily the case. Indeed, when Sidney and Cynthia Nolan arrived on Hydra to join Clift and Johnston, they found themselves living in one such mansion, that of the Ghika family. The Ghikas were of Albanian origin and had been on Hydra since 1628, and several of the family had been prominent in the War of Independence. By the mid-1950s, the Ghika mansion—high on the hill to the west of the port in the area of Kiaffa, and overlooking both Hydra Port and Kamini—had been inherited by Greece's most prominent mid-century modernist painter Nikos Hadjikyriakos-Ghika. Ghika was a cosmopolitan internationalist and an intellectual painter who by the 1950s was holding solo exhibitions in Paris, London and New York.

Like many wealthy Hydriots, Ghika maintained a primary residence in Athens, but he was a regular summer visitor to his Hydra house, where he worked in a large, beautifully lit studio [See Plates 2 and 3]. Important in the development of Hydra's association with the arts, Ghika's house became a focus for visitors, many of whom were prominent in the international arts scene on both sides of the Second World War. When Ghika was a resident on Hydra, he hosted a retinue of leading artists, writers and intellectuals, and when not using the mansion, he would make it available for their longer-term use. Among the many who enjoyed Ghika's hospitality were writers Henry Miller, Lawrence Durrell, Rex Warner and Norman Mailer, photographer Henri Cartier-Bresson, pioneering modernist architect Walter Gropius and British neo-romantic painter John Craxton.

Henry Miller visited Ghika for a weekend in November 1939 while travelling with Greek poet George Katsimbalis and recorded his impressions of his host's house in *The Colossus of Maroussi*.

> Madame Hadji-Kyriakos, Ghika's wife, laid a wonderful table; we rose from the table like wine casks without legs. From the terrace, which was distinctly Oriental in flavor, we could look out on the sea in drunken stupefaction. The house had forty rooms, some of which were buried deep in the earth. The big rooms were like the saloon of an ocean liner; the little rooms were like cool dungeons fitted up by temperamental pirates.

The long-term visitors to those many rooms would eventually include the Nolans, who, for the seven months they lived in Ghika's mansion in 1955 and 1956, 'united' the stream of visitors to the house with the then small group of expatriates living near the port. Ghika had befriended Nolan in London in the early 1950s, and when Nolan received an invitation to use the house, the decision for the couple to spend time on Hydra with their friends, the Johnstons, was made considerably easier. The Nolans arrived on the island in November of 1955, following war hero and travel writer Patrick Leigh Fermor and his partner Joan Eyres Monsell as guests in Ghika's house. In a letter written from Hydra in mid-1954, Fermor described the mansion in detail, including the sights and sounds afforded by its great height.

> [It is] a large house on a steep slope with descending terraces like a Babylonian ziggurat, a thick-walled, whitewashed empty thing surrounded by arid reddish rocks and olive and almond and fig trees and the mountainside goes cascading down in a series of tiled roofs and a church cupola or two to the sea, which juts inland in a small combe ten minute walk below (quarter of an hour up!) … The sun sets in the most spectacular way over these mountains and the sea, and every night Joan and I watch it from the top terrace drinking ouzo, then eating late—about 9, when it is dark—by lamplight at the other end of the terrace.

> There has been a full then a waning moon the last few nights, making everything look insanely beautiful.

Eyres Monsell departed for England in August 1955 with classicist Maurice Bowra as a travelling companion. Bowra, who was Warden of Wadham College, Oxford, later informed the young Australian composer and Wadham initiate Peter Sculthorpe that he knew Australia well and claimed (falsely) that a town in Queensland had been named after him—knowledge he apparently gleaned from George Johnston with whom he had become acquainted. Fermor himself departed Hydra in mid-September in the company of socialite and memoirist Lady Diana Cooper, who had visited the island with photographer Cecil Beaton.

Fermor had lived in the Ghika house on and off for the two years preceding the Nolans' visit, and would do so again after they departed. During Fermor's residency, the house continued to be a magnet for other British literary figures who came to share in his good fortune at being so well accommodated. That Fermor and others were either resident in, or frequent visitors to, Greece was in part due to the activities of the British Council in Athens. The Council had opened officially in 1939 and then closed with the German invasion of Greece in April 1941. When the Council reopened in 1944, it was tasked with establishing postwar cultural ties between the UK and Greece. Fermor was unemployed and looking for a new occupation in 1946 when he won the position of Deputy Director for the British Institute of Higher Education Studies created under the auspices of the Council, while Bowra had made his way to Greece as Chair of the British Council Humanities Advisory Committee and to lecture at the Institute. Fermor's immediate boss was Rex Warner, novelist, classicist and, with Lawrence Durrell, translator of Greek poet (and later Nobel Laureate) Giorgos Seferis. Seferis accompanied Miller and Katsimbalis to Ghika's house for their 1939 visit and later wrote the poem 'Les anges sont blancs', which centres on that occasion. Warner was, at the time, the husband of Barbara Hutchinson, who would become Ghika's second wife. Fermor also developed a warm friendship with Katsimbalis, who was editing a literary

Ghika's house. (James Burke)

magazine out of the British Institute and who was himself associated with numerous writers and artists, including Ghika.

Ghika thus welcomed to his Hydra house a flow of British visitors, many of whom had passed through the British Council in Athens. These included historian Patrick Balfour; novelist and biographer Nancy Mitford; art historian Roger Hinks (remembered for his part in the ruinous 'restoration' of the Parthenon Marbles); critic Cyril Connolly and writer Barbara Skelton; travel writer and explorer Freya Stark; and poet Stephen Spender. Spender, returning the favour, would later write of Ghika that "when it comes to his paintings of Hydra and Greece, Ghika is simply the best modern painter of Greece, and it is difficult to think of any past painter to compare with him". Fermor, for his part, would write much of *Mani*, his classic 1958 travel memoir of the southern Peloponnese, at Ghika's house, describing it as a "perfect prose factory".

The first that many Australians would hear of Hydra came in an article in *The Australian Women's Weekly* in February 1957, which reported on the Nolans' ex¬perience in the Ghika house. Written by novelist and journalist

Ronald McKie, the article, titled 'A home that Homer would have liked: Australian artist's house on island in Aegean Sea', describes idyllic island living marked by its cheapness and the relaxed and romantically blessed Mediterranean setting. Tapping into expectations of how someone of the Nolans' renown and sensibility might pass their time in such a location—"painting, gardening, visiting other islands, fishing with sponge divers, bringing up their stores from the village on donkey-back"—McKie complemented this lifestyle account with a description of Ghika's mansion and its setting.

> On the pink, white, and grey island of Hydra, the Nolans lived in a house built by Albanian pirates two centuries ago. The house, with 30 ft. high walls, is on a hillside, set in a wild terraced garden packed with almond trees, cacti and wildflowers. Below the garden the rocky headlands of Hydra dip into the sea that changes color from royal-purple to pewter-grey during winter storms. Against this background from the Odyssey the Nolans lived and worked…

There is no record that McKie visited Hydra, and it is likely his source was a discussion with Cynthia Nolan conducted after the couple returned to Australia in early 1957. Certainly Cynthia's enthusiasm for Hydra that permeates the article was genuine. In a letter to Pat Flower written from Hydra, she gushed about the island, proclaiming, "I tell you I like it all".

> [T]he white two-storey houses that have a blue haze for those twenty evening minutes, the kites that jerk up into the blue and white sky, the brilliant mainland that you can touch across the satin ribbon blue, or pewter, or yes, wine-red Aegean, the naked mountains that glow and stand up like cardboard cut out against a primrose cloud. Sorry, I am in love again, besotted, swooning, unable to embrace enough. Every day the madness grows.

While Clift herself would some years later also use *The Australian Women's Weekly* to extol her experience on Hydra, she would likely have seen McKie's article (if indeed she was aware of it) as another irritating example of Cynthia

Nolan seeking publicity for her husband's career. The Nolans, in the guise of Henry and Ursula Trevena, play an important role as fellow expatriates in *Peel Me a Lotus*, where Ursula is portrayed as constantly and annoyingly attending to the needs of her husband's talent. It is perhaps not surprising that there was some tension between Clift and Cynthia Nolan. While their husbands were established friends and bonded on the basis of their Melbourne working-class backgrounds and a shared interest in the mythical possibilities of the great European civilisations, there was less to cement a relationship between their wives. Johnston and Sidney Nolan were five years apart in age, but there were fifteen years between Clift and Cynthia Nolan, and a considerable gulf in terms of their social backgrounds. In Cynthia's willingness to sublimate her own ambitions as a writer in order to support her husband's career, Clift likely also saw a shadow of the woman she feared she herself might become. As Clift's pregnancy advanced over the winter of 1955–56, she worried about the prospect of never resuming an independent career, and this fear likely added a personal edge to her sour assessment of Ursula Trevena's role in catering to "gallery managers, publicity agents and the potential buyers of Henry's lesser works".

McKie's *Women's Weekly* article was accompanied by three photos, including one of Cynthia in the "terraced garden" of the Ghika house and another of Nolan painting (incongruously in a white shirt, tie and "stained apron") on the house's terrace [See Plates 4 & 5]. It is likely that this joint portrait was taken by Johnston or Clift, given the few other candidates for the role on the island at the time.

As Clift and Johnston commenced the search for an island house of their own, Clift found she envied the Nolans' circumstances. In *Peel Me a Lotus*, she describes approaching the Ghika house in a manner that made her admiration clear:

> As we came over the last rise, through the ruined tiers of houses built like forts or palaces, this house on the mountainside seemed indeed very beautiful. Within the great protecting walls pink vapour puffs of almond blossom wafted down over five stepped terraces to the very doors of the square, white dwelling whose foundations rise from the mountain gorge.

From the Ghika house, high on the hillside, Clift finds that "The view from the house is breathtaking … I must turn again to the sweep of the blue gulf below, the jagged peaks of the islands breaking the foam, and the far dim dream of the mountains of Arcady." In addition to admiring the position and scale of the "wonderful, twenty-room mansion loaned to them by a wealthy Greek who is an admirer of Henry's painting", Clift also coveted the convenience of running water and modernised sanitation that was so rare on the island.

> It was built in the period of the island's greatest prosperity on a wild mountain slope overlooking the gulf, and the owner has recently added a bathroom with flush toilets and beds with inner-spring mattresses to the charms of lofty rooms, fine carved furniture, and rare carpets.
>
> I think that Ursula can't believe her luck. A bathroom again! Tiled stoves and carpets! A real studio for Henry! After all the years of stumbling in Henry's wake through an endless succession of shoddy furnished flats, European hotel rooms, cheap pensions, and the guest-rooms of friends, it must seem incredible luxury.

Clift judges her friends' use of the house as a marker of Trevena's mounting success and perhaps an indication of something to which she and George might yet aspire. Indeed, *Peel Me a Lotus* includes a further hint at the rivalry between the two women, as, according to the book, the Trevenas develop an interest in buying an island house and then return in October 1956 (after Clift and Johnston have purchased their house) to do exactly that, with Ursula declaring that the house "must have some decent rooms where one can hang pictures, and then workrooms for Henry. And a garden, of course." It is therefore the Cynthia Nolan character who is placed in the position of envying her friend's ownership of an island house, but this was entirely a narrative ruse, as Cynthia never returned to Hydra even when her husband did, and there is no evidence the Nolans seriously contemplated buying on the island.

There was, however, no sign of personal tension in a series of photos apparently taken by Johnston and Nolan (the two men don't appear together in any of the images) picturing the two couples sharing a meal in the sunshine on

Martin Johnston, Sidney Nolan, Charmian Clift and Cynthia Nolan on the terrace of the Ghika house, 1956. (Johnston and Clift Collection)

the expansive terrace of the Ghika house while Martin Johnston enjoys the view over the town through binoculars. A copy of one of these photographs in the National Library of Australia carries the note: "Dinner with a friend on a roof overlooking the blue Aegean sea is one of the pleasures of life on a Greek island". The only indication that the Johnstons and Nolans may still have been adapting to the island lifestyle is that Sidney Nolan wears a tie and Johnston a bow tie—seemingly odd choices given the location and full sunshine.

Another to enjoy the view from Ghika's mansion, although briefly and apparently only once, was Leonard Cohen. Before the Canadian left London for Hydra in April 1960, he had met Jacob Rothschild of the prominent British banking family. Rothschild had instructed Cohen that when he made it to Hydra, he should seek out his mother Barbara Hutchinson, who by this time had successively divorced the 3rd Baron (Victor) Rothschild as well as her second husband, Rex Warner, and was living with Ghika. Once settled on Hydra, Cohen took the climb to the mansion to make the introduction, only to be rejected without gaining entry on the grounds that not only had Mrs Hutchinson not been informed of Cohen's impending visit, but she had little interest in "his sort of Jew" (although exactly who it was who rejected Cohen changes in the telling—according to other versions it was either Jacob Rothschild's sister or a servant).

While Cohen might have been denied entry to the Ghika mansion, he did find himself warmly welcomed into the many-roomed house (a substantial 'captain's house' rather than a true *archontiká*) of George Lialios. Lialios, who was to be a significant figure in Cohen's island life, was an example of the educated and intellectually inclined Greeks who forged a link between Hydra's international visitors and the island's established families. Lialios was not a Hydriot; his family was from Patras in western Greece and also had considerable land holdings on the Peloponnese. His father was a composer and musician, and Lialios had been born in Germany, studied in Cologne, spoke Greek, German and English, and had a strong interest in philosophy. He first came to Hydra in 1954, meeting Fermor and others at Ghika's house, and several years later acquired his large house high above the harbour—a house he had found "partly a ruin and partly magnificent". Lialios befriended Axel Jensen and Marianne Ihlen after their arrival in 1958, and began introducing these newcomers to some of the wealthy Hydriot families with whom he had a comfortable affinity.

In return, it is likely that Jensen or Ihlen introduced Lialios to Cohen. A close friendship quickly developed between the two men, who were apparently given to passing evenings in quiet conversation and even complete silence. Lialios would attribute their closeness to both men having roots in

Nikos Hadjikyriakos-Ghika on his terrace. (James Burke)

ancient cultures of the eastern Mediterranean, claiming that "we could sit together in silence, a virtue which is rare with western people. We never spoke unnecessary words." The idea of Lialios and Cohen passing time in companionable silence high above the *agora* supports Redmond Wallis's sense that Cohen was somewhat reclusive and given to avoiding the rowdier expatriate gatherings on the *agora*.

Someone who had more success than Cohen in gaining entry to the Ghika house was James Burke. Ghika was resident on Hydra in September 1960, and Burke took nearly sixty photos at his house, including on the terrace, in the studio and in the house proper. While Ghika is prepared to stand before the camera, for the most part these portraits are among the least engaging that Burke took. With apparently no one present to serve as a distraction or external point of engagement for his subject, Ghika looks towards the camera in a generally disengaged manner. Only in several of those taken in the studio does he appear more animated and engaged with something other than the

Nikos Hadjikyriakos-Ghika at home. (James Burke)

lens. The external photos taken on the terrace are more effective, at least in portraying the spectacular height of the house above the port and town, and the interior images capture the generous proportions of the studio and the distinctive architectural detailing of the house, with walls adorned by Ghika's own paintings and vibrantly decorated door frames. As Burke recorded in his notes, "[the] entire house … has been thoroughly Ghikarized".

The house continued to be enjoyed by Ghika and his guests for less than a year after Burke's photographs were taken. While the exact circumstances surrounding its destruction by fire remain something of a mystery, the story that is often told involves a deliberate act of arson. According to this version of events, the marriage of Ghika and Hutchinson in 1961 was the final straw for a staff member loyal to Ghika's former wife, and who took revenge on the newlyweds by razing the house to the ground and reducing a large collection of the owner's paintings to ashes in the process. The wilder theories even hinted at a curse Cohen was said to have put upon the house following his front door rejection. The truth is likely more prosaic, involving an intoxicated housekeeper and a lamp with a naked flame, but the result was the same, and the imposing, cliff-like foundations and basement walls of the mansion are all that remain over half a century later: burnt-out, fenced-off and desolate on their rocky promontory. It is said that Ghika was so devastated by the loss that he never returned to the island, although this is also likely untrue. Today the incinerated ruin is visited by locals and visitors alike, who make their way to the hillside to take in the view, pick flowers and ponder.

Interestingly, Ghika is not mentioned at all in Wallis's diaries and only fleetingly in *The Unyielding Memory*. Wallis's accounts are far from being comprehensive records of their author's time on the island, so care needs to be taken as to what this apparent 'absence' might mean, if anything at all. At the very least, it might lead to speculation that Clift and Johnston came to have a role amongst Hydra's foreign visitors that paralleled and continued Ghika's hospitality. They all brought together from afar, and for various periods of time, people with loosely shared interests, values and pursuits, using the island as a place for nurturing artistic and intellectual achievement while providing an agreeable sociability and a tolerant moral climate. It is the case that when the Johnstons took up their role at the centre of Hydra's expatriate and visitor community, they were adding to, rather than instigating, the island's reputation as an international meeting place for artists and intellectuals.

Those who gravitated around the Ghika mansion weren't the only constellation of international visitors drawn to one of Hydra's grand houses. There was another very substantial island house that also hosted a slew of high-profile guests and was generally more accessible to the island's struggling expatriates. This was the house of Mrs Katerina Paouri.

The Paouri mansion, overlooking the eastern side of the port, had been built by nationalist hero Lazaros Coundouriotis for his sister during the War of Independence, before being acquired—in need of repair—by Paouri immediately prior to the Second World War. Paouri was a woman of considerable wealth who, at the time, was in possession of not only her own substantial house but also a number of other properties on the island. So prominent was the Paouri family that Katerina not only had money, but at the time she was convinced she *was* the money, sharing the story that a younger version of herself in traditional island garb, looming large before a sketch of Hydra, graced the 1000 drachma note. Evidence suggests it is more likely to have been the daughter of the note's designer [See Plate 6].

By the time Johnston and Clift arrived on Hydra, *Kyria* Paouri enjoyed her status as a patron of the arts and, in this role, took an interest in the island's visiting writers and artists. Paouri also had a reputation for entertaining and frequently used her house for high-profile social events that brought together members of the island's established families and expatriates along with other visitors and celebrities who were passing through. It has been said that her annual spring cocktail party was considered the unofficial start of the Hydra 'season', during which her own entertaining included a constant round of noon cocktails and afternoon teas.

Peel Me a Lotus makes it clear that Johnston and Clift were part of these gatherings from their first year on the island. While Clift does not name individuals or houses, she does include a sly reference to Paouri when she reports receiving an invitation from a "stout, blonde woman" who claims to have "something blue to every room. For the Evil Eyes". Paouri was certainly stout and blonde by this time and famed for the use of a particular shade of blue to paint the doors and windows of her several island properties. The colour she used is commonly referred to as loulaki blue—the blue of the 'evil eye'—and is frequently used on other Greek islands as an intense counterpoint to whitewash. On Hydra, Paouri for a time claimed sole use of loulaki blue for her properties, with the island's police reportedly prohibiting its use by others.

Clift's familiarity with the houses of Hydra's wealthy is caught beautifully in the 'June' chapter of *Peel Me a Lotus*, as she describes the established families abandoning the heat of the city and opening their island houses for the summer months of elaborate entertaining.

> Several of the great houses have already been opened up for the summer. The aristocrats are in their rightful places, high, high on the soaring cliffs, where for a few months they will be able to forget the concrete monstrosities clanging up in Athens and the big American automobiles and shiny chromium bars where the new-rich congregate.
>
> Here nothing is changed: the Venetian chest, the pierced panels that enclose the winter bed-cupboard, the dull smoulder of gold caught in the light that burns always before the ikon-box, the silk-smooth flagstones in the hall. Here in the tiled courtyard the geraniums still spill their acrid blood-red flowers from stained stone urns, the willow-pattern plates hang eternally on the whitewashed wall, the polished flintlock at the turn of the stair. Snippets and waste from old ancestral leavings.

Clift noted that in cases where the family heirlooms had been lost or sold off as fortunes diminished, these things were now being bought back, or at least replaced, as some of the mansions transferred to new ownership. She reported that "At least four houses have been sold in the last year to wealthy Athenians" and were now being meticulously re-stocked with "the things the old families were forced to sell". Once again, it was the updated plumbing that drew her wishful admiration.

> Why, there isn't a lamp or a spoon in them that isn't in character, except perhaps for the luxurious tiled bathroom and the hot water service run on Buta gas and the amusing bar-barbeque converted from the old bakehouse.

The residents of these great houses—some descended directly from the admirals who had led the fight for independence and the creation of modern Greece, others who had made their money in that remade nation and were keenly buying into the island's history and traditions—enjoyed a side of island living that was far removed from those who provided the manpower on the port or handled the donkeys or resided at the naval academy. Although some within the island's artist community may have been poor, they nonetheless had entry into this world. As Clift recognised, the established Hydriot families had access to the education and travel that meant they were, in Hydra's terms, part of a cosmopolitan elite with more in common with the island's international visitors than with most Hydriots. They therefore found that the artists and writers were a more natural choice when it came time to fill their mansions with the summer parties. As Clift wrote, "Your hosts are gentle, cultured, gracious people, Englishly English or Frenchly French at will, with nothing in their easy manners or perfect accents even to remotely connect them with the fiercely whiskered gentleman in the exotic tasselled cap blazing away with a brace of pistols and glaring grimly from the gunsmoke-and-brimstone background".

With the Paouri house at its centre, Hydra during the summer provided a remarkably international and catholic social scene, devised to gather together those who were considered sufficiently novel, or entertaining and otherwise notable or interesting. It was therefore not surprising that, as a young, attractive couple with literary credentials, Axel Jensen and Marianne Ihlen were invited to the Paouri mansion for the island's swankiest parties soon after they arrived. Sometimes shoeless and t-shirted, they found themselves unexpectedly mixing with Athenian intellectuals and artists; major figures of postwar international art such Yves Klein, Robert Rauschenberg and Richard Serra; and the super-wealthy of the Greek shipping trade, including Aristotle Onassis and Stavros Niarchos.

Paouri's access to the international art set was enhanced in 1957 when American painter Timothy Hennessy and German-born artist Ioannis (Wolfgang) Kardamatis acquired a large house immediately adjacent to her own. The purchase also increased the number of houses on the island with an Australian connection. Kardamatis had been sent to Sydney from Germany in the late 1920s to live with his Greek immigrant father, where he proved his entrepreneurial mettle by conducting a "flourishing business … in hand-painted copies of the dirty postcards" he had picked up in Port Said during his journey to the antipodes. Kardamatis was, as his friend Robin Eakin (later Dalton) explained in her 1965 memoir, *Aunts Up the Cross*, a reluctant migrant "who had never wanted to come to Australia in the first place". Once out of high school, Kardamatis replaced the soft pornography business with the study of art, firstly with Antonio Dattilo-Rubbo in Sydney and then with George Bell in Melbourne, before returning to Sydney when he found his hopes of travelling to Europe thwarted by the war. Kardamatis eventually left Australia immediately after the end of the war, travelling to London, Paris, the Antibes (where he and Eakin helped Pablo Picasso display his first pottery exhibition) and Venice, where he rubbed shoulders with minor royalty and artists. It was here that Kardamatis met Hennessy, who married an Italian countess in 1955 in a lavish gondola ceremony. Kardamatis claimed credit for introducing the couple and presumably was the beneficiary of some of the wealth that flowed through the marriage and into the Hydra real estate market [See Plate 7]. Hennessy's much adored second wife, Isabella—a French woman of high social standing with whom he subsequently lived on a large estate in Ireland—was seemingly less tolerant than the countess of her husband's friends and their complex affections, as a result of which Hennessy and Kardamatis lost contact for some fifteen years. The two artists rekindled their connection after Isabella's passing and then moved between their houses in Hydra—where Hennessy covered every surface including the walls with stained glass patterns, while Kardamatis worked in gold leaf—and Avignon until their deaths.

Hennessy's abstract baroque style that found expression on the carpets, drapes, wall coverings and furniture of his Hydra house was a far cry from Paouri's ornately and traditionally decorated house, which features in a number of Burke's photographs. In several images, Burke seems to be primarily focused on recording the interiors, with the house's owner propped uncomfortably amongst her furnishings. These photographs capture the classic interiors of Hydra's mansions, with their air of self-conscious and carefully presented formality. If these interiors were a world away from the tastes expressed next door in Kardamatis and Hennessy's house, then they also display little of the casual and eclectic panache of the Johnstons' house that reflected the island location far more appropriately for modern eyes. Clift herself gently mocked the furnishings that were chosen to embalm the memories of the admirals and captains who had once been the masters of these mansions.

> See, this was the writing-table he used, just as he left it. And here is his pistol, his telescope, a contemporary lithograph of his ship in action against the Turks, the battered log-book with the thin brown spidery writing. And it is his ship's bell that rings as you enter the courtyard.

Another series of Burke's images depicts one of Paouri's social gatherings, where she entertains a small group of expatriates consisting of Clift and Johnston, David Goschen, and Carolyn Gassoumis and her toddler daughter, Athena. These images are a good example of Burke at his most photojournalistic, as he captures the sequence of events as the small group winds its way through the streets on the climb to Paouri's house; are welcomed at the front door by their host; enjoy refreshments on the terrace overlooking the harbour; reconvene in the house's tavern room for some further drinks; and finally depart and retrace their steps through the town's laneways.

Perhaps the most telling of these shots are those—over forty in all—taken on the terrace. Although Burke struggles in some of these images with the

Katerina Paouri at home. (James Burke)

bright backlighting provided by the sunlit harbour, his pictures nevertheless convey the stately and languid hour of the afternoon and capture an atmosphere of which Clift had written in *Peel Me a Lotus*:

> On terraces as big as state ballrooms you may drink tea at five o'clock in an atmosphere so still and unhurried that even the tea itself has a timeless flavour—brought in a clipper-ship, you suspect, stored in a carved chest, measured out in catties.

These photos also reflect the odd mix of formality and informality that was a feature of social exchanges between Hydra's elite and members of the artist colony. There is no obvious presence of the uniformed stewards noted by others, but nonetheless there is an air of ritual that is evidenced by the formal welcome at the front door; the carefully prepared table; Paouri managing the food and drinks; and the small group of visitors taking their departure escorted by their host. Those visitors, however, are noticeably dressed for comfort, with Clift in sandals and Goschen characteristically barefooted

George Johnston, Charmian Clift, Carolyn and Athena Gassoumis arriving at the Paouri house. (James Burke)

despite being elegantly jacketed—Burke reported that Goschen's jacket was "tweed" and his shirt, "saffron". Paouri's hospitality is shown to be generous, with a number of the images taken in the tavern room depicting her stretching up to the overhead wine barrels to pour her guests yet another drink. Perhaps due to the confined space, many of these 'tavern' pictures are oddly constructed, with Johnston and Clift shown cornered on one table, and Paouri and Goschen oddly partnered on another, an arrangement certainly not conducive to the relaxed conversation that Burke was presumably trying to capture.

Katerina Paouri, Charmian Clift, Carolyn and Athena Gassoumis,
George Johnston, at Paouri's front door. (James Burke)

We also have this gathering at the Paouri house to thank for a fine series of portraits of Clift taken by Burke during the terrace drinks. In a number of them, she is pictured in the company of either Paouri or Goschen, but in others she appears alone. In these photos, Clift seems serenely indifferent to the presence of the camera despite the obvious proximity and intensity with which Burke has fixed his lens upon her. Over half a century after their taking, these photos remind the viewer of Clift's reputation as a beauty, and they bring to mind Nadia Wheatley's observation that it was a beauty that transmitted photographically, with Clift being blessed with "that indefinable

HALF THE PERFECT WORLD

Carolyn and Athena Gassoumis, George Johnston, Katerina Paouri, Charmian Clift and David Goschen drinking "noon cocktails". (James Burke)

George Johnston, Charmian Clift, Katerina Paouri and David Goschen. (James Burke)

Charmian Clift. (James Burke)

thing which makes a certain face photogenic. It is clear that the camera loved Charmian—and that the feeling was mutual."

Rodney Hall was another financially struggling visitor escorted by Johnston and Clift to Paouri's house, where the hostess regaled the Australians with a story about one of her parties. It is a story—as Hall points out—told by Paouri at her own expense, but it also highlights a certain pride in the artistic types who found their way to her house.

> Katerina's saving grace was that she saw the funny side of her own misdemeanours. She told us one of her favourite stories when we had lunch with her and George and Charmian, and she said to us in her very hoarse Greek voice, 'I am famous for one thing,' she said, 'I have wonderful house parties and I once had Winston Churchill as a guest.' And she said, 'Not long ago, some friends of mine said they had a guest,

and could we bring our guest? He is Russian and he doesn't speak Greek and he doesn't speak English but he would love to meet you.' And they brought this awful old Russian man. She said, 'I took one look at him and I thought, 'My parties are too stylish for you.' Over the course of the evening he found someone to talk to and the party went off in the usual way, until her visitors left when she asked them would they sign her guest book. And the old man said through his friends, 'I've had such a lovely party, I would love to draw you a picture.' And Katerina said, 'I can't possibly spare you a page.' So he said, 'Alright, I'll draw you a little picture.' So he drew a postage stamp size square and he did a little drawing in it, and signed it and thanked her and went away. And she said, 'About a month later I'm having another party, and somebody opens my book, and says, 'Oh Katerina, look.' And she said 'What is it?', and he said, 'This is signed, and it was Marc Chagall.' 'Marc Chagall? And he offered to do me a full page drawing!'

Chagall's visit to the Paouri house is an incident that has considerable currency amongst those who remember Hydra at this time and has understandably been retold with variations. One expatriate who was an eyewitness to the occasion was Dinnie Blair, then living a struggling life on the island with her husband, Tore Pedersen. Blair recalls that:

> I knew Mrs Paouri very well, she comes from one of the wealthiest families in Greece. One evening I was invited to her palace up the hill for drinks, being tended to by god knows how many housemaids, being served retzina and moulding biscuits, they were almost green. Marc Chagall was there and as he signed the guest book he drew a picture instead. Mme Paouri checked it out, tore the page out, tore up the drawing and threw it in the fireplace, saying 'what trash.'

In an additional sequence of over thirty photographs, Burke captures Clift and Johnston, again in the company of Carolyn Gassoumis, as the only members of the foreign community present at a gathering at another of the *archontiká*.

House of Maria Kalergis. Carolyn Gassoumis, unidentified, George Johnston, Charmian Clift, Doris Papastratos, Maria Paouri, Betty Papastratos, Vanna Hatzimihali. (James Burke)

In this case, the occasion is evening cocktails at Mrs Maria Kalergis's house, which stands high on the western side of the harbour, opposite that of Mrs Paouri. Mrs Kalergis was the great-granddaughter of Nicholas Votsis, one of the wealthiest of the great sea captains and another who went on to become a hero of the War of Independence, and the house in which these photos were taken was the original Votsis mansion. Mrs Paouri is also present along with her daughter Maria and members of other notable Hydriot families. Burke recorded in his notes that this was a gathering of the "Cream of Hydra society" in a house full of "fine French furniture and Venetian ware".

In the numerous images Burke took, we see Johnston and Clift, together and apart, moving around the room, sitting and standing, with Clift quite smartly dressed and Johnston's clothes notably threadbare. The couple seems fully at ease in this company, chatting amicably and speaking intently with those present. Johnston appears to be as garrulous as his reputation suggests, with Clift less demonstrative but equally sociable. Carolyn Gassoumis, by contrast, often appears notably ill-at-ease, standing apart from conversations and clutching a drink tightly, with both her expression and posture betraying her discomfort.

The social gatherings at the Paouri and Kalergis houses were not the only time Burke had access to the houses of Hydra's established wealthy families. He also photographed Clift and Johnston visiting the house of Mrs Kiki Neophytos (a sister of Katerina Paouri) and took further photographs at the house of Mrs Neophytos' daughter, Doris Papastratos. These various gatherings photographed by Burke indicate that Hydra's social scene at the time was more integrated than has been suggested. The presence of middle-class and well-to-do Athenians with first or second homes on Hydra, coupled with the stream of established literary figures visiting and staying at the Ghika house, had long given the island a social and cultural veneer and integration rare amongst the Aegean islands. Although Clift and Johnston's Greek never progressed beyond a rudimentary level, they and other expatriates were well able to expand their social circle with English as a convenient *lingua franca*. There was also a stratum of Hydriot society that was not only able to speak English but which welcomed interaction with international visitors, whether they were long-term island residents or more casual short-term tourists. It may be that the number of photographs that Burke took of the expatriates mixing with Hydra's established families overstates the interaction, as it is likely that Clift and Johnston saw their access to these homes as a means of impressing Burke with their status on the island. There is, however, evidence from those who were there at the time that such social events were frequently attended by the island's international contingent, and that the Johnstons were indeed highly regarded and welcome visitors.

Times have, of course, moved on for even the most settled of Hydra's families and their *archontiká*. Not only has the Ghika mansion been reduced to a ruin, but recently the Paouri mansion was put up for sale. As island practice dictates, there were no outward signs of the house being on the market, but the indicators were nonetheless apparent—the closed shutters, a garden in need of weeding, a terrace built for entertaining devoid of decoration, and the loulaki blue paint on the doors and window frames fading and peeling.

*　*　*

Redmond Wallis recounts the experience of his main character Nick Alwyn being invited to lunch at the home of Katerina Paouri—including another version of the Chagall story.

> *The Alwyns were invited to lunch by Katerini, who had a large house adjoining their first house, above the naval school. They had never known her well. It was said that she had been a showgirl and had managed to hook some rich Athenian; it was certainly true that her house was grand and expensively furnished and she arrived accompanied by two or three maids and a handyman. Whenever she came to the island, which was two or three times a year, she gave a lunch party for selected foreigners. Katerini liked to dabble in politics and at the last election was said to have bribed every shepherd on the island to come down and vote for her candidate. She was a chubby little lady with peroxided and artificially curled hair, but she had a good heart and she was not averse to a bit of fun.*
>
> *When the Alwyns arrived the only other guests were Patricia, Doris and Nico. For a while they had to form a conversation group. Nico might earn marks for survival, thought Nick, but he was an arrogant, ill-mannered son-of-a-bitch, a smooth, artificially blond poseur. Then Stephanos and the four Australians turned up and he was able to move away. Stephanos probably had an ulterior motive for being with the Australians. George had intimated that he and his compatriots would drop around and see the*

Lamounises and their guests after Christmas dinner and Stephanos was doing his best to prevent that. It was Nick's bet that he wouldn't succeed.

Years before Paul told the Alwyns a wonderful story about Katerini. Marc Chagall had come to the island and Katerini had been told by Paul that he was pretty damned important, so she had invited him (with others) for drinks. When everyone was leaving Katerini produced her leather-bound visitors book and invited Chagall to write his name in it. Chagall whipped off a brilliant pencil sketch and signed with a flourish. Katerini looked at this in outrage and as soon as he was out the door ripped the page out and destroyed it: she, she told her remaining guests, with great dignity, wasn't going to have anyone scribbling in her visitors book.

Chapter Six

SOCIALISING AT KATSIKAS

There was no shortage of venues for Hydra's expatriates to gather for socialising, drinking, gossiping, arguing and flirting. During the long summer months, the *agora* opened up into a generous spread of tables and chairs spilling out of doorways and reaching towards the dockside as *kafenia* and tavernas competed for the seasonal tourist trade, while others operated from the alleys and side streets that rose away from the harbour.

There was one venue in particular that became the focus for expatriate social life—Katsikas, a one-stop *kafenio*, bar and grocery shop run by brothers Antony and Nick Katsikas and their families. Katsikas stood at the western corner of the dockside, immediately facing the harbour, where the wide promenade expanded into a small public square. It was separated from Tassos *kafenio* and the Poseidon Hotel by a narrow laneway known to the expatriates as Donkey Shit Lane. Here proceedings were watched over by the statue of Admiral Pavlos Coundouriotis, hero of the Balkan Wars of 1912–13, and an attendant lion—or, as Charmian Clift described it, the "ludicrous marble lion crouched pale and simpering in the square at the foot of that remote, far-gazing admiral who weathers all storms with disdain". According to James Burke, this area was known as "Katsikas corner", and he described the business that gave the corner its name:

> Katsikas is really more of an old-fashioned general store and it also provides relaxatives like wine, brandy and oozo. The drinks are served at tables on the quai in front of the store during the day, and in the stock room behind the store at night and in bad weather. The foreign

"Katsikas corner", looking east on the *agora*. Tore Pedersen about to walk up Donkey Shit Lane; Demetri and Carolyn Gassoumis, and George Johnston (backs to camera); Charmian Clift (bending); Charles Heckstall and Klaus Merkel (by wall). (James Burke)

> artists and writers who gather at Katsikas are referred to as the "Katsikas group" and they revolve around George and Charmian Johnston, who were the first arrivals and founding members of the Katsikas club, as it might be called.

As Burke noted, it was Johnston and Clift who led other expatriates to Katsikas when they chose it as their preferred place to socialise and drink soon after arriving on Hydra. Writing of her first island winter in *Peel Me a Lotus*, Clift reported that:

> Katsikas' Bar is six deal tables at the back of Antony and Nick Katsikas' grocery store at the end of the cobbled waterfront by the Poseidon Hotel, and it is here that we usually gather at midday among the flour-sacks and oil-jars and painted tin water-tanks and strings of onions and

Rear of Katsikas, n.d. (Redmond Wallis)

soft white festoons of cotton-waste: a sort of social club evolved from the necessity to relieve the boredom of an island winter.

The eclectic overabundance of general goods noted by Clift was characteristic of the shop's back room. Colin Simpson recalled a "half-dark cave of stalactite merchandise" where "Buckets, brooms and meat-safes hung from the ceiling and there were nails and whitewash brushes in boxes among the groceries and the ouzo bottles, and a heap of roped fishermen's floats in one corner". Little was intended for the tourist trade—the goods sold at Katsikas met the needs of locals for basic food and household and boating supplies, all of which provided a very mercantile yet domestic flavour to the inside gatherings.

FEBRUARY

Katsikas back room, *Peel Me a Lotus*. (Nancy Dignan)

Nancy Dignan, who produced the naïve but beguiling line drawings for Clift's *Peel Me a Lotus*, captured the essence of the Katsikas back room in her illustration for the month of February in the book's month-by-month chronology. Dignan depicted the heavily cluttered inside area favoured for winter gatherings, with a view through the shop providing a tantalising glimpse to the harbour-side and its *caiques*—a promise of the summer to come.

That Johnston and Clift became 'headquartered' at Katsikas inevitably made it the place to which international visitors gravitated. For while the expatriates' social lives were far from confined to one place, Katsikas became *the* place they gathered if they wished to fall within the orbit of the charismatic Australians. Leonard Cohen recalled in an interview with Australian journalist Marie Knuckey that the couple was always available at Katsikas to offer practical support and advice.

Winter at Katsikas. Sun Axelsson, Charmian Clift, George Johnston and Michael Piper (far right) with unidentified others, c.1963
(Johnston and Clift Collection)

> They [Johnston and Clift] were extremely helpful to all young people coming to the island. Many stopped at their table at Katsikas bar, to drink with them and get advice—on everything from where to buy their kerosene to what chemical to use to stop the toilet smelling. They were the focal point for foreigners on the island.

Marianne Ihlen and Axel Jensen were among those who discovered themselves at Katsikas and being helped by the Johnstons when they turned up on the island in January of 1958. As newly arrived foreigners they were directed to the Australian House, where the busy Johnstons invited the newcomers to meet them again later in the day in the back room at Katsikas. The two couples met as arranged, where Ihlen found herself seated amongst the shop's overabundance of hardware and foodstuffs, including "octopuses and sheep testicles" hanging to dry. Here Clift and Johnston befriended the young Norwegians, putting them in touch with the town's real estate 'fixer' and providing advice on surviving the Hydra winter.

If Clift and Johnston saw Katsikas as the ideal place from which to share their experience and dispense advice, they were certainly not alone in using it to conduct business. As Clift recalled, Katsikas was "where you hired masons and plumbers and consulted the caique captain about transporting goods from Athens and talked to the donkey men and bought water from the freighter and read your mail and arranged your social activities and entertained visitors and finally (when modernity hit) even took telephone calls from London or Australia".

Aspiring Australian poet and novelist Rodney Hall was another who first encountered the Johnstons in the rear of Katsikas, and his account provides further insight into the couple's hospitality and role on the island. Hall arrived in mid-winter, immediately after the Christmas of 1963, with his wife, Bet, and newborn daughter. The season made a poetic impression on Hall—in his poem 'Hydra' he wrote of "Midwinter: through this bitter morning/ customers stamp the market quay,/ the cold leaps up like a fish from the slab,/ while the trombone mules protest against/ the load of this, as of any day,/ and puzzle out the terraces". Amidst this winter chill, the Halls received the warmest of welcomes from the older Australians.

> We were walking this beautiful little *agora* on the waterfront and we went into a shop, a sort of grocery shop, called Katsikas, a shabby down-market little shop crowded with things, foodstuffs and sponges and things hung from the ceiling ... And while we were in the shop, choosing, we heard Australian voices from a back room ... and it wasn't immediately apparent there was a back room open to the public. And anyway we heard these voices and being a bit nosy I poked my nose in, while Bet stayed behind with the baby, and said 'G'day.' And there were these two people, these two middle-aged people, and they were very, very welcoming. I said, 'Well I've got my wife and baby,' and they said, 'Bring

them through, don't worry about Katsikas, he will follow you with the bill.' It was eleven in the morning and they were already socking into the retsina. And I mean they were lovely, they were so warm and welcoming and funny and clever. It was instant friendship. We loved them. We sat there and chatted for a couple of hours. And Charmian said, 'You've got to come and have lunch at the house, I've got salads.' So they carted us off to the house. And that began it—we just lived in their company.

Several months earlier, another young Australian couple, Robert Owen and Silver Collings, had an experience similar to the Halls'. The recently married art school graduates had left Australia for London, stopping off to visit Greece on their way. By chance, they landed on Hydra and, struck by the island's beauty and cheap accommodation, decided to stop over for longer than planned. As Owen remembers:

The next morning we noticed that there were a lot of other Europeans and English around. So we began … sitting at Katsikas Café for breakfast as they spoke a little English and over yogurt and honey, fresh bread, coffee and Metaxas, we soon got to know most travellers on the island.

Among the first of the "travellers" Owen and Collings met was Robyn Wallis, whose own story of arriving on Hydra was similar to that of the Australian couple. As Owen recalls, it was Wallis who pointed out Johnston.

Robyn had introduced us on one of those mornings while having coffee at Tasso's. George and Charm sat down to wait for the mail, and we got chatting. I was very impressed with George. In a letter home at the time I said he was a 'very humane and vital personality, the perception and wisdom of an owl, the kindness of a monk and the understanding of a poet.' Charmian was also very warm, open and full of life. Turned out she knew Silver's parents and we became quite close. They organised our stay over the winter in Bill Lederer's house overlooking the agora. As they both said we should stay the winter because it is very cold in England and if you want to do artwork, it's half the price of doing artwork in England and there's a nice community here. We got on very well so decided to stay a little longer which ran into around three years.

It was also the case that some Australian visitors who knew of the Johnstons—and perhaps intimidated by what they did know—chose *not* to meet them. Sydney- and London-based journalist Craig McGregor has written of catching a ferry to Hydra during a holiday in the early 1960s and being too shy to track down the couple. The visit did not, however, pass without an Australian encounter, as McGregor overheard Australian accents on the *agora*, leading him to poets Judith Green (Rodriguez) and David Malouf. As McGregor related of this fortuitous meeting, "We went swimming in the Mediterranean together, discussed Australian writing, and Judith and David showed me some of their latest poems", but none of the three young writers was to meet the island's two established Australian authors.

Despite Hydra's tight confines and limited social spaces, there was nothing inevitable about new visitors meeting each other or, indeed, mixing with the established expatriates. Del Kolve remembers of his own island summer that he and his fellow Oxford students were very aware of Clift and Johnston's presence and status, but, nonetheless, the two groups remained separate:

> We soon became aware of the Johnstons, and interested in them, because they lived full-time on Hydra, and they were writers and key figures in a small colony of expatriates. We 'sighted' them at tavernas and groceries, a clique clearly attractive, clearly interesting, but self-engrossed in each other and a changing, visiting circle of friends. They certainly were not interested in tourists, still few in number, visiting for a few days. That's probably how they initially saw us, though later, when we stayed on, they must have recognized we would be there some time. But they never introduced themselves to us, or offered a welcoming glance; we in turn never tried to introduce ourselves to them. They were living a bohemian life, with life-defining commitments; they were older, we were younger. They seemed very grand (in a provincial society kind of way), wholly self-involved, and we knew nothing of what they had accomplished.

While Johnston and Clift used Katsikas as the focus for their daily socialising—the place to meet friends, welcome visitors and dispense advice—they conducted their affairs in a way that subtly acknowledged their status as the senior members of the island's expatriates. Klaus Merkel recalls that the Johnstons were referred to as "the 'King and Queen' of the island", and remembers "talking with them or sitting in tavernas when they came down from their castle". When Redmond Wallis set the opening scene of *The Unyielding Memory* at Katsikas, he commenced with the new arrivals, Nick and Sue Alwyn, immediately rubbing up against the territoriality exerted by George and Catherine Grayson.

> He and Stephanos, Nick realised, had committed a cardinal sin; they had taken the table nearest to the door of Katsika's store, the table reserved for George and Catherine Grayson. These two were [the] Oldest Ex-Pats present, to use an army method of assigning temporary authority, and the table next to the door was theirs.
>
> After a moment or two, during which Stephanos made no move to rise and offer them their table back, they took the next one, moving it so that (after some shuffling and upheaval) it became part of the table next to the door and then, effectively, the big table next to the door. Then they sat down. They were not facing the way they preferred, straight down the agora to the sea, with good views to the left and right, but it would have to do, their expressions suggested.
>
> George turned his head to find Niko Katsika waiting.
>
> 'Good morning Niko,' he said in Greek. 'Cognac please.'

This small conflict over dockside space is a precursor to the intergenerational battle that ensues over the course of *The Unyielding Memory*, as the Graysons' role as the self-appointed leaders of the expatriates is eroded by more recent arrivals to whom they are seen to be an increasingly redundant presence. Nick Alwyn in particular eventually resents the Graysons, distancing himself from both the couple and the corner store 'scene' over which they preside.

HALF THE PERFECT WORLD

Charmian Clift and George Johnston at 'their' Katsikas table, as Demetri Gassoumis walks by. Charles Hulse seated to left, n.d. (Redmond Wallis)

Back room at Katsikas. L-R: Unidentified, Charmian Clift, Robyn Wallis, George Johnston, Redmond Wallis. (James Burke)

SOCIALISING AT KATSIKAS

Waiting for mail. Hydra's post-office at the time stood behind the Coundouriotis statue to the left of picture. L-R: Axel Jensen holding Tot (Axel Jnr), David Goschen, Robyn Wallis. (James Burke)

There were a number of quite practical reasons why Katsikas became the ideal meeting place for Clift, Johnston and others. These included its year-round long opening hours; the availability of both the back room for use in winter and the sun-drenched outdoor terrace for summer; the prime dockside location, with a good view of the incoming visitors disgorging from ferries; its proximity to the post office; and perhaps, most importantly, the willingness of the Katsikas brothers to extend generous credit to the island's longer-staying foreigners.

Certainly, the nearby location of the post office was important and, in its way, shaped the daily ritual at Katsikas. With many of the expatriates living an impecunious *poste-restante* existence, the lunchtime mail delivery offered not only the hope of news or cash from home, but for the writers amongst them, also the prospect of a manuscript acceptance or the delivery of royalties. As Johnston wrote in *Clean Straw for Nothing* (fictionalising Katsikas as Evangeli's):

> Nowadays we get down to the port about eleven-thirty to wait for the Athens steamer to arrive, because if it gets in on time they clear the mail before the *Taxydromeion* [post office] closes for the luncheon break and the long siesta. Mail has become a vital link with the outside world, the linch-pin of our survival in a way. We live *poste-restante* now, like the rest of the foreigners who crowd the tables at this hour outside Evangeli's corner shop. From here we can watch the grey mailbags being carried up the steps of the post-office, while drinking retsina or kokkinelli and wondering what the bags contain. Something for us? Money or the promise of it? More bills? Acceptance or rejection? Success or failure? Hope or despair? Another chance? The canvas bags … are bulky and misshapen by such possibilities.

Katsikas' dockside location also served as a place from where the established expatriates could keep an eye out for interesting new visitors. If summer brought the prospect of disruption to work and routine resulting from the extra activity, then it also afforded the promise of novelty and engagement in the form of 'new blood', some of whom might become part of the longer-term colony. As Johnston described in *Clean Straw for Nothing*, this could be a complex business—not only were the expatriates watching for new arrivals, but the expats were, in turn, increasingly scrutinised by the visitors, as the reputation of the island's counter-culture artists, writers and misfits who lead a sybaritic existence grew to the point where they themselves became an 'attraction'.

> While we await the clearing of the mail we study the passengers landing from the longboats which are rowed out beyond the harbour entrance to meet the trim white steamer. We have a practiced vigilance in this, too. We can pick the foreigners who are likely to stay and these we scrutinize carefully for their possibilities of interest or disruption. We are less concerned by the day or overnight tourists, who saunter with studied speculation around our tables, sometimes approaching us with diffident or bumptious enquiries: we are an established and recognized 'foreign

colony' now, bohemians to them, and artists and existentialists, outlandish oddities, rejectionists, dropouts from their own social systems, mavericks, even decadents, a genuine tourist attraction of the island.

If, as Johnston noted, the foreign colony had a reputation as bohemians, artists and existentialists, then their propensity to marry talk and argument with the long hours at Katsikas was where that reputation was grounded. Preferably sitting outside and facing the *agora* from beneath the store's windows with their distinctive oval tracery, the expatriates found Katsikas to be the ideal location for the enactment of their rambunctious social lives. As the spring and summer months progressed, and as their numbers swelled with the influx of seasonal residents, they gathered in the sunshine to talk and to drink, to watch and to wait, often to return in the evening to talk and to drink again, and to wait some more. Clift wrote of the hours lingering on the *agora* that

> mostly we talk, individually, severally, and at last all together, hurling and snatching at creeds, doctrines, ideas, theories, raging through space and time like erratic meteorites rushing on in the full ignorance as to either our origins or destinations, until at last we come to the blazing point of exhaustion.

And as with so much else to do with the foreign community, Johnston was at the centre of the talking. Robert Owen recalled that "George was a great storyteller, god he told wonderful stories", and Leonard Cohen remembered that "George was a magnificent talker". As many have attested, Johnston was ever-ready to offer a display of his magnificence, and with the talk went the drinking, and with the drinking went the arguing. Johnston and Clift stood out in these regards as well, as their drinking became more excessive over their years on the island. Likely this was the result of a number of reasons—tension within their own relationship; growing concern over their financial circumstances; and frustrations with their unrealised literary ambitions. It was also likely a result of their *need* for alcohol to sustain each day and to maintain the talk, the sociability and their place at the centre of every table. The blazing public rows that ensued sometimes included others but often involved only Johnston and Clift hurling barbs and insults back and forth.

When absent, the Johnstons could themselves be the subject of talk, which was not always flattering. In a diary entry for July 15th, 1960, Wallis notes how it becomes apparent, while the couple are briefly away in Athens, that "George & Charm have haters, in their absence [they have] been very thoroughly done over by everyone we've spoken to".

> George chiefly on the grounds he can't write—which he can't, not the stuff he wants to write, anyway—and Charm is her greatest creation, Charmian Clift, the great Australian woman novelist. Charmian is very curious. She is, potentially at least, a better writer than George but she has and is deliberately creating a picture of herself—a parody—which one feels she hopes will appear in her biography some day. The head of a literary coterie, beautiful, brilliant, compassionate but still the mother of 3 children, running a house. Sweating blood against almost impossible difficulties—a husband inclined to unfounded jealousy, the heat, creative problems, the children, the problems foisted on her by other people, an abortion (which she had in Athens recently and keeps referring to obliquely) George's previous pneumonia and t.b.—and yet producing great art. The daughter of a peculiar man from a little four-roomed shack in a tin-pot Australian fishing village, writing from the heart, eschewing silly intellectual ideas. Bah.
>
> The funny thing is that I always took them to be an agora-act. But Lena [Folke-Olsson] says she's like it with George at home, even when they think they're alone. … Lena says there's fearful competition between the two and Leonard voices the idea of sabotage on Charmian's part (make a lovely book, this) which may well be right. She comes down to the agora and she must know George hasn't made it yet—and passes the definitive (always wonderful) opinion of George's latest book before anyone else has read it. So how can you criticize the book honestly? Particularly when Charmian won't let you make any comment

Summer talk on the *agora*. Charmian Clift, George Johnston, Chuck Hulse, Magda Tilche, Polyxena Katsikas, Gordon Merrick, n.d. (Johnston and Clift Collection)

at all adverse without jumping in to fight George's battles for him. Oh, there's lots more.

After only three months on the island, Wallis had pinpointed the troubling complexities of the Johnstons' marriage—including the tension-inducing dichotomy between competitiveness and supportiveness; the struggle to balance family life with their literary ambitions; the pressure resulting from their self-appointed role as 'leaders' of the expatriate group; and the personal stresses within the relationship which paired Johnston, constantly troubled by ill-health, with Clift, who was prone to seeking consolation (real or imagined) with other men. Wallis also reflected on the battle within Johnston himself, as to whether he should write what he believes is needed to maintain the family finances as opposed to "the stuff he wants to write".

Of course, not all the dockside talk was driven by existential angst, literary one-upmanship, or the world-weary posturing of escapees from modernity, and not all of it was laced with acrimony and competitiveness. Much of it was light-hearted, flirtatious, gossip-laden—the usual grist of daily life milled by shifting personal circumstances and relationships. Whether at Katsikas or elsewhere, it was easy to simply enjoy the beauty, revel in the talk and pass the time, with nothing so necessary that it detracted from the moment, and no work so pressing that it could not wait another day. It was a place where, in Clift's words, the endless talk drifted on after dark while "outside the brilliant circle of the electric globe, the dark water laps and laps with the soft swish of silk and the night presses down around the town, warm and close like a cloak, soft as velvet, heavy with salt and the scent of white flowers". The island's expatriates and visitors found themselves given over not only to the intoxicating beauty of such moments but also to relationships that were intense, fluctuating and, in some cases, on the edge of social convention. To these intellectually ambitious and liberal-minded young men and women, Hydra provided the opportunity to shrug off their middle-class upbringings and surrender to the enticement of artistic bohemianism. As Cohen recalled:

> Everybody was beautiful and young and full of talent and covered with a kind of gold dust. Everyone there seemed to have very special, significant, unique qualities. These are naturally the feelings of youth, but in this setting, in this glorious setting at Hydra, all these qualities that youth naturally can claim, they were magnified, and they sparkled, and everyone to me looked glorious, and all our mistakes were important mistakes and all our betrayals were important betrayals and everything we did was informed by this glittering significance. That's youth.

James Burke took numerous photos both outside and inside Katsikas. He knew at the outset that it was an important part of the island's story, with his pitch to *LIFE* referring to the "lively waterfront group which revolves around Australian Johnston and makes headquarters at grocery store-wine shop on busy quai". Many of Burke's photographs centre on the expatriates as they mix idly over drinks and meals and gather spontaneously to observe the daily social rituals that garlanded their island lifestyle.

SOCIALISING AT KATSIKAS

Evening at Katsikas, including Charles Hulse, Charmian Clift, Jason Johnston, Gordon Merrick, George Johnston, Leonard Cohen, members of the Katsikas family and others, c.1960. (Johnston and Clift Collection)

It would seem, however, that not all such gatherings that Burke photographed were entirely spontaneous. Amongst the occasions at Katsikas he recorded was one attended by Nikos Hadjikyriakos-Ghika. Photos show Ghika arriving with his partner Barbara Hutchinson; being introduced by Johnston; conversing with the gathered members of the expatriate colony, particularly fellow artist Demetri Gassoumis; and then departing. There is about these photos an uncommon air of an 'event' that may have been contrived for the camera. Ghika was not a regular at such gatherings, and he stood apart from the island's foreign artists in a number of ways. He was, of course, Greek, and he most definitely was not a struggling artist battling to complete his work amidst the distractions of the harbour-front gatherings. As a member of one of Hydra's established wealthy families, he made his regular home in Athens, visiting the island occasionally and occupying the family

– 209 –

George Johnston introduces Nikos Hadjikyriakos-Ghika
to Chris Rand at Katsikas.
(James Burke)

mansion high above the town. As Burke reported, "He usually stays up there, not because he is exclusive but simply because it's a long haul up and down between the house and the waterfront agora". As captured by Burke's camera, this gathering appears to be marked by a quasi-formality, with the expatriates seen standing and rearranging chairs as Ghika arrives and is introduced by the presiding Johnston.

The reason for such an 'occasion' might be explained by the presence of two other Athens-based visitors, Chris Rand and Brian Bojenell. Rand was a long-time travel writer for *The New Yorker* who had joined his friend Burke

SOCIALISING AT KATSIKAS

Demetri Gassoumis chats with Nikos Hadjikyriakos-Ghika (rear left) at Katsikas. Marianne Ihlen and Tot (Axel Jnr) are seated at the window; George Johnston and Barbara Hutchinson are standing at the right. In the foreground are Chris Rand (L) and Brian Bojenell (R). (James Burke)

on Hydra for several days accompanied by Bojenell, a Greek-American managing the Athens office of Pan American World Airways. Rand was in the middle of a year spent collecting material for articles about Greece, which appeared in *The New Yorker* and later made their way into his 1962 travelogue *Grecian Calendar*. Rand's book extolled the attraction of both "dry Greece" (the mainland) and "wet Greece" (the islands) and described the rapid growth and impact of tourism on the country. The account he provided of "two delightful evenings in the cafes" of Hydra was brief, and in addition to noting the presence of Ghika and other Greek artists and intellectuals, he also mentioned:

three foreign writers: an Australian, a Swede, and an American Negro. The Australian, George Johnston, has lived on Hydra for several years now, and he and his wife have both written prolifically there—she has written a book about Hydra itself called *Peel Me a Lotus*, which seems a good tag-line for this whole foreign occupation of the islands.

Katsikas was not a place at which only the foreigners socialised. Many locals were also found in the back room and at the dockside tables, and inevitably on occasions the two groups came together. Burke's photographs and notes recorded one such gathering:

> An evening session in 'Cub Room' of Katsikas, the stock room in back of the grocery store where foreign artists and writers meet for wine and song along with Katsikas' regular Hydriot clientel. There are some of both—foreign and Hydriot—at this session.

Burke took some three dozen images depicting a fluctuating group sitting around a sole guitarist, many obviously engaged in the singing, others apparently more interested in the talking and the drinking. He noted that the guitarist and others were Hydriots, and there was a young woman who was "an artist from Athens", a "French painter", and American Inge Schneier. While Clift and Johnston are not present in these photographs, it seems they were at Katsikas on similar occasions, with Clift writing in *Peel Me a Lotus* of evenings when the Katsikas back room was taken over by Hydriots and their songs.

> Sometimes Vassilis the crippled sponge-diver joins in, or Tzimmy the pedlar … Vassilis sings, stretching wide the gaping hole of his mouth over two yellow teeth that look like the temple at Corinth; the young labourer Apostoli sings to the plaintive accompaniment of his guitar; in the dark corner the old men sing, quaveringly and off-key. And sometimes we sing too—folk songs half remembered or the nostalgic dance tunes that date our love days.

Gathering in the back room of Katsikas, including Inge Schneier in profile at right.
(James Burke)

Leonard Cohen was at the centre of one of the most-storied meetings at Katsikas, which took place some time in May of 1960 and commenced his decade-long relationship with Marianne Ihlen. At the time, Ihlen was in the throes of separating from Axel Jensen while also coming to terms with new motherhood, with the couple's child not yet six months old. As Ihlen later recalled of her first meeting with Cohen:

> I was standing in the shop with my basket waiting to pick up bottled water and milk. And he is standing in the door way with the sun behind him. And then you don't see the face, you just see the contours. And so I hear his voice, saying: 'Would you like to join us, we're sitting outside?'
>
> And I reply, 'thank you,' and I finish my shopping. Then I go outside. And I sit down at this table where there were 3–4 people sitting, who lived in Hydra at the time. He was wearing khaki trousers, which were

a shade more green. And also he had his beloved, what we in the old days called tennis shoes. And he also always wore shirts with rolled up sleeves.

And so began at Katsikas, in the early months of the 1960s, one of the decade's fabled counter-culture romances, sealed (and almost over) by the time Ihlen acquired inadvertent fame when her portrait appeared on the back cover of Cohen's second album, 1969's *Songs from a Room*. Ihlen had previously achieved a footnote in 1960s pop culture by being the subject of the enduring love song 'So Long Marianne' from Cohen's debut 1967 album, *The Songs of Leonard Cohen*, but now she was unmasked as the 'muse' to the man gaining renown for his beautiful melodies, poetic lyrics and lady-killing charm. In *The Unyielding Memory*, Wallis provides memorable introductory descriptions of the couple's alter-ego characters that capture the root of their immediately mutual attraction. Of Margaretha (Ihlen): "If you liked Scandinavian blondes, Margaretha was your meat. Her hair was so blond it was almost white, her eyes so blue they matched the sea, her teeth so perfect they looked like pearls set in heaven, her figure so good it made your mouth dry." And of Saul Rubens (Cohen):

> He interested Nick, because he seemed to be so self-contained, mildly amused by what he saw around him, passionate about work, and deliberately enigmatic. His public utterances were always somewhat noncommittal or pregnantly oblique: he was, Nick thought, usually doing precisely what he, Nick, also did, sitting back to record how people acted and what they said. But he was also seeking approval, such as that lavished on him by the Graysons, and he never showed any sign whatsoever of getting involved in the kind of *fasserias* that centred around the Graysons: he was, to use a word coming into fashion, cool.

Cohen and Ihlen's romance was to be 'public' only in hindsight, as for much of the decade, Cohen's career developed in relative obscurity, with what recognition he had coming from his poetry and fiction rather than his fledgling songwriting. But the picture of the starkly blond and elfin Ihlen, sporting only a white towel and a half-formed smile as she fingers the keys of Cohen's typewriter in his Hydra studio (seated at a table Cohen was given by the Johnstons to help the young Canadian settle on the island) was sufficient to imprint for the Woodstock generation an image of a beguiling Nordic *ingénue* who inspired the lovelorn lyrics from this most melancholy of men. If Cohen's recording and performing days still lay ahead of him in 1960, then he also took a small step in that direction at Katsikas. It was here, according to legend, where Cohen initiated his solo performing career when, at Johnston's instigation, he sang for his fellow expatriates during the summer of 1960.

(In an odd bit of pop-culture serendipity, *Songs from a Room* was not the only celebrated album of 1969 to carry an image with Hydra connections. When archetypal late-1960s supergroup Blind Faith released their debut (and only) album that year, it received as much attention for the cover as it did for the music. The cover photograph depicted eleven-year-old Mariora Goschen, the Hydra-born daughter of David and Angela Goschen, naked and gazing into the camera without expression while holding the cold, sleekly-crafted steel form of a stylised spacecraft. The cover was banned in the US, but photographer Bob Seidemann's stark juxtaposition of pre-pubescent innocence with the hyper-metallic technologies of modernity has since been recognised as a classic of 1960s graphic art. It was a far cry from the low-key charm of the picture of Ihlen gracing the Cohen album, and thereby a reminder that the tumult of the 1960s ended up in very different places).

Cohen was also involved in one other meeting at Katsikas that would have lasting significance—and for this meeting Burke was again present with his camera. The short and tempestuous marriage between Ihlen and Jensen had reached a crisis in May when Jensen departed Hydra with his lover Patricia Amlin. By August, Jensen was back on the island, only to find Ihlen partnered with Cohen. Burke's caption notes explain the meeting that he photographed:

Axel Jensen, Tot (Axel Jnr), Leonard Cohen, Marianne Ihlen, unidentified, at Katsikas. (James Burke)

> In the rear stock room of Katsikas' grocery store, where everything from lumber to soap is kept … Axel Jensen and his wife Marianne met one morning in mid-September to work out their marriage separation. Canadian poet and friend Leonard Cohen was on hand and also Tot, the Jensen's baby. … The separation was successfully worked out (only squares and the non-beat type have difficulty with these little personal affairs) and a few days later Tot was shipped back by an airline pilot friend to Marianne's mother in Oslo. … We won't go into the other details, such as Axel's American painter girl friend (who'll be coming back from the States this winter) and Marianne's affair with the yacht captain, etc., etc.

Burke took a number of images of this meeting between the separating couple and the new lover, which appears, based on the photographic evidence, to have been the relaxed affair that his notes suggest. Perhaps a little coyly, Burke does not indicate that, by this time, Cohen and Ihlen were established in a relationship—something of which he could not have been ignorant. The photographer's notes also report that following this meeting to settle the end of the marriage, "Marianne stayed on Hydra a couple more weeks before heading for Norway in Axel's car with another friend". That unnamed friend was Cohen.

These were the last images that Burke would take of the Jensen baby. The child had been baptised earlier in the year with the names 'Axel Joachim', but was now known by the non-specific 'Tot', with Axel Snr believing that children should grow to choose their own name—he would eventually become Axel Jnr. As Burke noted, shortly after this meeting, Tot was sent to Oslo to be with Ihlen's mother, an arrangement made possible after Ihlen struck up a conversation with Scandinavian Airlines System aircrew at Katsikas. Ihlen learnt that the crew members were soon to return to Norway as passengers, and they agreed to accompany the baby back to Oslo airport where his grandmother would collect him. Having seen out the Hydra summer, Ihlen and Cohen would be reunited with Tot some weeks later after they completed their drive from Athens to Oslo.

Polyxena Katsikas chats with Charmian Clift and George Johnston.
(James Burke)

In many of the photographs Burke took at Katsikas, members of the Katsikas family can be glimpsed in the background, either going about their shopfront business or tending to the needs of customers. In one series of photos, Burke brings Antony Katsikas and his wife, Polyxena, more intimately within Johnston and Clift's range. In several photographs, the seated Clift is depicted lightly embracing the standing Antony Katsikas, and in others, the Australian couple is seen chatting amicably with Polyxena.

Johnston and Clift had good reason to feel affection for the Katsikas family, such was their generosity in extending them credit. The Johnstons were not alone in being the recipients of such kindness—Ihlen recalls that she and Jensen received a year's credit soon after establishing themselves on the island, and Wallis's diaries record details of his Katsikas bills that caused him considerable anguish as he prepared to leave the island. When Colin Simpson visited Johnston and Clift in 1962, the couple regaled him with details of their credit from Katsikas, which included leaving for England in late 1960 with the debt unpaid and returning still impoverished six months later to find the Katsikas brothers offering them cash to tide them over. Johnston recalled to Simpson how a windfall from the sale of *Closer to the Sun* in the US later that year allowed them to repay their debt and host a dockside party that "went on for two days". Simpson believed he knew how the Katsikas debt had been incurred, telling the Johnstons' Sydney friend and novelist Ruth Park that during his visit, "It was embarrassing, unbearable. Vile quarrels and then a booze-up. Even though they were totally broke they bought grog instead of groceries and invited strangers to share it. I got out of there …".

Despite being repaid in 1961, Johnston and Clift's debt to the Katsikas brothers had well and truly returned by early 1964, with Johnston's departure for Australia fast approaching. On this occasion, the cause of Johnston's leaving, the imminent publication of *My Brother Jack*, was also his financial salvation. Rodney Hall witnessed the moment of Johnston's fiscal relief and the final settlement of the Katsikas debt.

> Shortly after we got there George got this telegram from Billy Collins, congratulating him on *My Brother Jack* and telling him that they were going to do 100,000 hardbacks or whatever it was in London, and the cheque is in the mail. And three or four days later the cheque arrived and Charmian said to us, 'We have got a little ceremony tomorrow and would you like to come and be with us.' I said 'What is it?' And she said 'You'll see.' And so we had to be at the house early, at 9 o'clock, and they were all dressed up in their Sunday best. So we knew that there was a major occasion, and we all trooped down to the little bank on the agora, which was only open a couple of days a week. And Bet and I waited outside while George and Charmian went in to bank the cheque. And they came out a little while later looking very rosy and cheery and said,

'Now this is what you came for. We now have to go to Katsikas.' So we trooped along the agora to the corner of the laneway where Katsikas had his shop and they went in and announced to him that they had a cheque and would he give them their bill. It took him a moment to process what they had said, because they only spoke English. And then it dawned on him, and he said 'Yes,' in a very courteous, restrained way, and he got out the book, because their best customers had a whole book to themselves with receipts and things. He got his abacus out and started doing all his calculations, and this took some time. Charmian said, 'You know, every month Katsikas gives us our bill for the previous month, and every month we thank him for it, and we don't pay. And over all the years we have been doing this, never once has he said I can't keep supplying you because you don't pay me anything.' And they bought everything there, all their groceries, their green groceries, and their alcohol. And the alcohol bill would have been something. Everything that was bought at Katsikas was on this account. And he added it all up, and it was some thousands of pounds sterling. In Greece at the time it was an enormous amount of money. So he gave them a bill, and Charmian wrote out the cheque, which she and George presented. Katsikas had tears in his eyes. And, by gesture, he asked for her shopping basket, and she passed it across. It was a high counter, with all sorts of stuff stacked on it, and he reached across, took the basket, and filled it up with gifts—dried figs, Metaxas brandy and other presents. And then he walked around to give them the basket and then invited them into the bar for a drink. It was a beautiful ceremony. And you know, we only have *My Brother Jack* because of an obscure grocer called Katsikas.

But for all the generosity of the Katsikas brothers; the extravagant sociability; the many long and bountiful days and the years of drinking and talking; the *frisson* of forming new relationships; and the thrill of occasional success, there were also undeniable tensions on the *agora* that went further and deeper than alcohol-induced arguments and lovers falling out.

The danger that Katsikas and the wider dockside scene created for Clift, Johnston and others intent on achieving something creative was the distraction it gave rise to from the work at hand. In *Peel Me a Lotus*, Clift reveals much about her fears around her own unrealised literary ambitions as she reports the opening salvo of the battle that would trouble the couple over the coming years—the struggle to free themselves from the temptations of regular sunshine, long afternoons on the *agora*, cheap alcohol and endless conversation in order to pursue their goal to create something substantial and important.

> It has become an obsession with both of us to try and avoid that tainted arena of the waterfront with its traps of tables and wine flasks, where still the shafts of spite and envy and malice break and splinter, and still under the loops of naked bulbs the dislocated psyches creak and crack, and obscure philosophers are trotted out, the negligent poems never completed, the revolutionary paintings never begun, and the interminable verbal catch-ball with esoteric phrases about linear values and plastic form that inflame George to a white-heat of fury.

While Clift and Johnston might have tired of the "tainted arena", they were also irresistibly drawn to it. Whether it be the need for relief from the intensity of their marriage with its constant rivalries and jealousies; or the irresistible opportunity to rub their own sometimes fragile egos against the "dislocated psyches" of the "obscure philosophers"; or the psychological need to sustain their positions as the de facto leaders of this increasingly disorderly contingent; or simply a compulsive desire for the many pleasures the dockside offered despite its capacity to sap time and energy, it was a ritual that engrossed, sustained and depleted them for almost a decade.

What did unfold over the course of the years was a gradual erosion of Clift and Johnston as the focus of the Katsikas circle. In the first years of their occupation, the couple served as the unchallenged gravitational centre of the foreign population, which, at times, was so small that this role was without status or interest. As the resident foreign population steadily grew and then swelled noticeably during the extended summers, Clift in particular seems to have felt pressed to maintain her and Johnston's position. Eventually, in the final months of their residency, the idea that there might be any gain in playing this role had become unthinkable. By 1964 Hydra's social scene had multiplied and fractured, and with the advent of a generation of bars catering to the needs of a younger set more interested in partying than talking and with various drugs replacing alcohol as the social lubricant of choice, Katsikas gradually became less interesting as latecomers went in search of more vibrant entertainment.

If Johnston's association with Katsikas had been marked by extravagant sociability and exuberance, then the circumstances of his leaving were very different. In Wallis's draft of *The Unyielding Memory*, Nick Alwyn recounts a final conversation with George Grayson when he finds him sitting alone at Katsikas on the eve of his departure and "shit-scared" of the success that would finally befall him:

> he was scared, scared of going back to his roots where they would finally give him his due, where he could lord it over those who doubted him, over his competitive wife, where money would no longer be a problem, and who was scared, frightened at 52 years of age, of how he would cope with the adulation, the people, the noise, the pace, the pressure. Or was it something worse? Had George been so long away from his country that he thought its people still rejected the creatively successful, that it was not adulation that awaited him, but at best derision, the old Antipodean trick of levelling down?

It is a passage that closely reflects Johnston's own recollection of this time. In *Clean Straw for Nothing*, as David Meredith waits to return to Australia, Johnston wrote that he "felt sick, old, tired, and fearful, and he had no song of any sort upon his lips".

The time of Johnston's departure was a period of transition in many ways for Hydra, including for a family business such as Katsikas that had previously depended on local trade. With newer and more glamorous bars and restaurants competing for the ever-increasing tourists, businesses located in prime sites on the dockside found they had to adapt. When Colin Simpson returned to Hydra in 1967, he noted that the Katsikas brothers had converted their shopfront to a "big restaurant"—the shop itself survived, but, in a concession to changing times, "had gone around the corner and now sold mainly souvenirs". Simpson chose to have dinner at the new restaurant, and sought out the Johnstons' former benefactor.

> I found Antoni Katsakis and he and his wife and daughter were delighted to hear of the Johnstons, and he wanted me to take them in Sydney a gallon of retsina—which would have cost about twenty dollars as excess luggage by air, and which I couldn't carry anyway. So he selected the biggest sponge in the shop and sent that.

Almost certainly Johnston and Clift would have preferred the retsina.

In Sydney in December of that same year, Clift found herself thinking back with both nostalgic wonder and real concern, as she prepared for her Australian Christmas and pondered what might have become of Katsikas' back room and its clients since the military coup earlier in the year. Clift was seemingly unaware that the back room, with its glorious array of overabundant foodstuffs and hardware, was no more—a victim not of the colonels but rather the inevitable progress of tourist-based commerce.

> All this makes me think, inevitably, of other Greek grocers' back rooms, and other Christmases, and my heart is so torn and hurt for Greece and my Greek friends at this moment that if I could help them I would willingly transpose myself to the other back room I know best, hung with plaits of onions and garlic, festoons of cotton waste, ecclesiastical organ-pipe arrangements of beeswax candles, rusted tin hipbaths, spiked coffee roasters, bundles of whitewash brushes, shovels and brooms, and it wouldn't be fine pale sherry I would be drinking but a rough retsina out of a copper beaker while working out my Christmas shopping list. …

Kyria Kali, "ancient and spry", n.d. (Redmond Wallis)

Bunches of little children would burst through the side door like ragged posies, raggedly chanting the ritual Christmas carol, interminably long and interminably boring, but profitable in reward of drachmas, nuts, sweets, and fizzy *gasoza*. Kyria Kali, ancient and spry, would make risqué suggestions to the police captain, who would be expansive and jolly and very willing to accept a glass of wine or ouzo. All through the morning the back room would fill up with wharf labourers, muleteers, masons, carpenters, visitors from Athens, foreign artists, schoolteachers, citizenry of high and humble degree, and there would be singing and eating and drinking and argument, and great goodwill would prevail.

I wonder what goes on in the back room these days. Perhaps the back room is proscribed as a possibly dangerous fermenting ground for political dissension. Under the new regime would the police chief accept risqué suggestions from a wicked old lady, or a glass of wine from a bearded foreigner? Would such gatherings be allowed at all, even at Christmas? One thing I do know is that Melina Mercouri won't be gracing the back room this Christmas, as she did so often, or Theodorakis, or many many others who seem to have disappeared without trace, many many friends of whom we hear nothing any more.

In its current incarnation, Katsikas carries on as the Roloi Café, a bar-cum-restaurant indistinguishable in style or purpose from its neighbours. The renovations that many years ago removed the famed back room have produced a more functional open space, although a keen eye will detect the ghost of former dividing walls. The distinctive oval windowpanes that framed the view of the *agora* have given way to a more regular design, and the post office that served as the conduit for expatriate hopes has been repurposed to take advantage of the commercial possibilities afforded by its location. One thing that has not changed, however, is that 'Katsikas corner' is prime island real estate, with the view taking in, as always, the long stretch of bustling dockside commerce; the blazingly coloured *caiques* and pleasure craft; the comings and goings of ferries and yachts; the stoop-shouldered patience of the donkeys; the terraced embrace of the town; and the comforting backdrop of the Peloponnese seen across the narrow stretch of gull-spotted gulf. It remains a place to sit, to watch and to talk.

***

In this passage from *The Unyielding Memory*, Redmond Wallis introduces "Soumala's", which Wallis also sometimes refers to by its proper name, Katsikas.

> *The centre of agora life for the few foreigners who lived on the island lay at its western end. The post office, their lifeline to the outside world, was situated there and from the tables outside a grocery store called Soumala's*

they could watch the grey mailbags being carried or dragged along the agora from the ferry and up the steps into the taxidromeion and calculate from their number and size how long it would be before the mail had been sorted. Then, casually, one or two of them would climb up the steps and collect the rejection slips, cheques, bank drafts, bills, letters of acceptance and notes from home to which they attached so much importance.

The tables outside Soumala's also served as a vantage point from which to see who, if anybody, had arrived on the ferry. At the height of the season some new arrivals were snapped up by island women at the far end of the agora and led to rooms near the naval school, and thus did not immediately get as far as Soumala's, but most of the year they were attracted or directed to the other end, or were heading for the one comparatively modern hotel up behind Soumala's, and thus passed in review before the foreigners. The pleasure of inspecting them and speculating on their intentions had to be foregone in the winter; then the foreigners gathered in Soumala's back room, close to the old iron stove. Few people of any interest arrived in the winter, however, and those that did, and were on the island for any length of time, eventually found their way to the back room.

Thus Soumala's was not only a grocery store: it was also a bar, a social club, in a small way a cafeteria (for mezes of bread, cheese, olives, tinned meat and tinned fish could be had), a hardware shop and, not least, a kind of bank. Yanni Soumala, tall, unshaven, boss-eyed, the possessor of a mouthful of displaced or broken teeth, liberally stopped with gold, was prepared to extend credit. By some miracle, no foreigner had ever welshed; and it was an unwritten law, enforced by all the moral persuasion a group of passionately interested expatriates could muster, that no one ever left the island without settling his Soumala's bill.

Chapter Seven

SINGIN' AT DOUSKOS, SWINGIN' AT LAGOUDERA

While the Katsikas grocery store-cum-bar was the focus of expatriate social life for the time George Johnston and Charmian Clift were on Hydra, it was far from the only place where they would gather. Redmond Wallis's diaries refer to a number of similar venues such as Grafos, Tassos, Lulus and Quintos, which were also visited frequently. Another of the alternatives was the Xeri Elia (Dry Olive) Taverna, which was and is commonly known as Douskos, taking the name of the family that has owned and run the business since 1825.

Douskos is located several minutes' walk from the *agora*, up the narrow laneways leading from the south-east corner of the dockside, and in the 1950s and early 1960s, it was one of the few eating and drinking venues found away from the waterfront. James Burke noted that for the expatriates Douskos "is, next to Katsikas itself, the favourite Hydra hangout". It is likely that Douskos was preferred when relief from the dockside activity was needed, and photographs featuring the island's visitors suggest it was a place they gathered in the evenings. Although Douskos doesn't enjoy the water views that are a part of many other social spaces on the island, it nonetheless opens onto a delightful public courtyard that has long been shaded by several large trees to give relief from the summer sun, and which also provides a welcoming outdoor space for evening meals. For Johnston and Clift the tavern had the additional appeal of being a very short walk from their house.

An evening of song in the Douskos courtyard. George Johnston (back to camera) and Charmian Clift are at either end of the table. Sue and Mungo MacCallum sit to Johnston's right, 1963. (MacCallum Collection)

Not only is Douskos renowned as Hydra's oldest tavern, but it is also now indelibly associated with the island's artist colony because of an evening in the summer of 1960 when a group of international residents and visitors were joined by James Burke and his camera. Since Burke's Hydra photographs have surfaced, it is these Douskos images that have been the most widely reproduced and distributed. Those that are most frequently seen, particularly since the singer's death in November 2016, feature Leonard Cohen, seated with a guitar at the centre of a small group of expatriates, with Clift immediately beside him. The full set of Burke's photos taken on that evening at Douskos—there are some 140—provides great insight into the social lives of the expatriates. On this evening, Burke started photographing as the island's international visitors commenced their evening inside the tavern. A series of images depicts the group sharing dinner, undoubtedly looking like any similar group of young people of their day enjoying each other's company, conversation and food (reported by Burke to be "spaghetti").

Dinner at Douskos. L-R: Robyn Wallis, Fidel Caliesch, Carolyn Gassoumis, Demetri Gassoumis, Charmian Clift, Charles Heckstall, Redmond Wallis.
(James Burke)

Once the revellers have moved into the courtyard, we witness the activity across the course of the evening, as they sit grouped around the guitar, laughing and singing, smoking and drinking, pulling up chairs, changing places and walking in-and-out of frame, while firstly Cohen and then Axel Jensen take turns strumming a guitar (borrowed from the tavern) and leading the singing. As Burke recorded, "Singing and wine-drinking outside Douskos continues until early morning".

There were at least eighteen foreigners gathered in the Douskos courtyard on that evening, and they formed a very international group. They included Australians (Johnston and Clift); Americans (Demetri and Carolyn Gassoumis, Fidel Caliesch, Charles Heckstall, Inge Schneier); Norwegians (Axel Jensen and Marianne Ihlen); New Zealanders (Redmond and Robyn Wallis); an Englishman (David Goschen); a Canadian (Cohen); a German (Klaus Merkel); and possibly other nationalities as well. Burke's photos record an apparently harmonious and convivial evening, with this youthful party

L-R: Charles Heckstall, Leonard Cohen, Charmian Clift, George Johnston,
Axel Jensen (back to camera), Marianne Ihlen, Inge Schneier.
(James Burke)

clearly comfortable in each other's company. Most of those present were in their twenties—Johnston, then forty-eight, and Clift, thirty-seven, were almost certainly the oldest—and in generational terms, the pictures present an amalgam of the 1950s Beat generation together with what we now recognise as an incipient form of 1960s counter-culture—the advent of which is hardly indicated by the coats and ties worn by Cohen, Wallis and Jensen, three upper middle-class young men from widely spread points of the globe.

For Johnston and Clift, revelling in their roles as the unappointed leaders of this contingent, such an evening must have represented the very lifestyle—the exotic appeal of a foreign summer, the heightened sociability, the ardent conversation, the embrace of cultural difference—they had been seeking when they abandoned firstly, the monochrome cultural sterility of postwar Sydney, and secondly, drab, cold and expensive mid-1950s London. Evenings such as this, Burke's photos suggest, were the expatriate's reward.

SINGIN' AT DOUSKOS, SWINGIN' AT LAGOUDERA

While Burke's Douskos photographs include many of the key players of the Hydra artist colony at that time, these are 'Leonard Cohen' photographs: it is Cohen who is the focus for Burke's camera and, commanding the guitar, he is also the centre of attention amongst the small group of onlookers. While his career as a guitar playing singer-songwriter was still some years away, these pictures capture his fledgling ability to engage an audience. Only Johnston and David Goschen, both sitting in the rear and often looking away as they engage in various conversations, seem to be outside Cohen's immediate audience. By the time Jensen takes up the guitar, the small crowd appears to be dispersing, gradually dwindling in size over a number of images.

For Cohen, this must have been a high point of his time on Hydra. Only five months before, he had arrived by chance at a place where he was immediately comfortable and embraced by both the place and the people. In a sequence of events that could hardly have been anticipated during the lonely and cold London months with which his year commenced, he now found himself in a place of great beauty; he was in the throes of buying his house in the sun that would provide a secure island foothold for the years to come; and Marianne Ihlen, the woman with whom he would share that house, sits before him, looking on with loving attention as her new man delights his audience. Within days of these photographs being taken, Cohen would turn twenty-six, and, although he wasn't wealthy, his finances were made buoyant by the life jacket of a government grant, providing the freedom to come and go as he pleased.

In a 1988 filmed BBC interview conducted in the studio room of his Hydra house where he had done his living, loving and work a quarter of a century before, Cohen reminisced about his new life at the dawn of a new decade.

> I just got off here, and somebody spoke English and I rented a house for fourteen dollars a month. I met a girl, and I stayed for eight or ten years.
> Yeah, that's the way it was in those days.

What reading those words can't convey is the manner of their delivery. Cohen's occasional claim that he is the least sentimental of men ("I have no

Redmond Wallis, Charles Heckstall, Klaus Merkel, Leonard Cohen, Charmian Clift at Douskos. (James Burke)

interest in the past, and I have very little interest in the man I was then") is supported by the matter-of-fact delivery of the first two sentences, but then immediately contradicted by a profound reverie in which his eyes and mind wander transparently to the past. The concluding sentence is a shrug-of-the-shoulders wisecrack which goes straight to the heart of his longing—whether for Hydra, for Ihlen or for the 1960s, or perhaps all three, it is difficult to know. Although as Cohen also told the BBC, "We didn't know it was the '60s then. We just thought it was ordinary time."

Ten years after Burke photographed Cohen playing to less than twenty people on Hydra, the 1960s were over, and the singer bookended his decade by performing one of the most-storied gigs of his career on another island and to some 600,000 people. The occasion was the third Isle of Wight Festival in late August 1970, which remains the largest and perhaps most unruly music crowd to gather in the UK. That Cohen followed The Moody Blues, Jethro Tull and Jimi Hendrix on a program that also featured The Who and Sly and the

Family Stone is a good measure of how far the world and youth culture travelled over that decade. Many things had also changed for Cohen during the intervening years: his career had been launched with two acclaimed albums that catapulted him onto the world stage and established his reputation as one of the decade's essential singer-songwriters; his romantic relationship with Ihlen had withered; and his ties with Hydra were loosening. It was also a decade that neither of Cohen's Hydra mentors would survive, with Clift having died the previous year and Johnston passing away just a month before.

Although Cohen's house was on the other side of the port from Douskos, the tavern seems to have been an important part of his imaginative geography of the town. As he expressed in his poem 'Duskos Taverna 1967', it is a place that called to him with its promise of just the sort of music-centred and leisured sociability depicted in Burke's photographs.

Dusko's Taverna 1967
They are still singing down at Dusko's,
sitting under the ancient pine tree,
in the deep night of fixed and falling stars.
If you go to your window you can hear them.
It is the end of someone's wedding,
or perhaps a boy is leaving on a boat in the morning.
There is a place for you at the table,
wine for you, and apples from the mainland,
a space in the songs for your voice.
Throw something on,
and whoever it is you must tell that you are leaving,
tell them, or take them, but hurry:
they have sent for you -
the call has come -
they will not wait forever.
They are not even waiting now.

Leonard Cohen entertains at Douskos. Also present are Klaus Merkel, Redmond Wallis, Charles Heckstall (partly obscured), David Goschen, Charmian Clift, George Johnston, Carolyn and Demetri Gassoumis, Fidel Caliesch, Marianne Ihlen, Inge Schneier, Axel Jensen (partly obscured), and Christopher Booker (?).
(James Burke)

While Cohen's concise poem relies for its effect on the expatriate's dream of the rustic Mediterranean courtyard tavern in which one passes balmy and convivial evenings with little care for tomorrow—a dream that continues decades later to drive mass tourism to Mediterranean Europe—one also finds in the poem indications that this is not a space for visitors alone, but one that remains essentially local. Douskos is a place for "someone's wedding", or the site for marking the passage of expatriation in the other direction, when "a boy is leaving on a boat in the morning". If the viewer looks further at Burke's pictures, beyond the immediate circle, outside the brightly-lit focus of the courtyard and against the tavern wall, we see a number of Greek men quietly observing the expatriates' sing-along. Their shadowy, almost spectral presence, whereby they simultaneously both fit comfortably within the frame while being relegated to outsiders and observers, reminds us of the particular conditions of expatriation that prevailed on Hydra. This was a time and a place in which separation between the locals and the visitors was hardly feasible but also mutely enacted and respected on an occasion such as this.

One member of the Douskos group photographed by Burke bears a striking resemblance to English journalist and cultural commentator Christopher Booker. Booker was then working as the jazz critic for London's *Sunday Telegraph*, and achieved greater notoriety the following year when he co-founded and edited the satirical magazine *Private Eye*. In 1963 Booker would wed novelist Emma Tennant, whose family had a long association with the Greek islands and in particular Corfu, as chronicled in her 2002 memoir *A House in Corfu*. The couple spent some weeks on Hydra in the summer of 1964, and although their marriage would only last several years they achieved a degree of permanence by having small parts in Wallis's *The Unyielding Memory* as Peter and Matilda Winton. There is evidence in *The Unyielding Memory* that Booker had previously visited the island prior to the Wallises leaving for London in 1961. (Wallis's choice of the name 'Winton' proved to be prescient of Hydra's literary future. In 1988 Australian novelist Tim Winton spent six months on the island writing his 1991 novel *Cloudstreet*, which won Australia's annual Miles Franklin Award for the year's best novel twenty-eight years after Johnston's *My Brother Jack*. Winton's 1994 novel *The Riders* was partly set on Hydra).

While Douskos represented a traditional aspect of Hydra and one form of the expatriation fantasy for those who, in Clift's phrase, "dreamed of islands", a number of new venues also emerged during these years, providing for a different sort of social experience and a different type of island dreaming. These new ventures targeted an affluent and youthful crowd of short-term visitors whose interest in Greek mythology may have extended no further than *eros*.

The first and eventually most well-known of them was the Lagoudera Marine-Club, spectacularly located on the western side of the harbour entrance. While Lagoudera opened in 1959, a similar business had been tentatively launched at the same location a year earlier, in a building that had previously been used for boatbuilding and as a waterside refuelling depot.

This first bar—apparently without a name, or at least one that has been lost to history—had been created by Paolo and Magda Tilche. In his 1958 *Pictures from Greece* account of Hydra's flourishing writers' colony, Vasso Mingos briefly detailed the couple's respective backstories and their plans for an island bar. Magda, described by Marianne Ihlen as "tall and gorgeous, with flaming red hair and colourful clothing" and by Mingos as a polyglot "one-time swimming champion … and a former Bratislava actress" who wrote short stories in her "basic language" German, had fled Czechoslovakia for Paris in the aftermath of the Second World War. It was in Paris that she met Egyptian-born Italian Paolo who was then running the Rose Rouge night club in the Saint-Germain-des-Prés quarter. Established in the mid-to-late 1940s, the club proved popular with both Parisian existentialists and France's leading jazz players. A decade later, *Variety* magazine suggested that Rose Rouge was shifting its focus to the tourist trade, informing its American readers that the current revue, presented by Paolo Tilche, "has its quota of stripped girls" and that while acts by singer Betty Reilly and a "feverish Africano ballet" offered interest, the umbrella spinning choreography of the Yves Joly hand ballet troupe, once a big crowd pleaser, was beginning to wear thin.

While Tilche's club was popular with the punters, it was increasingly unpopular with his competitors, particularly the original Rose Rouge located on the Rue de la Harpe and owned by Féral (Francois) Benga, a gay Senegalese cabaret dancer. That club also attracted the modernist Parisian crowd not least because Benga himself was a perfect example of everything his patrons wanted in their *l'art nègre*. The two venues operated in peaceful coexistence until the mid-1950s, when things soured to the point that both closed their doors for good in 1956. If Mingos knew of these intriguing details, he chose to abbreviate them, simply quoting Paolo Tilche's explanation that "Other night-club owners, alarmed by the growing popularity of the Rose Rouge, began to be unpleasant so I decided to leave France". The Tilches eventually made their way to Hydra, and while Paolo harboured "a secret desire to write screen plays and become a movie director", his more immediate concern was to support his family by opening a bar in a converted island boathouse.

As it happened, the first incarnation of the Hydra bar that would become Lagoudera was finished with the aid of voluntary labour by other expatriates and opened with considerable flourish. Unfortunately, it was to remain open for only a matter of weeks during the summer of 1958, during which Paolo Tilche fell into both the arms of another woman—reputed to be an Egyptian princess—and unspecified trouble with the police from which he decided to flee. The island bar was immediately shut, and Magda, faced with a second bar closure as well as a future without her husband, was forced to spend several months in an Athens prison as a result of Paolo's wrongdoing. Magda returned to Hydra after her release and resumed her place within Hydra's expatriate community, only to be ordered off the island for a period in 1961.

While many of Hydra's expatriates were facing forms of exile, it was Magda Tilche who best represented the restless modernity that swept through large parts of Europe after the war, rendering people stateless by necessity or choice. Steve Sanfield called Hydra a "home for the homeless", and it became just that for Tilche as she found security amongst the island's insecure contingent of foreigners. For her, Hydra was a refuge from the large European cities from which she had become estranged. Tilche found comfort in singing Russian-Jewish folk songs with Leonard Cohen and had a particular friendship with Marianne Ihlen, the younger Ihlen being attracted by the exotic vibrancy of a women who "became like an older sister". Tilche eventually ran an antiques store in a lane near the port and married and had a child with local man Theodoros Anargirou, who is mentioned in Wallis's diaries as a real estate fixer and go-to guy for the expatriates, a suspected thief and general rogue who Wallis clearly distrusted. Magda, however, found a secure place on Hydra, eventually passing away in the island's home for the aged in 2005.

(Paolo Tilche's forays into the Mediterranean leisure business didn't end with his Hydra bar. In the early 1960s, Tilche and his new partner Myriam Beltrami opened a guesthouse on another small, rocky, out-of-the-way, traffic-free island—this time, the Aeolian island of Penarea. So successful was this business that it expanded into the substantial Hotel Raya, which was designed by Tilche's Milan-based architect cousin, also named Paolo Tilche. The hotel

Magda Tilche, c.1963. (Redmond Wallis)

was responsible for Panarea developing a reputation as an 'artists' island'—a term laden with irony as, in Panarea's case, it refers to holidaying celebrities escaping the prying cameras of the paparazzi rather than a struggling underclass. Tilche passed away some years ago, but, unlike his Hydra venture, the Hotel Raya lives on as a legendary 'celebo-boho retreat' of the Mediterranean).

The Tilches' short-lived bar had to wait another twelve months for its next incarnation, which came when it acquired a new owner, Babis Mores. According to the legend of Lagoudera, Mores first visited Hydra in 1958 and immediately fell in love with the island. When he returned and found that the defunct bar was for sale with all its fittings, he moved quickly to create a new type of island entertainment with a venue designed to appeal to more affluent tourists tempted by the promise of a cosmopolitan Mediterranean glamour that

Plate 1: Charmian Clift and George Johnston.
(James Burke)

Plate 2: Nikos Hadjikyriakos-Ghika in his studio.
(James Burke)

Plate 3: *The Studio in Hydra* (1959). Nikos Hadjikyriakos-Ghika.
(©2017 Benaki Museum)

Plate 4: Sidney and Cynthia Nolan on the terrace of Ghika's house, 1956. Nolan is painting *Untitled* [*Hydra*] (1956). (Bauer Media Pty Limited / *The Australian Women's Weekly*)

Plate 5: *Untitled* [*Hydra*] (1956). Sidney Nolan.
(©The Nolan Trust / Bridgeman Images / Sotheby's Australia)

Plate 6: A Hydriot maiden (Katerina Paouri?) adorns the currency.

Plate 7: Marianne Ihlen (during her brief period as a brunette), Charmian Clift, Ioannis (Wolfgang) Kardamatis, Timothy Hennessy and George Johnston, 1958. (Johnston and Clift Collection)

Fun is in the Air...in Greece

Islands like this one...*Hydra*...are part of your visit to Greece!

*Brilliant sunshine, balmy climate, sparkling blue-green seas
...the very _air_ is tonic.*

You can't stay inhibited when you stay in Greece. Ask anyone who has vacationed there.

Everyone who returns from Greece speaks of the reviving freshness of the air itself...and the pure, delicious drinking water the Greeks themselves so highly prize.

You *must* have fun in Greece...because everybody does. You simply can't resist the Greeks' spontaneity in bursting into song or dancing, anytime.

And...with the drachma at 30 to the dollar, you can enjoy all the comforts of smart new hotels, delicious food and wines, glorious golden beaches...and a variety of night life.

Each day of your stay is filled with the 3,000-year-old antiquities of Greece. Her ancient temples and altars and amphitheaters hold you spellbound.

♦ ♦ ♦

Do let your Travel Agent tell you how much fun it is going *to* Greece, staying *in* Greece! Picture-literature from National Tourist Organization of Greece, 120 East 56th Street, New York 22.

Where ultra-moderns gather...

GREECE
...close to every Capital of Europe!

Plate 8: "Fun is in the Air", 1962. (*Sports Illustrated*)

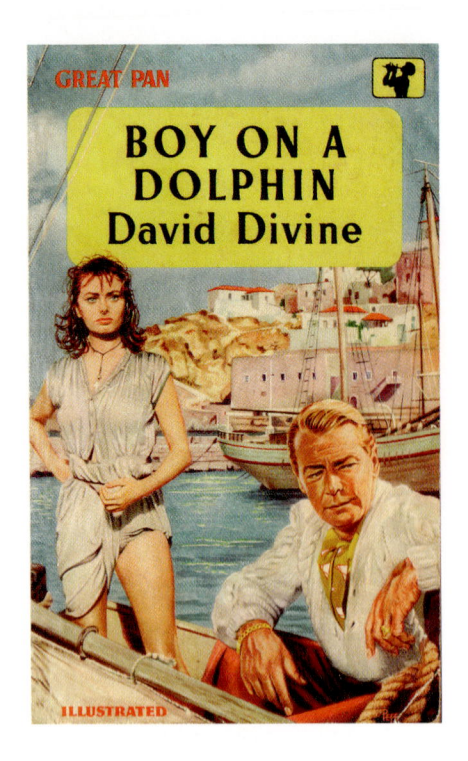

Plates 9–10: Hollywood comes to Hydra. Above: movie tie-in edition of *Boy on a Dolphin*, 1957, features Sophia Loren and Alan Ladd on Hydra harbour. Below: Melina Mercouri and Anthony Perkins on the *agora* during the filming of *Phaedra*, 1967. (James Burke)

Plate 11: *Stormie Seas* under full sail, 1958.
(Vasso Mingos)

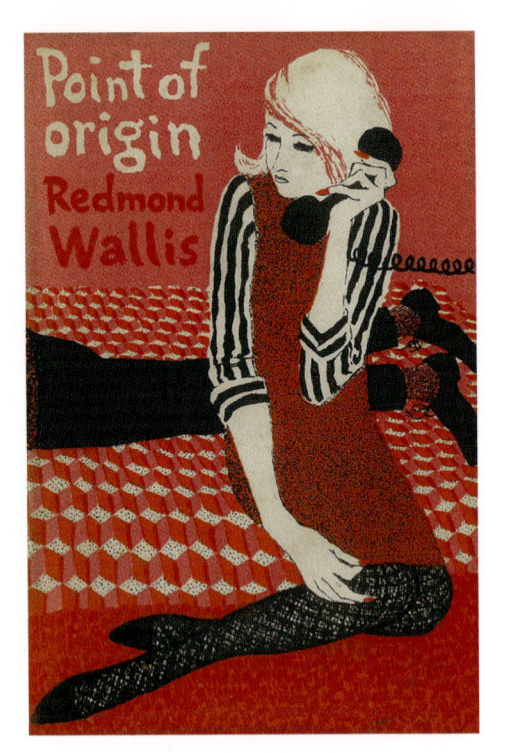

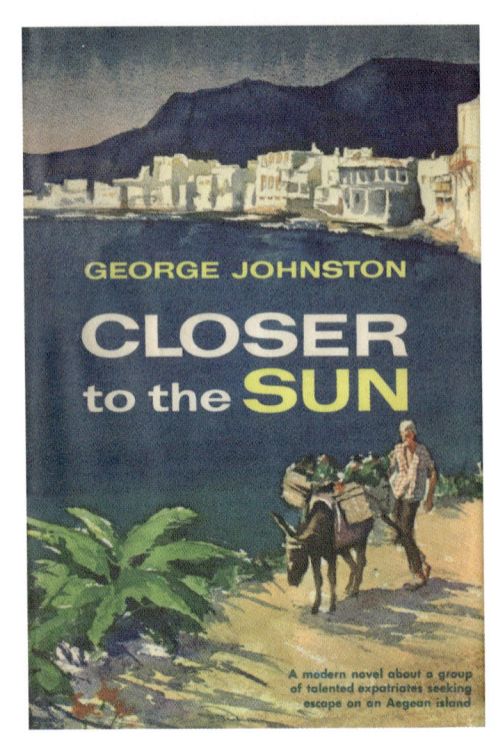

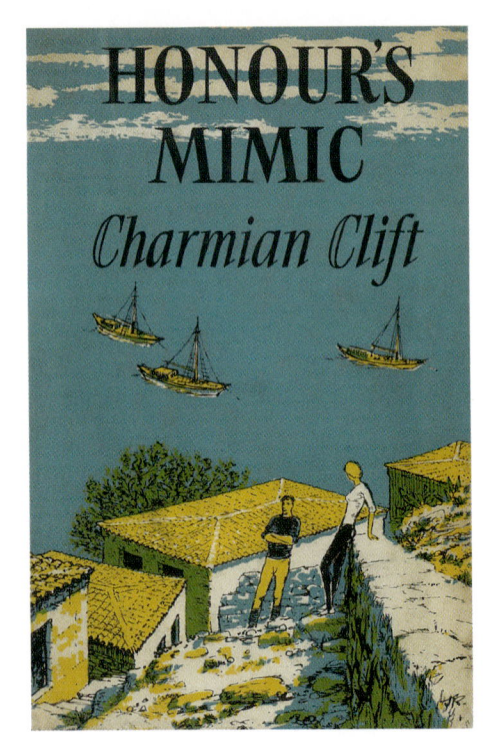

Plates 12–15: Top left: Axel Jensen, *A Girl I Knew* (London: Andre Deutsch, 1963)
Top right: Redmond Wallis, *Point of Origin* (London: Bodley Head, 1963)
Bottom left: George Johnston, *Closer to the Sun* (New York: William Morrow and Company, 1961)
Bottom right: Charmian Clift, *Honour's Mimic* (London: Hutchinson, 1964)

had hitherto been unknown to Hydra—and to the Greek islands. The opening of Lagoudera took place in May 1959 and, happily for Mores, coincided with a period of international visibility for the island following the release of two widely seen films, *A Girl in Black* (1956) and *Boy on a Dolphin* (1957).

Importantly, Mores had a flair for running his new business. His goal was to make Lagoudera the social centre of Hydra—and, indeed, of the Saronic islands—and from the outset, he promoted his new bar as a 'must visit' destination for those who might have otherwise been seen at the western and central Mediterranean resorts of Marbella, Portofino or Capri. To be successful in attracting a new type of wealthier and higher spending clientele, Mores realised he could not depend upon Hydra's beauty alone; he needed a radically different type of venue and experience from the island's traditional taverns with their reliance on cheap alcohol and occasional guitar strummers.

Mores coupled his ambition for Lagoudera with a very useful hobby, in that he was a keen amateur photographer. From the outset, he obsessively photographed the goings on in his bar and the wider Hydra social scene. These photographs served a dual purpose. Firstly, Mores realised their power to attract business, and he made sure the best of them—particularly those featuring political figures, pop-culture royalty, or actual royalty—were fed to newspapers in Athens to guarantee that Lagoudera became an ever-more desirable place to be 'seen'. Secondly, Mores used his photographs to create an archive of Hydra in the 1960s by compiling annual volumes that permanently recorded the various comings and goings of both the famous and the unknown. His many photos were cut up, juxtaposed, thematically overlaid and haphazardly annotated to form a rollicking post-modern collage of memories capturing the carefree spirit of island hedonism.

Mores's entrepreneurial talents extended to working the ever-increasing number of smart yachts that entered the harbour, meeting them as they moored and plying those on board with promotional material for his bar-cum-nightclub. These various strategies succeeded, and *Pelagos Magazine* (the official touristic publication of Hellenic Seaways, which runs daily ferries to Hydra from Piraeus) recalled of those heady days:

> Lagoudera hosted internationally famous names, VIPs in the arts, politics, business and international aristocracy. They danced, drank, ate and jumped into the sea fully clothed, a trend initiated by Babis. Names such as Henry Fonda, Peter Ustinov, Elizabeth Taylor, Jeanne Moreau, Douglas Fairbanks, Eddie Fisher, Leonard Cohen, Dimitris Myrat, Aleka Katseli, Andreas Barkoulis, Aliki Vougiouklaki … Maria Callas, Ralf Vallone, Anthony Perkins, Rossana Podesta, Jules Dassin, Melina Mercouri, Jacqueline Kennedy, Aristotle Onassis, Stavros Niarchos, the Empress Soraya, the Count of Barcelona … These and many others (the list is endless) participated in the fun at Lagoudera, some in supporting roles and others as protagonists.

Not all of these names are widely recognised nearly six decades later, but, at the time, they represented the emerging European and international 'jet-set', even though Hydra remained resolutely beyond the reach of jets or, indeed, any other sort of aeroplane. And where the jet-set landed, mass tourism quickly followed. The ferries became more frequent, the visitors more exotic, cocktails replaced retsina, and pop and rock music blared across the once silent waters of the night-time harbour. Hydra became the first Greek island to develop what would become known as 'night-life'.

This was a development with the potential for culture shock. Del Kolve was a witness to *the* significant event in 1960, Lagoudera's first full year of operation, when Elizabeth Taylor visited. Kolve's account registers the response of himself and other island visitors, and also the Hydriots who found themselves not only face-to-face with an international celebrity, but also entering for the first time a venue very different from the island's established taverns.

> The big celebrity sighting of the summer was the arrival of a yacht with Elizabeth Taylor and Eddie Fisher on board. They had recently married shortly after the scandalous breakup of his marriage to the much-loved Debbie Reynolds. Around 7pm, just as the island was buzzing with the news, the couple took a tender into the harbour and visited Lagoudera, the one bar that had some style, served cocktails, played sophisticated

music (sambas even!) and catered to well-off tourists. It was a place we went only if someone invited us, but some of us went to see Liz and Eddie, along with an assortment of local folk, fishermen and workmen who were entering the bar for the first time. They didn't order drinks, but just stood there, pressed up against the walls, staring in silence, as did we. Liz and Eddie were glamorous indeed, but also understandably uncomfortable, and they didn't stay long. One witnessed the price of fame.

Predictably, as time passed, it was not only wealthy tourists and younger day-trippers who gravitated towards Mores's spectacularly sited bar but also many of the established expatriates in search of a more vibrant and youth-oriented experience than that provided by their traditional gathering places. An evening sitting out at Katsikas drinking cheap ouzo and talking at length with George Johnston suddenly had less appeal as the younger and more beautiful people passed by on their way to Lagoudera. The generational difference that Clift had described several years earlier in existential terms in *Peel Me a Lotus* was now suddenly apparent as a widening social gulf.

The impact of Lagoudera and the changes that followed were swift. Redmond Wallis's diary for 1960 and 1961 makes only brief mention of Lagoudera, and Katsikas remained the centre of his social world. By the time he returned in 1963, it was a different matter. As he later recalled, "the swinging sixties … would not really strike Hydra until after we left in September 1961 (and would be in full swing when we returned in August 1963…)". Or as he writes in *The Unyielding Memory* of his return to the island:

> The island is full of tourists, among them are a fair number of flaunting pooves and ladies on the make. The bars are wide open, erupting with the noise of jukeboxes, and the agora is almost impossible to walk along as the bars' owners increase their catchment area.

In an unpublished 1963 Hydra travelogue, Wallis described the new generation of bars that rapidly opened in the wake of Lagoudera's success.

Party life. Anthony Perkins, George Johnston and Charmian Clift and unidentified others, 1961. (Johnston and Clift Collection)

For the sophisticated, there are five bars on Hydra serving foreign spirits, at Athens prices. They are, in order from where the boat docks, the Portofino, Lagoudera (which also has an art gallery, a handicraft shop, and a room where people can retire and read without being asked to drink), the Dolphin, the Siroco, and the Castello. The Siroco lies beyond Spelia on the way to Kamini. It tends to get dark and intimate in the small hours of the morning.

While foreign spirits and Athens's prices were new to Hydra and likely a deterrent to some established expatriates, the promise of somewhere "dark and intimate" appears to have been a powerful attractor to the younger generation. While Wallis still frequented Katsikas and other traditional tavernas, it seems he prioritised a daily visit to Lagoudera, Dolphin (Delfini), Siroco or Portofino, and sometimes several on the same evening, mainly in pursuit of women, and the difference in the atmosphere that he describes is stark when compared to the homely pleasures of the back room or dockside of Katsikas, or the courtyard of Douskos.

SINGIN' AT DOUSKOS, SWINGIN' AT LAGOUDERA

Charles Heckstall and Rosemary Whitman at Portofino. (James Burke)

One of the island's new venues, Portofino, had opened in the summer of 1960, shortly before Burke's visit, and he used the tavern's generous window space for a series of images featuring Charles Heckstall and Rosemary Whitman. While Portofino's aged stonework and gnarled fig tree indicate the building's venerable age, there are also signs that change was afoot—not least of all in the presence of Heckstall and Whitman, but also with the patently 'on-trend' chairs that were a far cry from the rustic ladder-backs found at Katsikas, and in the haphazardly wrought business sign bearing the bar's name and evoking an even more glamorous Mediterranean harbour.

It is in Hydra's nature that it can never sustain an entirely segregated structure for socialising—the town is too small, the venues too integrated, the desirable locations too many. So, it is no surprise that, despite their considerable differences, the social worlds of Katsikas and Lagoudera overlapped. Nor is it surprising—given they shared an urge to slip within the gravitational pull of the 'stars'—that Clift and Johnston, dressed in their finest, were photographed partying, most likely in Lagoudera, alongside Anthony

Jules Dassin (left), Melina Mercouri (back to camera), Tony Randall and Gordon Merrick at Katsikas, 1962. (Merrick Collection)

Perkins when movie cameras returned to Hydra in 1961 to film Jules Dassin's *Phaedra*.

Other photos show the stars moving in the opposite direction, with Melina Mercouri, Jules Dassin's wife and the real star of *Phaedra*, and others, including Tony Randall, relaxing alongside established expatriates at Katsikas the following year during the filming of Morton da Costa's *The Island of Love*. For the time being, Lagoudera and Katsikas would exist together, both sharing the harbour-front and rubbing shoulders alongside other established taverns and new nightclubs. But it was clear that a change had come, and Hydra would never be quite the same again.

The site of Lagoudera continues to entertain island visitors—it is now the restaurant Omilos, which uses its website to proclaim its heritage as the "most famous Bar-Restaurant in Greece". The entertainment may now be a little more sedate; the visitors less likely to be a rollcall of Europe's most chic and beautiful; and the food improved from the heady days of Lagoudera when Babis Mores put his mother in charge of the kitchen. But the view still takes in a wide expanse of the Saronic Gulf, Hydra's famed harbour remains as magnetic as ever, and the venue retains its reputation as the birthplace of a new type of Aegean sophistication.

* * *

Redmond Wallis recounts an event from Lagoudera's early days, that of Babis Mores enticing the then-favoured beacon of pan-Eurasian glamour, Princess Soraya of Iran. Princess (formerly Queen) Soraya was recently divorced from her beloved husband, the Shah, on the grounds of her infertility.

> *Another dark beauty, Queen Saraya, divorced two years before, paid them a visit. Babbi, an Athenian who had opened a bar called Lagoudera, the first of its kind, designed to be sophisticated and fun, and who was struggling to imbue it with chic and reputation, gathered together what he believed to be a representative collection of artists and beatniks (which were pretty much the same thing in Babbi's eyes), most of them like the Alwyns, to provide local colour. Queen Saraya, beautiful, but infinitely sad and totally silent, her features part obscured by a headscarf and dark glasses, sat at one end of the bar, supported by what seemed to be minders, while the local foreigners made the most of the free drinks Babbi had offered as bribes and one of them did artistic things on an acoustic guitar. It had been a dull evening, and the queen had gone back to her magnificent steam yacht after half an hour or so, still looking sad.*

Chapter Eight

TOURISM

Whether it be Provence, Andalucía, the Amalfi or Tuscany, the desire for a life lived fully, simply and authentically in an 'unspoilt' Mediterranean pocket of an otherwise overly crowded and hyper-modernised world is ingrained in the contemporary western dreamscape and travel literature. This romantic impulse is driven by a yearning for a lifestyle cleansed of materialism, consumerism and urban alienation, and replaced by stable communities, centuries old pre-industrial traditions, long and glorious summers, seasonal abundance, rustic dishes to-die-for, and, ultimately, of being accepted by a cast of gruff, amusing, wise and rascally local characters.

The worm that burrows deep into the bud of such longing is the reality of mass tourism. In an age when tour buses push further into distant corners of tranquillity, when cruise ships nose their way into ever remoter ports and bays, and when Airbnb has become the currency of rural hospitality, it is increasingly difficult for travel writers to convey the sense of both 'separation' and 'belonging' that differentiate the traveller-author from the tourist. This problem is not new, and faced Charmian Clift when she reflected on her Hydra life in *Peel Me a Lotus*.

In that context, it is not incidental that Clift chose to begin her narrative, without preamble, in the early months of 1956 when Hydra was gripped by winter and devoid of tourists. The depth of the season is evident as she gazes across to the Peloponnese where "a thick crust of snow swept down through the dark pine forests to the sea". These frosty surrounds provided the island with an aura of sequestered artistic expatriation that Clift cherished. Writing of the six foreigners on Hydra in that winter—herself and George; Henry and

Ursula Trevena (Sidney and Cynthia Nolan); and Sean and Lola Donovan (Patrick Greer and Nancy Dignan)—Clift establishes their solidarity based on the novelty of being thrown together as sort of 'anti-tourists' drawn into close proximity by their commitment to removing themselves from an increasingly alienating urbanism.

> Every one of us, in his particular way, is a protestant against the rat race of modern commercialism, against the faster and faster scuttling through an endless succession of sterile days that begin without hope and end without joy. Each of us has somehow managed to stumble off the treadmill, determined to do his own work in his own way. Sitting among the bean-sacks in an island grocery store, we have become very fond of one another, in the manner of people who by their very presence bolster up the other's sometimes flickering convictions.

This wintry vision of artistic solidarity is emptied of visitors except for "winter strays" who wander through in an out-of-season sojourn to Hydra's art school.

Clift's account of Hydra in the winter of 1955–56 describes a low-key start to the expatriate colony that would gather numbers and notoriety as the seasons passed. Five of the six 'stayers' for that winter were Australian, and the Nolans, Greer and Dignan were there because they had followed the Johnstons. It is therefore feasible that Clift, Johnston and their children might have found themselves the only foreigners on the island over the desolate months of that first winter. Having almost no Greek and with Clift's pregnancy advancing, it would have been an extraordinarily lonely experience for this prodigiously sociable couple.

Even in the early summer of 1956, as the family waited to see what the 'season' would bring, Clift remained focused on the small group of fellow expatriates with whom she and Johnston shared their swimming spot at Spilia.

> It is a diverse and tantalizing collection of human beings sprawled about these rocks and ledges on a hot cliff far from their native lands, insurgents all who have rebelled against the station in which it pleased God to

place them. What devious roads brought them to this small island, what decisions and indecisions, what driftings, what moments of desperation and hope? And what are they looking for? What do they expect to find here, an Australian journalist, an Irish school-master, an American misfit, an exotic outsider from the St.-Germain des-Pres?

The rhetorical questions asked in that paragraph are telling; they are not the sort of questions asked of tourists, and they are revealing of Clift's own insecurities, her own "flickering conviction". As someone who has decided not to come and go, as tourists inevitably do, but rather to come and stay, the questions remained to be answered: what is *she* looking for? What does *she* expect to find? How will *she* cope with "moments of desperation and hope"? Clift knows that it is not simply enough to have escaped from elsewhere and to be here; she and Johnston are not visitors in search of novelty and diversion, but rather they have chosen to settle their family and live here in search of … *something*.

One of the key narrative threads of *Peel Me a Lotus* emerges in Clift's account of the tourist influx in the summer of 1956. That Hydra attracted tourists during the summer should not have been a surprise for Clift. After all, she and Johnston had visited and then settled on the island the previous August, at a high point of the tourist season. They had also travelled to several Greek islands including Hydra in May 1954 as Johnston collected material for *The Cyprian Woman*, a novel that conspicuously satirises the region's reliance on tourism. For the novel's hero, unproductive filmmaker Stephen Colvin, the tourists are "whizzing through the place, catalogue in hand, as if it were the Chelsea flower show … Too hot, too tired, too bustled about, too organised. And so scared of missing one little thing that they end up by missing it all." For the alluring but frivolous Erica Kostandis, who works as a guide for busloads of uncomprehending tourists, her clients are simply "petulant, ugly, thick-bodied sheep".

But just as Kostandis needs the tourists she openly despises, so too Clift's narrative in *Peel Me a Lotus* needs the transient island visitors in order to propel her themes of settlement and belonging. The tourists allow Clift to distinguish herself and George from those who have come to Hydra encumbered by touristic indifference and with simpler motives of recreation or scenic diversion. Their presence establishes a hierarchy of escapism, and Clift is able to make the point that her dedication to her literary craft goes hand-in-hand with settlement and integration—experiences of a different order from holiday-making, island-hopping or day-tripping.

Initially, as the tourist season builds, the newcomers seem to be a welcome novelty as Clift and Johnston happily share their favourite waterfront cafés, tavernas and swimming spot with a young, eclectic and noticeably international bunch of engaging misfits. As the summer progresses, however, and ferries disgorge ever greater numbers of tourists from Athens and further afield, Clift encounters the problems of the serial distractions that result when tourism impacts a small community in a confined space. The challenge is that she and Johnston have gone to Hydra with a real purpose—to make a home, raise a family and earn a living by writing—but now she confronts their increasingly precarious circumstances as their refuge from modernity is engulfed by that most modern phenomenon: mass tourism. For although Hydra delivers on its Mediterranean promise—Clift does not fail to write about the ever-present sunshine; the abundance of cheap produce; the reassuring enactment of authentic local ritual—she is all too aware of the danger the tourists pose to those looking for a dedicated working life. In a telling passage, she goes to the heart of the couple's predicament, juxtaposing their situation as committed writers when they encounter the enticements of the *agora*, heavy with tourists and seductive with the promise of long, romantically charged but existentially fraught evenings of talking and drinking.

> Warm, mad, and wonderful the nights, wearing the soft bloom of purple grapes. The water lapping dark, and a huge mad moon extinguishing behind the sharp mountain edges like every dream one ever had. What are we doing here under the mad moon watching the promenade pass and repass—the linked girls, the complacent citizens, the gay tourists,

> the self-conscious artists, the few groups of aristocrats come down from their lofty palaces to mingle with the village people? They all have their places. They belong. Why did we have to protest, burn our bridges, isolate ourselves, strip off our protective colouring as if it had been a decontamination suit? Why? Just to sit eternally and eternally around the plastic tablecloth playing verbal pitch and toss, baiting, being baited, being bored, drinking too much wine, becoming too angry or too tired to stop.
>
> 'Let's go on! Let's go somewhere else!' someone cries gaily. 'There's music tonight in Yanni's *taverna*. Let's go and drink some more and dance'.
>
> But we must get up so early in the morning, we demur. There is the baby. We've got a lot of work on at the moment.
>
> 'Oh, come on!' They are already moving. 'Let down your hair for once!' … They shrug and go off laughing into the night, looking for music, for dancing, for wine and still more wine, while we—proved yet again to be priggish, dull, respectable spoilsports—go home a little drunker than we ought to be, feeling vaguely worsted, jangling with some unspecified resentment, indefinably *tainted*.

Once again Clift asks "What are we doing here?" and other difficult questions as she contemplates a summer that provides both what she craves and what she fears. At the heart of Clift's anxiety is the expatriate's dilemma of belongingness, where—contrary to logic—even the tourists can have more of a place, more of a *reason* to be on the island than those who have expatriated. Although buying a house, having children in school, and giving birth on the island marked out the Johnstons as 'different' from most foreigners, it is also the case that they were hybrids—not a tourist and not a local; neither a temporary visitor nor guaranteed of permanence; neither a resource to be exploited nor someone who benefits. As long as she rubs shoulders with tourists, Clift understands she is cocooned within, but separate from, a group who have no need to 'belong'. With excess time and money, the tourist's role on the island extends no further than the enjoyment of a novel environment and the

Neither tourist nor local. George Johnston (centre, background) strides through the *agora* crowd of Hydriots and visitors. (James Burke)

need for social diversions. Clift, on the other hand, is constantly reminded of the unsettling liminality that is the fate of those expatriates who have an existential need to feel at home.

Insofar as Hydra had a tourist tradition by the mid-1950s, it was one that was already associated with the arts. The island's School of Fine Arts opened in 1936 as one of a series of similar institutions dotting Greece's islands in order to attract international visitors looking to flavour their Aegean holiday with some cultural activity. Prolific English travel writers Eric Whelpton and Barbara Crocker Whelpton noted as much in their 1961 guide to Greece and its islands, writing of Hydra that "The cafés and taverns on the quayside are unpretentious, but exceptionally cheerful, because of the presence of the colony of painters attracted here by the summer school of the Athens Academy of Arts which provides accommodation for students".

Certainly, the Greek National Tourism Organisation promoted Hydra as an artistic destination. In a pamphlet published in October 1960, visitors were informed that "In recent years … and especially since a branch of the School

Klaus Merkel (far left) with students at Hydra's School of Fine Arts. Director Perikilis Vyzantios is at far right. (James Burke)

of Fine Arts has been functioning in the Tombazi mansion, artists from all over the world have begun to gather in Hydra". The previous month James Burke, armed with instructions to photograph the island's "glamorous and ordinary tourists", had scaled the stairs to the School of Fine Arts, where he took three dozen photographs of a group of youthful artists bathed in sunlight and sketching under the watchful eye of the school's director, Perikilis Vyzantios. Vyzantios was instrumental in establishing the school and had been its director since it opened. He was also a friend of Nikos Hadjikyriakos-Ghika and had a small role in Henry Miller's *The Colossus of Maroussi* as Pericles Byzantis.

Arguably in these Art School images, Burke is practicing his own art, with the sunlight rather than the artists themselves being the true subject. It is a light that Redmond Wallis described as having a quality of "opalescent, impenetrable, shimmering milkiness", which "shattered the very air and dispersed it in fine particles".

However, a new generation of postwar travellers was looking for reasons for island travel other than the arts. In his 1958 travel book *The Morea*, Robert Liddell—who worked for the British Council in Athens before moving to the University of Athens's English department and translating the work of Greek poet Constantine P. Cavafy—noted that "a modish interest" had developed in Hydra, which was increasingly attracting tourists for reasons other than its artistic tradition.

> Lately the tourist trade has increased: the Argo-Saronic steamers no longer discharge all their passengers on to the quays of Aegina, Poros or Spetsai; Hydra has its share of them. For some years it has been a favourite haunt of artists, and recently it has attracted other tourists, who fill the hotels or lodge in private houses; a beautiful house may be hired cheaply for the whole summer, and not long ago could be bought for a song. It is not altogether suitable as a tourist centre; if you do not lodge near the quay you will constantly have to go up and down steep, ankle-breaking steps. And if you are not prepared to plunge off rocks into deep water, you must make a long caique journey to Mólos, for a bathing-beach. Moreover the little town, shut in its amphitheatre of rocky hills, is apt to cause claustrophobia … Yet Hydra has a greater dignity and tranquillity than that of the other islands. The romantic beauty of the little town, and the wonderful sea-scape to be seen from its edge, hold many people captive there for months; it could never be left without a pang.

As postwar tastes in Mediterranean tourism shifted towards island-hopping leisure, Greek tourism authorities increasingly promoted attractions other than the country's rich cultural heritage. The idea of Hydra as a sun and fun-filled holiday destination was evident in promotional campaigns such as one from 1962, which ran in *Sports Illustrated* and other high circulation American magazines [See Plate 8]. The advertisement, from the Greek National Tourism Organisation, pitched the inexpensive pleasures on offer in Greece, and on Hydra in particular. Alongside a fleeting mention of its ancient monuments, the country (and island) is sold as a place for "ultra-moderns", where "fun is in the air".

Johnston wrote in *Closer to the Sun* of the seductions and impact of such advertisements.

> To these people [the expatriates] seasonally are added the bright flocks of swift-skimming tourists who, in spring and summer, attracted by a tourist poster which describes Silenos as 'Poseidon's Playground,' briefly visit the island to take photographs, to swim and disport in the memorably clear and fantastically blue water which bathes the sheer-falling rocks of the island's outer shell, or to behave with carefree immorality which the city conventions deny them.

In his later novel, *Clean Straw for Nothing*, Johnston wrote again of the influence of advertising on island tourism although, in a deft touch, narrator David Meredith positions the expatriate artist community as being in itself a tourist attraction:

> It is extraordinary to realize, now we are a genuine foreign colony growing more numerous every week, now tourists pour in by every boat, now even the Government travel brochures feature the place as a 'colourful haunt of bohemian artists and writers from all parts of the world,' that when Cressida and I came to settle just five years ago we were the only foreigners here and the island was shunned by tourists.

Not everyone, however, saw the presence of the artists as a touristic drawcard. For Leslie Finer, writing in his 1964 book *Passport to Greece*, it was the very presence of this group—or, more to the point, those attracted by this group—that led him to dissuade the casual tourist from lingering on Hydra. Finer suggested that a day or two spent on the island "will not be wasted", but that:

> the ultimate disqualification of Hydra as a fit place for a relaxed vacation is the obtrusive presence on the island of a motley foreign colony, bizarre in dress and behaviour, which performs the empty motions of bohemian tradition created long ago by a few real artists and writers

who found inspiration in Hydra but who have long since been driven out by the inanity of their imitators.

How easy it was to confuse or conflate various elements within the Hydra tourist scene was apparent when the April 1964 issue of *Motor Boating* magazine—self-proclaimed as "America's authority on modern boating"—reported that Hydra had attracted "1000 yachts" in 1962, and was "now an artists' and movie colony" and *the* island to visit and mingle with the "Bohemian jet-set". While *Motor Boating* might have missed the nuances of Hydra's international contingent, it was right in linking the island's increasing popularity with the film industry, since two high-visibility films had recently added to Hydra's international recognition factor.

The first of these was renowned Cypriot director Michael Cacoyannis's *A Girl in Black* (*To Koritsi Me Ta Mara*) released in 1956 but filmed in the late summer of 1955, soon after the Johnston family arrived on Hydra. The Greek-language film was widely seen in Europe, and was the first Greek film to receive substantial international recognition when it was nominated for a Golden Palm Award at the 1956 Cannes Film Festival; and if an article published in April 1959 in *The Australian Women's Weekly* is correct, *A Girl in Black* almost led to ten-year-old Martin Johnston becoming a reluctant movie star. As reported in an unattributed article (likely by Ruth or Charles Sriber), Cacoyannis first noticed Martin when he politely refused a small part in the film—"'I'd rather read my books', the boy told him gravely". When Cacoyannis later needed to cast *The Wastrel* (1961), he remembered Martin and believed he would be ideal to play "the son of the … dissolute father". In an effort to entice Martin's participation, Cacoyannis returned to Hydra with Frederick Wakeman, the author of the book on which *The Wastrel* was based. After a long walk that saw Wakeman and Martin discuss the script, the author coaxed from the boy a pledge to play the part, gifting him an expensive watch that Wakeman spontaneously slipped from his wrist. A plan for Martin and Clift to travel to Bermuda for the filming never eventuated, and the film was made with another boy in the role. (While Martin had passed up the opportunity to feature in *A Girl in Black*, Shane Johnston did find a small role. The starkly blonde Shane stands out amongst the Greek children in the drowning scene that serves as the film's climax. Cacoyannis went on to make an even more significant contribution to Greek tourism with his 1964 film, *Zorba the Greek*.)

Martin was once again dragged away from his books when the next film crew arrived on Hydra. That film, the Jean Negulesco directed *Boy on a Dolphin*, based on a novel by David Divine, was filmed in 1956 and released in 1957 [See Plate 9]. *Boy on a Dolphin* marked the first time Hollywood had ventured to Greece to shoot on location, and the movie, in DeLuxe Color and Cinemascope, made a major impact, not least because it featured Sophia Loren in her first English-language role playing alongside an established American cast led by Alan Ladd. This time Martin wasn't offered an acting role but, according to *The Australian Women's Weekly*, he was called upon to help "actress Sophia Loren to learn Greek for her part", presumably a reference to the song '*Ti ein' afto pou to lene Agapi*' that Loren sings. *Boy on a Dolphin* itself may have been underwhelming, but a large audience discovered that both Loren and Hydra looked spectacular on the big screen.

Whereas Clift makes no mention in *Peel Me a Lotus* of the Cacoyannis film, she wrote at length about the filming of *Boy on a Dolphin* in the book's concluding sections, although neither the film nor its stars are named. Coming at the end of the family's first full year on the island, when they have already been overwhelmed by the summer tourists, the impact of this Hollywood-funded intrusion on their island haven was startling. Conjuring up potent images of a D-Day styled invasion, Clift described the island—her home—as being under siege.

> Incredibly, it is happening. Like an invading army they are coming, with great weird landing-barges that nose grimly into the tiny scoop of harbour, and bear down on the moorings where the wine boats were blessed a week ago. … [S]lowly, inexorably, the monstrous maws open and down the ramps roll the first wheels these cobbles have ever

> known—jeeps, truck, trailers, half-tracks, strange, shrouded instruments, wheeled lamps. The ordinance of the conquering army.

While this disturbing operation might be temporary, Clift sees evidence of a lasting impact as the island is mimetically transformed to display an *ersatz* version of its own intrinsic appeal. The "make-believe waterfront" has become "the queerest fantasy world", cleaned up and re-painted to look more real than itself, and where the locals are now employed to pretend to be themselves, with their habitual actions halted midstream and repeated over and over for the benefit of the camera. Clift realises that the making of the film is predictive of the island's touristic future, whereby Hydra and the Hydriots will be permanently deployed to perform as they once were—or at least as they are imagined to have been.

Even those who have no role in the movie find themselves transformed by being the subject of Hollywood's gaze, so that Clift understands that she is being treated (almost certainly to her satisfaction) as "indigenous" and that "one finds oneself unprotestingly playing the assigned role". The power of the camera's all-seeing eye scrutinising their small world is irresistible, so that when Clift is invited to a party in honour of the film's stars she overlooks her one good cocktail dress—a remnant of her London years—in favour of dressing "in character", in "old cotton pants and a clean, patched shirt".

For those locals in the right line of work, being "in character" means moving quickly to take advantage of this rare opportunity. As if rehearsing their future roles in a more commercial world, the catchcry is suddenly "*dollaria*" as everyone from Nick Katsikas to Lefteri the house painter, to Dinos the builder, to Tzimmy the peddler jostles for the profit that is to be made from Hollywood's annexation of their island backwater.

Clift is quick to point out that the locals' search for profit is one side of a 'knowing' interaction that is taking place as both the filmmakers and the Hydriots benefit from each other's presence. Yet she also realises that there is more to this exchange than a transient and mutually beneficial exploitation, and that the making of the film will have more disturbing impacts from which there is no retreat. Clift records a remark by one of the film's crew that "it's quite a little paradise you folks have found for yourselves", to which another responds, "I think it's just too bad we are going to ruin it all for you ... Because we *will* ruin it. *Apres nous le deluge*! It's inevitable believe me! ... God, when I see a sweet little unspoilt place like this, and think what will happen to it after we have gone."

There is no way of knowing if Clift has accurately reported her conversation with the Hollywood dream-merchants, or whether it is simply a projection of her fears for what a more tourist-focused future will mean for her secluded island life. Either way, it indicates that this moment was seen, even as it was unfolding, as a turning point for Hydra's tourism. As predicted, the daily ferries and the smart yachts arrived in increasing numbers, and new businesses replaced the old, as travellers, tourists and gawkers came looking for the hybrid world of harbour-side village authenticity and the wide-screen, technicolour, cocktail-sipping cosmopolitanism depicted in *Boy on a Dolphin*. The former Hydra could provide with ease, while the latter would soon be met by a smarter set of new bars and restaurants, such as Lagoudera, Portofino and Delfini.

Redmond Wallis was one observer (and participant) who recognised that Hydra was transforming into a tourist destination in a way it never had been before. Having left the island in the summer of 1961, Wallis turned his hand to travel writing with the aim of replenishing his exhausted finances. He drafted a 2500 words essay about Hydra that he submitted (without success) to travel magazine *Go!*, which chimes with Liddell's earlier assessment of the island as an emerging, unconventional tourist destination. Wallis wrote in the knowledge that it was tourism that had brought him and Robyn to Hydra on their way to London, when they carried packs that blended Wallis's army training with his upper-middle class background and which included tents, ground sheets, nylon rope, aluminium plates, a collapsible frying pan, one white shirt (for Wallis) and tweed slacks (for Robyn). Wallis's article pointed to the same blending and shifting of Hydra's tourist demographics that had been observed by Clift and Liddell, but at a slightly later time when the island had been the setting for yet another movie, *Phaedra* (1962), starring Melina Mercouri and Anthony Perkins [See Plate 10].

> The island of Hydra lies three hours south of Athens and some three miles from the eastern coast of the Peloponnese. Six years ago it was just another relatively unknown and undistinguished Greek island, a spot on a map of the Saronic Gulf known only to a few Grecophiles and with no particular claim to be included in a classical tour. But in the last two years its fame has grown to such an extent that its visitors last year included Elizabeth Taylor, Queen Saroya, and the first lady of America, Mrs John Fitzgerald Kennedy. Jules Dassin, Tony Perkins and Melina Mercouri made a film there—the second, incidentally, for parts of "Boy on a Dolphin" were shot there. Nowadays anyone who is anyone in the "smart set", or in the fringe belt of art, has been or is going to Hydra.
>
> Until the beginning of last year, Hydra was at the stage that Capri was when Norman Douglas wrote "South Wind". Perhaps it was even a little more rustic than Capri at that time. Of its 2800 inhabitants about a dozen were foreigners engaged in some sort of artistic endeavour. The most famous was Nikos Hadjikiriakos—better known as Ghika, the painter who designed the sets for the Royal Ballet Company's recent performance of "Persephone". The island's other claim to fame was more than one hundred years old. But two years ago the pseudo-artists, the commercial and the successful artists, and the ordinary tourists began to drift in. The touring yachts followed them. The culmination was Jackie Kennedy. Hydra is now a smart place to go—as Greece is.

Wallis then adds what might have been the 'kiss of death' for his aspirations to have his essay published, as he reels off a list of Hydra's log-of-claims to remain under the tourist radar when compared to the attractions of other islands. He concludes, like Liddell, with an argument that despite (or perhaps because of) what it lacks, the island nonetheless possesses a degree of existential exceptionalism.

> Those who intend to go to Hydra should do so with the clear idea that they are not going to see the best of Greece. They are not, indeed, going to see an island typical of Greece. There are other much more beautiful islands—Skiathos and Skopelos in the Northern Sporades, for example, or Crete, or Corfu. Besides these Hydra is an almost treeless, barren rock. There are other places where the Greeks are much more hospitable—again Crete is a notable example—but then Hydriots are of Albanian stock. There are other places where classical treasures abound—Hydra has none—and other places where folk arts are cultivated—Hydra does not bother. Hydra's charm, apart from its architecture, is a subjective one: the traveller either falls in love with it or hates it. Its only factual attractions are its history, the great houses that stand as symbols of that history, and the brooding solemnity of its hills in winter. For some people it is the only island in Greece.

It is certain that Wallis counted himself and his fellow expatriates—the Johnstons, the Gassoumises, Leonard Cohen and Marianne Ihlen and others—amongst those for whom Hydra was "the only island", and yet the essay proceeds without noticeable emotional investment, relating in a workman-like manner details about the island and its ferry culture, including routes, fares, timetables, and on-board catering—pies, sandwiches and confectionary are all for sale! At a time when Hydra had limited electricity and no telephones, the ferries were the most vital connection to the wider world—the same world that expatriates such as Clift and Johnston wished to renounce by settling on the island. But it was the ferries that were bringing *that* world to Hydra in the form of mass tourism.

When Wallis returned to Hydra after nearly two years in London, his first diary entry reported the increased presence of tourists and their impacts, describing an island "full of people, mostly English and French, mostly tourists, students etc, …, lots of tail, lots of marijuana and a certain amount of syphilis". All these people (and their sexual activities) are certainly at odds with images of Greece that the European travel market hawked as part of its

Robyn and Redmond Wallis at the Acropolis, 1961. (Redmond Wallis)

Grand Tour itinerary. For nineteenth-century travellers, Greece was preferably emptied of contemporary buildings, signs or people, while ancient monuments and ruins symbolised the desirable ideal of Greece as some eternal lightly-populated Arcadia. It is a view of Greece that Wallis's own tourist pictures, taken on the Athens Acropolis, seem to playfully acknowledge in the context of mid-twentieth century tourism.

It seems that anyone during this period who left and then returned to Hydra after even a short time noted the rise in visitor numbers. Colin Simpson went to the island in 1962 and then again in July of 1967 and observed undesirable changes that he attributed unambiguously to tourism. Writing after his later visit, Simpson recorded that "Ydra wasn't as tourist thronged in 1962 as it is now", and he found that by 1967, the tiny harbour had turned into a sort of marine parking lot ... The café tables had bred into hundreds of outside cafés that had not been there before. Everybody sitting in them was young and there was a great prevalence of beards and very long hair on girls in sexy gear.

What the Hydriots made of their island increasingly teeming with tourists, particularly younger visitors with exposed flesh and an insatiable appetite for leisure, may be gleaned not only from Clift's writing in *Peel Me a Lotus*, but also from Burke's photographs. Burke was interested in tourism as a phenomenon—he had signalled as much when pitching the story to *LIFE*—and once at work he took many photographs of the 'ordinary' tourists as they disembarked from the ferries in large numbers. They are the sort of images that might have been captured—then and now—in destinations around the globe as incoming tourists spill off ferries, buses and trains and wonder, what happens next? In the case of Hydra, it is a question that has been answered for decades by the short trek along the dockside to reach the shops and restaurants on the *agora*. (Among the hungry visitors to Hydra was Leslie Finer, who, in addition to being unimpressed with the artists' colony, also reported his disappointment with the island's culinary offerings, writing that, "My experiences in Hydra foodwise have not been very happy ... considering the number of guests it receives, [Hydra] seems to import very little of what it lacks"). The absence of luggage in Burke's photos indicates these are day-trippers, perhaps a mix of Athenians and others, making a journey to the two or three islands (usually Hydra, Poros and Aegina) they could visit in the course of a day.

While Burke might have ventured into the field as a detached observer, some of his photographs are far from disinterested. The image he took of a single man on the dockside facing an oncoming tourist crowd is framed in such a way that it sets up a distinct spatial division between the solitary figure and the approaching throng whose collective advance is about to overtake the intervening space. The presence of the lone Hydriot might be read as a form of solitary resistance, a last attempt by an elderly local to stand between his

TOURISM

Tourists disembarking from the *Saronis*.
(James Burke)

Resisting or abetting the tourist onslaught?
(James Burke)

town and the commercialisation that will see it (literally it seems) overrun by tourists. More likely, however, his motive is very different and he is looking to do some business; perhaps touting donkey rides, or a restaurant, or a room for rent—whatever it takes to make some '*dollaria*'. As Del Kolve recalls: "As we got off the boat, we were greeted by housewives holding up signs saying 'Room for rent' in various languages, and rented a room on the spot. It cost, as I recall, about 45 cents for the night".

Certainly, in *Peel Me a Lotus* the Hydriots are represented as pragmatic, adapting their lives to make room for, and profit from, tourism, although not entirely without some expression of concern. In particular, Clift recounts the competitive jousting between two entrepreneurial locals, Creon and Socrates. The former is a one-time sponge baron who retains his influence as the town's notary public and occasional financial 'fixer' for approved expatriates; the latter is a carpenter-turned-estate agent who makes his living by finding cheap property for purchase or rent.

> On Saturdays the *Sirina* lists with the weight of week-ending Athenians, family parties in funny hats and Gay Young Things carrying spear-guns and underwater equipment. The School is packed with artists. Maria is doing a brisk trade in souvenirs. Socrates has abandoned carpentry altogether. He trots up and down the quay in a frenzy of business, losing keys and forgetting appointments and promising impossibilities. Creon has changed into a white suit and white buckskin shoes and sits outside Soteris' coffee-house, brusque, business-like, ready to offer his services as an adviser and interpreter to any foreigner who looks respectable and appears to be in difficulties.

Creon is educated, travelled and speaks English acquired from schooling in Constantinople (Istanbul). He is comfortable in the company of the expatriates and is a regular at their Katsikas gatherings. Whereas Socrates sees every foreigner as simply an opportunity to do business, Creon distinguishes between his "respectable" friends who are on the island to stay and those who are merely tourists with scant regard for the island or its customs.

Lunch at Katsikas. Tourists and one of Hydra's scrofulous cats.
(James Burke)

'That's all right,' says Maria shrewdly. 'But Father's old now and doesn't see that times have changed. The island is coming on. Athenians are buying houses. There are more tourists every year.'

... 'Tourists?' Creon snorts dismissively. 'Bums and perverts, my girl! Bums and perverts! There's not a moral or a penny piece among the lot of them! The island is finished, young woman, and don't let that fool Socrates tell you otherwise.'

Amongst the tourists depicted in Burke's photographs there are no obvious "bums and perverts"—presumably those Clift herself wrote of less pejoratively as "young men in tight pants, and interesting-looking people of uncertain age

Young backpacker couple. (James Burke)

and sex who wear their hair smartly jagged and carry artists' portfolios". The photographs show evidence of a mix of nationalities, and while both young and old are to be seen, the average is seemingly skewed towards middle age, and their activities seem no more perverse than dockside rambling and dining.

Perhaps in order to represent further variety in the tourists, Burke consciously directed his lens towards several younger couples, aware that they represented a different sort of island tourism that supposedly was in keeping with Hydra's beat appeal. Seemingly unbeknown to his subjects, Burke trained his camera on one particular young couple, who apparently represented for the photographer another of tourism's more youthful variegations.

Burke photographed the couple strolling along the dockside; taking in the sights and atmosphere of the *agora*; and then heading towards the ferries prior to departure. Burke's notes record that this photograph depicts a "Beat type tourist couple leaving Hydra after brief stay", but to the modern eye there is nothing notably Beat about their appearance aside from their youth. While this couple is almost certainly not part of the ascendancy of "bums and perverts" predicted by Creon, they are an example of another type of tourist transforming the economic and social future of the Aegean islands. They might now be called 'backpackers', a term that gained currency during the 1960s as hippies and their followers set out for Asia, with Greece a stop on this 'trail'. As the American foreign affairs journalist and social historian Robert D. Kaplan later wrote, "Greece was where you came to lose your inhibitions … a terrain of lust and passion and hallucination. The Greek tourist boom of the early 1960s was a precursor of the drug cult and the sexual revolution." Despite the Junta's efforts to deter these independent, alternative travellers, in the late 1960s enclaves such as Matala on the island of Crete flourished, with caves above a small fishing village becoming a 'hippie-Hydra' and providing for several months a home for another Canadian singer-songwriter, Leonard Cohen's by then former lover Joni Mitchell.

Burke also documented yet another form of incipient tourism that was coming of age on Hydra—leisure boating. Perhaps the most obvious difference between photos taken of Hydra's harbour over the postwar decades was the astonishing growth in the number of leisure craft moored at both the main dock and the mid-harbour breakwater. While *Boy on a Dolphin* might have depicted, and deployed for its plotline, a harbour full of working *caiques*, one of the film's impacts was to attract to the island a very different type of craft and seafarer. As Clift wrote in *Peel Me a Lotus*, "In the little jewel-green scoop of harbour there are yachts at anchor now, sleek, beautiful, expensive toys with tall masts from which droop the still, bright folds of the flags of Italy, of France, of Panama, of the U.S.A." Burke took a series of photographs aboard one of these leisure yachts docked in the harbour. Whereas on the *agora* Burke might have been simply one more photographer among numerous photograph-taking tourists, he must have had an invitation to access these select on-board gatherings that carried a sense of exclusivity, if not glamour.

Edgar and Ann Bronfman (seated at rear), William and Patricia Green (front), Everett Kovler and Dr Herman Tarnower (right). (James Burke)

In his caption notes sent to *LIFE*, Burke bemoaned that he had just missed Elizabeth Taylor's yachting visit and that unfortunately no one so "celebrated" turned up in Hydra Port during his island visit. As it happened, however, the American yachting tourists he photographed, while perhaps not attaining Taylor's global fame, were of more than passing interest and perhaps more typical of the moneyed travellers finding their way to Hydra.

They included Edgar and Ann Bronfman. Edgar Bronfman was a major Canadian-American businessman and philanthropist whose family wealth derived from the Seagram's distilling business, and who later became the influential president of the World Jewish Congress. Ann Bronfman (née Loeb) was a banking heiress with family connections to both American Express and Lehmann Brothers, and who also devoted her life to philanthropy. Also pictured was Bronfman's friend S. William Green and his wife Patricia. Green was a Harvard Law School graduate who would go on to be a seven-term Republican congressman from Manhattan. The Bronfmans and Greens are joined in several photos by Everett Kovler— another distilling company executive who, through his role at Jim Beam, popularised bourbon in Europe in the 1960s and 1970s—and by cardiologist Dr Herman Tarnower, who would achieve a different form of notoriety as the author of the popular 1978 fad diet publication *The Complete Scarsdale Medical Diet plus Dr. Tarnower's Lifetime Keep-Slim Program*. It is an indication of the particular form of tourism recorded in these photos that the group is joined in several by a personal guide, Athens-based Naya Koussoula.

Burke completed his notes accompanying these images by lamenting the fate of other Mediterranean hotspots such as Costa Brava and Capri, "where well-heeled tourists and celebrities not only visit but have virtually taken over from the artists and writers who discovered the places". Burke's prediction seems to join the conversation that Clift started in *Peel Me a Lotus* when she concluded of Hydra, without obvious irony or hint of self-implication, that "This beautiful little port is to suffer the fate of so many beautiful Mediterranean ports 'discovered' by the creative poor. … We are in the process of becoming *chic*".

Many of Burke's photos, whether of day-tripping Athenians, youthful backpackers or the well-heeled yachting types, provide evidence that he was interested in thinking about, and recording, an experience intimately associated with the photographic image. Burke, more than most, was aware of the extent to which the rise of mass tourism was encouraged by the ubiquity of the camera and of travel photography conventions, whereby tourists came not only to *see* but also to embalm (or replace) the moment of seeing with the quasi-permanence of the image, to the point where the photograph became a touristic end in itself.

It is therefore noticeable that Burke repeatedly photographed tourists paused in the act of picture-making. The portable camera technology that heralded the democratisation of photography coincided with the emergence of mass tourism, and the *mise-en-abyme* on which Burke's pictures turn— photographs of tourists taking photographs—indicates an awareness of the

Tourist photographer. (James Burke)

history and effects of his professional medium. Not only does photography have a part to play in drawing tourists to Hydra as a desirable destination, but these photographs also represent the extent to which photography structures how Hydra is 'seen' with, and without, a camera, codifying visual experience beyond what is pictured and the photographer doing the picturing.

Once again it is a subject on which Burke and Clift appear to have been in agreement. In an essay titled 'Getting Away from It All', Clift describes the tourist's desire to "snap the colour slides, buzz off a few feet" as symptomatic of their goal to "wring the island dry of its history, economy, local customs and quaint folklore". Clift also related (and only possibly exaggerated) an encounter with a tourist-photographer:

> I still remember, and still with dazed disbelief, an American gentleman in dazzlingly gay gear, hung about with more cameras, meters, recorders, dilly-bags and gadgets than I have ever seen before, standing on the waterfront of our small Greek island and demanding of the donkey

boys that they bring him a camel instead. It turned out, upon fascinated enquiry, that he had lost a whole page of his tour schedule and confidently believed himself to be in Egypt.

The interplay of cameras featured by Burke also has a part in imagining the expatriate community in the context of the late summer tourism on another occasion that the photographer documented. If Clift was keen to establish the difference between the expatriates and the various strands of tourism in *Peel Me a Lotus*, then Burke's photographs of a donkey ride to Hydra's hilltop monasteries both complicate and confirm that desire for dissimilarity.

Hydra has some half a dozen Orthodox monasteries, of which the two most commonly visited are Profitis Ilias (Prophet Elijah) and Agia Efpraxia. The two monasteries lie close together and are visible from the port, floating high above the town. For tourists with sufficient time, a visit to these monasteries, usually as small groups escorted on donkey-back or mule-back, remains a popular way of seeing something of the island beyond Hydra Port. Burke photographed just such a party as they climbed the rocky paths winding upwards away from the town. In this case the group, in addition to Burke and a small number of attending 'donkey boys' and their boss, consisted of longer-term residents Leonard Cohen and Marianne Ihlen; Redmond and Robyn Wallis; sisters Sue and Maryann Davis; Inge Schneier; and one unidentified man.

In Burke's photographs, those in the small party pass through the upper reaches of Hydra town; gradually ascend ever higher with spectacular views over the town to the Saronic Gulf and the Peloponnese; visit the two monasteries; shop for souvenirs from the nuns at Agia Efpraxia; and then take the return descent on foot. From all appearances, this is simply a typical group of tourists doing what many thousands have done before, and making the most of their island visit. Together the group is not 'playing' at being tourists but rather conventions of tourist photography are being trained on them, as Burke works to get the best shot of his subjects, moving ahead to photograph the advancing party and finding the ideal position from which to picture the ascent against the spectacular Aegean backdrop.

HALF THE PERFECT WORLD

L-R: Marianne Ihlen, Leonard Cohen, Sue Davis, Robyn Wallis, Maryann Davis and Redmond Wallis. (James Burke)

TOURISM

L-R: Sue Davis, unidentified, Leonard Cohen and Marianne Ihlen.
(James Burke)

Sue Davis and Leonard Cohen with unidentified boy.
(James Burke)

L-R: Sue Davis, Robyn Wallis, Maryann Davis, Marianne Ihlen and Leonard Cohen at the Monastery of Profitis Ilias. (James Burke)

It is possible that this trip was contrived for Burke's camera as a way of depicting a typical tourist experience while also capturing the views from the high part of the island. Indeed, this could explain why Johnston and Clift are not present on this occasion. Johnston wrote of just such an outing in *Closer to the Sun*, making very clear that he scorned it as an undertaking strictly for tourists rather than those who, with whatever justification, considered themselves 'islanders'. In Johnston's novel it is Mike Meredith, a visitor to Silenos and brother of expatriate David Meredith, who suggests a donkey ride to "the monastery of the Prophet Elijah", but it is David who has to draw on his local knowledge to "organise the cavalcade". It is evident that David has no interest in joining the party, while his wife Kate declines with the excuse that "it was the day when the mainland market-boats called at Silenos". Clearly the Merediths have no desire to be part of the excursion because they do not see themselves as tourists, but without Kate it "was left to David alone to escort the grotesque column, left to him to meet the startled eyes and gaping mouths of the peasants".

TOURISM

Tourist cavalcade, including Maryann Davis, Sue Davis and Leonard Cohen.
(Redmond Wallis)

Burke was not the only person who carried a camera on that excursion. Redmond Wallis also took a number of photographs as the party wound its way to the hilltop. Unlike Burke's photographs, which place him outside the party as an objective observer, Wallis's images are in keeping with a tourist's experience—they are taken from the back of his donkey and from his place near the rear of the small cavalcade, depicting the rest of the party proceeding before him.

From Wallis's camera we see the excursion as a touristic novelty—in one photo Robyn Wallis and Maryann Davis look back towards the camera, as if

Sue Davis and Robyn Wallis. (Redmond Wallis)

Wallis has called to them to turn so that he can take their picture from his place at the rear. This experience seems therefore not to be an everyday occurrence—as such an experience cannot be for a tourist—and a reminder that for long-term visitors there was still something novel to be found in an event that placed them in the role of 'tourist' that David Meredith so vehemently resisted. In this case, the depiction of the riders as touristic outsiders is highlighted by the constant, controlling presence of the locals, for whom this is an unremarkable event, whether it be the donkey-boys walking alongside—presumably encouraging the donkeys and instructing the riders—or the nuns as they display their tourist wares to potential customers. Viewed together, Burke's and Wallis's photographs suggest just how permeable the categories of 'tourist' and 'expatriate' might be.

When Clift began so early in her time on Hydra to fear the changes that would follow in the wake of *Boy on a Dolphin*, she could not have foreseen other factors that would support that change: the advent of global jet travel; the 1960s explosion of global youth cultures; the ninety-minute hydrofoil shuttle from Piraeus; and the unstoppable momentum placing the Greek islands at the centre of international tourism. She might also have been surprised by her own future reconciliation with the movie industry and Hollywood.

When Hollywood and Warner Bros. came calling once again in 1962 for the filming of Morton DaCosta's *Island of Love* (1963), the whole Johnston family, sensing the opportunity for some '*dollaria*', were signed up as paid extras. It was this need to replenish the family coffers that seems to have induced a change of attitude towards tourism on the part of the Johnstons. At some point, it occurred to them that this unstoppable growth in tourism created another market for their writing. In June of 1961, Clift wrote to publisher David Higham asking if *Peel Me a Lotus* could be brought back into print, in a letter that expressed an enthusiasm for tourism distinctly at odds with the book she was promoting.

> Fabulous things are happening to this island, which by next year may well become one of the most fashionable resorts in the world, and Lotus is the only book about it. I am asked a dozen times a week by tourists where they can buy a copy … It seems crazy that it should be out of print just now, when … the tourist expectation is fabulous for the summer.

When this approach failed, Clift and Johnston set about co-authoring *The Serpent in the Rock*, a Hydra travelogue specifically targeting the tourist trade. Overcoming their distaste for the island's summer visitors, they produced a ninety thousand-word manuscript that was apparently a blend of Hydra history, folklore and personal testimony. In this case, the collaboration even became a family endeavour as Martin was needed to translate various Greek sources as his parents unravelled the island's story. The manuscript for *The Serpent in the Rock* was dispatched to Johnston's New York agent in May 1962, and the couple was hopeful it could be readied for the coming summer. As it turned out, they received little encouragement from agents or publishers on either side of the Atlantic, and the manuscript was eventually withdrawn. Hydra, it seems, was considered too uninteresting or little known in New York and London for the book to be thought saleable.

All copies of *The Serpent in the Rock* appear to be lost. While it might have had little appeal to publishers at the time, it would no doubt make for fascinating reading over half a century later—particularly with regard to any observations the authors might have made about the changing face of their island as it adapted to the realities of postwar affluence, mass-mobility and a growing taste for exotic travel.

* * *

In *The Unyielding Memory*, Redmond Wallis captures the year-on-year growth of island tourism, including the transition from a summer influx to a year-round presence. Wallis also notes how these changes disrupted the social patterns and moral codes of the established foreign colony.

> *That winter, Nick was later to decide, marked the moment at which the island ceased to be a haven for the creative poor and became a playground, mirroring the world beyond. The shadow of change fell over the old foreign colony, alliances were permanently damaged, and as the days shortened and the weather worsened the pace of life failed to abate, as it always had before. New attitudes challenged what had generally been accepted as a basis for civilised behaviour. In the year to come, breaches of that civilised base, if conducted as they had been in the past, would look curiously old fashioned. It was (hindsight was to suggest) not unrealistic to say that the old foreign colony—George and Catherine, Kaycha and Theodoros, Patricia and Stephanos, Paul and Lee, even the Alwyns—were from a*

different age, in agreement about an antiquated set of morals and mores to be as much honoured in the breach as in the observance. As the island's reputation spread (and, his own reputation growing, Saul Rubens contributed, however innocently, to that), so two new strands entered island life: a strand of young, Athenian sophistication, monied, connected, a strand evinced previously only by George Karraridis, an Athenian who, it was said, was related to the Greek royal family, and a strand of young cosmopolitan, eastern-philosophy-studying hippies, none of whom were short of a dollar or two. The first winter they had been in England the island had been, Patricia reported, deserted; the second year she had written to the Alwyns about sensitive, intelligent and educated artists, philosophers, musicians and a few pleasant bums, who played guitar jazz and knew how to twist: this third winter's crop was less extrovert, less musically competent, more inclined to do interesting things in the privacy of their own (rented) homes. Most moved on, but some stayed: just as the winter began, six fresh faces appeared, two American and four Australian.

Chapter Nine

SAILING *STORMIE SEAS*

On Saturday May 13th, 1961, a party of Hydra's expatriates boarded *Stormie Seas*, a two-masted forty-three-tonne schooner, for a three-week journey through the Aegean [See Plate 3]. As Redmond Wallis wrote, it was "a wonderful once-in-a-lifetime trip", with their course "swinging up from the island past Sounion through the Gulf of Euboea and on up to the Northern Sporades and back home via Mytilene and Kos". The costs involved in chartering a yacht such as *Stormie Seas* would usually have been prohibitive; however, an early season lull in demand saw Sam Barclay, the yacht's owner and captain, propose to take them on the cruise for "the price of the fuel and their keep". It was an offer too good to refuse, and one that gave this small and fortunate group the island-hopping experience they often dreamed about. It was also an occasion that played into, and possibly exacerbated, some of the mounting tensions between core members of Hydra's expatriate colony.

Barclay, who lived in the nearby port of Spetses when not sailing the Aegean on *Stormie Seas*, was well known to Hydra's expatriates, and not only because his chartering business often brought him to 'their' island. He was, by any measure, a dashingly romantic and memorable figure ideally suited to his role as a seafaring skipper. In available accounts, Barclay comes across as someone who has just stepped out of a swashbuckling adventure from another time.

A 1958 article by 'Rover' (the *nom de plume* of Athens-based photojournalist Vasso Mingos) in the English-language monthly *Pictures from Greece* established that the thirty-eight-year-old Barclay was the great-grandson of the founder of Barclays Bank, before quickly distancing its subject from the

Stormie Seas in Hydra Port, c.1960. (Redmond Wallis)

office-bound world of metropolitan high finance. "Sam", the article notes approvingly,

> is in his element when he has his hand on the tiller and his bare feet firmly planted on the heaving deck of his schooner. Had he lived during the reign of the first Elizabeth, he might have developed into another Sir Francis Drake or another Sir Walter Raleigh. In our era of nuclear-powered ships, operating a schooner yacht for private charter seems to be the only occupation that fits in with his inclinations.

In *The Unyielding Memory,* Wallis recasts Barclay as Bill Crouch and describes the seafarer in similarly heroic and romantic terms. Perhaps borrowing his imagery from that earlier article, Wallis writes that Crouch "would

Sam Barclay skippers *Stormie Seas*, 1958. (Vasso Mingos)

have made a first-rate Elizabethan pirate. He was more than six feet in height, blond, wiry, burnt brown by the sun." Even if Wallis had not read Mingos's article, his buccaneering characterisation of Barclay was no doubt informed by common knowledge regarding his subject's colourful past.

Barclay's Aegean adventures began in the latter stages of the Second World War when he volunteered for the British-Greek Levant Schooner Flotilla, running traditional but heavily armed *caiques* in support of commando and partisan operations in the German occupied Aegean. Working mainly at night and spending days under heavy camouflage, the Flotilla boasted some dozen *caiques* that were operated by British Royal Navy sailors, Special Forces and Greek volunteers, and charged with causing maximum disruption to Axis operations.

It is likely that Barclay first met Mingos during this period, as they had a shared history in Special Operations circles. Mingos had been recruited by British Intelligence in Alexandria and dispatched to Greece as part of another clandestine operation assisting partisan resistance. The operation was a debacle, and many agents were quickly rounded up by the Germans and imprisoned. According to Mingos's son, Michael, family legend has it that after being sentenced to death, Mingos managed to escape and, with the help of partisans, returned to Egypt by submarine. He later lived in Athens, working as a photojournalist, until his early death in 1962.

Barclay's experience with the Flotilla left him with a great knowledge of the Aegean, and he decided that he "liked the islands, the people, the climate and the ships". It also gave him a plan for his postwar life. With many of the Aegean island trading vessels destroyed, Barclay saw an opportunity. As Mingos wrote:

> War's end found Greece with most of her *caiques* sunk. The few that were left were able to command high freights. This gave Sam Barclay the idea of rigging up a trading ketch, *Bessie*, and going into the freight business. He did a roaring trade with the islands until conditions returned to normal and wartime losses in shipping were made good.

While not mentioned by Mingos, Barclay continued to work in support of British naval operations during the years of the Greek Civil War. Skippering *Bessie* with help from his friend and first mate, Charles Landery, the supposed cargo-carrying activities were effectively a ruse to run supplies and arms from Athens to Salonika (Thessaloniki) as part of the British support for Greek government forces fighting the communist-backed Democratic Army of Greece.

Barclay was aware, however, that gun running and cargo carrying provided a limited future, and began to plan for his Aegean life post-*Bessie*. The answer was in tourism, and Mingos described how Barclay set about designing a vessel to use for sailing the Greek islands for leisure.

> *Stormie Seas* was the ship he acquired after selling *Bessie*. Entirely designed by himself [Barclay], it combined the outwards shape of a Greek *trehandiri* with the underwaterline of a Norwegian *redingskoite* that made it fit to navigate the high seas.

Wallis's diary also gave an account of the building of the forty-eight-foot schooner, noting that *Stormie Seas* was constructed in "1949 to Sam's design in Piraeus". Having gone to the trouble of designing his own vessel, Barclay was not about to stint on the details, using select timbers from the island of Samos—reputed to be Greece's best source—for the hull, and building the deck and hatches from the finest teak salvaged from a wreck in Tobruk.

Mingos's narrative of *Stormie Seas'* construction in *Pictures from Greece* also highlights the romantic gesture of Barclay building his schooner as his courtship with Scottish-Irish Eileen Hay developed. Eileen had travelled widely with her father who worked as a Shell Company engineer, and that experience "gave her girlish charm that aura of romance an adventurous fellow like Sam was bound to fall for". As *Stormie Seas* was being built, Hay's family resided in a neighbourhood overlooking the boat-building yards of Piraeus, and Hay is quoted in *Pictures from Greece* as saying that "By the time she [*Stormie Seas*] was ready to go in the water, I was ready to marry him".

In the meantime, British security operations hadn't lost interest in Barclay and his particular skills, and were intrigued that he was building what looked like a traditional trading *caique* above the waterline, but with a considerably deeper draught and larger storage areas below deck. Barclay later related, in an interview with politician and historian Nicholas Bethell, how with the intervention of MI6 *Stormie Seas* came to be much more than a typical schooner.

> While we were doing this [building *Stormie Seas*], we were approached by the 'firm', who knew about our previous work and knew we were building a boat. We said we had other plans, but we would think about it if we ran out of money … The Greek shipbuilders grossly underestimated the cost of building *Stormie Seas* in order to get the contract.

When it was half done, they announced it was going to cost a lot more. We ran out of money. So we told Pat Whinney [Secret Intelligence Service Chief] that we were on. We went down to Malta under sail and MI6 paid for the installation of a very big engine, the cabins and the rest of the boat.

As Ben Macintyre recounted in his history of postwar British spy operations, under the command of Barclay and his partner John Leatham, *Stormie Seas* was ostensibly a leisure boat, "the sort that rich men charter to take their friends on eastern Mediterranean cruises", and yet "in the saloon below [were] concealed compartments and dummy fuel tanks", and a place where "radio equipment and code-books" were stored. Moreover, *Stormie Seas* boasted "a mighty ninety-horsepower engine … and enough munitions to start a small war".

Between 1949 and 1951, *Stormie Seas* was used—often with Hay and the couple's dog Lean-to on board—to transport and supply an anti-communist guerrilla unit conducting secret operations inside Albania, with the first of these missions proving to be disastrous. As historian Rhodri Jeffreys-Jones relates, on a moonless night in early November 1949 *Stormie Seas* undertook the "first Anglo-American covert operation of the Cold War". Below deck were nine Albanians trained in Malta by MI6 and the US Office of Policy Coordination (a division of the newly formed CIA) and waiting for their opportunity "to step ashore and start an insurgency against the Hoxha regime". What they hadn't counted on was the Albanian army chief, Beira Maluka, getting wind of the plan. Within three hours of disembarking from *Stormie Seas*, three of the men had been killed by waiting troops, and another had disappeared.

Despite this initial misadventure, *Stormie Seas* continued to sail in the service of MI6. However, even with the large engine the schooner was eventually determined not to be fast enough and removed from the sea drops. Barclay, Leatham and *Stormie Seas* were now redirected to execute an extraordinary episode in British propaganda, which involved launching balloons at sea that were designed to shower Albania with 'information' leaflets. As Barclay recalled:

> We used to sit about 20 miles offshore and wait until we got the signal from London that the wind was right … Then we had to weigh out the correct amount of pamphlets … The boys in London presumably imagined thousands of Albanians picking these pamphlets out of the skies, reading them and then preparing themselves for the liberation that was to come by land, sea and air.

Barclay would later claim that "In my view the whole thing was a joke from the beginning".

All this time Barclay was also working on his second interest—sketching and painting. When Charles Landery published an account of their shared adventures aboard *Bessie* in *Whistling for a Wind* in 1952, it was Barclay who provided the illustrations. It was also in 1952 that Barclay was finally able to convert *Stormie Seas* for the task for which she had been intended—carrying wealthy tourists through the Aegean during an annual season from early April until the end of October. Mingos concluded the *Pictures from Greece* article by noting that although *Stormie Seas* had travelled as far afield as France and Spain, her usual beat was the Aegean, where "To islanders she has become a familiar and friendly sight".

Hydra was one of the islands firmly on *Stormie Seas*' Aegean itinerary, and in the course of these visits Barclay befriended George Johnston and Charmian Clift. By this time the Barclays also had on board their son James who Mingos photographed in Hydra for his article. Out of frame, James Barclay would no doubt have played amongst the docked boats and along the cobbled lanes with Martin and Shane Johnston while their parents socialised and the Johnstons brought the Barclays up to speed with the island's goings-on during their seafaring absences. (Over several summers James spent time living with the Johnston family as his parents plied their seasonal trade).

Barclay's involvement with Hydra's expatriates grew when he and Eileen met Axel Jensen and Marianne Ihlen in the early months of 1958 and assisted

James Barclay at Hydra Port, 1958. (Vasso Mingos)

the Norwegians in finding labour needed to repair their newly purchased island house. It was a 'friendship' that would rapidly become more complex. The relationship between Jensen and Ihlen was frequently tempestuous, and on several occasions Jensen left his partner for other women. This was the situation in which Ihlen found herself in early September 1958 when Jensen announced that a new dark-haired companion would be joining them on Hydra. Ihlen responded by dyeing her own hair dark, but when this ploy did nothing to deter her errant partner she fled for some time alone in Athens.

It was while in Athens that Ihlen had a chance encounter with Eileen Barclay who immediately regaled her with a story and a problem. The story was that she had taken a "fantastic new lover"; the problem was that she was committed to an upcoming six-week voyage cooking and cleaning aboard *Stormie Seas*. In the same month that *Pictures from Greece* was extolling the Barclays' idyllically romantic on-board lifestyle, Eileen was explaining to

Ihlen that not only did she have a new man but also that she "was tired of life in a primitive Greek house in the winter and drifting on the waves like a vagabond in summer". In order to have time with her lover while Sam was safely out of the way, Eileen pleaded with Ihlen to take her place on the trip that was to sail from Piraeus and then along the Turkish coast. For Ihlen the invitation was "like a gift from the gods", and the next morning she found herself setting out aboard *Stormie Seas* as help-mate to Barclay—a role that also included caring for young James.

Ihlen would later recall her voyage with Barclay aboard the *Stormie Seas* to her biographer, Kari Hesthamar, as a sun-blessed and star-dappled respite from her troubled relationship with Jensen.

> Along the side of the schooner hung baskets of live lobsters. There were big English brunches and late dinners in small whitewashed towns. The stars above gave the endless Greek night sky a pale glow. The sky was three-dimensional: beyond the stars there were other stars, and beyond those yet more stars. They sailed along the coast of Turkey, heard wolves howling under the full moon and wandered among the colonnades of ancient temples in the company of lumbering tortoises.

Not surprisingly, the two rejected and lovelorn sailors found themselves seeking solace in the course of this trip, and Ihlen and Barclay became lovers, with Hesthamar relating that "Marianne's encounter with Sam was fleeting and without strings". Almost immediately after the voyage was completed Ihlen returned to Jensen—the dark-haired lover having quickly drifted out of his life—and the couple were married in Athens in late October 1958.

This was not the end of the contact between Ihlen and Barclay. The newly wedded Ihlen and Jensen found themselves in need of an income, and, with Marianne's recently acquired skills as a ship-hand, the couple (along with regular deckhand Mitso) were signed on by Barclay in the early months of the 1959 season. It was an experience Barclay related affectionately in an undated postcard (almost certainly from March 1959) he sent to the Johnstons from their former island home of Kalymnos.

Sam Barclay and Marianne Ihlen aboard *Stormie Seas*, 1958.
(Ihlen Collection)

George, Charmian, Martin, Shane & Jason JOHNSTONE
HYDRA
GREECE

I feel terrible not having written before this but now we are in Callimnos I cannot delay any longer. All the sponge caiques are frantically fitting out, great bustle and stir and a mass of gay colours, every now & then a sad little drab one that is not going with the others, sails in tatters and weed on the bottom. So far everything has gone wonderfully on the trip. The weather has been nearly perfect. We have been by Sunion, Khalkis, Stylis (Thermopolae), Skyathos, Skopolos, Skyros (delayed two days by weather), Samos, Kusadasi (Turkey), Bodrum, Kos and now here. We have eaten like fighting cocks on this trip and Marianne's cooking has been terrific, all with no apparent effort at all. Axel works like a black, mostly in the cabins, which are now polished & shining so that you can see your reflection almost everywhere you look, on the floors, door knobs, everywhere. Axel and Mitso get on very well. Axel gives Mitso cigarettes and Mitso bosses Axel around which makes him feel like a bosun and so everyone is pleased. Mitso is very slow with the sails and Axel is very quick. Mitso steers a straight course whatever the weather, Axel can only just see the compass so everything evens itself out. It has been blowing strong from the west these last two days which is dead on our nose so we have been delayed in Kos. Bobby Bevan was getting very red and impatient, he is a business tycoon but a nice tycoon, and the situation was only saved by Marianne's cooking. He is very fond of eating. And of drinking. The number of demijohns that we have emptied since leaving Piraeus is terrific. I hope, if all goes well and we are not delayed again by the weather, that we may be able to look in briefly at Hydra on the 5th [of April] or thereabouts. I do hope that all goes well at Hydra and wish we could be with you for Easter. I have never known far enough ahead where we were going to ask you to forward mail. Please hang on to it now until we come. We saw Grace & Becky in Kos. They were well and quite enjoying life. Lots of love to you all from all of us. Sam, Axel & Marianne

The 'Bobby Bevan' referred to by Barclay was almost certainly wealthy businessman and sailor Robert 'Bobby' Bevan, a major figure in mid-century UK communications and advertising. Bevan shared a pedigree with Barclay in that the Bevan family had been amongst the original owners of what became Barclay's Bank, which during the eighteenth century had traded as Barclay, Bevan and Bening.

Its casual racism notwithstanding, Barclay's postcard suggests an intimacy between those aboard *Stormie Seas* and the Johnston family stationed on Hydra. That closeness would play out in various ways over the ensuing years. One tangible outcome of the 1959 voyage was that Jensen and Ihlen conceived a child aboard *Stormie Seas*, and the following year Sam Barclay would become the child's godfather. Barclay meanwhile maintained his affection for Ihlen and, following the breakdown of his marriage to Eileen, he eventually proposed to Ihlen in early 1961, by which time her own marriage to Jensen was also over. Ihlen gently rejected the offer as she had now established her relationship with Leonard Cohen.

The friendship between Johnston and Barclay was also borne out in 1962 when Johnston, writing as Shane Martin, dedicated *A Wake for Mourning*, the last of his Professor Challis detective novels, to "the other SAM and the *Stormie Seas*". *A Wake for Mourning* takes place on a charter boat captained by Sam Brewster, and the "other Sam" was of course Sam Barclay, whose romantic entanglement with his former ship-hand was common knowledge. The plot of *A Wake for Mourning* turns on a sea journey undertaken by a bunch of New York gangsters ostensibly accompanying the ashes of their fellow gangster Giuseppe Simione, who has been twice-murdered (all is explained by a case of stolen identity and an empty funeral urn), to their resting place on the fictional Aegean island of Kastókos.

Supplementing this melodramatic narrative is Sam Brewster's desire for crew-member Josephine Portland. Portland, bored of being in Rome "with a crazy bunch of my brilliant exiled compatriots who don't know whether they belong to the lost generation of Scott Fitzgerald or the lost generation of Irwin Shaw", had known Brewster only three days, but she accepts, as did Ihlen, the offer to work on the boat as a cook and factotum to the main gangster. Brewster's passion for Josephine is barely repressed throughout the novel, until a life-threatening gun battle confirms their mutual desire: "His fingers fell in a tight grip on her shoulders, and then he lifted her, and held her tightly as she clutched him, sobbing. 'Oh Sam!' she breathed. 'Oh Sam, darling!'" In the world of the novel's narrative, establishing this union restores a sense of order that the boat trip has put into disarray, with Challis telling Sam, "You lose more than half your charter money. But you *do* get Josephine. So you're way ahead". Extending beyond the pages of the text, this dubious commodification of the main female character in the name of romantic love might be read as a compensatory fantasy for Barclay, and another instance of Johnston lifting a story from the life of those around him and placing it in fictional service.

According to Wallis's diary, planning for an Aegean trip commenced in January of 1961 when Clift and Johnston were in England. At the time, Wallis and his wife, Robyn, were contemplating moving on to London themselves, until Demetri and Carolyn Gassoumis persuaded them to stay. They offered to lend the Wallises money and enticed the couple with the idea of a voyage around the Aegean on a *caique* they were considering buying. Wallis's diary entry described the projected passenger list as "C[arolyn] & D[emetri], Fidel [Caliesch], us [Redmond and Robyn Wallis], Carolyn's brother Jim [Gibbons] and wife Beverly, Stu Barnes, and Carol, his wife". Cohen and Ihlen were away from Hydra at this time, having departed for Oslo the previous October. Cohen would then spend the early part of 1961 on a very different island, Cuba, where he went to witness first-hand the impact of the Castro revolution and was briefly arrested after finding himself in Havana at the time of the Bay of Pigs 'invasion'. He and Ihlen would not return to Hydra until August 1961.

Wallis, always on the lookout for income, also recorded his hope that the yachting adventure would provide an opportunity for some travel writing and photographs that could be sold to "American glossies". He also added, with somewhat salacious anticipation, that it "Could be really fascinating if the Johnstons come back, because they've always wanted to do this and I don't think they'd be invited—and Carolyn recently refused George a loan. They'd hate our guts." Given Johnston's well-known love of boats and boating, and his established friendship with Barclay, Wallis's dramatisation of the Graysons' exclusion from the proposed voyage in *The Unyielding Memory* takes on a personal and even malicious edge:

> 'Can you imagine being stuck with George and Catherine on a boat for three weeks?' asked Stephanos.
>
> 'They've always wanted to do that,' said Sue. 'Sail around the Aegean, stopping wherever they felt like. They're going to be very upset.'
>
> 'Not as upset as I would be if they came,' said Stephanos.
>
> 'Maybe they'll stay in England for a while,' said [Patricia]. 'Maybe they'll just not be around.'
>
> 'They won't stay in England for four months,' said Stephanos.
>
> The Graysons had been offered a cottage in the English countryside by a gentle upper-class lady who had bought a house on the island and thought they might need a break.

'No,' said Nick. 'Oh, well, just have to put up with it if they get annoyed.'

Clift and Johnston did return to Hydra in mid-April, a month before the party set off, but their response to the news that a group of fellow expats was sailing off around the Aegean aboard *Stormie Seas* is unknown. Having only so recently returned to the island, they were likely preoccupied with resettling themselves and their children, and perhaps they were more interested to learn at the end of April that Johnston's novel *Closer to the Sun* had been sold to the American Literary Guild selection and would see him get a half share of the $25,000 advance. There is more than a shade of *schadenfreude* when Wallis records in his diary news of the advance and adds, a little too gleefully, that the book had received "lousy reviews in England".

At some point the proposal for the Gassoumises to purchase a *caique* fell through, or was at least replaced by Barclay's offer of a cruise on *Stormie Seas*. Barclay would set the course for the trip, thereby giving him an opportunity to visit destinations away from the more well-known islands favoured by those who usually hired his services. In addition to Barclay and three crew members (including Mitso), the party consisted of those identified in January: the Wallises, Gassoumises, Fidel Caliesch, Jim and Beverley Gibbons, and Stu and Carol Barnes (about whom little is known). With thirteen aboard, *Stormie Seas* exceeded her usual capacity, and the crew and the Wallises made room by sleeping on deck.

Wallis's plan for the trip to serve as the basis of a saleable travel story was soon discarded, overtaken by "the sheer pleasure of the experience", and his diary went largely dry during this period. The only account of the trip is that which he left in *The Unyielding Memory*, although typically the description of the journey reads like a form of diary transcription, revealing the bare facts of the itinerary but quite devoid of personal or emotional engagement. Nevertheless, it effectively suggests the gallivanting pace as they encountered the people, places and legends of the Aegean.

They sailed on to Chalkis, and then on a loop that took them up via Edipsos through the Northern Sporades and back through the Dodecanese. The islands' names rolled off Nick's tongue: Skiathos, Skopelos—so beautiful they began to talk of buying houses—to Iliodhromi or Alonissos, which simply meant 'another island.' From the cove where they anchored, which contained nothing beyond a white shack, they climbed up to the village on the crest. It was supposed to have a population of 1,700 but did not look like it. They received a very warm welcome … Women were thrashing grain with a mule on a round oval patch of ground, the only flat piece of land anywhere. They ate lobster cooked on the beach. They had intended to visit Mount Athos before Alionissos, but the *meltami* had forced them to shelter: it was still blowing: Bill got Nick up at 2:30am to help him move the boat; he got back to bed half an hour later, but at 6am Bill got him up again: the *Delfini* went lee rail under at times. They put into a place called Kuphos and spent the day on make and mend. Two days later, the weather better, they sailed past Mount Althos and stopped to climb up Dochyaria. The monks gave them ouzo and spoons of sweet jam in glasses of water and Nick drank from a well that did miracles. There was also a miraculous icon, which Mitsou kissed. By the beginning of the third week in May they were at Plati where the women went ashore, breaking the rule that no female beings were allowed on Athos. They visited Vatipedou, after some fuss with a policeman and a customs officer, who thought they should have permits. Nick saw the sign of the yin and the yang on the wall: it came from Byzantium and had no special significance for the monks. Here there was a cup—the cup of Michael Paleologus—which was alleged to neutralise poisons. It was cut from a block of jasper the dark green stone streaked with red, flecks of gold, its handles dragons.

Thassos, Limnos, Lesvos, in Mtilene Nick bought a knife with a catch of song engraved on its blade—and on to Chios…

Andros, Kea, Zea, Mitsou's home island. At Andros they were anchored in a quiet bay when a vast white motor cruise came in. Two radar-equipped patrol boats and a speedboat were lowered over the side and while the patrol boats headed out to sea, to look for fish, the speedboat screamed across the water to them. The sailors told them the cruiser was owned by Kyrio Goulandris, and gave them some red mullet. Everyone was deeply offended by the presence in their quiet, deserted, beautiful bay of this piece of conspicuous consumption, but fortunately it motored out again after an hour or so. Nick, Sue and Henry slept ashore on the beach in their sleeping bags. They got back to the island on June 3.

In contrast to the sequential cataloguing of the voyage that Wallis provides in *The Unyielding Memory*, his photographs from the trip convey the sense of relaxation and camaraderie the voyage must have involved. Of those photographs, several are taken from the bowsprit and depict the languid art of sailing in smooth seas. The broad deck of *Stormie Seas* serves as a generous space on which to take in the sun, with the schooner's 'crew' engaged in easeful relaxation and conversation.

Other photographs taken by Wallis on the trip are portrait shots that suggest the amiable relationships between the photographer and his subjects as they enjoy the early summer weather. Insofar as *The Unyielding Memory* touches upon the more personal aspects of the trip, it is with regard to a matter that would occupy Wallis considerably for several years to come—his (Nick Alwyn's) mounting desire for Beverley Gibbons (Cindy) who he describes as "undeniably beautiful, a hazel-eyed brunette with a pert mouth, a swift-tongue to go with it, and a good figure". Perhaps more to the point, he discerns that there is little to connect Cindy to her academic husband, and that "Nick got the impression Cindy's idea of activity might have focused on men". Wallis captured portraits of both Beverley and Jim Gibbons relaxing alongside *Stormie Seas*' rigging, and of his good friend Demetri Gassoumis as he emerges from below decks into the full Aegean sunshine.

Carol Barnes, Sam Barclay, Fidel Caliesch and others, *Stormie Seas*, 1961.
(Redmond Wallis)

Stu Barnes (standing), Demetri Gassoumis and Fidel Caliesch, *Stormie Seas*, 1961.
(Redmond Wallis)

Stormie Seas, 1961.
(Redmond Wallis)

Beverley Gibbons, *Stormie Seas*, 1961.
(Redmond Wallis)

Jim Gibbons, *Stormie Seas*, 1961.
(Redmond Wallis)

Demetri Gassoumis, *Stormie Seas*, 1961.
(Redmond Wallis)

Sam Barclay, *Stormie Seas*, 1961.
(Redmond Wallis)

Almost certainly the most arresting portrait that Wallis captured aboard *Stormie Seas* is of its skipper, Sam Barclay. Looking at this image nearly six decades later, it is easy to imagine Wallis seeing Barclay in exactly the romantic mode his adventurous history invites—the photograph is less a portrait of the man than it is an expression of his personal legend. Barclay's face is placed in the centre third of the shot, with the roping and other equipment enough to signal the nautical context and serve as a reminder of his wartime heroics. The low camera angle emphasises his stature, framing his profile and horizon-scanning gaze against the open sky. The viewer's gaze, on the other hand, is directed upward, in admiration of the subject with his look of dreamy determination. There is no doubt this is a yachtsman's yachtsman.

More than innocent snaps of a fun holiday, Wallis's photos also speak to the tensions on Hydra between the island's expatriates, and the absences are as significant as those whose presence was recorded by the camera. That Fidel

Caliesch, for example, is pictured and was invited aboard the *Stormie Seas* adventure, when Clift and Johnston pointedly were not, underscores existing allegiances and antagonisms. Caliesch, an American artist (and art dealer), seems to have had a major falling out with Johnston. Wallis records in his diary for the previous year that Johnston had labelled Caliesch a "sycophantic little tale-bearing shit" for apparently shooting "his mouth off about George to Chuck [Hulse] and Gordon [Merrick]". What he allegedly said is unknown. For his part, Caliesch wrote to Wallis on January 22nd, 1963, when he was in San Francisco and the Wallises were in London. His letter gossips about the whereabouts and behaviours of Hydra friends and acquaintances, including the Gassoumises, and praises Wallis on the publication of *Point of Origin*, singling out the dust jacket as being "more handsome than any Charm, George or Axel ever got" [See Plates 12–15].

In turn, in a comic short story written in the early 1960s, 'Vale, Pollini!', Johnston gave the suspiciously familiar-sounding name of Carol Caliesch to a self-professed philosopher (he distributes a business card made out with that moniker) who turns up on Hydra and thoroughly falls for the expatriates' efforts to expose his intellectual pretensions. Even when physically apart, the rivalries and friendships that shaped their lives on Hydra, and which the voyage on *Stormie Seas* intensified, continued to play out.

Although Wallis's plans to write a travel narrative based on the *Stormie Seas* adventure were scuttled, he also considered writing a novel set on Barclay's boat. While aboard *Stormie Seas*, Wallis made only one diary entry, for May 28th, in which he jotted down ideas for a thriller, a "locked room killing" that depended on the schooner's beneath-deck layout. In these notes, Wallis collated facts about *Stormie Seas* and included rough sketches of the craft.

For the plot Wallis hit on the unlikely idea that the yacht's lavatory was the ideal setting for either a deadly bomb explosion or for lethal poison to be injected through a ventilator, presumably as the intended victim went unsuspectingly about their ablutions. Wallis did express doubts about how

Robyn Wallis and Fidel Caliesch, c.1960.
(Redmond Wallis)

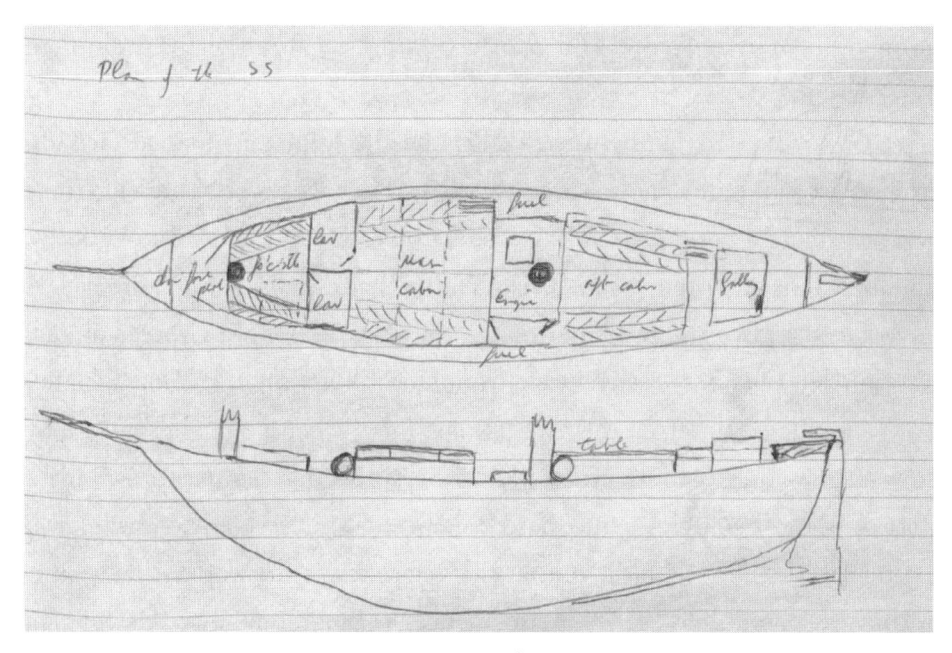

'Plan of the SS', 28th May, 1961.
(Redmond Wallis)

this locked room set-up would target the "right victim". In attempting to resolve this problem, he considered fudging the dimensions of the lavatory's air duct, which would otherwise prove "too small to take DDT bomb", as though stretching the truth of this detail would somehow unravel the thriller's otherwise unimpeachable claims to verisimilitude. It is unsurprising that Wallis's planned thriller never progressed beyond this diary entry.

Arriving back at Hydra on June 3rd, *Stormie Seas*' party was home in time to intersect with a much more high-profile yachting tourist, Jacqueline Kennedy. The US First Lady and her entourage arrived on Hydra on the morning of June 9th as part of a heavily publicised tour of several islands. She spent the day at the port where she was welcomed with ringing church bells, a small festival and a clamour of school children and local dignitaries. She was said to be impressed, and announced she would love to return with her children. The next morning, Kennedy moved on to Mykonos, where the press contingent included James Burke, who took numerous photographs of the glamorous visitor with one of the island's most famous citizens, Petros the Pelican. Kennedy's Aegean tour was another milestone in the rapidly growing profile of Hydra as a choice destination for socially prominent internationalists.

The growing tension between Wallis and the Johnstons that surfaced in Wallis's account of the *Stormie Seas*' voyage had not always been present. There are records of a previous sea-based adventure, in 1960, when the Wallises, the Johnstons and others were consolidating their bonds. Among the papers in Wallis's archive is a program for the National Theatre of Greece's annual Epidaurus (Epidavros) Festival, held from June 19th to July 10th, 1960, together with an undated ticket for the play *Hecuba*. Ihlen recounted in her biography how the Hydra expatriate group had all been reading *Hecuba* (indicating a sort of island book club with shared intellectual interests), and that she in particular identified with the central character's tragic story. At Ihlen's urging, a trip was planned to see the performance, as biographer Kari Hesthamar, relying on Ihlen's recall, would later relate:

Gordon Merrick (white shirt) escorts Jackie Kennedy, 1961. (Merrick Collection)

The friends decided to visit the amphitheatre at Epidavros to see the drama performed in Greek. Beside Marianne and Leonard there were George and Charmian and their children, the American author Gordon Merrick and his partner Chuck Hulse, and the Swedish woman Lena Folke-Olsen, who would later have two children with Axel Jensen. None of them had much money, but they scraped together enough to hire a traditional caique to take them to Napflio in the northeast Peloponnese.

Ihlen was familiar from her travels aboard *Stormie Seas* with other classical theatres in the region, but she found that, at over two millennia old and capable of holding fifteen thousand spectators, "Epidavros exceeded everything". As, so it seems, did the experience.

> The night was velvety warm. Marianne sat close to Leonard. Enveloped by the dark she heard Hecuba whisper to her and the hovering white figures who sang directly to her heart. Marianne didn't feel the effects of sitting on cold stone until the performance was over several hours

Picnic, 1960. (Redmond Wallis)

later. The little group tumbled out into the night with the rest of the audience, and rode in the taxi back to the blue and white caique that awaited them in the harbour at Napflio. They unpacked food and wine from their woven baskets. Ate and drank under the stars while the night became morning and then sleep overtook them.

No mention is made in Ihlen's account of the presence of the Wallises, but Wallis's diary entry for July 15th reports that he and Robyn attended a performance of the play—although in stark comparison to Ihlen's romantic account of the occasion, Wallis describes a performance that was "ruined for me by spending the entire performance looking for Robyn, who had got the trots, in the ladies". Wallis's photographs offer what can only be a visual record of the *caique* excursion to Epidaurus and the picnic that Ihlen recalled so vividly.

Wallis's photograph of the picnic finds him momentarily playing the role of a still-life artist. The careful tiering of the food and the neat crossing of the forks suggests a purposeful arrangement by those fingers waiting at the photograph's margins, as does the pleasing scatter of the eggs amongst the darker vegetables and fruits. Indeed, the very presence of the photograph suggests that this was no ordinary meal. Wallis was not in the habit of shooting food scenes, and that he took the image marks out this picnic as something special, both for the photographer and likely those kneeling at the picture's edges.

All of Wallis's other available photographs from this trip are taken on the *caique*. These are happy holiday memories that the personal camera records, something acknowledged in a group photograph by the bearded Cohen's tilt into the frame, responding perhaps to a request from the photographer to hurry up and get into the shot.

In these photographs, the tight space provided by the *caique*'s bow establishes the composition's confined parameters, which in turn creates a sense of shared (if cramped) on-board *joie de vivre*. The open smiles and relaxed postures communicate the excitement that this short trip must have provoked, both for the reason for their going and for the rare opportunity to escape the confinement of their island home.

In another picture from the same excursion, a guitar-playing Cohen is placed squarely in the centre of the shot and is also seemingly the centre of attention, as attested by the momentarily neglected pamphlet and half-raised mug in the foreground. In *The Unyielding Memory*, Nick Alwyn declares Cohen to be "as revolutionary as the songs he sang"; and Mungo MacCallum recalled, "In those days Cohen sang mainly union songs—Old Paint, the horse with the union label, was a specialty". If only photographs could sing.

While most other photographs taken on that voyage picture the passengers in varying combinations as a group at play, another distinctive image features Johnston and Clift at rest, being observed by Gordon Merrick. Sailing on a tranquil sea beneath a casually erected shelter, Clift lies in full repose amongst scattered rugs, as does Martin Johnston, asleep alongside his parents. Johnston

From bottom centre (clockwise): Robyn Wallis, Marianne Ihlen, Lena Folke-Olsson, Leonard Cohen, Gordon Merrick, Shane Johnston, Martin Johnston, Sandro Tilche, Redmond Wallis and Magda Tilche, 1960. (Redmond Wallis)

(L-R): Leonard Cohen, Lena Folke-Olsson, Charmian Clift, George Johnston, Gordon Merrick, Marianne Ihlen, Magda Tilche, Robyn Wallis, Theodoros Anargirou, Shane Johnston, Sandro Tilche, Martin Johnston and Redmond Wallis, 1960. (Redmond Wallis)

Leonard Cohen, 1960. (Redmond Wallis)

Gordon Merrick, Charmian Clift, George Johnston and Martin Johnston, 1960.
(Redmond Wallis)

has put aside a book and gazes lazily out to sea. For Clift and Johnston, the trip would have been a significant event, for as much as they loved Hydra, it conspicuously lacked those great monuments of classical Greece such as Epidaurus to which they were so attracted. Being in the Aegean gave them much that they needed, but *sailing* the Aegean—even briefly—must have hinted at so much more.

Reading this picture more closely, it becomes apparent that the canopy, in addition to providing shade, serves to identify and sequester Clift and Johnson as a couple and, with Martin, as a family. Merrick is posed awkwardly, sheepishly even, and is seen to be entering or even intruding on the space the Johnstons claim with their relaxed, trusting poses. The sense that both Merrick and the photographer are trespassing is underwritten by Clift's closed eyes, which contrast with the reciprocal gazes of Merrick and the photographer positioned at the borders of the shot. Yet, for all their looking, it is likely that neither Merrick nor the photographer notes Clift's hand gently holding her husband's near-hidden foot, a gesture that comes to us now weighted with the knowledge that months before, while Johnston was in Athens receiving treatment for tuberculosis, Clift was having an affair on Hydra with American Chip Chadwick, a transgression that would severely strain their marriage.

Merrick was also a keen sailor. Thanks to the ongoing income generated by his best-selling 1947 novel *The Strumpet Wind*, Merrick owned, with Charles Hulse, a small yacht, also named *The Strumpet Wind*, on which they entertained friends such as Cohen and Ihlen.

Among the novels Merrick wrote on Hydra was a trilogy, released by romance publishing house Avon and sold in US supermarkets. It focused without disguise on the relationship between two men, Charlie Mills (a painter) and Peter Martin (an art dealer). The second novel in the trilogy published in 1971, *One for the Gods*, has Charlie and Peter charter a boat, *Cassandra*, with an unhappily married couple, the Kingsleys. This small group cruises the Greek isles, the experience of being at sea prompting in Charlie moments of extended reverie "on a flat and lazy sea".

Marianne Ihlen, Gordon Merrick and Leonard Cohen on board *The Strumpet Wind*, mid-1960s. (Merrick Collection)

Charlie studied the land around them, but couldn't make heads or tails of it. There were islands everywhere and hazy promontories and landmasses that were part of the mainland. ... They drifted while Charlie reduced his vision of the past to its real visible scale. Here, great empires had risen and fallen, navies had clashed, armies had marched, momentous moments that in Charlie's mind required huge canvases to reenact had all taken place within spitting distance of each other.

The photograph featuring Merrick with Clift and Johnston on board the *caique* is languorous by comparison to the action that takes place on *Cassandra*. The men's sailing experience sees them involved in various sexual encounters that extend beyond, and threaten, their relationship. An eventual reconciliation occurs on Hydra after a chivalrous fistfight: "Charlie was hurting before he realized that Peter was in earnest. He fought back, smashing his fists into the hard body. He was careful not to land any punches near his eyes or mouth", until their "mouths met and they kissed at length, holding each other in spite of their drained and aching bodies. Their mouths parted and Peter laughed. 'How D.H. Lawrence can we get?'" For Charlie, the fight awakens a clear acknowledgment of his queer desire—"I am in love with a man"—and the (re-)union between Peter and Charlie is consolidated by both men's names being placed on a housing lease, a contractual, place-specific domestic arrangement resolutely at odds with the undisciplined desires their sea-faring has unleashed.

Inevitably for an island-dwelling boat lover, George Johnston was another who dreamed of a yacht of his own. Clift registered her husband's intense interest in boats in *Peel Me A Lotus* in the context of noting Hydra's many boats that are found "In the sheds and basements, in lanes and doorways, there are little boats lying upside down or on their sides in every state of repair". Clift writes of coming across George,

> squatting beside an upturned hull and can of hot tar. A wrinkled ancient stands by with a tolerant smile, watching George caulk seams. On George's face is an expression of infinite love.
>
> 'When the royalties come in,' he says, 'we'll buy a boat of our own'.
>
> But he spits three times carefully and crosses his fingers.

Johnston almost certainly had in mind a small yacht, but the royalties were never so generous. Instead, in 1957 he managed to purchase a fishing dinghy. According to Nadia Wheatley, Clift christened the vessel *The Slithey Tove*, and it allowed the family "to explore little coves away from the busy tourist trap of the swimming hole near the town". It might not have been exactly the craft Johnston wished for, but it was only one of many occasions in which his Aegean dreams fell short of reality.

There is no record of what became of *The Slithey Tove*, but *Stormie Seas* had a distinguished third life after her days in the service of MI6 and Aegean tourism were over. In 1967 Sam Barclay returned to the UK after selling his

Shane Johnston at the oars of *The Slithey Tove* (?), n.d. (Johnston and Clift Collection)

beloved schooner to pioneering marine archaeologist Peter Throckmorton, a man whose credentials as a swashbuckler equalled those of Barclay himself. *Stormie Seas* retained her name under Throckmorton's ownership and plied the Aegean as a wreck-hunter, often with James Barclay helping to crew the yacht that as a child had been his summer home. *Stormie Seas* was an integral part in several of Throckmorton's most exciting discoveries—including in August 1975 when he discovered the so-called Dokos Wreck just off the coast of Hydra. Having been dated to c.2200 BC, the Dokos Wreck remains the oldest marine wreck yet found, and Throckmorton's momentous discovery forged a final link between Sam Barclay's distinctive schooner and the island that he knew so well. It also triggered events that would eventually lead to *Stormie Seas*' next phase of life, well removed from the Aegean waters she had graced for quarter of a century. Throckmorton, disgusted by the Greek authorities' failure to protect the Dokos Wreck from looting, abandoned Greece in 1976 and chose instead to take the *Stormie Seas* wreck-hunting in the Caribbean.

HALF THE PERFECT WORLD

* * *

Yachts, it seems, were never far from George Johnston's mind. In this passage from *The Unyielding Memory*, Redmond Wallis recounts an argument on the subject between Johnston and Mungo MacCallum. This is one of a number of passages in the manuscript where Wallis was yet to replace characters' 'real' names with those of their fictional counterparts.

> *Last night Demetri and Carolyn, Robyn and I went down to the port and sat with George, Charmian and Chuck. There was an air of hostility. The big yachts were running for shelter into the harbour, heeling over outside the breakwater as they manoeuvred to get inside. Mungo and Gordon came back to their seats and there followed a big discussion of the definition of 'yacht'. George protesting to Mungo, thirty years his junior, that 'yachts' was used in Australia for everything from twelve or so feet upwards. Mungo, denying this, said 'yacht' was the only one-syllable in the English language for this sort of thing and when Mungo asked him rhetorically how many one-syllable definitions there were in the English language George said 'Fuck, shit, food' and seemed to consider his point proved. There was a pause while the conversation went on without him and then, for some reason, he looked George straight in the eye and said 'I have the National Geographic book at home called "Men, Ships and the Sea", which lays these things down very firmly. And so it should.'*

Chapter Ten

DEMETRI'S POOL

In October 1963 Bob Dylan recorded his anthem for a generational revolution, 'The Times They Are a-Changin'', calling upon people, "Wherever you roam / And admit that the waters / Around you have grown". Certainly the times were changing on Hydra in October 1963, and much of the debate about this change concerned the town's waters, where someone had managed to grow their share for a reason entirely new to the island—filling a swimming pool.

As is often the case when rapid change is afoot, community concern becomes focused on a single, representative issue. On Hydra that issue arose when Demetri Gassoumis decided to build a swimming pool. For an island with constant problems supplying sufficient clean water, this was an audacious and even provocative act. It was even more contentious because of who Gassoumis was and the singular status he enjoyed on the island.

Demetri's father, Kleomenus (Mike) Gassoumis, had been raised in a village in central Greece before leaving to seek better opportunities in the US, where he arrived in time to join the armed forces in World War One. He eventually returned to Greece, as so many first-generation immigrants did, in search of a wife. He met Demetri's mother, who was from an established Hydriot family. The couple married on Hydra, before Gassoumis took his wife back to the Bay Area of San Francisco, where Demetri was born in 1933.

After a preliminary trip to Hydra in 1959, Demetri reversed his parents' migration by moving to the island the following year with his wife, Carolyn, and their baby daughter, Athena. Having recently graduated from the California College of Arts and Crafts in Oakland, Gassoumis was looking to earn his living as an artist, and he came to Hydra, by island standards, a wealthy man. Demetri had married well in that Carolyn was from a well-to-do family as a result of her father's successful career in medicine. She also came into her inheritance early when her parents were killed in an air crash (likely the result of an on-board bomb) over the Gulf of Mexico in November 1959. Carolyn had already been suspicious of the easy wealth of her upper middle-class Californian upbringing, and the tragic and possibly murderous death of her parents only cemented her willingness to embrace an Aegean lifestyle as a form of 'dropping out'. Demetri, on the other hand, was any nation's ideal second-generation immigrant: thankful for every convenience or luxury that his family's adopted country had to offer and confident they were a gift to be shared with the world. Gassoumis was a reflection of the Greeks who Henry Miller scorned in *The Colossus of Maroussi*: those who (in Miller's somewhat prejudicial assessment) gave up the natural dignity, pride and insouciance of a Greek peasant life in exchange for the wealth and ease of America, only to return to Greece and pass their time deriding their former countrymen for their poverty and ignorance.

On arriving on Hydra in the summer of 1960, the Gassoumises were immediately welcomed into the expatriate community. Demetri was a passionate young man, full of ideas and enthusiasm and with a great talent for the social currency of the Hydra colony—talking. The newly arrived couple was supported by George Johnston and Charmian Clift, and quickly became an integral part of the expatriates' daily gatherings on the *agora*. The Gassoumises particularly befriended Redmond and Robyn Wallis, fellow newcomers of similar age and related interests, and they would eventually find their way into Wallis's *The Unyielding Memory* as Stephanos and Patricia Lamounis. *The Unyielding Memory* introduced the Lamounises with a snapshot portrait that explains that what attracted Stephanos to Patricia was her teenage embodiment of American glamour and success, while Patricia was intrigued by Stephanos's cultural hybridity exemplified by his exotic adoption of 1950s American youth style.

Demetri Gassoumis, n.d. (Redmond Wallis)

[Patricia] was tall and slim and her features had been shaped by the country whose philosophy she had questioned and whose boundaries she had fled. She had high cheekbones, a wide mouth, white, shining, perfect teeth, long, straight, blond hair and grey eyes. Stephanos said he had married her because she was rich, white, anglo-saxon, the highest being to which the son of a Greek migrant could possibly aspire. [Patricia] admitted freely that when she had met Stephanos at the age of 15 she had been totally overwhelmed by his DA haircut, Californian shades, sideburns, drape suit and crepe-soled stompers. He had been so different, so gorgeous, that she had been hot for him instantly. She was now twenty-six years old and had been married to Stephanos for ten years.

The unfolding relationship between the Alwyns and the Lamounises is at the centre of *The Unyielding Memory*. In particular, the novel traces the influence of the charismatic Stephanos Lamounis over Nick Alwyn, as Alwyn finds himself increasingly attracted to Lamounis's libertarian approach to marriage, relationships and sex. Alwyn gradually realises how conservative his New Zealand upbringing has been; chafes at the thought he has married too young and in haste; and envies the space the "thrustingly heterosexual" Lamounis has within his own marriage for "cutting out". Unsurprisingly, Alwyn's journey closely mirrors Wallis's own embrace of the liberal attitudes to personal relationships he witnessed on Hydra, including the often-flagrant infidelities within the expatriate colony. On the evidence of Wallis's diaries and the many photographs he took of Gassoumis, it is clear the two men enjoyed an intense if waggish friendship similar to the one imagined for Alwyn and Lamounis in *The Unyielding Memory*, with Gassoumis shaping Wallis's rapidly evolving attitudes to life.

Once settled on Hydra, Gassoumis found he had access to the full gamut of island society in a way that was difficult (or impossible) for other expatriates. He was at once both an outsider, as a non-Hydriot-born artist and as a member of the expatriate community with an American wife, and an insider, as a fluent Greek speaker and a member of a family with longstanding connections to the island. Gassoumis's ability to speak Greek was important to other expatriates and he was often called upon to negotiate various transactions on their behalf with officialdom and the police, particularly with regard to residency permits. He also helped his friend Leonard Cohen negotiate and finalise the purchase of his island home.

Additionally, Gassoumis was in the unusual position of being able to financially support at least some of the impecunious expatriates. Wallis's diary and *The Unyielding Memory* both record a number of instances where Wallis received loans from Gassoumis, including a diary note from January 1961 that the Gassoumises were providing him and Robyn with 1500 drachma a month to help cover their living expenses of about 2000. The margins of Wallis's diary include frequent calculations relating to the repayments of these debts, a situation that persisted for some years and eventually included Robyn undertaking tutoring work with the Gassoumises' daughters, Athena and Cassandra, as a form of repayment.

Gassoumis, in keeping with his hybrid nationality and identity (Wallis wrote that Stephanos "could switch his personality instantly and effortlessly from American to Greek"), was ambivalent about his new island location. While it provided an ideal environment to pursue his art and to experiment with new relationships, he was certainly not keen to leave behind the material comforts afforded by postwar American technologies. Gassoumis therefore set out to acquire a sizable island home that would allow him to establish his place amongst Hydra's well-heeled residents and to indulge his desire for a comparatively affluent 'American' lifestyle—a measure of the success achieved by his family's migration.

James Burke captured a series of images that reflects the Gassoumises' search for a 'renovator's dream' on Hydra. When *LIFE* magazine's George Caturani approved Burke's photo shoot, he suggested various subjects, including the expatriates "perhaps househunting". Burke responded with several photo sequences, including Demetri and Carolyn Gassoumis with the Johnstons as they scour the town in search of a house. The photos depict the two couples wandering the town's laneways looking at houses; stopping to admire a view over the harbour; then (according to Burke's notes) "Carolyn Gassoumis and Charmian Johnston peering in window of one of Hydra's old ruined mansions, figuring how it might be restored", before "entering through window of old empty Hydra house which Gassoumises would like to buy", and finally, sizing up "the great ground-floor kitchen, which has lovely archways".

These photos not only depict the Gassoumises looking for their permanent slice of island life, but also show Johnston in the role that came naturally to him—helping Hydra's newcomers get established and perhaps enticing them into making their expatriation permanent.

House hunting Hydra style. The Johnstons and the Gassoumises. (James Burke)

Carolyn Gassoumis, Charmian Clift and George Johnston
finding out what is inside. (James Burke)

The Johnstons and the Gassoumises consider the possibilities of the "great ground floor kitchen". (James Burke)

This house-hunting scenario must have been common on Hydra as holiday-makers used their leisure hours to size-up the possibilities of turning an island sojourn into an ongoing lifestyle. The Gassoumises were about to make the dream a reality. Soon after, they purchased their island home, although not the one "high above the waterfront" depicted in Burke's photographs, but rather lower down with a short and gently inclining walk to the south-east corner of the harbour. As it happened, it was also only a short distance from the Johnstons' house.

Having acquired his house, Gassoumis set out to turn it into a landmark in terms of Hydra's development. As Nick Alwyn narrates in *The Unyielding Memory*, the Lamounises were "living reasonably well and working towards living a great deal better". Whereas other expatriates accepted the need to live quite simply—and as Clift and Johnston had demonstrated, adapt their homes to reflect their island location and limit renovations to improving the

Demetri and Carolyn Gassoumis in the 'American' kitchen, and unidentified woman, c.1963. (Redmond Wallis)

ablution facilities—Gassoumis was determined to bring a slice of Californian sophistication to the island. His plans included renovating his large new house to incorporate all the latest interior design trends and labour-saving devices favoured in California, most of which he would have to import from the US. Firstly, he needed to renovate his new house to a suitable standard—walls came down and new ones went up; a new staircase was built; floors were replaced; modern bathrooms were installed; and a model kitchen was placed at the centre of the home. What Stephanos Lamounis achieved, Wallis wrote, "imposed a Californian pattern on a Greek fabric".

Gassoumis's ambitions did not stop at the interior of the house. He would also create a new type of outdoor space previously unknown on Hydra. The external plans started with a lawn, a remarkably exotic touch by island standards where exterior spaces were given over to paving and cobblestone—choices that responded to the readily available materials, the terrain and the chronic lack of water. Gassoumis, however, saw no obstacle to his quest to bring America to the Aegean.

> Stephanos was deep into the detail of renovating his house.
> 'See, the front will be down in Bermuda grass, with just the two cypresses and maybe a couple of flower beds.'
> 'What's Bermuda grass?' asked Nick.
> 'Aw, come on, Nick, you know what Bermuda grass is.'
> 'No, I don't.'
> 'It's tropical grass, it grows close to the ground, like outwards, not upwards like ordinary grass. Miami's full of the stuff. OK, so we have a lawn out front. Then the whole of the ground floor is going to be kitchen, dining room and living room, all open.'

(If Gassoumis was going to have grass, it followed that he would be needing a gardener. It was a role Australian artist Robert Owen took on briefly when he was employed as a caretaker while the Gassoumises were absent. Fellow Australian artist and eventual long-time Hydra resident Bill Pownall speculated to Owen, in a 1965 letter written from London, about some of the possibilities of his role:

> You must write about your experiences as Gazoumis gardener. I can see it now … 'Robert was cutting the grass with long rhythmic muscular strokes. He could just see the corner of the pool, where she lay, indolent in the sun.' Three pages and then a row of asterisks. Bloody censors.

Pownall might have lifted his ideas for Owen's projected novel from his own recent reading. In the same letter, he mentions that he has just read Gordon Merrick's 1958 novel *The Hot Season*, which has as its protagonist an American Embassy intelligence officer with an unfaithful wife. He thought it was "very readable at various levels", and then asks after both Merrick and Gassoumis).

The scale of the house renovations and delays in importing material from the US meant that plans to be in the house by Christmas 1960, and then Easter 1961, came and went. The Gassoumises rented elsewhere (the house vacated at short notice by David Goschen) before eventually moving into their still incompletely renovated house during the summer of 1961. The town would now learn that Gassoumis's plans for the house's outside areas did not stop at Bermuda grass. He set out to create, as the crowning and most obvious statement of his successful homecoming, the one extraordinary feature that would set his house apart from all others on Hydra—the first swimming pool.

Not only was the astonishing idea of a pool shaped by Gassoumis's American experience and imagination, but he would only be satisfied if all of the associated hardware could be imported from the US. As Wallis described the situation in *The Unyielding Memory*:

> The house Stephanos and Patricia had bought was … L-shaped, on two storeys, and surrounded by a two-metre-high whitewashed wall that enclosed a front garden and a back yard. There was a small cottage at the back. It was Stephanos' intention to turn the back yard into a swimming pool, the rooms beside it on the shorter arm are of L to be pool rooms with, above them, accessible from the main house, a bathroom

Carolyn and Cassandra Gassoumis enjoy the Bermuda grass, c.1963.
(Redmond Wallis)

and dressing room for Patricia. Anything available in Greece was, in Stephanos' opinion, Mickey Mouse, and so he was preparing to fly from the States, on an ordinary flight, as personal baggage, an entire kit for the largest available domestic pool made, along with its pumps and ancillary equipment. … Dragging a 19th century Greek house into 20th century California was a considerable undertaking, but it did not seem to faze Stephanos.

As Wallis also wrote, "Of all the luxuries Stephanos had sought to impose upon the island's simplicity, the pool was the most complex". What Gassoumis planned was not only a pool, but one with all the conveniences necessary for complete swimming comfort, including electrically driven water pumps; a filtration system; underwater lighting; and floodlighting for the courtyard. In addition, he had also installed an electric waste disposal system into the house. All this was too much for the town's unreliable power supply and so, in addition to the many other challenges, a small courtyard cottage was converted to house a generator. This equipment was also shipped in parts from the US, assembled in Athens and transported to the island.

If progress on the house had been frustratingly slow, then so too was headway on the pool. In order to create the necessary space, a small orchard had to be removed from the generous courtyard, with only a couple of decorative fruit trees and a single palm remaining. Excavation of the site was then slowed by the pool's considerable size and depth. Photos taken by Wallis of the still-empty pool indicate that it was some ten feet deep in parts, deep enough to allow the use of a springboard—presumably also imported from the US. Not only did excavation have to be completed by hand, but the large amount of unwanted soil could only be removed on the backs of donkeys and mules. And not only did it take time to import the pumps, filtration system and generator from the US, but there were further delays in Greek customs that were only resolved by payment of substantial import taxes. Gassoumis also had other distractions during this period. In 1962 his mother died—never having seen the changes her son was bringing to the island of her birth—which required Gassoumis to travel to the US for an extended period, and he used the trip to dispatch more materials and furnishings to Hydra.

The complexities Gassoumis faced not only included the logistics of building the pool but also the need to negotiate the reactions of a town that was uncertain if it was ready for this degree of American comfort. As Wallis recorded in *The Unyielding Memory*, fellow expatriates were particularly wary of the encroachment of such obvious 'American' luxuries and values into their small haven of isolated resistance.

> For a long time Stephanos had spoken of the pool as if he had his tongue in his cheek, spoken of it deliberately in front of the homes-and-gardens set, typified by Paul and Lee, knowing the status it possessed in their eyes and yet spoken of it with his full-lipped hooded smile that conveyed to them he was not serious, a full-lipped hooded Levantine smile because only he (and Patricia) knew that he was.

'But can you imagine it?' he had said. 'In August, when you guys can't even get into the sea at Spelia, I'll be lying by beautiful, clear, fresh water with no one around except people I want, listening to the hi-fi. Can't you just see it? The palm tree and the tile surround and all those beautiful chrome fittings. It will be a beautiful thing.'

'It will look exactly like Las Vegas and if there's one thing we don't want on this island it's Las Vegas,' Paul had said, and encouraged the others to laugh.

But I love Las Vegas!' Stephanos had protested. 'Las Vegas is a beautiful place. I want it to look like Las Vegas.'

No one seriously believed him, then.

They had a very good reason not to believe Gassoumis would build his pool, because in addition to the many other challenges, the pool required the one thing that was in notoriously short supply on Hydra—fresh water. The island's lack of a reliable water supply had long troubled the town and, with many established wells drying or brackish and the number of tourists increasing each dry season, the concern about the availability of drinking water was rising. Most houses collected water in their *sterna* (usually found in kitchens), but in summer these might run dry or become undrinkable. Most islanders therefore relied, at least for part of the year, on having clean water delivered by donkey, with water sourced either from the wells of *Kala Pigadia* or shipped from Athens. Needless to say, it came at a considerable price.

The other method used for transporting water was in the form of ice blocks. With restricted electricity supply, refrigeration depended on the availability of ice and ice chests for cold storage. The island supported an ice works to meet demand, and ice was commonly delivered to the dockside businesses and nearby houses by being towed in large blocks at the end of a rope. It was a method that worked best for those, such as the Johnstons, with a house that could be reached without steps. Clift wrote in *Peel Me a Lotus* of the constant battle to claim the prized blocks of ice:

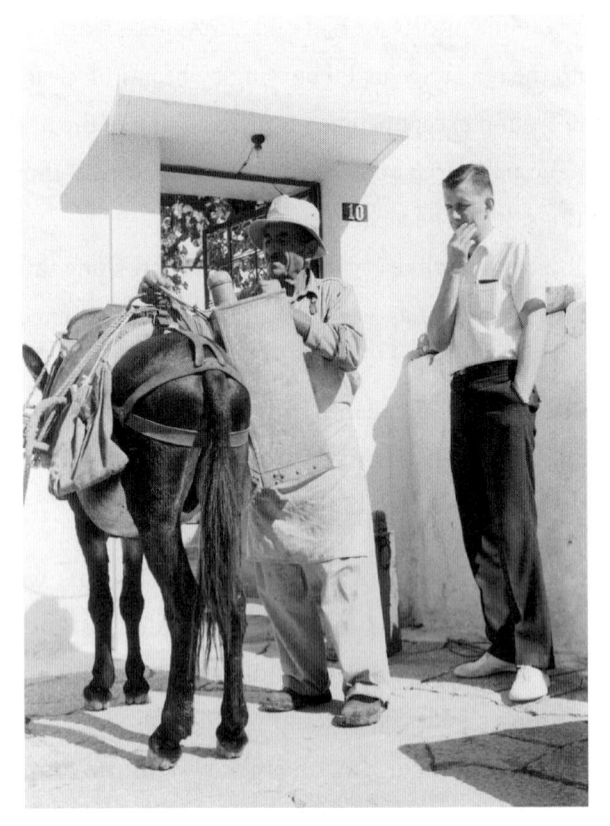

Konstantinos Roussis delivers water to Bob Maxwell.
(James Burke)

George has to go to for the ice the moment he is out of bed. The ice factory is as inadequate as the town's electricity plant, and every morning the crowd gathers at dawn, three hundred people who know full well that there will be no more than a hundred half-blocks of ice for distribution.

When Costas opens the doors everyone surges forward, and the weaker men and all the women and children are trampled under or swept aside. ... George gets a block three times out of five, but then he is very tall and in his youth took part in a football scrum every Saturday afternoon. He comes home from the ice scrum panting and excited, dragging the prize behind him on a length of frayed rope ...

DEMETRI'S POOL

Dragging the ice block. (James Burke)

So scarce was clean water over summer, and so irregular its transportation from Piraeus, that it was a role for the mayor to determine which of the competing needs had priority. And such were the sensitivities regarding water use that the whole town was quickly aware of what was going on behind the high walls of the Gassoumises' courtyard as the lawn was established and the pool built—and they didn't like it. Whereas the pool was designed to serve as a measure of Gassoumis's wealth and a declaration of his 'taste', it also succeeded in winning the enmity of the town's population. Rodney Hall recalled the response to the building of the pool:

> It was an interesting situation, where for Demetri it was clearly a homecoming as a successful person. He never needed to work again, and so he immediately slotted into the community as one of the few rich men there, and Carolyn had no place in that, and no place with the women in black. So Carolyn basically lived in the expatriate community. They bought a quite large house near the *agora* and had a swimming pool, to the outrage of the population because fresh water was at a premium.

We and George and Charmian and everyone else bought water from the donkey man who brought it down from the sweet spring up the mountain. All the houses had a well, and whatever rain they got was collected in the well, and that was used for washing up and bathing. But your drinking water came by donkey, so water was a precious commodity. And here come these rich people who put in a very large swimming pool, and although it was invisible from the roadways because of the walls, everybody knew it was there, and it was like a living sore, it was a scandal. Demetri I think found a certain notoriety in that but Carolyn found it a burden. Not that she didn't want the pool, she loved the pool, but she knew that it wasn't appreciated.

Charmian Clift would also recall the troubles created by the pool, explaining Gassoumis's passion for his project as an expensive consolation for Hydra's absence of taken-for-granted Californian luxuries:

> on Hydra … a rich Californian friend of ours, with the whole Aegean on his front doorstep, was building a Hollywood-style swimming pool in his backyard. He planted a lawn too when all vegetation was seared with heat and the wells had run dry and every drop of household water had to be pumped up from intermittent water-tankers at great cost. The pool and the lawn were his talismans. Luxury is only a question of degree. Some sort of personal compensation for residence in the Kingdom of Lack.

The final challenge facing Gassoumis was therefore the greatest of all—finding the water with which to fill his pool. When the Wallises returned to Hydra in mid-1963, they moved in with the Gassoumises for some weeks and found the pool, two years after its commencement, 'finished' but forlornly empty, with the generator and filtering system installed but standing idle. The property by this time had two wells containing brackish water, a sterna and roof tanks for the storage of clean water, and the newly installed pumping system that included a complex arrangement of taps that could be used to direct, mix or separate the flow as water was directed to the household, the lawn or the pool. What it couldn't provide, however, was the sizeable volume of clean water required to fill the pool.

When Gassoumis took up his case for water with the mayor, he found that the official, sensitive to the concerns of other residents, deemed the empty pool to be of secondary importance. During the hottest weeks of the summer of 1963, Gassoumis's frustration grew as the pool stood ready but empty. Gassoumis was not, however, about to surrender his dream—not only had he already invested heavily in the pool, but that investment only raised the stakes in terms of his need to mark his presence on the island by creating an oasis of Californian style and sophistication. As Wallis wrote of Gassoumis's alter ego Lamounis:

> The pool dominated his life because it alone of the separate projects finished or going forward within the four stone walls surrounding the house would serve almost all his ends. The Bermuda grass lawn might be an extravagance, the waste disposal unit a novelty, the pumping system an exotic wonder, and all these things might be unique as far as the island was concerned, but the pool was to be a gem beside which they would be dull, cheap, unworthy of their setting.

The problem of the much-needed water was further complicated by the pool's method of construction, which required the long-finished concrete shell to be plastered and then the pool to be filled before the plaster had fully dried. Gassoumis therefore needed to have his workforce available to complete the plastering immediately prior to the water being delivered. As Wallis wrote:

> [T]wo infinitely variable factors had to be precisely combined: the availability of Giorgio's workgang, and the presence of the water boat with just thirty tons surplus to the requirements of the naval school, the restaurants and the dry sternas of the town's people. For three months of the second summer Stephanos tried to create that surplus by cajolery, bribery and threats. On the few occasions he succeeded Giorgio's gang was otherwise engaged.

Finishing touches. Demetri Gassoumis and unidentified worker, 1963.
(Redmond Wallis)

Gassoumis's chances of eventually acquiring such a large amount of water were helped when, in the summer of 1963, a new form of water delivery to Hydra commenced, involving a large canvas water-filled 'sausage' drawn behind boats from Piraeus. From the harbour, water was then decanted on the dock or pumped to various parts of the town. Eventually, as the hottest days of summer passed, the mayor relented, Gassoumis prevailed, and both the water and the workforce were secured. Wallis's diary recorded that the final touches were quickly made to the pool as "we etched it with hydrochloric acid". Photographs taken by Wallis indicate that Gassoumis took a very hands-on approach to the task—likely his doubts about the quality of Greek equipment and machinery extended to a distrust of Greek craftsmanship when it came to the finer points of pool construction.

DEMETRI'S POOL

Demetri Gassoumis (2-R), with unidentified workers and the nearly completed pool, 1963. (Redmond Wallis)

The presence of local workers in Wallis's photographs of the nearly complete pool is a reminder that even though the pool troubled many Hydra residents, it was far from being a straightforward equation. One photograph shows Gassoumis in the company of nine workers, spanning several generations. They are pictured beside the still-empty pool, appearing relaxed and proud of their participation in this notorious project and, no doubt, pleased for the work regardless of what it signalled about the island and its future—or perhaps *because* of what it signalled about the island and its future. Issues of water aside, it was hard to resent foreigners (if that is what Gassoumis was) when they spent so extravagantly and used their wealth to provide employment at the same time as they introduced to the island the luxurious rewards of American modernity.

Poolside with friends. Demetri Gassoumis, Robyn Wallis, Leonard Cohen, Marianne Ihlen and Carolyn Gassoumis, 1964. (Redmond Wallis)

Gassoumis's water was finally pumped up to his pool overnight on August 26th and 27th through canvas piping that snaked its way uphill through the narrow streets for several hundred metres. As Wallis soon reported in his diary, "we've been in it ever since. Write all morning, from rise or so until 12:30–1. Quick swim before lunch, then lie around or swim all afternoon and by five or six when the temperature drops I'm ready to write again."

In addition to being a personal triumph for Gassoumis, the completion of the pool was also a watershed for Hydra in that it marked the emergence of a new form of social space. The island's sociability had been largely built on the

Robyn Wallis, Leonard Cohen, Marianne Ihlen, Demetri Gassoumis and Carolyn Gassoumis, 1964. (Redmond Wallis)

necessity to share the public spaces of the taverns and *kafenia* of the *agora*, the wide expanse of the dockside promenade, and the swimming spot at Spilia. Whereas the expatriates previously reported gleefully of the intense socialising on the *agora* and of the long days sporting with incoming tourists, they were now developing other, more private, options. Wallis wrote in his diary that such was the tourist throng when he returned to the island that "[I] Want to hide behind Demetri's walls", and, as quoted above, one of the arguments that Lamounis uses to defend his pool in *The Unyielding Memory* is his dream of "lying by beautiful, clear, fresh water with no one around except people I want, listening to the hi-fi". Whether it be the choice to own rather than rent, the option to build a pool rather than share a beach, the setting of ever-higher perimeter walls, or the convenience of a hi-fi and recordings over public music-making, social space was increasingly made personal and private, and used as a defence against the influx of tourists and travellers, and (potentially) as a means of avoiding other expatriates.

Even as Gassoumis was finally enjoying the benefits of his completed pool, the house was already on the market. Buying property on Hydra in the early 1960s might still have been comparatively affordable, but renovations were expensive given the need to have all building material transported from the mainland, and excessively more expensive when it required heavy equipment to be transported from the US. Gassoumis claimed the pool alone had cost $40,000 at a time when substantial island houses in good repair might be acquired for a fifth of that amount. The Gassoumises also had money tied up in other property in the US that could not be released to support their Hydra investment. Selling such a property on Hydra at the time would be impossible if Gassoumis hoped to retrieve anywhere near the amount he had invested, but they put it on the market for £25,000 and focused on institutional buyers. The asking price emphasised that while expatriates were bemoaning the rising prices, they were nonetheless part of the 'problem' as they invested in houses that set new standards for the island and pushed the cost of both property and living ever higher. As a result, it became ever more difficult to use Hydra as a base for the hand-to-mouth living of struggling artists and writers.

Unsurprisingly, the Gassoumises' pool was only the first on Hydra. Stand on a high point above the town today and you will find the view dotted with pools. These are almost all built to a small size, with the scale of the courtyards and compact building lots restricting them to little more than 'plunge pools'. Pools on the scale of that built by Gassoumis remain a rarity, and even in 2018 only one of the island's hotels, Bratsera, boasts a pool. Swim in the Bratsera pool today or use the hotel's courtyard restaurant and you might also hear splashing coming from elsewhere—it is separated only by a single high wall from the pool that Demetri built.

DEMETRI'S POOL

Of the various members of the expatriate community featured in Burke's and Wallis's photographs, few would have such a continuous presence on the island as Demetri Gassoumis. There was a time during the mid-1960s when Greece became uncomfortable for him as the military used his Greek nationality to try and force him to undertake national service, and then with the coming of the Junta he left to work on his art in New York. By the mid-1970s, however, he had once again returned to Hydra, purchasing another house in the area of the town known as Four Corners. Demetri Gassoumis spent the remainder of his life sharing his time between Hydra and California—maintaining his trans-Atlantic identity until the end—and painting successfully across a range of styles and subject matter. He held his last exhibition on Hydra in June of 2014 and passed away in 2015, with his estate donating a number of paintings and home furnishings to both the Hydra Archive Museum and the Coundouriotis Museum.

* * *

In two sections from *The Unyielding Memory*, Nick Alwyn observes the island's lack of fresh water and Stephanos Lamounis's struggle to find enough for his newly completed pool.

> [Stephanos] had, on one of his trips back from the States, done exactly what he said he would do: air-freighted to Greece, aboard the same aircraft, all the equipment needed for the pool except for the generator. It had taken him six months to get the equipment through Greek customs, six months and duties sometimes running as high as a hundred per cent. … The third cottage had been turned into the equipment room—pump, filter, generator—and the hole for the pool had been dug so that the date palm stood just behind the diving board and the two other trees remaining from the orchard, an almond and a peach, stood at the other end, in front of the French windows that opened from the main living room.
> That done, Stephanos sat down to wait for water.

HALF THE PERFECT WORLD

The problem was that the island, like most Greek islands, was a stone dropped into the Aegean (by God, the Greeks said, when he had finished the world) and had virtually no water. The islanders lived on rain water, collected as it had been for generations. When the first rains came, they were allowed to wash the roofs and the terraces clean. Then, this done to the householders satisfaction, the wooden bungs stuck in the holes leading off the terrace to the sterna below were removed and soon the sound of water cascading into the tank would fill the house. Most of the sternas held something like twenty tons of water, almost all of which was needed to get through the hot dry summer until the rains came again.

*

The pool was filled at two o'clock in the morning. Stephanos turned on the spotlight and sat in a chair by the French windows, drinking vodka and lime and watching the clear water gush from the huge canvas hose. Nick shared his moment of triumph. The night was warm and clear. A full moon was poised above the chapel high above Spelia. It gave the night sky a curiously blanched-out aspect. It hurt to look at the moon.

The spotlight fell into the pool, broken up by the black rippling water. The date palm at the far end, heavy with rotting fruit, was orange-black. Except for the noise of the generator, the noise of the water, and the more distant hum of the boat's pumps, the night was silent.

Nick and Stephanos were silent too. There seemed to be nothing to talk about. Occasionally Stephanos said something to the men from the boat, usually an injunction against letting the hose lie on the bottom of the pool and scour the new plaster, but most of the time he simply sat, sipped and smiled. Patricia and Sue were in bed in the darkened house…

Stephanos wouldn't let anyone swim until the pH balance of the pool was right. He christened it himself at dawn, but by the time Patricia was up the ban was in force. He had an indicator kit with a colour chart showing him what colour a test solution would be if the pool was too acid, just right, or too alkaline. The water was far too alkaline and he and Nick wrestled a carboy of hydrochloric acid out to the side of the pool and then poured in a carefully measure quantity. Stephanos started the pump and switched in the filter. If the pH got out of balance, he explained to Patricia, you got algae. Black algae was the worst, it got stuck in the white plaster and ruined the pool's appearance. Surface algae you could clear more easily.

Chapter Eleven

AT WORK

While there were reasons to question the quality of what George Johnston had written prior to leaving London, his work ethic was indisputable. When Johnston and Charmian Clift arrived in the Aegean in November 1954, he already had some eleven books to his name including the novels *High Valley* and *The Big Chariot* co-authored by Clift. Of these titles, a number had been knocked-out rapidly during the war, largely based on a recycling of Johnston's newspaper reportage, and his more recent fiction had been produced under pressure as he worked long hours with his journalism and editing roles in Sydney and London.

On the evidence of Johnston's fiction to this point, his facility with words was accompanied by stylistic and thematic uncertainty. His readers might have praised his control of atmosphere and some impressive descriptive passages and set pieces, while criticising his poorly conceived plots, inconsistent characterisation and sometimes unconvincing dialogue. It was also striking that none of Johnston's fiction published by this time had an Australian setting or resonance. Neither the lack of stylistic confidence nor the use of 'foreign' settings was about to change with his final London novel, *The Cyprian Woman*.

The Cyprian Woman is a lightly rendered romance-turned-crime novel written in the wake of the Greek holiday that Johnston and Clift had taken in May 1954, and it was Johnston's first novel with a Greek-Aegean setting. Whatever retrospective interest the novel holds is because of what it reveals about Johnston's mindset at the time—his disillusionment with the drabness of 1950s London is palpable, as is the appeal of the lovingly described Aegean coastal setting. Johnston also crafted a plot that gave him ample opportunity to show off his learning about Greece imbibed from his wide reading on the subject and his recent travel. *The Cyprian Woman* is set in the ancient Peloponnesian coastal city of Nauplia (Nafplio), the first capital of modern Greece. A plotline that includes a novelist, Christine Lambert, who has recently published a bestseller set in classical Greece, allows Johnston to weave in references to Greek history, archaeology and mythology, and his personal engagement with the subject is revealed in the regular name-dropping of various destinations—including Hydra—he and Clift had recently visited. *The Cyprian Woman* was also notable as the first of Johnston's novels to focus on adultery and the figure of the cuckold, themes that would be staples of his later fiction.

Despite some engaging elements, *The Cyprian Woman* is once-more clumsily plotted, with the central characters suffering from confused (and confusing) motivations, and it was another of Johnston's novels to sink beneath the weight of its author's busy working life. Johnston felt the same way, and later recalled realising that if he was going to produce work of genuine quality, then he could no longer continue to write in his spare time.

> Well I thought, you are getting old and you have written a hell of a lot of books, and it's high time you tried to write a good one. I had lost enthusiasm for the newspaper work at that time and it was a moment of decision.

As soon as Johnston and Clift reached Kalymnos, they set about working on a second Greek novel—the one they went to the island to write—the co-authored *The Sponge Divers* (published in the US as *The Sea and the Stone*). Despite the co-author credit for Clift, *The Sponge Divers* was largely Johnston's work. When later queried about her development as a writer, Clift related that *The Sponge Divers* "was a phony collaboration because I was beyond the stage where I could collaborate any longer and I wanted to do my own work, my own way". The opportunity for Clift to emerge as a writer independent of her husband came with her decision to write *Mermaid Singing*, a travelogue cum memoir of the family's time on Kalymnos.

Progress on both *The Sponge Divers* and *Mermaid Singing* was rapid despite the challenges the family faced in adapting to their Greek home, language and lifestyle. In a February 1955 letter to her London friend Jo Meyer, Clift reported that "George at least works like buggery", and that "he's saturated in the atmosphere and the people and the drinking and the talk and the singing and the stories and every day when he sits down to work it just pours out onto the typewriter". Progress was such that the manuscript for *The Sponge Divers* was dispatched to London for final typing in March and was with the publishers by the beginning of May. In an effort worthy of Johnston himself, Clift had largely completed *Mermaid Singing* by the end of summer in the same year.

Despite his hard work, *The Sponge Divers* wasn't a great step forward for Johnston. The plot centres on Kalymnos's rapidly declining sponge industry and its various impacts when the island has little else to sustain its economic, business or social structures. The key outsider is Australian writer Morgan Leigh, who sets out to observe and write about the island's changing fortunes but inevitably becomes enmeshed in the lives of those most affected. *The Sponge Divers* has some excellent set pieces, and convinces the reader that Johnston had absorbed both the history of Kalymnos and the contemporary complexities of island life. It is let down, however, by being over-written in parts, and having characters, particularly the Kalymnians, who struggle to be more than stereotypes. *Mermaid Singing* was more successful. While it is quite clinical, almost anthropological, in its descriptions of life on Kalymnos, it is also insightful about Clift and Johnston's own circumstances as expatriated outsiders adapting to a place and a lifestyle that are, on one hand, beguilingly beautiful and disarmingly simple and, on the other, extraordinarily harsh and at times bewildering.

Considered in tandem, the two books do have the effect of providing real insight into Kalymnos and Greek island living. It is apparent that Johnston and Clift could have had few illusions about what living long-term in the Aegean would mean, as both books depict 'characters' coming to terms with the isolation, struggling economies, lack of services, and conservative and difficult to penetrate social structures.

The circumstances of the Johnstons' expatriation changed when they moved to Hydra in August 1955, and then conclusively when they bought their house early the following year. As neither *The Sponge Divers* nor *Mermaid Singing* would sell sufficiently well to secure their finances, the house purchase was only made possible by the sale of Johnston's 'The Astypalaian Knife'—an unremarkable story based on a knife Johnston had been gifted on Kalymnos—for the remarkable sum of eight hundred and fifty US dollars. According to the Johnstons' friend Charles Sriber, the couple first thought that the money would provide "enough to spare for Charmian to have her baby in the maternity hospital [in Athens]. But, at this time, there was a beautiful house for sale on Hydra, very cheap. The Johnstons decided to buy the house, instead of paying maternity hospital bills." The windfall from 'The Astypalaian Knife' not only provided the couple with the finances to acquire their Hydra house, but also gave them much needed confidence that earning a living from writing while remaining in the Aegean was viable. According to Sriber, as a sign of that commitment, after purchasing their Hydra house "The first thing they did on moving in was to nail the Astypalaian knife to the wall of their living-room".

Despite their recent productivity and success, it is apparent that Johnston almost immediately felt the pressure of supporting his young family. As important as the money received for 'The Astypalaian Knife' was, it did not cover the purchase price of the house, which consumed whatever other savings the couple had available. Johnston therefore elected to turn to writing crime novels, with the hope of targeting a market for rapid sale and maximum return. Less than a year after moving himself and his family to a remote island in order to have the time to write high-quality literary fiction, Johnston was already prioritising commercial necessity over artistic ambition. Clift wrote sympathetically of her husband's plight in *Peel Me a Lotus*, noting that "In actual fear of poverty for the first time in his adult life he is doomed to write not what he wants to write but what he knows will sell". Published under the pseudonym of Shane Martin (derived from the names of his two elder children), the novels were based on the character of the diminutive and aging Professor Challis, a US born academic archaeologist with a speciality in Minoan civilization who, therefore, has good reason to spend much of his time in the Aegean, where he encounters the impact of modern crime (and of modernity more broadly) on the most ancient of cultures.

Johnston would produce five Shane Martin novels, commencing with *Twelve Girls in the Garden* and concluding with *A Wake for Mourning* (published in the US as *Mourner's Voyage*). Exactly how much the Shane Martin titles contributed to the family's finances is unclear, although it can be concluded that they were sufficiently profitable for Johnston and his publishers to persevere to the extent they did. They were certainly not, however, the type of fiction Johnston had in mind when making the decision to write full time, and subsequently they have been dismissed by critics as revenue-raising "potboilers". It is not a term that Johnston shied away from. As he noted in an interview after returning to Australia:

> It all began in this beautiful romantic adventurous dream as these things always do, and one was going to an island to write the book that would naturally be a best seller and all that sort of thing, but it wasn't … We pretty much sort of got broke. It was pure survival then. So I wrote potboilers because you had to boil the pot.

Unfortunately for Johnston, the Shane Martin novels appear to have been too close to prewar styles of 'Golden-age' detective fiction by the likes of Agatha Christie and Dorothy L. Sayers to appeal to very large numbers of mid-century readers. By the time Johnston reached the Aegean, Ian Fleming had already published the first two of his hugely successful James Bond novels, thereby setting a standard for 1950s mass-market fictional heroes. In terms of reader appeal, Challis, the ageing professor of classical studies—he is sixty-six at the outset of *Twelve Girls in the Garden*—was severely disadvantaged when compared to the youthful and glamorous warriors in the geopolitics of the Cold War, such as Bond. So while *Twelve Girls in the Garden* might have been praised by *Manchester Guardian* reviewer Frances Iles (pseudonym of influential English crime writer Anthony Berkeley Cox) as "an intelligent thriller for sophisticated readers, especially those with Hellenic yearnings", such a seemingly favourable notice was a kiss-of-death in the battle for mass-market supremacy. Traditional crime fiction at the time was a tough market for authors with *belles-lettres* aspirations.

Irrespective of Johnston's motivations, the Shane Martin novels nonetheless have interest as examples of mid-century genre fiction not altogether surrendering literary aspirations. Their broad thematic concerns with the 'clash' of societies or civilizations that are historically out of step, and with the capacity for ancient civilizations to irresistibly imprint themselves across millennia, are also found in the novels Johnston published under his own name during this period. As a consequence, the Shane Martin novels should be read not as separate from Johnston's other fiction but rather as an integral component within his considerable body of work. It was only the final novel, *A Wake for Mourning*, written several years after its predecessor and at the urging of his publisher, that was prodigiously bad, devoid of Johnston's usually reliable narrative virtues that might have mitigated the contrived and confused plot.

It is arguable that, within their limited ambitions, the earlier Shane Martin novels were as successful as the others Johnston published contemporaneously, such as *The Darkness Outside*. *The Darkness Outside* was the first of Johnston's novels published under his own name to be written entirely on Hydra, and makes for a useful comparison with the Shane Martin books in that it shares the same archaeological premise, with its hero (and narrator), the brilliant American Elliot Purcell, being an expert in Pre-Sumerian Mesopotamian civilizations. The action is entirely confined to the scene of an archaeological dig in modern-day Iraq, undertaken by Purcell and five colleagues, including the dour, conscientious and honourable Australian Rudy Levin. The novel's action relies upon another unconvincing plot device (the inexplicable arrival of a delirious old man who spreads fear when he rambles nonsensically about swarming hordes from the east) and eventually dissolves into a largely pointless conclusion. It does have interest in that it reiterates themes around the trans-millennial 'clash of civilisations' that were central to the Shane Martin novels, and it is also perceptive in its observations about the psychological games that emerge when a small international group of men and women are cut off from the outside world for a considerable period. For this element, Johnston had his own experience of Hydra winters to call upon, and this is put to good effect as characters confront the pitfalls of fraying tempers, fragile psyches, shifting alliances and none-too-clandestine sexual liaisons. *The Darkness Outside* also includes one of the clearest statements of Johnston's agnostic worldview, which is hinted at in the novel's title and voiced by Purcell as he attempts to convince Levin of the futility of pursuing some ultimate archaeological discovery.

> There are only some things of purpose, only a few things. Everything else is blind, whirling in a void, inexplicable. Put your finger behind to see how it works. There's nothing there. Nothing. God isn't there. Man isn't there. Magic isn't there. Not even a piece of clockwork mechanism. Nothing. Darkness and the wind, maybe, but nothing else.

When Johnston first arrived on Hydra it was not only his own worldview and work with which he was concerned. The arrival of Sidney and Cynthia Nolan three months later delivered to the island another artist with a work ethic that matched Johnston's. The Nolans were visiting Hydra for reasons apart from their existing friendship with Johnston and Clift—the trip was specifically planned around Nolan and Johnston's shared fascination with Greek mythology. It was an interest intensified by the publication earlier that year of Robert Graves's *Greek Myths*, which Nolan now planned to use as the basis of a series of paintings relating to Trojan history. At Johnston's instigation, Nolan also read an article about Gallipoli by Johnston's fellow Australian war correspondent Alan Moorehead, which had appeared in *The New Yorker* in April of that year, noting the proximity of Gallipoli to Troy and describing similarities between the two campaigns. Moorehead was, at the time, living nearby on the island of Spetses and completing his book on Gallipoli. The outcome was that Nolan undertook a quick trip to the Turkish peninsula, including Gallipoli, and then immediately returned to Nikos Ghika's studio on Hydra to commence work on paintings that fused elements of classical mythology with Australian iconography derived from the Gallipoli campaign. As Johnston later recalled in a piece published in *Art and Australia*:

> He [Nolan] painted away as if in a ferment of excitement for five months, experimental sketches in oils or inks on heavy art paper mostly, hundreds and hundreds of studies concerned with nude figures interlocked and grappling, centaur-like horsemen, desiccated skulls and bones in formalized masks and helmets, the harsh edges of dry rock and brittle, snagged vegetation against burning bright skies. There was no thought in his mind of a finished painting. 'I am just trying to work it out,' he would explain, surveying a vast floor carpeted with a hundred separate sketches. 'It will take a long time … maybe ten years before I'm ready to have a proper go at it.'

Johnston also recalled Nolan's frustration with the project and how "in a rare outburst of emotional passion he had flung his sketches down and cried, 'You can't paint it! You need metal and a forge, it's got to clang!'" But it was a frustration Nolan was prepared to live with, as the Gallipoli paintings would occupy the artist for some twenty years and eventually run into the hundreds, creating a legacy that is matched only by his Ned Kelly paintings in their contribution to Australia's self-image.

Gallipoli was not the only subject that consumed Nolan's energy while on Hydra. He also found time to produce numerous sketches and paintings of the island and town, several of which memorably capture the broad sweep of the vista of the town and Saronic Gulf as seen from the Ghika mansion. While many of Nolan's Gallipoli sketches expressed the drama, terror and 'clang' of battle, his paintings of Hydra often display a very different temperament, reflecting both the bucolic surroundings in which the Nolans were living and the agreeable change of pace away from the major art centres of Europe.

The seven months Nolan spent on Hydra provided him with both opportunity and inspiration, and his association with the island and Johnston would continue. Nolan made a short visit to Hydra in late 1958, and when the Johnstons returned to England in late October 1960 in order to retrieve their financial situation, Nolan both tried to persuade them that they would be best served by returning to Hydra to pursue their work and then eased the way for them financially. Nolan also visited Hydra in 1963 to discuss with Johnston his design of the dust jacket for *My Brother Jack* (a painting that would directly reference the Gallipoli series), and on his arrival in Australia to promote the book, Johnston would return the favour by scripting the film, *Toehold in History* (1965), which used Nolan's paintings to illustrate a re-telling of the Gallipoli story. The film was produced and directed by Dahl and Geoffrey Collings (who had their own Hydra connection through their daughter Silver), and sponsored by the Australian carrier Qantas—an arrangement that was part of Johnston's negotiations with the airline in return for his passage back to Australia.

In addition to feeding Nolan with subject matter, Hydra was also an ideal place for the artist to work. The Nolans' visit spanned from autumn of one year until the following spring, and during this period the island was a quiet place with a mundane daily life. With few other foreigners wintering on the island, Nolan and Johnston discussed Greek mythology, Homer, Graves, Gallipoli and Troy late into the night as "the *retzina* circled and wild winter buffeted at the shutters of the waterfront taverns", and they had little to keep them from their work. In a scene in *Peel Me a Lotus*, Clift has Henry Trevena—the character based on Nolan—display the impressive results of his season's work in the studio of the mansion house in which he is living and working.

> In the studio Henry had spread out his winter's work for inspection: five hundred small sketches in oil paint on the stiff white sheets of heavy art paper that he buys in bundles of a thousand at a time.
>
> The islands are there, the rocks, the goats, the spikes, the thorns— Greece actual. But most of the studies are concerned with Greek myth, browbeaten into tractability. Icarus occurs again and again. ...

Work done for the day. George Johnston outside Katsikas, n.d. (Redmond Wallis)

The sketches are terribly impressive. It occurred to me, not for the first time, that Henry might well turn out to be one of the really important artists.

Following the pattern established in this first year, the extended winter months would remain the 'writing season' for Johnston and Clift, the period when they were most free to dedicate themselves to their work. If they were to work at all over summer, with the ever-expanding summer tourist season peppered with the distractions of new arrivals and a busier social life, it would be before the day's libations commenced in the late morning—a scenario that also required them to be sufficiently recovered from the excesses of the previous evening.

Even as they found themselves unable to resist the sociability visitors afforded, Clift and Johnston were often scornful of those with whom they mixed. The couple's dedication to their craft was the point of difference that Clift in particular saw between herself and Johnston and those others who drifted through Hydra with aspirations, or pretensions, to an artistic life. An anecdote from Redmond Wallis in *The Unyielding Memory*, focusing on Leonard Cohen, underscores Clift's attitude to the island's writers and their work.

Earlier in the narrative, Catherine and George have instructed Nick Alwyn on Saul's (Cohen's) special status: "Saul Rubens wasn't seen on the *agora* very often. He was, said the Graysons, who clasped their acquaintance with him to their bosoms protectively, almost as if they were afraid the rest of the foreign colony might take him away from them, writing a book of poetry, to be called 'Alms for Eichmann' ['Flowers for Hitler']." From the beginning of the acquaintance between the two men, Alwyn finds Rubens fascinating because of his commitment to his craft. Nick believes that, "This one is going to come very close to being a great writer".

The acclaim Cohen received after the publication of *The Spice-Box of Earth* in May 1961 saw him return from Canada to Hydra to avoid the attention, several months after he used a Canadian government grant to finance a trip to Cuba. This Cuban trip instigates a strained conversation between Alwyn and George and Catherine Grayson in *The Unyielding Memory*, with the Graysons voicing a change of heart about Saul who seems, in their eyes, to have flouted his artistic commitments by becoming interested in politics.

> 'I used to love Saul,' he [George] said … 'but it's gone now. I think he's insincere and uncommitted. There was a time when Saul was in a position to do something worthwhile with his life, when he had real talent, but he's pissed it away by accepting state money and spending most of his time getting involved in politics instead of concentrating on his poetry.'
> … Catherine gave him [Nick] a superior little smile … 'Commitment is more than just saying you're a writer or a poet, Nick, it's dedicating yourself to something body and soul, being prepared never to compromise

your position. Saul has to learn that, and he has to do it, if he wants to make his mark, going to Cuba isn't enough.'

Whether this exchange is verbatim or complete fiction (the former is more likely although, given Cohen's later reputation, Alwyn's retrospectively imagined forecast has the canny effect of reflecting positively on Alwyn himself), it suggests a commitment to work that underpins Clift's understanding of her own purpose for being on Hydra. That said, it is certainly the case that despite the Graysons' purported misgivings, Cohen won respect throughout his career for his meticulous approach to his craft, and he was able to work diligently even given Hydra's many diversions. As he later recalled of this period of his life:

> My days were very clear, because I was writing novels, putting books of poetry together, so the days were very, very orderly. We'd get up early, I'd have breakfast and I'd go to work. And a sandwich would be brought to me. I think I was on speed too so I wasn't eating very much. And the day would proceed like that. I had a quota, I think it was three pages a day—I *know* it was three pages a day.

As Cohen indicated, drugs were easily come by on Hydra at this time and another potential distraction from work, and when he wasn't writing he was often smoking hashish with his friends Steve Sanfield, Nana Isaia (a Greek artist, and later a poet and translator, who arrived on the island in 1964) and Sheldon Cholst. Cholst was a New York psychiatrist and aspiring poet who had done jail time in England for his drug involvement. In 1964 he published a rather startling volume of poetry titled *Hydra: summer season—sixty two, poems and drawings*. The poems include earnest hymns to Hydra's donkeys ("I think I am a donkey too / but a freed one"), unexpected comparisons between women and French salamanders, and an offbeat meditation on "Marianne, Marianne, Marianne / Who has an Axel and a Leonard". Another memorable associative poem about Hydra includes lines that leave readers to wonder what feedback Cohen might have provided on his friend's poesy:

I play music when I kiss
Silent music upon the lips and mouth
My tongue plays upon a girls teeth
As if I played a xylophone.
I have bitten lips as if they were
The tastiest meat this side of heaven
I have sucked upon lips as if they contained
Rare juice of pomegranate which I don't think
I've tasted yet
I have munched upon lips as if they were
Delicious crackers and I were starving …
I have reached depths unheard of by others
For my tongue is long …
I do not like to eat cooked tongue
It seems a crime to cook tongue
But fresh—and alive—I roll it around in
My mouth and taste its rare ecstasy …

There is no reason to believe that Clift ever read this particular volume. Had she, she might well have used it as indisputable evidence of all that was wrong with the island's *poste-restante* visitors.

Both Cohen's work focus and drug use extended well beyond Hydra. In a diary entry for January 11th, 1962, by which time he was in London, Wallis recorded that "Leonard Cohen dropped in from Hydra on Tuesday. Remarkable the stimulus I get from him. … He makes me feel—as he feels—that I can't afford to waste time on anything not being written at the absolute peak of my ability, on anything in any way frivolous." In addition to inspiring Wallis with his work ambitions, Cohen also used this visit to introduce Wallis to marijuana. In a March diary entry, Wallis reported that he had been "Smoking marijuana with Cohen", but he decided that he was "not too fond of this stuff. Exactly like being drunk except good physical control and hardly any mental control at all." It was also, he noted, a "Great laxative".

Wallis, like Clift, Johnston, and perhaps all of Hydra's writers and artists, found himself working against the island's many distractions. While Wallis found it difficult at times to maintain his resolve, he was quick to dedicate himself to his writing once he and Robyn decided to extend their stay, and he was determined to complete a novel before departing for London at summer's end. Wallis's diaries and workbooks offer a detailed insight into his work ethic, recording enough of his aspirations to make it clear that, contrary to Clift's sceptical evaluation of the young men then washing up on Hydra, Wallis was setting a course for a long and influential literary career.

In a diary entry for April 18th, 1960, less than a week after arriving on Hydra, Wallis announced "So here we are & all I have to do now is find something to write about", and set out an ambitious schedule to complete a novel by mid-September, including two drafts and three weeks for "final revisions". This entry also includes his first attempt to produce a plot outline: "Boy meets girl, boy loses girl, boy gets syphillus".

Wallis commenced writing properly on April 25th, and several days later offered another plot draft, more sophisticated than the first and at least gesturing towards the final content of the novel.

> This is a novel about two different societies, Christchurch & Wgtn, & how they corrupt a young man—thru his own inadequacy. He comes from a moral background, sort of falls for a girl from one of the best Chch families. Doesn't want to go on with it. She is killed in Ballantyne's fire. He goes to Wgtn & with the knowledge acquired thru' loving her, harder & more assured now, fits into the business rich society of Wgtn. He marries a silly girl, who is yet more subtle than the Chch one, and hooks him. This is a tragedy.

Wallis also noted that he was writing four thousand words a day and that "4000 a day is easy and I must pick it up". By May 14th he reported having written sixty thousand words and "Finished the first part of the book", but that "it stinks" and that there is a "Hold up on where to go from here. Not an incident, plot in my head." At this point Wallis comprehended the enormity of the task he had set himself and, while he continued to write quickly, he also recognised the problems that he was encountering. On May 22nd he noted:

> This book has possibilities. Trouble is, that unless it is very good, it won't sell because the story (and theme) is not really original—just in a new setting and handled slightly differently. If it was really good, of course, it would almost be literature. Robyn looks at me last night and says 'Do you realise if you kept on writing you would be NZ's first man of letters?' Oh, sure. But I have a funny feeling, unusual in me, that I could be quite good, if I did keep on. If only I had more intelligence!

Disregarding his self-proclaimed intellectual limitations, Wallis announces that he is striving for something new in New Zealand fiction, noting that "It occurs to me that having noted years ago that I wanted to write 10 good NZ novels to give NZ lit a basis, I'm going to be well outside the mainstream of my national lit", and that he is writing "one of the first NZ novels to deal directly with ideas".

Firstly, however, he needed to finish the novel on which he had embarked. A month after starting his optimism waned and he declared that he has been writing "shit".

> Why on earth did I have to write about someone so stupid, if so young, and why does the story have to be so commonplace and bloody uninteresting. I feel like dropping the whole thing—a month and a day after the start—and start something else.

Despite this threat to abandon the novel, Wallis continued working, reporting on June 5th that the first draft was finished. He immediately started to redraft, and on July 15th declared that "it is incomparably better but still only so-so. ... I have the horrible feeling I may have to work on this for months yet." Just over a month later, on August 22nd, he reported that he "Finished 2nd draft of Point of Origin yesterday", his first reference to what would be the novel's published title. He noted that the novel "has been written twice, completely, in 4 months, almost to the day. Too fast", but that it is "salvageable".

By late summer it was apparent to Wallis that his original timetable for completing the novel was beyond him and, although chronically short of cash, he decided to extend the couple's stay. He now commenced a complete re-write of the novel, aiming for a more modest two thousand words a day, but as winter set in and many of the foreigners left the island, Wallis's diary records his growing self-doubt about the quality of his writing.

Despite this crisis of confidence, Wallis continued planning future novels and in his "literary notebook" he makes mention of "When I get around to writing the Hydra stories"—the first indication that he was planning to fictionalise his time on the island. Finally, after months of re-writing, Wallis recorded in his diary, with great precision, "6.30pm June 29 [1961], wrote the end to Point of Origin". The following day, after posting the manuscript, he noted that "I've learnt so much that the next one will be incomparably better". With the novel's overdue completion, the Wallises immediately left for London, where in March the following year they received the news that *Point of Origin* would be published in the US by Houghton-Mifflin—the months of hard work and self-doubt on Hydra had paid off. The couple eventually returned to Hydra in the second half of 1963, assisted by a £500 writer's grant from the New Zealand government, thereby disregarding the Johnstons' warnings about writers accepting subventions.

Another who might be discounted as being among the young men Clift scorned as lacking dedication to their art is Rodney Hall, who tells the story of how he gifted to the Johnstons a sequence of poems he was working on as atonement for an offence he inadvertently committed against Martin Johnston. Hall relates how he and a number of other expatriates gathered at the Johnstons' house for a festival celebration. During the festivities, Martin put Joseph Haydn's trumpet concerto on the record player. Hall commented casually that while Haydn was a great composer, this piece was his "one vulgar work". Johnston immediately summoned up an incandescent rage, taking the comment as a criticism of his son. In a display of mutual indignation, Clift ordered Hall, his wife and baby out of the house. Hall recalled that, to redeem the friendship:

> I collected a whole group of poems, I think there were about twelve of them, and typed up a fair copy, and bound them together with a dedication sheet, dedicating it to them. And I had a new manila folder, so I enclosed the little swag of poems in the manila folder with the dedication, and we went around to the house. Bet got a bunch of flowers on the way, and we went around and left them at the house with the flowers.

The Halls were promptly forgiven and presented in turn with a basket of goods by Clift, which she carried while "coo-eeing" her way up the hill in search of their house. Johnston, presumably, was at home writing.

James Burke's photographs include some two dozen images of Johnston at work at his typewriter in the light-flooded studio room of the Hydra house, bringing to mind Clift's testimony that "The studio is his action-post for all the morning", and that "While I work I can hear the dull thudding of George's typewriter up in the studio—that familiar intermittent chatter that has been the background to all my married life". Burke's images project Johnston's self-identification as a serious author whose purpose for being on Hydra was to write. With both Johnston and Clift priding themselves on how much harder they worked than other expatriates, these images appear designed to emphasise to doubters that their move to Hydra was determined by the need to find an ideal creative environment rather than a leisured island lifestyle.

Burke's photographs depict Johnston pounding at the typewriter with two-fingered intensity, his ever-present cigarette replaced by a pipe in order to keep his hands free for the task. At the time the images were taken, Johnston was awaiting the publication of his novel *Closer to the Sun*. The book was notable for three reasons. Firstly, it was the only novel that Johnston would write while on Hydra that directly referenced his island experience. Johnston renames the island Silenos, but for the most part, characters—other than Meredith, his wife Kate, and the *agent provocateur* Mouliet—are only very

George Johnston at the Remington. (James Burke)

loosely based on individuals on Hydra. Secondly, it introduced readers to the character of David Meredith, who would be reprised in Johnston's following novel, *The Far Road*, and then go on to be the central figure in the Meredith trilogy that commenced with *My Brother Jack*. Thirdly, it continued the use of 'the brother' as an important narrative device in Johnston's novels—in this case David Meredith's brother Mark, who serves as the rational counterpoint to the emotionally tempestuous David.

Johnston's creation of David Meredith, his enduring alter ego, was a transitional moment in his development as a writer. The precise timing of Meredith's emergence is relevant, as *Closer to the Sun* was written in the aftermath of a major health scare for Johnston in late 1959 that included a period of treatment and recuperation in Athens. It was an incident that appears to have re-committed Johnston to the importance of producing work of lasting quality, and he found in Meredith a means of channeling all the desire, self-doubt, insecurity and frustration that had hitherto dogged his life and literary ambitions. At the time he was concluding *Closer to the Sun*, Johnston produced a very fine short story 'The Verdict', also featuring Meredith, which provides a pitiless account of the protagonist's confrontation with his own mortality as he spends a day alone in Athens waiting for what he believes will be a cancer diagnosis. While contemplating his predicament, Meredith provides a scarifying assessment of the meagre return for his "restless, driving obsession with work" and of his long-deferred ambition "to produce something 'worthwhile'". In the face of his failure and the fragile state of his marriage, Meredith momentarily sees death as an appealing way out, a chance to side-step his responsibilities and the pressure to succeed.

> And the joy of it was that he would no longer have to try to tilt his blunted little lances at those windmills of contemporary writing. He could round it all off as an ex-newspaperman turned commercial novelist and let it go at that, with some garish covers on some inflammatory paperbacks and a little money coming in as insurance for his dependents, and to hell with delusions of literature and a remembered name.

There is irony in Johnston not attempting to have this excellently conceived and modulated story published when it might have presented his best defence against the self-accusation of mediocrity. Almost certainly, however, there were elements—particularly those reflecting his sexual inadequacy in his relationship with Clift—that even he might have considered too self-revealing. The story would be resurrected a decade later in an abbreviated form as a section of *Clean Straw for Nothing*. In the meantime, the concern about his accomplishments as a writer would develop into a central theme of *Closer to the Sun*, but this time in conjunction with a focus on Kate Meredith's sex life rather than her husband's.

What Meredith doesn't reveal to his wife for much of the novel is that his inability to write is partly the result of his growing certainty that she is involved in an affair with the character Achilles Mouliet, a French artist. Mouliet was based on Frenchman Jean-Claude Maurice, who was to be a provocation in the Johnston-Clift marriage for several years. Maurice had arrived on Hydra in the summer of 1956, and in *Peel Me a Lotus* Clift made clear her fascination with the hedonistic and libidinous Frenchman, who appears as the character Jacques, from the moment he arrives on the morning boat.

> His feet were bare, and he wore only a pair of patched jeans; a rag of a scarlet shirt, and one gold ear-ring. Rather slowly and sleepily he shuffled along the quay, carrying a big-artists portfolio, a mule saddle-bag in bright stripes and a tabby cat in a netted basket. Had he chosen to arrive in the faun-skin of Dionysus, wearing an ivy-crown, and carrying a fennel-wand, the effect could hardly have been more electrifying.

Clift's response to Maurice over the course of the book expresses the contradictions of her own desires. On the one hand, he is the embodiment of the shallow, self-obsessed and unproductive war generation who have little substance in their work; on the other hand, his youthful beauty, licentiousness and commitment to personal freedom captivate the pagan and libertarian side of Clift's personality and are an antidote to her fear of being bound by her role as a mother, tethered to an increasingly ill husband, and adrift on a barren rock. If Johnston had not suspected, based on his own observation, that his wife had a flirtatious sexual interest in Maurice, then he certainly would after reading *Peel Me a Lotus*.

It is unlikely there was any physical relationship between Clift and Maurice in the summer of 1956, but when he returned to Hydra two years later there certainly was. The affair appears to have been conducted quite publicly (there was little choice amongst the Hydra expatriates) and unsurprisingly brought enormous stress to an already tempestuous marriage. However, it is in his own handling of the Maurice character, Mouliet, that Johnston brought to *Closer to the Sun* something that would trouble his marriage until its end—his use of fiction as a weapon of accusation and punishment targeting his wife. In what amounts to an audacious statement of intent, Johnston introduces Mouliet's boat arrival in almost exactly the same terms as Clift had used for Jacques—the jeans, the ear-ring, the portfolio of art, the packages and the cat in a basket are all present, as is the association with the figure of the faun, with Johnston writing that "his brown face was the face of a faun, or of an old

Greek god, a face with the pagan look of an ancient angel". Later, in his telling of the consummation of the relationship between Kate and Mouliet, Johnston draws from Clift's evocation of Dionysus in order to evoke the transgressive pagan spirit of their coupling: "He looked exactly like the bronze image of the god Dionysus she had once seen in the Louvre, the god young and naked and beautiful".

It is clear that Johnston's 'borrowing' is something other than a form of low-level benefit from having read Clift's book. Rather, it is a way of signalling—to Clift certainly, but also to others—that Jacques and Mouliet are one and the same, and that this fiction aligns to the 'reality' of Clift's memoir, thereby confirming that Clift's infatuation portrayed in *Peel Me a Lotus* reached the physical conclusion Johnston had feared. It was also an indication of the extent to which Johnston's work, which was intended to be the vehicle by which the couple would pursue their shared dream, had the potential to be a corrosive element in their relationship. The inter-textual link between characters would be fully explicit when Johnston came to write *Clean Straw for Nothing*, in which he also adopts the name Jacques for the same "quick, handsome, faun-like" character, and emphasises that "his physical appeal to women was irresistible, but Cressida's captivation was much more …".

The reality for David Meredith in *Closer to the Sun*, and indeed for Johnston at this point, is that the prospect of leaving the island and recommencing a career on Fleet Street was precluded by the very financial stress that also made it necessary. The family was, as Clift had warned, effectively "marooned". Johnston's situation is reflected in a number of James Burke's images in which the hard-working author is framed in such a way that he appears to be 'imprisoned' in his writing room by the vertical bars of the room divider. In the most striking of these images, Johnston apparently explodes in frustration at the task before him.

In contrast to the carefully curated image of a 'serious author' hard at work that Johnston assisted Burke to produce, an element of the calculated revenge that Johnston took on Clift in *Closer to the Sun* is that Kate Meredith

A blank sheet of paper in an unresponsive typewriter. George Johnston expresses his frustration. (James Burke)

is stripped of any role as a writer—she is represented as no more than a housekeeper and carer to the children. Johnston would have been aware of the hurt this would cause his wife who, in addition to having her infidelity laid bare, also found her role in the family and within the island's expatriate community reduced to that of factotum to the struggling artist, whose prospects for success she is depicted as recklessly turning upside-down as he alone battles to provide for the family.

It is notable that this role separation between David and Kate Meredith in *Closer to the Sun* is repeated in Burke's photographs of Johnston and Clift. In addition to the numerous images of Johnston at his typewriter there are also other photos, taken inside and outside the house, where he appears in his full creative armour as the brooding, hard-drinking, hard-smoking man of letters. Clift, on the other hand, is given no function as 'author' in any of Burke's photographs, and in most images of her taken in the house she appears in the kitchen and engaged in domestic duties. It is impossible to know exactly how or why Burke's images were constructed as they are, but the result reinforces the impression of Johnston as the creative force with Clift in a supportive role.

The reality, however, was quite different. While Clift maintained the household and children, she was also constantly engaged with her own writing. In the early months on Hydra she completed and dispatched the manuscript for *Mermaid Singing*, and then almost immediately commenced work on *Peel Me a Lotus*. Although Clift's goal remained to write fiction, she found a very comfortable metier with the amalgam of travel writing and memoir, and although not blessed with Johnston's ease in turning out words, she succeeded in drafting, rewriting and preparing for publication two of the finest books from the couple's body of work. By any assessment, *Peel Me a Lotus* is the indispensable starting point for an understanding of the period that Clift and Johnston spent on Hydra, even though it covers only the first year they were on the island. Featuring numerous passages of fine descriptive writing, it draws its real strength from the clear-eyed appraisal of the circumstances in which the couple found themselves and of the peculiarities of expatriation more generally. For a writer with an inherently romantic temperament, and working in a genre that relies on romantic conventions, Clift managed nonetheless to dig away at the 'realities' that slowly undermined the idealism with which the couple approached their Aegean lives. While both Clift and Johnston were immediately enchanted by Hydra and its potential to provide them with the artistic and personal lives for which they longed, it is also apparent from *Peel Me a Lotus* that Clift quickly foresaw the pitfalls and dangers that inevitably awaited—some of the couple's own making and others over which they had little control.

In a repeat of a problem that plagued Clift and Johnston during their time on Hydra, both *Mermaid Singing* and *Peel Me a Lotus* were well regarded by publishers and favourably reviewed but sold in modest numbers. With the authors being geographically outside the Anglo literary realm, many standard promotional activities were impossible, and it seemed there was only so much that could be achieved in building an author's profile without the drip-feed of personal visibility and the associated column-inches. Undaunted by the public reception of her earlier books, Clift had the manuscript for her first sole authored work of fiction, *Walk to the Paradise Gardens*, to her agent by April of 1959. *Walk to the Paradise Gardens* was noteworthy in that it was the first book by either Clift or Johnston to have an Australian setting, with 'Lebanon Bay' clearly modelled on Clift's hometown of Kiama.

From there Clift's focus shifted to a Greek island setting as she commenced her second novel, *Honour's Mimic*. By the time she was working on that novel, Clift was finding writing fiction to be increasingly difficult. Not only was she diverted by assisting Johnston in editing and proofreading his drafts, but she would later describe how she "ran into an absolute writing block" at this time. Unlike the pace the couple usually set, the writing of *Honour's Mimic* would consume nearly four years.

The island depicted in *Honour's Mimic* is unnamed. Descriptions reveal similarities to both Kalymnos and Hydra, but as a social setting, the island is clearly based on Kalymnos, with its reliance on a sponge-diving industry dominated by a small number of wealthy and influential families, and a largely British community of expatriates. The main female character is Kathy Bassett, an Australian woman married to an Englishman, who finds herself staying on the island in the home of her Greek brother-in-law, Demetrius, and his wife, Milly (sister of Kathy's husband). Demetrius and Milly have created an island house that is a displaced slice of England, where it is the norm to sit around on a "glazed chintz sofa pouring Earl Grey's tea from a silver pot". The plot is driven by the ill-matched love that forms between the free-thinking Kathy and Fotis, an out-of-luck sponge diver with a wife and eight children.

The novel is notable for passages of fine writing; its unsentimental portrayal of doomed love; its exploration of distinctions of ethnicity, class and gender; and as yet another novel by the couple that has infidelity at its heart. In terms of Clift and Johnston's own marriage, troubled as it had been by betrayals on both sides, it was provocative for Clift to feature a loosely autobiographical character in an adulterous relationship. While it has not been suggested that the events depicted are true to Clift, it is inevitable that for Johnston the echoes of his wife's relationship with Maurice and other island infidelities would have been undeniable and taunting.

As noted, Clift's delay in concluding *Honour's Mimic* may have been as much due to the assistance she was providing to Johnston as to her case of writer's block. In early 1960, Johnston began writing a book that he was (again) convinced would reverse his fortunes and reputation. As he wrote to his daughter Gae in Australia during February, "your Old Man might turn out to be a real novelist yet! I have the feeling I am on the verge of writing something worthwhile." This "something worthwhile" was the novel *The Far Road*, which told the story of Johnston's horrific encounter with mass-death while working as a war correspondent in Western China in 1944. There was to be nothing pot-boiling or frivolous about this novel, which related with unrelieved intensity a story as harrowing as any produced about Australian experience in the Second World War. As Nadia Wheatley observed, Clift's role was to not only push Johnston to write this demanding book but also to make herself "available as sounding board and emotional backup as George got this horrific tale down on paper". In this case Johnston's dedication of the novel, "for Charmian, in earnest", was hard-won.

Although *The Far Road* was commenced on Hydra, it was completed during the Johnstons' English sojourn in late 1960 and the early months of 1961. It seems to have been the only work-related positive to come from that six months of respite, other than an increasingly desperate Johnston commencing the final Shane Martin novel. That Johnston called upon his alter-ego character of David Meredith once more for *The Far Road* was indicative of both the novel's autobiographical element and his increasing investment in the Meredith character. Whereas Johnston later expressed a view that *Closer to the Sun* had been let down by his own ambivalence in handling the novel's autobiographical underpinnings, there was no such hesitancy evident in the intensity with which Meredith's doubts and fears are exposed in *The Far Road*.

The result was Johnston's finest novel to date, and finally an achievement in which he (and Clift) could take real pride. It was, however, another case where positive reviews failed to generate sales, and the novel was almost certainly the poorest selling of Johnston's career. If it is true that the Shane Martin novels missed their moment, then the same can be said for *The Far Road*. Coming just as the 1960s began to swing, there was little appetite by readers to be thrown back to the horrors of one of the least understood theatres of the all-too-recent war. *The Far Road* was always destined to be a difficult book to retail.

Although Johnston and Clift had been buoyed by their return to Hydra in mid-April 1961, this lift in their spirits was short lived and did little to relieve the mounting stress of their island living or the conflicts within their own relationship. Both of these issues were exacerbated by the passing of another summer with its ever-increasing influx of tourists, and by Clift embarking on another affair of which Johnston soon became aware. The couple's excessive drinking and public arguments became more frequent, and there is evidence of occasional physical confrontations. As the summer of 1962 waned, Johnston's health problems once again worsened when, as usual, the cold and damp winter exacerbated his respiratory difficulties.

At the time, there could have been few less-likely candidates amongst contemporary Australian writers to produce a serious tilt at the 'Great Australian novel'. The prematurely-aged, consumptive, alcoholic and increasingly homesick novelist with a perilously fractured marriage and a recent track record of declining readership seemed well beyond his most capable years. By any measure, the eight years in the Aegean had failed to produce the quality of work of which he and Clift dreamed, without even providing the compensation of a steady income.

As always, however, Johnston found an escape, and hope, in his work. With the growing awareness of his mortality leading him to turn his mind increasingly towards his own country and his childhood, in late 1962 Johnston commenced work on the novel that would become *My Brother Jack*. After several false starts that sketchily traced David Meredith's childhood, Johnston found his range with the realisation that Meredith could serve as the vehicle through which he could channel his whole life story. The ongoing emergence of Meredith, together with the novel's themes and structure, may not have been a totally unexpected revelation. As Johnston later claimed, partly refuting his reputation for speed, the work of writing *My Brother Jack* had effectively been going on for years.

> I spend a long time sitting around, drinking grog, smoking cigarettes, thinking about what I want to write. In fact *My Brother Jack*, I thought for seventeen years about that before I tackled it. … And then one day you are still having that grog or smoking that cigarette and suddenly you know how to do it.

As Johnston climbed once more into the literary trenches he again found Clift at his side. A crucial component of the Johnston and Clift myth is the extent to which they worked cooperatively on *My Brother Jack*. Almost from the outset both realised that this was 'the one'—the book they had gone to Hydra to write. It was Johnston's story, but more than ever he needed Clift to encourage, prompt, read, and edit. Famously, the two worked in tandem as Johnston battled with his memory to create the vivid word-pictures of suburban interwar Melbourne that were crucial to the book's authenticity and appeal, with Clift eliciting ever more precise detail from her fragile husband. As *The Australian Women's Weekly* later reported when Johnston was interviewed shortly after Clift's death in July 1969:

> 'Charmian sat on a stone step on a cushion and we talked and talked and remembered and remembered, and I wrote "My Brother Jack"' … There were no books of reference on the island. George had to undertake a monumental feat of recall, to bring back Melbourne, Australia, in the grip of the Depression. 'It was tough—but if I gave myself to memory it worked, in a most uncanny way. I'd try to remember a street, and soon I'd be able to bring back all the shops. And although Charmian was 11

years younger than I, she could remember the Depression, as a little girl. I'd ask her, 'What sort of clothes did your sister wear? What sort of slang did you use?"

Copies of *My Brother Jack* had been forwarded to Hydra by Christmas 1963, and several years ago a copy gifted by Johnston to Clift was offered for sale. It carried the inscription: "Charmian—a Christmas ago it was impossible. Without you it was impossible. And always will be … without you. Much love. George. Christmas, 1963. Hydra." Once again Johnston had acknowledged, whatever the problems that plagued their marriage, the considerable debt he owed his wife.

Certainly, the couple's collaborative memories were essential to the success of *My Brother Jack*, both as a work of considerable literary merit and in attracting a large Australian readership. As a novel that spans the two World Wars and the intervening years of the Great Depression, it drew upon crucial nostalgic touchstones for several generations of Australians that were evoked by the meticulously described accounts of Melbourne life. *My Brother Jack* resonated then, as it does now, with the emotional pull of an Australia that had changed, and that would go on changing ever more rapidly up to the point of publication, and in the years since.

Characteristically for Johnston, however, the novel's real strength is found in its unflinching scrutiny of the central character. For the first time, David Meredith is represented with first-person narration, and the impact is palpable in terms of the immediacy and authenticity this lends to his 'life'. Whether or not the reader knew (or now knows) of Johnston's life story and therefore reads the novel autobiographically, Meredith's narration carries a stamp of genuine experience as he does battle with his fears, frailties and deep insecurities that are again thrown into relief by the character of a brother, in this case the eponymous Jack.

My Brother Jack also casts additional light on Johnston's decision to expatriate. For although it is the novel that describes Meredith's Australian years, it is also written in anticipation of the later fiction that will describe his expatriation. Johnston flags Meredith's future life almost at the novel's outset in a passing reference to "Only the other day, [when I was] sitting in the sun outside a waterfront coffee-house on a Greek island where I have been hiding for several years …". The novel touches upon the many 'triggers' to Meredith's expatriation, including his "traditional sense of isolation from the things that were happening in Europe"; a first marriage that leaves him abandoned in the suburban wastelands of Melbourne; his mounting disenchantment with a conservative and insular Australia; and his inner demons that see him disenchanted with his apparently enchanted life. Part of the achievement of *My Brother Jack* is that Johnston imbues Meredith with significance, so that the arc of his life is a story that makes sense not only in personal terms but in its representation of national narratives and discontents. To the reader, Meredith's decision to leave Australia in the postwar years therefore seems both rational and reasonable for someone of his disposition.

My Brother Jack was critically and commercially acclaimed internationally, but it was in Australia that it became a publishing sensation, making a 'celebrity' of Johnston. It was a success on a scale that had long seemed beyond its author, but it was also an achievement that highlighted his previous protracted failure. For if *My Brother Jack*'s obvious merit is seen as justifying his decision to move to the Aegean in order to produce "something worthwhile", then having used the cosmopolitan sweep of his previous fiction in a failed attempt to gain international recognition could be seen to have been misguided, time-wasting and self-defeating. The singular success of *My Brother Jack* meant that everything else that Johnston wrote on Hydra was immediately seen as irrelevant and forgotten—a form of protracted juvenilia.

In addition to Johnston and Clift's considerable body of published work completed on Hydra—fourteen books in all—there were also, not unexpectedly, several 'false starts' and incomplete or discarded drafts produced by both. Of these, the most notable is Clift's novel *The End of the Morning*, which was conceptualised as an autobiographical coming-of-age fiction in which she was to introduce her character Cressida Morley. The work on this novel, which had commenced in 1963, was seemingly derailed by Clift's commitment to assisting Johnston with *My Brother Jack*. As Nadia Wheatley has astutely observed, however, the difficulties Clift faced when she returned to the novel were compounded by Johnston having 'borrowed' Cressida Morley for his own uses in *My Brother Jack*.

> The problem arising was that Charmian Clift regarded Cressida Morley as being her own alter ego character. And if Johnston was developing Cressida—how could Clift? It was as if there were two sculptors chipping a figure out of the one block of stone, but one sculptor worked much faster than the other, so that his side of the shape was developing while the other side was still inchoate.

While Clift continued to work on *The End of the Morning* almost up until her death and was awarded a grant from the Commonwealth Literary Fund in late 1968 to enable her to complete the project, the novel remained fragmentary. The surviving drafts of sections of *The End of the Morning* are now housed in the National Library of Australia.

* * *

In *The Unyielding Memory*, Redmond Wallis includes several sections that recount the competitiveness between Hydra's writers, and, in the process, reveal something of his own rivalry with Johnston and the fraught relationship (professionally supportive and personally corrosive) between the Graysons. In these two passages, Wallis recalls periods during which Grayson (Johnston) is writing "The Islanders" (*Closer to the Sun*), and a book "about the writer's brother" (*My Brother Jack*).

> 'Isn't it a delightful day,' she said, in a deep, rounded voice that, Nick knew, his wife thought was affected, the voice of a woman who had decided to be a woman writer, and a cultured one at that. There wasn't a hint of Australian in it, and yet Catherine, like George, was a dyed-in-the-wool Australian.

She stretched dramatically, looked at Nick, and said: 'So how are you getting on, Nick?'

'Pretty good, I'm churning out four thousand a day without much effort. In fact, I'm going to push it up.'

'Good, I'm so glad. It's wonderful when it flows like that. George has the same facility, don't you darling?'

'Well, I'm trying to slow down with this one,' said George. "It's going to be important, I don't want to hurry it.'

'What's it about?' asked Nick.

'He's writing about the island as us,' said Catherine. 'As it really is, as we really are, it's going to be wonderful, so true, not like anything he has done before.'

'Got a title?'

'It's called "The Islanders" at the moment,' said George.

Sue, who had a good ear, had already registered Catherine's view of her husband as a writer. She said, 'Are we all going to be in it?'

Catherine gave her a calculating look, decided to ignore the question, and said: 'I'm doing the sexy bits for him, aren't I, darling?'

'Tarting them up a bit,' said George with a self-deprecating grin. 'I'm not very good at sex scenes.'

'It's probably just lack of practice,' said Catherine. And then, with a throaty laugh: 'Oh, darling, I didn't mean that!'

The inquiry after work-in-progress was a necessary part of social life on the island. The Graysons took it in turns to write, one doing the household chores and looking after the three children while the other worked. George spent longer on the domestic stuff than Catherine did: he could knock out a pot-boiling detective story in a couple of months; Catherine, more literary, took eight or nine months and, the Grayson's finances being what they were, wasn't given the chance all that often.

*

AT WORK

Katsika's back room was so full of his stock-in-trade that sitting at one of the tables—there was room for only three—was like being aboard a space craft laid out by an early writer of science fiction. It was cramped and almost as if everything the astronaut might require had been placed ready to hand so that minimal effort was needed to reach it. It was where the foreign colony retired in the winter and in this crowded environment, which in its way was a museum of island existence, Nick sat, ostentatiously rubbing knees with Kaycha, while he talked to George about his new book, a book that purported to be about the writer's brother, but which Nick saw as disguised autobiography. Nick, who had liked it, said so; George, perhaps inevitably, assumed the praise to be unqualified and donned a modest expression.

'But George, how could a man like Burton get to be a successful journalist, a war correspondent for Time no less, with so little apparent equipment?' asked Nick, moving his knee once again against Kaycha, who moved her knee in response.

'That's how it was,' said George. 'I could write, I had a sense for colour, I wasn't always too worried about the facts if the story was a good one. I was lucky.'

'Burton's a little dull,' said Sue. 'I know he's your hero, but he doesn't exactly excite passionate interest in what happens to him.'

'Yeah, right,' said Nick.

'Well, it's a very honest book,' said George, with a defensive note in his voice.

'Oh, yes!' said Catherine, who had been listening to the conversation without contributing. 'Burton's portrait is beautifully drawn and just so right.'

This, as her listeners recognised, being a compliment to the writer but an adverse criticism of the man, it demolished the chance of further conversation on the same topic. Nick glanced at his watch.

'Well, we're supposed to be at the Campbells,' he said.

The Campbells, down to their last drachma, gave them soup and bread for dinner.

Chapter Twelve

LEAVING

In addition to the writing of *My Brother Jack* being the culmination of the Johnstons' time on Hydra, it also instigated the end of their expatriation. The novel was published in England in January 1964, and Australian publication followed in March, by which time George Johnston was back in Sydney. As he told Hazel de Berg in an interview, there were two things that had kept him tied to Hydra, and both were resolved by this last roll-of-the-dice triumph.

> Having at one time been a sort of a big pea in the journalistic world here [Australia] I vowed I wouldn't come back with my tail between my legs or cap in hand or asking for a job. Well I didn't have much credential at this stage to justify myself having been away. And the other more important point perhaps, was that I didn't have the fare back, because by this time we had another child and when it is a family of five full fares to come ten thousand miles, it's a lot of dough. And that's it, I didn't have the fare back.

As the writing of *My Brother Jack* progressed, Johnston became convinced that it would restore both his pride and his finances, thereby providing the opportunity to return to Australia. It was also the case that the effort he made in imaginatively re-creating the Australia that he knew as a child and young man reinforced his desire to 'go home'.

> I'd written books set in the places I knew—in China, Assam, Burma, Mesopotamia, Tibet, England, France, Italy, Greece. Then quite suddenly I found myself wanting to desperately to write a book about Australia.

> So I wrote *My Brother Jack*—from a distance of 10,000 miles in space and 14 years in time. And that started it. The infection developed into chronic, incurable homesickness.

As Johnston also recalled, "By the time I was half way through *My Brother Jack* there was no question in my mind, but as soon as the book was done I was making arrangements to get back home". These arrangements were, as it turned out, considerable, and included Johnston negotiating a deal for a free fare from Qantas; recording an interview (now lost) conducted by Redmond Wallis; giving another interview with John Hetherington that ran in the *Age* literary pages; both he and Clift writing pieces for the Australian press about their time on Hydra and ruminating about their forthcoming repatriation; and inveigling British Pathé into making a newsreel, filmed both on Hydra and at Sydney Airport, recording his return.

My Brother Jack also settled for Johnston the question of 'what next?' After spending twenty years scrabbling for subject matter and a coherent authorial voice, the answer was to continue telling the story of himself and Clift, using the characters he now had at hand, David Meredith and Cressida Morley. As he was writing *My Brother Jack* Johnston already conceived the novel as the first part of a trilogy that would encompass in turn, his life leading up to his expatriation; the expatriated years of London and Greece; and then the return to Australia. Johnston therefore *had* to return to Australia in order to complete the structure for his life's work, and his deteriorating health meant that although only in his early fifties he was aware he had limited time.

As Johnston planned, the trilogy covers the full stretch of David Meredith's life. *My Brother Jack* concludes with Meredith and Morley commencing their relationship and with their expatriation clearly signalled. *Clean Straw for Nothing* recounts the couple's disillusionment with postwar Sydney; their moves to London and the Aegean (with Hydra referred to simply as "the island"); their fragile relationship as they become enmeshed in alcohol addiction and sexual rivalry; and Meredith's mounting homesickness and return to Australia. *A Cartload of Clay*, incomplete and posthumously published, traces Meredith's wanderings through suburban Sydney as he reflects on his career, postwar Australian life and Morley's death.

In *Clean Straw for Nothing*, the narrative drive—outside the deteriorating relationship between Meredith and Morley—comes from Meredith's uncertainty about where he might live, as he struggles to keep afloat the ideals that drove his move to "the island". One of the issues sparking friction between Meredith and Morley is the possibility they might go back to Australia. Even as they are getting established on the island, Morley is emphatic that her expatriation is permanent while Meredith is ambivalent.

> 'Can you really settle and belong, as an alien?' Stephanos asks quietly.
> 'Don't you ever feel you want to back to your own country and your own people?'
> 'Never,' says Cressida. …
> 'And you, David?' asks Stephanos.
> 'Oh, occasionally.' I hedge a little. 'Vaguely.'
> 'Never!' Cressida didn't hedge.

Johnston's mounting homesickness was exacerbated when Sidney Nolan visited Hydra twice in 1963 to discuss his cover design for *My Brother Jack*. Nolan, by this time, was a true internationalist, fulfilling what was likely Johnston's own one-time dream of maintaining a career in the global centres of art and literature while travelling often to Australia. Having previously encouraged the Johnstons to remain on Hydra, Nolan now seemed determined to tempt them back to Australia, something achieved when he burnt some eucalyptus leaves to evoke the smell of the Australian bush. Johnston recalled the incident in *Clean Straw for Nothing*:

> [T]he moment the aromatic pungency of the burning leaves struck his nostrils he experienced for an instant a real pang of hunger for something experienced and lost far back in time, and staring into the fire at the darkening curl and shrivel of the scimitar leaves he saw again the blue hazes of hot big distances and brown leaves in a tangle of fallen bark.

Johnston was not alone in his vulnerability to the powerful emotional tug conjured up by those burning leaves. Clift also recorded this incident in her essay 'After the Hodmadods', describing an identical response to that of Johnston: "he [Nolan] put a match to them and burned them and held them under our noses and I was ready to cry with longing for the spiky wild strange grey bush tunnelled with harshness and silence".

But homesickness and the promise of long-desired literary success were not all that was driving Johnston and Clift's decision-making. Another reason why the couple left Hydra at this time—and chose to leave permanently—is the extent to which they were being ostracised by the very expatriate community they had fostered, to the point that staying on the island was hardly an option. By mid-1963 many of the key players of Hydra's international colony had accumulated long and complex personal histories that tested the goodwill of even this famously liberal and forgiving group. In this environment, it was the increasingly erratic, alcohol-induced and self-absorbed behaviour of the Johnstons that strained friendships and eroded their central role among the established expatriates.

Evidence of Clift and Johnston's mounting isolation is registered in Redmond Wallis's correspondence and *The Unyielding Memory*. In the latter, when Nick Alwyn returns to the island in 1963 after a two-year absence, he immediately recognises the changes that have taken place. He finds that Hydra has "ceased to be a haven for the creative poor", and that a "shadow of change [has fallen] over the old foreign colony". While Alwyn's first period on the island had been focused on the foreign contingent and the occasionally fractious sociability that centred on the Graysons, he now finds the old social structure in disarray and the key role previously exercised by the Australian couple quickly eroding.

In the first conversation between Alwyn and George Grayson after Alwyn's return, they discuss Grayson's forthcoming novel "that purported to be about the writer's brother, but which Nick saw as disguised autobiography". From this point on, a considerable plotline of *The Unyielding Memory* is concerned with George's high hopes and anxious wait for the publication of this new novel; the increasingly fraught state of the Graysons' marriage; and the deteriorating relationships between the Graysons and other expatriates. While Alwyn notes the mutual support the Graysons continue to give each other on literary matters, *The Unyielding Memory* provides an unstinting account of the issues troubling their marriage, including alcohol abuse, drunken public brawling and Catherine's brazen infidelities that are discussed and debated by the other expatriates (as is George's impotence).

The deterioration of the Graysons' relationships with other expatriates is as telling as the slow unravelling of the Graysons' marriage. Just as George stands on the cusp of the success of which he and Catherine have long dreamed—the very dream that took them to the island—the couple is increasingly shunned due to their drunkenness and fighting. In one pivotal scene, George responds to a discussion about his current reading by proclaiming,

> 'I'm sick of being taken for the village idiot' and then, accusing Stephanos and his generation of doing nothing except 'masturbating against the wall.' Catherine had passed out on his lap. Paul said, the next day, the sooner certain people get off this island and we can have a rational conversation, the better.

While some were beginning to wish the Graysons/Johnstons off the island, the Wallises were settling back in. After a period staying with Demetri and Carolyn Gassoumis, they then moved into Leonard Cohen's house in September 1963 after it was vacated by Steve Sanfield. Wallis thereafter wrote regularly to Cohen, providing his landlord with an account of the troubled goings-on amongst the expatriates, including the worsening relationship between Clift and Johnston ("George and Charm are at the point of killing each other again") and their gradual isolation from the other expatriates.

Wallis recorded, both in his correspondence with Cohen and in *The Unyielding Memory*, that as Clift and Johnston's status waned, the focus of their social lives shifted to a number of young Australians who had recently arrived on the island. Amongst those who arrived during 1963 were artist William

Pownall; future journalist and political commentator Mungo MacCallum and his wife Sue; artist Robert Owen and his sculptor wife Silver Collings; Sydney couple Ian and Jan McNay; and, at year's end, poet and novelist-to-be Rodney Hall and his wife Beth. During this period, Johnston and Clift, finding themselves increasingly at odds with the established expatriates, remained as welcoming as ever to these newly arrived Australians. Their affection for the young Australians was returned, but as fond as Rodney Hall was of the Johnstons, he recalls the roller-coaster of drinking and fighting that was overwhelming the couple's marriage and damaging established friendships.

> They were darling, warm, wonderful people, but they were alcoholics. Being in the house with them you would hear downstairs these rows when they began, these terrible rows with crashes and bangs, stuff being broken, shocking rows. But by the morning they would be absolutely lovey-dovey and all over each other.

It seems that Johnston and Clift—reacting to their growing estrangement from other friends, and with Johnston preparing to depart for Australia—were consciously surrounding themselves with fellow Australians. In a letter to Cohen dated January 4th, 1964, Wallis noted—with some exasperation—their growing number, recording the extent of island disharmony when the Australian contingent mounted a display of Yuletide nationalism:

> Christmas Eve: two parties, the Johnstons with four other Australians (there are now, with children, 15 on the island—I can't stand it) ... So, dinner is on the point of being mounted at Demetri's when the soft sound of 'Waltzing Matilda' sung by six lusty Australian squares plus an itinerant Yank is heard outside and before you can say 'Dearie me' the group is in the house waving a homemade Australian flag. Just too, too embarrassing. The group proposes to sit and sing songs while we eat. Carolyn summons all her reserves and says it would really be a much better idea if they came back later. The group departs. 'No we won't come back later,' says George. Very frosty post-Christmas it was, on the port.

Such flag waving was untypical of the Johnstons, although Clift did write later that she had been known to sing 'Advance Australia Fair' at dinner parties across the world to mirthful audiences astonished by the anthem's less than patriotically inspiring lyrics. In the same article she praises 'Waltzing Matilda', the song used to celebrate her final Hydra Christmas, as an air to be sung "with enjoyment and even gusto (particularly in foreign parts where it goes down very well at an inter-racial hootenanny I have found)". Perhaps she had forgotten, or chose to overlook, the frosty response her Christmas rendition had received on at least one occasion. That the Johnstons partook in such patriotic carolling indicates the psychological states they had reached by the winter of 1963–64—Johnston as he prepared to leave for Australia, and Clift as her role as unofficial leader of the expatriates evaporated. Johnston's impending departure could only have made Clift even less certain about her 'place' on the island.

As if to underline the fractures within the established expatriates, a letter 'home' by Robert Owen in early 1964 indicates that, unsurprisingly, the newly arrived Australians had a distinctly different attitude towards the Johnstons and their freely offered Christmas cheer than did other expatriates:

> Well! We had a swinging festive season (with the necessary adjustment) at the Johnston house. An all Aussie Xmas, logfire, candles, turkey, Huntly & Palmers plum-pudding, real mistletoe and holly, not to mention large Flagons of 'ritsina' and 'cockanelli' (red wine).

Owen went on to report that the prospects for Australians generally appeared good on Hydra, with even Wallis's close friend (and another who was tiring of the Johnstons) Demetri Gassoumis praising their energy.

> Hopes are pretty high at the moment as we have made some very good contacts … Theres a big interest in Aussie art over here, not just the galleries but the Artists we have met … A very good American painter Dimitri Cosumemus (American born Greek) says he has never seen so much vitality and freshness from one country. Every-day someone

Silver Collings and Robert Owen selling jewellery on Donkey Shit Lane, February 1964. (Owen Collection)

is asking about Aussie, boy its quite overwhelming I'm beginning to wonder myself.

Whatever Johnston's problems were with some of his old island friends, he must nonetheless have been in good cheer that Christmas, as the first copies of *My Brother Jack* reached the island. Wallis reported the novel's arrival in a letter to Cohen, seemingly unable to hide his peevishness at the success that awaited its author.

The blurb on MBJ compared George to Thomas Wolfe, James Joyce and someone else I can't recall. The front cover of the Bookseller says MBJ is the GREAT AUSTRALIAN NOVEL. All this is an extremely interesting insight into just what a goddamned publisher can do if he wants to make money. Collins are spending money like water: I'm sure George will make a small fortune.

Wallis also recorded in *The Unyielding Memory* an occasion called to celebrate the arrival of Grayson's novel. The Alwyns drop in on George and Catherine and "[find] the four Australians there and George as drunk as a skunk: he'd got the first copies of his book and he was celebrating. The blurb compared him to 'Richard Mahony,' with whom Nick was not familiar, Joyce, Wolfe and Dickens." The Australians then move on to Katsikas where George is subjected to some pointed barbs from other expatriates about his new book, but is "too pissed to care".

While Wallis's complaints about Johnston dated back to soon after the New Zealander first arrived on Hydra in 1960, that they now reached a new level may be related to Johnston's impending success. Certainly one way of reading the Nick Alwyn character in *The Unyielding Memory* is as a struggling writer jealous of the success that is about to befall Grayson and as part of a personal rivalry that is symptomatic of the wider competitiveness between the island's writers. This competitiveness is compounded by various sexual rivalries—most evident within the Graysons' marriage with its public infidelities—and the insecurities that are revealed as even the best of friends, Nick Alwyn and Stephanos Lamounis, begin a sexual jousting involving each other's wives and new women arriving on the island.

The self-doubt also extends to Grayson's anxiety about his own literary reputation. In an incident set at Katsikas, Grayson is portrayed as envying the commercial and critical success achieved by two other writers, Saul Rubens and Bill Sullivan, the latter based on the American author William J. Lederer, whose controversial 1958 book *The Ugly American* was adapted for the big screen in 1963 with Marlon Brando as its star. The state of affairs Wallis describes are such that even as Grayson awaits the publication of his own *tour de force*, he is neurotically concerned about his reputation. The evening begins with "George and Catherine getting drunk":

> Sullivan makes a play for Catherine. Then something happens and Catherine says she's leaving and won't be stopped. George starts crying and says everyone likes Sullivan's book better than his, and he's a good writer and so on.

Lederer was at work on his own 'Greek novel' at the time, telling his editor in a September 1963 letter that "the novel is about Americans but it takes place in Greece and I believe it will be good for Greek tourism". It was not until 1984 that Lederer published such a novel, *I, Giorghos*, which sees its burnt-out American protagonist 'find himself' on Hydra. The novel's impact on Greek tourism was likely indiscernible, however *Kirkus Review* memorably noted that it was "Soggy with watered-down Zen and California-therapy jargon: a well-meaning but embarrassing soul-journey, only slightly enhanced by the Greek-isle backgrounds".

While Wallis was airing his grievances with Johnston in his correspondence with Cohen (letters that would be recycled in *The Unyielding Memory*), Johnston, true to his nature in encouraging younger writers, continued to support Wallis as he attempted to place his second novel, *The Submissive Body*. In a letter dated September 11th, 1963, Johnston wrote to George Ferguson at Australian publisher Angus and Robertson signalling his intention to return to Australia early the following year, and also "to let you know of my interests in a young New Zealand novelist, Redmond Wallis", who he describes as a "writer worth watching". Unfortunately, Bodley Head thought otherwise, in the same month sending Wallis the unwelcome news that it was rejecting *The Submissive Body*. When other publishers responded with a similar verdict, Wallis withdrew the novel on the basis that he had higher hopes for another manuscript, *Bees on A String*. Neither novel would see publication.

Despite their mounting personal differences, Wallis was still capable of giving Johnston a hand. As Johnston planned his return to Australia, he turned his mind to preparing some pre-arrival publicity, for which he conscripted the assistance of his fellow journalist. Wallis reported what followed in a letter to Cohen:

> Collins are going to push My Brother Jack in Australia and so George got all fired up with the idea of going out and helping with the publicity. You know George—as soon as he gets an idea he goes overboard. So he wrote to Qantas to organise a free ride and in the meanwhile I interviewed him for Australian radio … it took us two and a half days to get twelve minutes of interview and George was in bed for five days after that—but the end result, even if I do say so myself, wasn't bad.

Wallis also informed Cohen that the island's strained personal relationships were anything but mollified by Johnston's impending departure. In a letter dated February 29th, Wallis told of the bitter prelude to Johnston's leaving:

> The hostilities on the island at present are fantastic. George and Charm were invited the day before George left to Chuck and Gordon's, and Carolyn and Demetri too. Little lets-be-buddies lunch party. Demetri sent a note up refusing for various excellent reasons. Said he couldn't see any point in it. It was fun because the night before Charm had had a little party for George, to which everyone, it seems, but C and D and Robyn and I were invited … Oh yes, we all love each other very much. Chuck and Gordon claim they are not going to have any more to do with Charmian, that they're tired of her falling into her food etc.

In *The Unyielding Memory*, the narrative of George's departure is more elaborate and includes several expatriates refusing to attend a farewell party, with one stating that "he couldn't be bothered being exposed to George's horseshit", and that he "doesn't think he'll even bother to see George off tomorrow". Nick Alwyn, although himself part of the bickering and the general displeasure with George, does recall that four years earlier it was George who had convinced him to stay on Hydra, advice for which he "had always been grateful". He also provides a grudging appreciation of George Grayson's commitment to his writing where others had failed:

> [George was] a man who had suffered the slings and arrows of outrageous critics and who had now, finally, written a book in which he truly believed and got it right. A man who had battled ill health, money problems, marital problems, the scorn of his peers and had won through.

While Alwyn has no personal regret for Grayson's departure, he nonetheless registers that it is a defining moment for Hydra and its expatriate community, and that the island that had been perceptibly changed by George's arrival will also be altered by his leaving. For Alwyn, George's departure is another marker of the transformations overwhelming the island, which "had somehow lost something and would never be quite the same again, the shift of personnel and attitudes which had begun the previous autumn was now complete and the future no longer predictable".

The antipathy reached by early 1964 between Johnston and other members of Hydra's foreign colony was about to be made worse, and at Johnston's instigation. In an article published in Sydney's *Sunday Mirror* to coincide with his return, Johnston leant on various national stereotypes to take a final hyperbolic swipe at the island's non-Australians. In the process he re-inscribed national identity—for his Australian readers, at least—as an integral part of expatriation. Johnston caricatured his fellow islanders as:

> The sick, neurotic Americans, homogenised and plastic wrapped into resentful futility; the blasé Continental, all too ready to settle for a wearisome decadence; the climate-worn Britisher, angry and aggressive about the wrong things; the inferiority-harried Canadian, scrabbling for his Government culture-grants; the over-clean and over-civilised Scandinavian, insensately grabbing at Mediterranean grubbiness and pagan license; the chip-on-the-shoulder South African with his load of racial guilts bigger than his rucksack; the earnest New Zealander, trying to shed the conventional as a snake sheds its skin.

This was ungracious of Johnston, containing as it does barely veiled references to those who had been his friends for some years, including Cohen and Wallis. In contrast with this litany of national baggage carried by the international members of the Hydra colony, he praised the demeanour and creative endeavour of the recently arrived Australians:

> But the blunt fact that has presented itself more forcibly is that the Australians stand head and shoulders over everyone else for dynamic vitality and for an undeniable sense of belief in a destiny and of really going somewhere. The Australians who come here all work, and work damned hard, all show resource and initiative and imagination, all have ideas that are at least different from other people's, all display a purposeful sense of wanting to get somewhere and not away from something.

Those remaining on Hydra did not miss the appearance of this article, as Johnston may have wished—Wallis's mother sent a copy from New Zealand. Wallis's reaction is narrated by Alwyn in *The Unyielding Memory*:

> The story had been timed to appear two or three days before George got back. In it, George had got in what Mark Twain might have called 'a few licks' at those on the island he thoroughly disliked, managed to plug Australia and Australians, and had also indulged in a little advance publicity for his book.

Wallis then quotes in full what he refers to as the "payback paragraph" (quoted above), before Grayson/Johnston "embarked on the 'kissing-the-tarmac' part of the article, the business of getting the Australians to treat him as a dinkum bloke and not some poncey intellectual bastard with ideas above his station". Even though well-removed from Hydra, Johnston had clearly not lost his ability to disconcert the island's non-Australian contingent.

Johnston's heightened rhetoric on nationality was, as Wallis accurately reasoned, part of the public atonement demanded of the returning expatriate. After all, Johnston had a book to promote, and in order to unlock the marketplace he had to make amends for having turned his back on Australia. *My*

Brother Jack was sold to the Australian public, with some truth, as the book that he had to go away to write, a returning gift from a notoriously prodigal son.

A second story reporting Johnston's return, this time based on an interview with journalist John Hetherington, appeared in early February in the *Age Literary Supplement*. Once again Johnston stressed that he was essentially unchanged by his time on the Greek island, arguing that despite more than a decade away "we go on *being* Australians—a different people, a race apart". With his pathway to repatriation prepared, Johnston left Hydra on February 23rd and departed Athens for Sydney on the following day.

While Johnston had a commercial need to re-embrace Australia, it would seem that he was also genuinely disillusioned with Hydra and its potential to sustain creativity. In a letter dated April 13th, 1964, designer and filmmaker Dahl Collings wrote to her daughter Silver and son-in-law Robert Owen on Hydra, following a dinner with the recently returned Johnston. (Collings and her husband Geoffrey had known Johnston and Clift before they left for London). Collings reported that during a late-night conversation, Johnston spoke of Hydra's "claustrophobia" and warned that "young people … [should not] stay too long on Hydra", as it "stops you from moving freely through the places that are vital for your learning and work". This was not advice given by a man yearning for his Greek island home or unaware of the problems associated with his own decade of having lived so remotely.

Whatever thoughts Johnston now harboured about Hydra, or that his Australian friends might have had about his choice to move there, that he returned bearing *My Brother Jack* was his ultimate redemption. His frail physique and obvious ill-health might have vindicated some judgements made about his decision to take his family to such a poorly developed part of the world, but his unexpected late-career shot at the great national novel provided evidence that he had used his expatriation in the service of his art and his country. And he found Australia receptive—the publicity generated by Collins; his own efforts to promote his return; and the enthusiastic response the novel had already received in London, ensured considerable fanfare as

Johnston stepped back on Australian soil in Sydney. Within weeks he was at the Adelaide Festival, enjoying star billing alongside another repatriated novelist, Patrick White. George Johnston, working-class boy from the Melbourne suburbs, had suddenly, and against the odds, attained the national recognition that justified his years of being "marooned".

It is a measure of the interest in the couple's return that several days after Johnston's article was published in the *Sunday Mirror*, Clift's account of their repatriation appeared in *The Australian Women's Weekly*. Whereas Johnston had focused on his confidence in Australia and hopes for the future, Clift was more cautious, clearly regretful for the home she was abandoning and concerned about how her children would adjust to this "foreign land" as they left behind all that was "familiar" and "incredibly beautiful". Like Johnston, Clift also took the opportunity to ruminate about the young Australians who had found their way to Hydra, what their demeanour told her about the progress of her home country, and how her children might adapt to this unfamiliar environment:

> And in sitting and chatting to these pleasant young people, many of them brand-new husbands or wives—and even in a couple of cases a brand-new baby ... I liked these youngsters enormously. But in talking to them at a time when I am contemplating the sixteenth birthday of my own son, with its vexed questions of tape-recorders, Samian wine, and passport forms, I am inevitably led to wonder how my own three would have turned out with an Australian upbringing.
>
> And how will Australia strike them? As a foreign land? As home? For it is their country too. Martin and Shane were born in Sydney, at Darlington and Paddington respectively, names which peal as oddly in my ears as Calabria and Piraeus did once. 'I wonder how you are going to like it,' I say in my troubled moments, and they shout confidently, 'We'll love it!'

Contrary to Clift's bold declaration, the evidence confirms that her children were far from looking forward to moving to Australia, with Martin and Shane having no memory of their country of birth and Jason having lived only on

LEAVING

Shane Johnston and friends climb on the wine boats.
(James Burke)

HALF THE PERFECT WORLD

Jason and Shane Johnston buy ice-creams from Yianni Kerkiraios.
(James Burke)

Hydra and (briefly) England. On Hydra, the Johnston siblings had known the freedom their parents had hoped for when moving to the island. In his 1958 interview with Vasso Mingos, Johnston declared that one of the reasons for leaving London was to "give our kids the kind of free life, with plenty of sea and sunshine that you can't get in big cities". Hydra's compact spaces meant that when not being cared for by their parents or housekeeper Zoe Skordoras, the children could play on the port, run through the laneways, and swim from the rocks, with neighbours always keeping an eye out for them. Del Kolve recalls that "The Johnston children swam every day from the same cliffs I would go to. They were beautiful, golden, confident, enabled—children running free."

Not unexpectedly, the freedom the children enjoyed went hand-in-hand with their parents' lifestyle, and both were not without their consequences. Years later, Martin Johnston declared as much to interviewer Erica Travers:

> The way my parents lived has perhaps been disastrous for me in the long term, in that what they did was, they wrote very hard, I know, they were terribly hard workers—they wrote from say seven in the morning till midday, and then they went down to the waterfront and got pissed. And I suppose that's the pattern of life that I've followed ever since.

Clift remained on Hydra following Johnston's leaving, and proved to be an ongoing irritant to other expatriates as she planned her own departure. Wallis reported in a letter to Cohen in late February 1964 that the furniture that had been gifted to him by the Johnstons when he purchased his house was now being reclaimed:

> Next most important item is a determined attempt by Charmian to rape the place. She claimed to have furnished it for you and she's now talking of taking it all back. She took the flowery bed today, plus two mattresses ... and in passing observed that later she would collect the table in the studio, the bench around the kitchen table, and the bookcase ... She says she's taking the flowery bed back to Australia (she's out of her mind of

course) … Obviously this is basically malicious as the stuff isn't worth very much and anyone without malice would regard it as given away.

This incident is also recounted in *The Unyielding Memory*, where Catherine is described as having "turned up with a donkey boy at about 11am for the bed: white polo neck sweater, black trousers, hair all over the place and eyes like pissholes in the snow". Cohen's reply to Wallis suggested that he too was losing patience with the errant Australian:

> I'd like to pile it up on a couple of donkeys and send it down to her with a thank-you note. I leave this up to you: if she's being particularly obnoxious, send the lot back; if she's being merely bitchy, bargain for any pieces you need. And don't labour too hard to save the friendship, or the goods.

When Wallis wrote again to Cohen in early May he reported that "the question of the furniture hasn't cropped up again", but that Clift's behaviour was now causing concern for other reasons. Immediately after Johnston departed, Clift had met English painter Anthony Kingsmill in Athens, and within weeks he had moved into the Hydra house—something that was too much even for Johnston's friends who were well used to Clift's philandering.

> Not long after I wrote to you about Charmian she began to find solace with a number of guys, the most recent of whom, who's a nice guy, is still with her: hence she is wandering around in a nice, euphoric daze, part relaxation, part sex, part alcohol … Chuck I'm afraid grows more prudish day by day—there was a big fight at Grafos the night before last when he decided that it was his responsibility to read Charmian off about her sex life. Attacked both her and her boyfriend, Anthony—who's a good head, and played it cool.

This section of Wallis's letter to Cohen is quoted verbatim in *The Unyielding Memory*, as "Alwyn to Rubens", and is one of the final mentions of Catherine. If this flagrant infidelity on Clift's part shocked even her longstanding island

Martin Johnston reads the Greek sports pages. (James Burke)

friends, then its impact on her children, already coming to terms with the absence of their father and their impending return to Australia, was even more profound. Fifteen-year-old Martin coped by leaving for a period to live with friends in Beirut. He later recalled the difficult final stages as the old expatriate colony fractured, pinpointing the problem while distancing his parents from the cause.

> The foreign community was getting bigger and bigger, and beginning to tear itself apart with internecine squabbles and bitchery and … all sorts of sexual and alcoholic tangles, and generally beginning to be a pretty unhealthy sort of a place in which to live. My parents more and more felt this.

The problems referred to by Martin Johnston dominate the final sections of *The Unyielding Memory*. The focus shifts to the increasingly intense relationship between the Alwyns and Lamounises, as Nick Alwyn and Stephanos Lamounis throw themselves into the sexual opportunities and recreational drug taking brought their way as the swinging sixties overwhelm the island. There is no longer an 'expatriate community', with a sense of purpose and identity, but rather a cycle of repetitive days in which the men seek out the bountiful opportunities to satiate their desires while seemingly blind to their faltering marriages. A final reference to Catherine comes when Nick Alwyn encounters her at a party where she "ear-bash[es] Stephanos and Sue, who [sit] for a while beside her, saying how she'd set everyone up on the island and they'd turned their backs on her". Feeling betrayed by the very community she had nurtured, Catherine/Clift was leaving her beloved Hydra forever, with the pain of her departure sharpened by the sting of humiliation and exile that could not be eased by her husband's publishing triumph.

After nearly fourteen years abroad, Clift's return to Australia in August 1964, six months after her husband, was also somewhat chastening. Whereas Johnston had travelled as a guest of Qantas and had been feted on the basis of *My Brother Jack*'s highly anticipated Australian publication, Clift and the children assumed the role of migrants, taking a government assisted passage on a Greek steamer. As she wrote several months later:

> the ship on which we travelled was a migrant ship, and filled with other families also travelling hopefully or apprehensively from one world to another … By the time a migrant—and I am including myself and my Australian born children in the term—actually boards the ship that is to carry him to his brave new world the audacious bite of decision has long since been blunted, if not altogether gummed up, on the toffee-apple of bureaucracy. The freshness of adventure has worn off and uncertainty, alas, is practically all that remains.

While *My Brother Jack* had paved the way for Johnston's celebrated return and provided a pathway for his future writing, no such welcome or certainty awaited Clift. Her second novel, *Honour's Mimic*, was published that year, but received nothing like the critical or public acclaim given Johnston's novel. And with its storyline of Greek island life, sponge-diving fishermen and an incestuous expatriate community, *Honour's Mimic* must have seemed like a

Mungo and Sue MacCallum with baby Diana, 1963. (MacCallum Collection)

reminder of an abandoned past rather than a confident step into a new writing life.

Johnston and Clift did find that much had changed in Australia. For a start, Sydney now had its own bona fide libertarian and bohemian subculture in the form of The Push. Notably, however, The Push was dominated by individuals who were at least a generation younger than Clift and Johnston, both of whom would have been deeply suspicious of its domination by Sydney University students and alumni, a number of whom would go on to form the next generation of high profile literary expatriates. Indeed, as the Johnstons made their separate ways back to Australia, they were passed in transit by a younger generation—tourists, travellers and soon-to-be expatriates alike—who were heading in the opposite direction. As Mungo MacCallum reported, after reversing the migration of Clift and Johnston by moving from Hydra to

London, "We spent most of our spare time with Australian friends; our group from Sydney Uni had now moved almost en masse to the mother country". Expatriation was forever altered, swamped by the globalising advent of jet travel and its myriad impacts.

The emergence of the youth cultures that would so define the 1960s was emphasised in the months separating Johnston's return in February 1964 and Clift's in August, when Australia received high-profile visitors in the form of a tour by The Beatles. The group's irresistible rise and the pop culture explosion that followed transformed London and urban cultures across the world, but their Australian tour displeased Clift immensely. In early 1965, she wrote an essay expressing her distaste for the "Mersey Beat" music sweeping Australia's airways, describing the "lunatic volume of sheer noise", and her "thorough distaste for Beatles, Rolling Stones, Aztecs, Pinheads and the rest of them, Passed, Passing or To Come". The advent of The Beatles turned out to draw the line-in-the-sand for British postwar social reconstruction, and yet found Charmian Clift—idealist, libertarian and bohemian—in danger of looking like a conservative naysayer against the social and cultural forces that permanently shifted London from the long postwar gloom that had so negatively impacted her own experience of the city. As on Hydra, she was again at risk of finding herself locked out of a world she had either created or longed for.

Together, but in their different ways, Clift and Johnston had encountered some of the limits of 1960s cosmopolitanism, and were now required to make different sorts of accommodations in order to re-adjust to living in Australia. But whereas Johnston was a celebrated returnee, able to slip back comparatively comfortably into Australian life, Clift remained persistently troubled by the feeling that she was "here but not here", and "half alien and certain of nothing". Johnston continued to re-cement his relationship with the country of his birth by writing *The Australians*, a book published in 1966 that consciously re-inscribed numerous national myths based on a continental landscape totally different in scale and temperament from his recent island home. The year before had seen *My Brother Jack* appear on the national television broadcaster in the form of ten half-hour episodes, which, in a display of their continued ability to work in partnership, Clift had scripted. *The Australian Women's Weekly* reported a month after the first episode was aired that "Johnston is loud in his praises of the job his wife has done on the book".

> 'I couldn't face it myself,' he said, 'I had just finished the book, and in its original form it was completely unsuitable for TV. It is an introspective book of Davey's thoughts about his brother Jack. These had to be translated into action. Charmian has done a wonderful job. She should get all the praise.'

What Clift was praised for were the weekly articles she began writing for the *Sydney Morning Herald*, which positioned her on the cusp of belonging as she looked upon Australia from a somewhat removed and ambivalent position. In these short essays, Clift appraised the nation in its emerging diversity, finding it worthy of both admiration and condemnation as she compared it to her island life. Clift's articles and attitude endeared her to a generation of readers who, for reasons of temperament, ethnicity, gender or their own cosmopolitan impulse, shared her uncertain emotional attachment to their homeland.

When writing for an Australian audience on the pros and cons of raising children on Hydra, Clift casts herself and Johnston as "foreign parents", arguing that not only their Australian-ness but Clift's own habits of wearing trousers, smoking and drinking publicly—in short, not acting in a 'womanly' or 'maternal' fashion—were 'trying' for their children. And yet Clift positions herself as an outsider in Australia too. In her essay 'On Being a Home-Grown Migrant', she reported that "It is now all of sixteen months ago … that I struggled off a migrant ship with my three children and onto home territory for the first time in nearly fifteen years", and used this anniversary—and the advantage afforded the migrant, "even a home-grown one like me"—to reflect on the changes in Sydney's cultural landscape and to anticipate a future ushered in by fellow migrants that would see the city's stagnant suburbia "blossoming into exciting life".

'Trying' parents. Charmian Clift and George Johnston, c.1960 (Redmond Wallis)

This self-identification as the outsider in the mantle of the migrant, and a migrant who promises positive social change at that, is evoked again in a later essay, 'Report from a Migrant, Three Years After'. In this piece, Clift reflects on the national character and finds it wanting, particularly when it comes to political matters. Putting some distance between herself and those she observes, Clift writes that "Far from being anti-authoritarian as I had always believed, they [most Australians] actually seem to derive a sense of comfort and ease from unquestioning submission". So as not to disconcert her readers too much, Clift uneasily ends the essay with a patriotic declaration, "Three years out I wonder why I like the damn place so much".

Clift's observation about the passivity of Australians and the ambivalent note on which the piece concludes were underpinned by knowledge of the political unrest in the place that was never far from her mind. The years Clift and Johnston had lived on Hydra had seen a number of governments come and go in Greece, but in April 1967, a coup d'état led by right-wing generals took place in Athens, and its repressive brunt was felt well beyond the capital. Martin Johnston, still in his teens and in the throes of establishing himself as a poet, offered a modest tribute with the publication of an early poem, 'To Greece under the Junta'. More immediately, Greek migrants in Australia lobbied the federal government to apply diplomatic pressure for the restoration of constitutional and democratic rights in Greece, and to guarantee protection for Australian Greeks. Spearheading public activity in Australia was the Committee for the Restoration of Democracy in Greece, for which Clift and Johnston served as vice-presidents, and in whose service the fluently Greek-speaking Martin and Shane Johnston worked. Shane also worked as a secretary to the editor of Sydney's *Hellenic Herald*, an important publication reporting on the political troubles to Greek-Australians and mobilising their support.

At the same time, and in another corner of the world at New York City Town Hall, Leonard Cohen was also agitating, albeit for a different cause. It was on April 30th, 1967 that Cohen first performed as a professional singer as part of the National Committee for a Sane Nuclear Policy Against Vietnam War Concert at the invitation (and insistence) of Judy Collins. While Cohen held on to his house on Hydra until his death, he was an infrequent visitor from the late 1960s onwards, having moved to the US in 1967 to pursue songwriting, which set him on course for an itinerant life of touring, then a protracted 'retirement' to a Zen Centre near Los Angeles, before returning to the world stage for a celebrated final chapter of his career. Cohen also retained a house in Montreal, but never fully repatriated to Canada. His career, unlike Johnston's, never demanded it.

Cohen's former Hydra-house tenant, Wallis, also never returned to New Zealand to live. The need for the Wallises to improve their finances led to Robyn Wallis leaving Hydra for London to rejoin her job at *Vogue* in August 1964, the same month that Clift left to join Johnston in Australia. Wallis stayed on some weeks in order to complete his novel *Bees on a String*. In the weeks they were apart, Wallis wrote to Robyn, warning her of his decision to make a living by whatever means possible in order to write the sort of 'quality' fiction to which he was drawn—and which he had watched George Johnston struggle so desperately to produce.

> It's suddenly become crystal clear to me that I do have something to write about at last, something very important and that it can only be put down very slowly and without any consciousness whatsoever of the end result. It has to be done and whether the first publisher takes it or the twentieth or none at all it doesn't matter … I've realised that writing the way I want to write is the only thing that matters and therefore the fact that I live by being a bus conductor is unimportant.

Wallis's words turned out to be prophetic in a way. *Bees on a String* failed to find a publisher—although in his assessment it "came close"—and neither did any of the other adult-fiction manuscripts he would complete over the coming decades.

Wallis departed Hydra for good in early October 1964, and his leaving was another moment of difference in a watershed year that saw the fracturing of the old Hydra colony. Likely seeing him off at the port were Gordon Merrick and Charles Hulse, who—tired of being inundated by tourists—would themselves leave Hydra for Sri Lanka, never to return, with the couple dividing their time between a house they bought there in 1975 and a home in Normandy. The journey to London also proved a personal turning point for Wallis. On the seemingly endless train trip across central Europe, he had the time to strike up a relationship with Anna Mitrovic, who several years later became his second wife. After a period working for Australian Associated Press on Fleet Street he had a long career in editing and publishing. There is no evidence that he ever returned to Hydra.

* * *

LEAVING

Nick Alwyn describes the final stages of George Grayson's departure from the island.

> *[George] was dapper in a new blazer and told them he'd had a suit and extra trousers, the blazer, three pairs of slacks and another suit remodelled for 1,400 drachs. He would leave at midnight on Tuesday and arrive in Sydney at 8am on Thursday. Nick and Sue found they did not have a lot to say to him. What could one say at the point? Catherine came in, shaking like a leaf and then left to check the mail. The Alwyns stayed half an hour or so. As they too left, Nick told George to look after himself. They did not bother to go down to the boat to see him off. There had been people whom Nick had lost, had seen depart, knowing he would not see them again, and felt sorry, but he did not feel that about George.*

CONCLUSION

In 2014 it was the fiftieth anniversary of the publication of George Johnston's *My Brother Jack*, which was commemorated with lengthy commentaries in the Australian national broadsheet and other media outlets. That there was an anniversary at all says something about the enduring reputation the novel and its author enjoy in his homeland. If the writing of *My Brother Jack* required Johnston to direct his creative vision from far-away Hydra to inter-war Australia, then discussion about the writer and his book today inevitably turns the gaze the other way, from the novel's Australian setting to Johnston's mid-century Greek island expatriation. To speak of Johnston and *My Brother Jack* is to address the decision he and Charmian Clift made to live and work on Hydra, and its significance for their relationship, their children, their attitude to Australia (and the nation's to them), and their literary output.

The anniversary of *My Brother Jack* was only one recent indication of the extent to which Johnston, Clift and Hydra remain inextricably enmeshed and persistently present in Australia's cultural imagination. In late 2015, established artist Mark Schaller held an exhibition in Melbourne under the title *Homage to Hydra*, which featured paintings depicting numerous episodes (both real and mythical) from Johnston and Clift's Hydra years; in 2015, Melbourne musicians Chris Fatouros and Spiros Falieros debuted the show *Hydra: Songs and Tales of Bohemia*, marrying Leonard Cohen songs to a narrative about the Johnstons and the Hydra colony; and in 2016, it was announced that the Queensland Theatre Play Commissioning Fund would support:

> a work about the intense and tumultuous relationship between Australian writer Charmian Clift and war correspondent/novelist George Johnston, often regarded as Australia's Scott and Zelda Fitzgerald. The play will examine their time living on the Greek island of Hydra, their return to Australia and the relationship between life and art.

CONCLUSION

The sometimes romantic and sometimes querulous association between life and art and Hydra has also become one of the foundational stories of Leonard Cohen's often-repeated biography that has constantly been reaffirmed since his death in 2016. Although Cohen rarely returned to Hydra in the final decades of his life, the story of how he turned up on the island in 1960, fell in with the Johnstons, bought a house and met a woman has become an integral part of both his personal biography and the island history. In these narratives the poet-musician and the island are mutually inflected by an air of the exotic, the fanciful and the otherworldly. That the other major player in the Cohen-on-Hydra narrative, Marianne Ihlen, passed away shortly before Cohen, made their island romance all the more resonant for the many who reminisced about the couple's entwined lives in a time and place that are now seen as both formative to Cohen's artistic development and a rare moment of bohemian innocence on the cusp of great social change.

Cohen fans from around the world gathered on Hydra in June 2017 to present the island with a commemorative bench overlooking the sea not far from Spilia, at a place of which the singer was said to be particularly fond. The crowd-funded bench signalled a victory over island authorities, who had obstructed its construction for several years. Cohen's fans ultimately attained what entrepreneur Richard Branson—with his vision for a luxury island hotel—could not: a building permit. With interest in Cohen heightened by his passing, the event was solemnly reported by the international press, as was the decision to rename the street outside his island house in his honour.

In such accounts Hydra is described (yet again) as a place where time stands still, in this case arrested imprecisely in the 'early 1960s'. For some parts of the town, this abiding idea of a place out-of-time is not without truth. The contemporary Douskos, for example, seems little changed from the tavern of earlier years. Members of the Douskos family still preside, the menu remains 'traditional', and the courtyard is remarkably unchanged over nearly sixty years. A few new window shutters have been applied here and there, and the courtyard trees are considerably grown—the one beneath which James Burke photographed Cohen and Clift still stands, its substantial trunk supported by a small brick wall to keep it upright. The tavern continues to attract locals and visitors alike, and a warm summer night brings a wide smattering of languages. The printed menu includes a nod to the Cohen connection, graced as it is by one of Burke's photographs of that long-ago evening and Cohen's poem that bears the tavern's name. Linger in the courtyard and you are certain to see travellers point to the low wall where Cohen was pictured. Some sit on the same spot and re-enact the photographic moment, creating a tableau that fleetingly mimics the poses of Cohen and Clift and transports Burke's fragments of light, with their glimpse of past lives and times, across the decades.

Understandably, Cohen's part in Hydra's 1960s bohemian enclave continues to loom large in island narratives. Perhaps typifying is a 2014 *New York Times* travel article by novelist Lawrence Osborne. Osborne backgrounded a story about Hydra and its vibrant arts scene by giving an abridged history of the mid-century artist community, affording Cohen the foundational role in the establishment of the colony (with a passing nod to Gordon Merrick and Charles Hulse), and thereby effectively shifting its establishment to 1960. Osborne went on to set his 2017 novel, *Beautiful Animals*, on Hydra, wherein characters note the contemporary presence on the island of "old bohemians" who "all came because of Leonard Cohen", and Douskos is evoked as "the place where famous people once strummed their guitars under trellises", an image that rests entirely on Burke's photographs for its meaning. While not claiming to be comprehensive, such accounts erase the presence of Christian Heidsieck and Lily Mack, Patrick Leigh Fermor, Johnston and Clift, and others who had previously arrived on Hydra with a vision of wedding a bohemian Aegean lifestyle to the fulfilment of their creative ambitions.

Yet despite its rich postwar history of artistic bohemianism, contemporary Hydra is far from being a Disneyland of mid-century nostalgia for sentimental hippies or celebrity-struck tourists. It is, as always, a place where people live and work, write, go to school and take art classes, talk politics and play soccer on the expansive green pitch carved into the hills and discreetly hidden

CONCLUSION

from the view from the port. Greek tourism has inevitably moved on from the 1960s, and Hydra's time has, to some extent, passed. The locals' resistance to resort-style developments and the harbour's unsuitability for use by the ever-larger cruise ships that ply the Aegean, coupled with considerably improved access by both sea and air to more remote islands, eventually ensured that Santorini, Crete, Rhodes and Mykonos would surpass Hydra in terms of tourist facilities and international visibility. But while Hydra may no longer be among the most instantly recognisable of Greek islands, it continues to attract visitors in sufficient numbers to sustain the island's economy and its cosmopolitan gloss. The ferry ride makes for a pleasurable day-trip diversion from the crowds at the Parthenon or Plaka, and Hydra Port remains a beautiful destination with the promise of a donkey ride in the traffic-free streets adding novelty.

While tourists come and go, many Hydriots have returned to the island for the long-term, having previously left to pursue education and career opportunities but now looking to raise children in a safe and pleasing environment. Still others commute between the island and the mainland for work, joining weekenders every Friday on the late ferry from Piraeus. And at a time when the impact of Greece's debt crisis continues to be felt, and refugees from wars and camps in Syria and Turkey flee to the islands of the eastern Aegean, the presence in Hydra harbour of luxury boats and yachts alongside busy ferries, smaller cruise ships, water taxis and working *caiques*, is a potent reminder of the uneven forces of modernity that propel people to Hydra (and beyond), much as they did to James Burke during the few weeks in 1960 when he visited with his camera.

One way in which the island has very noticeably stepped out of the 1960s is the 'entry point' for island real estate. "See that place over there?" asked the current owner of the Johnstons' house to his researcher-guests, pointing from his rooftop terrace to a nearby hillside, "it's on the market for 4 million Euros". Such prices seem to realise the fear Vasso Mingos and Burke expressed all those years ago—"[T]his is likely to be Hydra's fate", Burke wrote in 1960;

"the creative poor will have to move on to find another cheap beauty spot where they can work". To some extent this prediction has come true, although the island continues to accommodate artists and writers, and to pride itself on their presence, both now and in the past.

While Leonard Cohen's death was an event noted around the world, others associated with the Hydra story as told in this book passed away in comparative obscurity. James Burke continued to work throughout Europe, the Middle-East and Asia, returning often to northern India, an area for which he carried a deep affection following his 1945 excursion to Tibet with Johnston. Early in 1964, Burke was photographing the Himalayas in India's Assam Province, close to the Tibetan border, when, as Johnston wrote in *A Cartload of Clay*, "he made a careless backward step while focusing his camera and lost his footing and fell headlong into a vast and deep abyss where the grey snout of a glacier groaned and creaked and mumbled". It was, Johnston added, "the right ending for Jim", to die in the part of the world that he loved best. An obituary in *LIFE* noted that Burke "was so quiet and self-effacing that it was hard to believe the dangers he had seen". Clift also wrote fondly of Burke in an essay soon after his death, recalling that "He used to wear thick bifocals and a baseball cap and hideous flowered shirts, and he was a brave and simple and good man and one of the finest photographers in the world".

Redmond Wallis's career as a novelist failed to fulfil his youthful ambitions, with *Point of Origin* remaining his only published novel for adults. He and Robyn divorced in the mid-1960s, and he went on to a successful career in editing and publishing, living for extended periods in London, Spain and France, and returning to New Zealand only briefly. Throughout his post-Hydra years Wallis never gave up writing fiction, and in 1992 he wrote to his longstanding (and likely long-suffering) literary agent, Sheila Watson, declaring that "I shall turn my 60's Hydra diary … into something first, poor old George Johnston, Charmian Clift, Gordon Merrick etc being dead". Although *The Unyielding Memory* was never completed, the extensive drafts and plot notes found in the Turnbull Library indicate that Wallis spent considerable time on the task. He eventually realised, however, that creating satisfactory fiction from his Hydra experience was beyond him, conceding that "The problem has always been that the reality was more powerful than any fiction I could invent, and turning fact into fiction has proved extraordinarily difficult". Wallis passed away in southern France in 2006.

On returning to Australia in late February 1964, Johnston was confident that *My Brother Jack* would gain him recognition as a major novelist. He was right, with the novel winning Australia's most high-profile literary prize, the Miles Franklin Award, as did its successor *Clean Straw for Nothing*. The return to Australia also precipitated a high water mark in Clift's career as she became one of Australia's premier newspaper columnists with a weekly feature in the *Sydney Morning Herald* that was syndicated to other capital city dailies.

While the couple's late-career success was significant, it was also somewhat illusory. Johnston's health was failing, and Clift and the children struggled to adjust to life away from Hydra. Despite the positive changes that had occurred in Australia in the years they were absent, it was still a form of surrender to a place and a lifestyle they had previously rejected. The couple had turned their backs on the material comforts of big-city living in order to pursue their writing, and then, when Johnston's writing finally succeeded, they chose to forego the way of life that had produced that success in order to promote the novel and optimise the benefits. Writing as David Meredith in *Clean Straw for Nothing*, Johnston noted how after moving to "the island" he had to "stuff [his] ears with wax against the beguiling siren song of money and self-importance and excitement". The wax eventually fell away and the siren led Johnston and Clift back to Australia, where they found themselves dashed on the rocks of alcohol abuse and their floundering relationship. Right to the end, the Johnstons' marriage remained troubled, unable to escape the personal flaws that had dogged it from the beginning or to recover from the various blows that were inflicted on it across the course of two decades.

Despite Clift's success on returning to Sydney, the effect on her was devastating. Not only did she miss her island life, but she struggled constantly with the pressure of newspaper deadlines and fretted about her inability to make progress on her long-planned autobiographical novel. She suffered a protracted depression and eventually took her own life in July 1969, at the age of forty-five. According to some accounts, it was the impending publication of *Clean Straw for Nothing*, which Clift knew would once again lay bare her island infidelities, which led her to take her life. Certainly her suicide note was a pain-drenched stab at Johnston and his determination to punish her for her perceived wrongdoing.

Johnston lived to see the publication of *Clean Straw for Nothing* but did not survive to complete his Meredith trilogy. He died from tuberculosis and related respiratory ailments just over twelve months after Clift passed away. The third volume of the trilogy, *A Cartload of Clay*, was published posthumously, with its status as an 'unfinished' novel providing an appropriate end-point for two lives that were semi-fulfilled and wastefully truncated.

The misfortune that befell Johnston and Clift also manifested in the following generation. Shane Johnston never fully reconciled with leaving Hydra and was often at odds with her mother. She took her own life at the age of twenty-five in 1974. Martin Johnston established a reputation as one of the finest Australian poets of his generation. He returned to Greece to live in the mid-1970s and again in the late 1980s, and for a number of years worked for the broadcaster SBS translating Greek films. He suffered from severe alcoholism for many years and died of complications from the disease in 1990, at the age of forty-two. Jason Johnston has kept his distance from the interest in his parents' lives, although his awareness of the wider legacy of his family's experience on the island is suggested by his consent to the donation of a store of family photographs to the National Library of Australia, including many taken on Hydra.

Examined in that way, the experience of Johnston, Clift and their children may seem like a slow and inevitable tragedy, alongside which the achievement of even their best and most-lasting writing is of little account. But such judgements narrow the attention to the commonplace reality of lives that run

CONCLUSION

amiss for any number of reasons, and of consequences that become far more 'predictable' in hindsight. The years in the Aegean may have been, at best, half perfect for Johnston and Clift, but it was on Hydra that they connected to a place, a lifestyle and a community that allowed them to live and express themselves intensely, and as they chose. Along with others with whom they shared those island years, they refused to believe their dreams were an illusion, or that belief in their own abilities and a leap-of-faith might not allow them to reach beyond the constraints of their birthright.

To give the (almost) final word to Clift, as she reflected on the journey that brought the couple to Hydra:

> I thought of the safe anonymity of the office desk, the furnished flat, the monthly salary cheque, the insurance policy, the hot, stale smell of the herd and the will-less, witless way one had shambled along in the middle of it. It had seemed a glad thing to declare against all that; to declare for individuality, for risks instead of safety, for living instead of existing, for faith in one's ability to build a good rich life from the raw materials of the man, the woman, the children, and the talents we could muster up between us. 'We will go and live in the sun,' we had said, and George had got up from his desk and walked out whistling.

The sound of that whistle has echoed across the decades—giving example and hope to ask more of life; courage to imagine a future free from the straightjacket of a stale inheritance; and a spur to embrace landscapes fit for bold new dreams. As the long postwar period spirals toward uncertain end points, it may be the only sound we can trust.

IMAGE ATTRIBUTIONS

Photographs attributed to James Burke are reproduced with the permission of Time & LIFE and Getty Images. Photograph of George Johnston and James Burke, Tibet 1945, is from the James C. Burke Collection, Stuart A. Rose Manuscript, Archives, and Rare Book Library, Emory Library, and is reproduced with the permission of Rosemary Burke and Jean Crawford. Cover illustration from *Honour's Mimic* by Charmian Clift was published by Hutchinson, and is reproduced by permission of Random House Group Ltd, © 1964. Cover illustration from *Closer to the Sun* by George Johnston was published by William Morrow and Company, and is reproduced with permission of HarperCollins © 1961. Nikos Hadjikyriakos-Ghika's *The Studio in Hydra* (1959), pastel, charcoal, pen and ink on paper, 0.45x0.545m, is reproduced with the permission of the Benaki Museum, Ghika Gallery, Athens. Photographs identified as being from the Ihlen collection are reproduced with the permission of Marianne Ihlen. Photographs identified as being from the Johnston and Clift Collection are reproduced with the permission of the National Library of Australia. Photographs identified as being from the MacCallum Collection are reproduced with the permission of Mungo MacCallum and Diana MacCallum. Photographs identified as being from the Merrick Collection are reproduced with the permission of the Princeton University Library. Photographs attributed to Vasso Mingos are reproduced with the permission of Michael Mingos. Sidney Nolan's *Untitled [Hydra]* (1956) is reproduced with the permission of The Nolan Trust, Bridgeman Images and Sotheby's Australia. The photograph of Sidney and Cynthia Nolan is reproduced with the permission of Bauer Media Pty Limited / *The Australian Women's Weekly*. Photographs identified as being from the Owen Collection are reproduced with the permission of Robert Owen. Photographs attributed to Colin Simpson are reproduced with the permission of the National Library of Australia. Photographs attributed to Redmond Wallis are reproduced with the permission of Dorothy Wallis. Cover illustration from *Point of Origin* by Redmond Wallis was published by The Bodley Head Ltd., and is reproduced by permission of Random House Group Ltd.© 1963.

Every effort has been made to identify copyright holders and obtain the necessary permissions to reproduce images. We would be interested to hear from anyone who believes their copyright may have been in any way infringed.

A NOTE ON SOURCES AND FURTHER READINGS

The following books and articles have informed our research:

Anonymous, 'I, Giorghos', *Kirkus Review* 19 March 1984.
Dimitris Antonakakis, 'The Speyer houses on Hydra', *A. James Speyer: Architect, Curator, Exhibition Designer*, edited by John Vinci, Chicago: University of Chicago Press, 1998, 59–71.
Nicholas Bethell, *The Albanian Operation of the CIA and MI6, 1949–1953*, edited by Robert Elsie and Bejtullah Destani, North Carolina: McFarland & Co., 2016.
Max Brown, *Charmian and George: The Marriage of George Johnston and Charmian Clift*, Dural: Rosenburg, 2004.
Artemis Cooper, *Patrick Leigh Fermor: An Adventurer*, London: John Murray, 2012.
Gregory Corso, *An Accidental Autobiography: the Selected Letters of Gregory Corso*, edited by Bill Morgan, New York: New Directions, 2003.
Robin Dalton, *One Leg Over: Having Fun–Mostly–in Peace and War*, Melbourne: Text, 2017.
Erica Doss, *Looking at LIFE Magazine*, Washington: Smithsonian Books, 2001.
Lawrence Durrell, *Prospero's Cell: A Guide to the Landscape and Manners of the Island of Corcyra*, London: Faber & Faber, 1945.
Robin Eakin, *Aunts Up the Cross*, London: Anthony Blond, 1965.
Robert Eisner, *Travellers to an Antique Land,* Ann Arbor: University of Michigan Press, 1991.
James Emerson, *A Picture of Greece in 1825, As Exhibited in the Personal Narratives of James Emerson, Esq., Count Pecchio, and W. H. Humphreys, Esq. Comprising a Detailed Account of the Events of the Late Campaign, and Sketches of the Principal Military, Naval and Political Chiefs*, London: Henry Colburn, 1826.
Patrick Leigh Fermor, *Mani: Travels in the Southern Peloponnese*, London: Murray, 1958.
Leslie Finer, *Passport to Greece*, London: Doubleday, 1964.
Alexander Freund and Alistair Thomas, eds., *Oral History and Photography*, New York: Palgrave, 2001.
Helle V. Goldman, ed., *When Were Almost Young: Remembering Hydra through War and Bohemians*, Tromsø: Tipota, 2018.
Patrick Greer, 'George Johnston in Hydra', *London Magazine* 1 November 1980: 109–115.
Kari Hesthamar, 'Interview with Leonard Cohen, Los Angeles', Norwegian Radio, 2005.
Kari Hesthamar, *So Long Marianne: A Love Story*, Trans. Helle V. Goldman, Toronto: ECW, 2014.
John Hetherington, 'An Australian author in Greece Returns to his native land', *Age Literary Supplement* 8 February 1964: 21.

Wilson Hicks, *Words and Pictures: An Introduction to Photojournalism*, New York: Harper, 1952.

Rhodri Jeffreys-Jones, *In Spies We Trust: The Story of Western Intelligence*, Oxford: Oxford University Press, 2013.

Susan Johnson, *The Broken Book*, Crows Nest: Allen & Unwin, 2004.

Robert D. Kaplan, *Balkan Ghosts: A Journey Through History*, New York: St. Martin's, 1993.

Kay Keavney, 'From George, with sadness', *The Australian Women's Weekly* 27 August 1969: 13.

Daniel Klein, *Travels with Epicurus: A Journey to a Greek Island in Search of a Fulfilled Life*, New York: Penguin, 2012.

Marie Knuckey, 'In search of Charmian's island', *Sydney Morning Herald* 1 June 1972: 24.

Katherine Koch, 'Hydra, in 1960', *Nowhere Travel Stories* http://nowheremag.com/2016/03/hydra-in-1960/.

Kostis Kornetis, *Children of the Dictatorship: Student Resistance, Cultural Politics, and the 'Long 1960s' in Greece*, New York: Berghahn, 2013.

John Laffin, *Middle East Journey*, Sydney: Angus & Robertson, 1958.

Charles Landery, *Whistling for a Wind*, London: Phoenix House, 1952.

Robert Liddell, *The Morea*, London: Jonathan Cape, 1958.

William Linton, *The Scenery of Greece and its Islands: Illustrated by Fifty Views, Sketched From Nature, Executed on Steel, and Described En Route*, London: the artist, 1856.

Celia Lury, *Prosthetic Culture: Photography, Memory and Identity*, London: Routledge, 1998.

Mungo MacCallum, *Mungo: The Man Who Laughs*, Sydney: Duffy & Snellgrove, 2001.

Ben Macintyre, *A Spy Among Friends: Kim Philby and the Great Betrayal*, London: Bloomsbury, 2014.

Craig McGregor, *Left Hand Drive: A Social and Political Memoir*, Melbourne: Affirm, 2013.

Ronald McKie, 'A home that Homer would have liked: Australian artist's house on island in Aegean Sea', *The Australian Women's Weekly* 20 February 1957: 17.

Constantine E. Michaelides, *The Aegean Crucible: Tracing Vernacular Architecture in Post-Byzantine Centuries*, Missouri: Delos, 2001.

Constantine E. Michaelides, *Hydra, a Greek Island Town: Its Growth and Form*, Chicago: University of Chicago Press, 1967.

Henry Miller, *The Colossus of Maroussi*, San Francisco: Colt, 1941.

Vasso Mingos, 'Island of writers', *Pictures from Greece* 29, June 1958: 4–11.

[Vasso Mingos] Rover, 'With red sails on the blue Aegean', *Pictures from Greece* 32, December 1958: 10–13.

Babis Mores, ΛΑΓΟΥΔΕΡΑ: Η ΧΡΥΣΗ ΕΠΟΧΗ ΤΗΣ ΥΔΡΑΣ, 1959–1967, compiled by Theodore Roubanis, Athens: Militos, 2010.

Bill Morgan, *The Beats Abroad: A Global Guide to the Beat Generation*, San Francisco: City Lights Books, 2015.

Nan Musgrove, 'A period piece of touching nostalgia transferred to the TV screen with loving care', *The Australian Women's Weekly* 22 September 1965: 18.

Ira Nadel, *Various Positions: A Life of Leonard Cohen*, Toronto: Random House, 1996.

A NOTE ON SOURCES AND FURTHER READINGS

Michalis Nikolakakis, 'Representations and social practices of alternative tourists in post-war Greece to the end of the Greek military junta', *Journal of Tourism History*, 7.1–2, 2015: 5–17.
Lawrence Osborne, 'Beyond the Sea', *New York Times Style Magazine* 21 March 2014, https://www.nytimes.com/2014/03/21/t-magazine/hydra-island.html.
Lawrence Osborne, *Beautiful Animals*, London: Hogarth, 2017.
Ruth Park, 'Nothing but writers', *The Independent Monthly* September 1989: 32–33.
Jill Piercy, *Brenda Chamberlain: Artist and Writer*, Cardigan: Parthian, 2013.
Christopher Rand, *Grecian Calendar*, New York: Oxford University Press, 1962.
Anthony Reynolds, *Leonard Cohen: A Remarkable Life*, London: Omnibus, 2012.
David Roessel, *In Byron's Shadow: Modern Greece in the English & American Imagination*, Oxford: Oxford University Press, 1997.
Tom Rothfield, 'Island legend for sale', *The Age* 1 October 1977: 20.
June Shelley, *Even When It Was Bad … It Was Good*, Indiana: Xlibris, 2000.
Sylvie Simmons, *I'm Your Man: The Life of Leonard Cohen*, London: Vintage, 2012.
Colin Simpson, *Greece: The Unclouded Eye*, Sydney: Angus & Robertson, 1968.
Adam Sisman, ed., *Dashing for the Post: The Letters of Patrick Leigh Fermor*, London: John Murray, 2016.
Graeme Skinner, *Peter Sculthorpe: The Making of an Australian Composer*, Sydney: University of New South Wales Press, 2015.
Aristodimos N. Sofianos, *Hydra*, Athens: I. Zacharopoulos, 1965.
Jorge Sotiros, 'Who cares for Cohen?' *Griffith Review* 29, 2010: 232–245.
Charles Sriber, 'It's all Greek to them: the knife became the symbol of the Johnstons' unknown future', *People* 14 May 1958: 15–16.
Charles Sriber, 'We'll never go back', *The Bulletin* 20 October 1962: 21–23.
Ruth Sriber, 'Australians find a dream life on the isles of Greece', *The Australian Women's Weekly* 20 July 1960: 15.
[Ruth or Charles Sriber (?)], 'Aussie boy prefers reading to acting', *The Australian Women's Weekly* 16 April 1958: 30.
Louden Wainwright, *The Great American Magazine: An Inside History of LIFE*, New York: Alfred Knopf, 1986.
Eric Whelpton and Barbara Crocker Whelpton, *Greece and the Islands*, London: Travel Book Club, 1961.
David Wills, *The Mirror of Antiquity: 20th Century British Travellers in Greece*, Newcastle: Cambridge Scholars Publishing, 2007.
Kostas Yannakopoulos, '"Naked piazza": male (homo)sexualities, masculinities and consumer cultures in Greece since the 1960s', in *Consumption and Gender in Southern Europe Since the Long 1960s*, edited by Kostis Kornetis, Eirini Kotsovili and Nikolaos Papadogiannis, London: Bloomsbury, 2016, 173–189.
Christian Zervos, Stephen Spender, Patrick Leigh Fermor, eds. *Ghika: Paintings, Drawings, Sculpture*, Boston: Boston Book and Art Shop, 1965.

Throughout, this book has engaged with the writings of authors who lived and wrote on Hydra. These people and texts include:

Brenda Chamberlain: *A Rope of Vines: Journal From a Greek Island*, London: Hodder and Stoughton, 1965.
Sheldon Cholst: *Hydra: Summer Season–Sixty Two, Poems and Drawings*, New York: Williams, 1964.
Charmian Clift: *Mermaid Singing*, London: Michael Joseph, 1958; *Peel Me a Lotus*, London: Hutchinson, 1959; *Walk to the Paradise Gardens*, London: Hutchinson, 1960; 'Home from the Aegean', *The Australian Women's Weekly* 16 February 1964: 7; *Honour's Mimic*, London: Hutchinson, 1964; *Images in Aspic*, London: Horowitz, 1965; *The World of Charmian Clift*, Sydney: Ure Smith, 1970; *Trouble in Lotus Land*, North Ryde: Angus & Robertson, 1990; *Charmian Clift: Selected Essays*, Pymble: Harper Collins, 2001.
Leonard Cohen: *The Spice-Box of Earth*, Toronto: McClelland and Stewart Ltd., 1961; *The Favorite Game*, Toronto: McClelland and Stewart Ltd., 1963; *The Songs of Leonard Cohen*, Columbia Records, 1967; *Songs from a Room*, Columbia Records, 1969; *Book of Longing*, Ontario: Penguin, 2006.
Rodney Hall: *Eyewitness*, Sydney: South Head, 1967.
Axel Jensen: *Icarus: A Young Man in the Sahara*, Trans. Maurice Michael, London: George Allen & Unwin, 1959; *A Girl I Knew*, London: Andre Deutsch, 1963.
George Johnston: *Grey Gladiator*, Sydney: Angus & Robertson, 1941; *Battle of the Seaways*, Sydney: Angus & Robertson, 1941; *Australia at War*, Sydney: Angus & Robertson, 1942; *New Guinea Diary*, Sydney: Angus & Robertson, 1943; *Pacific Partner*, New York: World Book Company, 1944; *Journey Through Tomorrow*, Melbourne: F. W. Cheshire, 1947; *Death Takes Small Bites*, New York: Dodd, Mead & Co., 1948; *Moon at Perigee*, Sydney: Angus & Robertson, 1948; *The Cyprian Woman*, London: Collins, 1955; *Twelve Girls in the Garden*, New York: William Morrow & Co., 1957 [Shane Martin]; *The Saracen Shadow*, London: Collins, 1957 [Shane Martin]; *The Man Made of Tin*, London: Collins, 1958 [Shane Martin]; *The Myth is Murder*, London: Collins, 1959 [Shane Martin]; *The Darkness Outside*, London: Collins, 1959; *Closer to the Sun*, London: Collins, 1960; *The Far Road*, London: Collins, 1962; *A Wake for Mourning*, London: Collins, 1962 [Shane Martin]; *My Brother Jack*, London: Collins, 1964; 'Home to land of bubbling vitality', *Sunday Mirror* 23 February 1964: n.p.; *Toehold in History*, director Dahl Collings, Collings Productions, Qantas Airways, 1965; *The Australians*, Adelaide: Rigby, 1966; 'Gallipoli paintings', *Art and Australia* 5.2, September 1967: 466–469; *Clean Straw for Nothing*, Sydney: Collins, 1969; *A Cartload of Clay*, Sydney: Collins, 1971.
Martin Johnston: *Selected Poems & Prose*, edited by John Tranter, St. Lucia: University of Queensland Press, 1993.

A NOTE ON SOURCES AND FURTHER READINGS

George Johnston and Charmian Clift: *High Valley*, Sydney: Angus & Robertson, 1949; *The Big Chariot*, Sydney: Angus & Robertson, 1953; *The Sponge Divers*, London: Collins, 1955; *Strong-man from Piraeus and other Stories* (includes 'The Astypalaian knife', 'The Verdict', and 'Vale, Pollini!'), compiled by Garry Kinnane, Melbourne: Nelson, 1983.

Gordon Merrick: *The Strumpet Wind*, New York: William Morrow & Co., 1947; *The Hot Season*, New York: William Morrow & Co., 1958; *One for the Gods*, New York: Bernard Geis Associates, 1971; *Forth Into Light*, New York: Avon, 1974.

Redmond Wallis: *Point of Origin*, London: Bodley Head, 1962. The Wallis archive held by the Turnbull Library includes some 56 folders of material. A complete listing is available from https://natlib.govt.nz/collections/a-z/manuscripts-collection. The folders cited in this book are *The Unyielding Memory* MS-Papers-9189-2; MS-Papers-9189-3; MS-Papers-9189-4; *Perspective One, 1962–1968, Analysis* MSX-6717; *Diary* MSX-6716; and *Letters and Background Material* 2003-189-37. This latter folder includes a nine-page "gossipy cv" that Wallis provided to the Turnbull Library.

During the course of this project we have published a number of articles in scholarly journals that cross over with the interests of *Half the Perfect World*, often providing additional detail. These include:

'Charmian Clift and George Johnston, Hydra 1960: the "lost" photographs of James Burke', *Meanjin* 73.1, 2014: 18–37.

'Australians in aspic: picturing Charmian Clift's and George Johnston's expatriation', *Journal of the Association for the Study of Australian Literature*, 15.3, 2015: 1–23.

'Desperately seeking Suzanne: photographs in Suzanne Chick's adoptee-narrative *Searching for Charmian*', *Life Writing* 12.4, 2015: 385–399.

'Google comes to Life: researching digital photographic archives', *Convergence: The International Journal of Research into New Media Technologies*, 21.1, 2015: 46–57.

'"New Zealand's first man of letters?" Rediscovering Redmond Frankton "Bim" Wallis', *Antipodes: A North America Journal of Australian Literature* 92.2, 2015: 293–308.

'"Taking the flowery bed back to Australia": the repatriation of Charmian Clift and George Johnston', *Australian Literary Studies* 31.3, 2016: online at https://www.australianliterarystudies.com.au/articles/taking-the-flowery-bed-back-to-australia-the-repatriation-of-charmian-clift-and-george-johnston.

'The case of a very loose-canon: the Shane Martin "pot-boilers" of George Johnston', *Southerly* 77.1, 2017: 56–76.

'George Johnston's Tibetan interlude: myth and reality in Shangri-La', *Journeys* 18.2, 2017: 1–27.

INDEX

Note: italicised page numbers refer to images.

A

Age 77, 78
Age Literary Supplement, The 371, 383
Agia Efpraxia (monastery) 100, 271
Amlin, Patricia 123–7, 215
Anagirou, Theodoros 24, 237, *306*
Androlakis, Emmanuel 107–9, *108*
archontiká (mansions) 43, 44, 56, 57, 166–92
Argus 1, 3
Arlen, Albert 5
Athens xv, 7, 16–8, 24, 28–9, 32, 34, 40, 63–4, 71, 84, 90, 95–6, 111–2, 116, 121, 123–6, 132, 147, 152–4, 158, 166, 168–9, 179, 198, 206, 209–12, 217, 224, 237, 239, 242, 249, 253, 259, 261, 269, 280, 283, 287–8, 308, 324–5, 341, 355, 365, 383, 388, 395
Athens School of Fine Arts (Hydra) 7, 144, 166, 247, 251–2, *252*
Australasian Post 2
Australian Women's Weekly, The 96, 169, 171, 255–6, 364, 384, 393
Axelsson, Sun 140, *197*

B

Balfour, Patrick 169
Barclay (Hay), Eileen 284–-8, 290
Barclay, James *57, 69,* 286, *287,* 311
Barclay, Sam 124, 280–7, *282,* 288–91, *289,* 292–3, *296, 299,* 300, 310–1
Barnes, Carol 292–3, *296*
Barnes, Stu 292–3, *296*
Barwick, Kester 29
Bayar, Celâl 111
Beatles, The 111, 392

Beaton, Cecil 19, 168
Beats (and beat) 15–17, 31, 90, 114, 116–8, 145–6, 266–7
Beltrami, Myriam 237
Benga, Féral (François) 236
Bessie (boat) 283, 286
Bethell, Nicholas 284
Bevan, Robert ('Bobby') 290
Blind Faith (band) 215
Bojenell, Brian 210–1, *211*
Booker, Christopher *234,* 235
Bowles, Jane 114
Bowles, Paul 114
Bowra, Maurice 168
Boy on a Dolphin (film) 239, 256–8, 259, 267, 277, *Plate 9*
Brando, Marlon 378
Branson, Richard 43, 399
Bratsera (hotel) 334
British Council 168–9, 253
British Pathé 371
Bronfman, Ann 268, *268*
Bronfman, Edgar 268, *268*
Bulletin 156
Burke, James 13–22, *14, 21,* 29–31, 41, 68, 73, 87, 89, 107, 109, 111, 123, 126, 127, 132–6, 137–8, 140–60, 175, 177, 182, 185, 188, 190, 193–4, 208–10, 215, 227–9, 252, 262, 266, 267–75, 277, 302, 317, 335, 354, 358–60, 399–400, 401–2
  and China 13, 15, 134
  meets George Johnston 13–4
  moves to Athens, moves to 16
  photojournalism training 15–6
  see also LIFE
Burke, Jim (James Jnr) 20
Burke, Josephine 161

C

Cacoyannis, Michael 255
Caliesch, Fidel 26, *130, 229, 234,
  292–3, 296,* 300, *301*
Callas, Maria 29
Cameron, Didi 100, 158–9, 163
Cameron, Peter 100, 158, 163
Cartier-Bresson, Henri 166
Case, Christopher 148, *151*
Case, Gene (Eugene) 148, 150–1, *151*
Case (Pease), Mary Jane 148–51, *149, 151*
Castello (bar) 241
Caturani, George 17, 18–9, 22, 317
Chadwick, Chip 308
Chagall, Marc 188, 191–2
Chamberlain, Brenda 100–1
  A Rope of Vines 100–1
Chappaqua (film) 16
Charalambopoulos, Ioannis 112
Charity Farm (UK) 158–60
Cholst, Sheldon 349–50
  Hydra: Summer Season—Sixty Two 349–50
Churchill, Winston 187
Clift, Charmian
  (photographs of) *xvi, xviii, 61, 62, 69, 75, 76, 86, 88, 89, 98, 119, 159, 173, 184, 185, 186, 187, 189, 194, 197, 202, 207, 209, 218, 228, 229, 230, 232, 234, 242, 306, 307, 318, 319, 394,* Plate 1, Plate 7
  alcoholism 205, 219, 403
  arrival on Hydra xv, 6–7, 246, 338, 341
  autobiographical writing 12, 361, 366–67
  childhood 86–7, 365
  expatriation xvii, 4–7, 55, 77–8, 85, 87, 117, 230, 246, 340–1, 360, 370, 372
  finances 63, 77, 99, 105, 158–61, 218–20, 341
  house hunting on Hydra 7, 55–6, 58, 317–9
  and Hydriots 234–5
  infidelity 122, 308, 357, 361–63, 388–9
  London 4–5, 51, 53, 56, 60, 63, 66, 81, 84, 86, 90, 95, 117, 257, 278, 392
  marooned on Hydra 116, 118, 357
  meets Axel Jensen 197–8
  meets George Johnston 2–3
  meets Leonard Cohen 196–7
  purchase of Hydra house 58, 60, 63
  relationship with George Johnston 2–4, 12, 53, 60, 61, 74, 75, 84, 219, 354, 356, 361, 393, 403–5
  repatriation 384, 390, 392, 403–4
  reviews 83, 360
  status on Hydra 207, 222–3, 230, 292–3, 300, 302, 373–6, 387
  success 393
  swimming 86–90, 93
  tourism 246–251, 256–8, 264–6, 267, 277–8
  travels 82, 116
  work ethic and writing 339–40, 360–2, 364, 366–7, 393
  works
    'After the Hodmodods' 373
    The Big Chariot 6, 83, 338
    The End of Morning 366–67
    For Your Information 2
    'Getting Away from It All' 270–1
    High Valley 4, 338
    Honour's Mimic 361–2, 390–1, Plate 15
    Mermaid Singing 6, 339, 340, 360
    'On Being a Home-Grown Migrant' 393
    Peel Me a Lotus 9, 11, 12, 41, 44, 46–8, 51, 56–7, 62–3, 73, 89, 92–5, 98–101, 104–7, 116–8, 171–2, 178–9, 183, 194, 212, 221, 241, 246, 264–5, 267, 269, 277, 310, 325, 341, 346, 356–58, 360
    'Report from a Migrant, Three Years After' 394
    The Serpent in the Rock 277–8

INDEX

The Sponge Divers 339–40
Walk to the Paradise Gardens 87, 361
Cohen, Leonard xiii, *xiv*, xv-xvii, *xviii*, 13, 18, 26–7, 30, 48, 79, 87, *88*, 90–2, 107, 109, 111, 114–5, 123, 126–31, *129*, *130*, *131*, 135–6, *135*, 138, 140, 145, 156, 163, 173–7, 196, 205, 208, *209*, 213–5, *216*, 217, 228–34, *230*, 232, *232*, 234, *234*, 237, 240, 271, *272*, *273*, *274*, *275*, 290, 292, 305, *306*, *307*, 308, *309*, *332*, *333*, 348–50, 374–5, 377, 379–80, 382, 387–8, 395, 398–9, 400, 402
  arrival on Hydra xv, 26, 127–8, 231
  Cuba 292, 348
  drugs 349–50
  house on Hydra 79, 128–32, 316, 374, 395
  London xv, 231, 350
  meets Charmian Clift and George Johnston 196–7
  meets Marianne Ihlen 126, 213–4
  singing and music 122, 135, 214–5, 228–32, *230*, *232*, 237, 305, *307*, 400
  work ethic and writing 349
  works
    'Duskos Taverna 1967' 233–4
    The Favourite Game 140
    'Flowers for Hitler' 348
    'So Long Marianne' 214
    Songs From a Room 214–5
    The Songs of Leonard Cohen 214
    The Spice-Box of Earth 348
Collings, Dahl 346, 383
Collings, Geoffrey 346, 383
Collings, Silver 199, 346, 375, *377*, 383
Collins, Judy 395
Collins, William (Billy) 219
Connolly, Cyril 169
Cooke, John Starr 127
Cooper, Diana (Lady) 168
Corso, Gregory 15–17, *16*, 115, 120, 156
Coundouriotis, Lazaros 34, 178
Coundouriotis, Pavlos 193, *203*
Courchinoux, Christiane 135

Courchinoux, Jean Marie 135
Craxton, John 115, 166
Cyprus 47, 105–6

D

da Costa, Morton 244, 277
Dassin, Jules 240, 244, *244*, 259
Davis, Maryann *130*, *131*, 154, *155*, 271, *272*, *274*, *275*, *275*
Davis, Sue 153–4, *155*, 271, *272*, *273*, *274*, *275*, *275*, *276*
de Berg, Hazel 370
de Watteville, Vivienne 147
Delfini (bar) 241, 258
Desanti, Dominique 135
Dessaix, Robert 29
  Corfu 29
Dignan, Nancy 9, 52, 196, 247
Divine, David 256
  Boy on a Dolphin (novel) 256, *Plate 9*
Dominion, The 24
Donkey Shit Lane 79, 112, 146, 194, 377
donkeys (and mules) 22, 23, 48, 100, 113, 118, 135, 144, *145*, 225, 264, 271, *272*, *273*, *275*, *276*, 324–5, *326*, 349, 388, *Plate 1*
Doss, Erika 20
Douskos (Xeri Elia) Taverna 227–35, *228*, *229*, *230*, *232*, *234*, 241, 399–400
drugs 90–1, 222, 267, 349–51
Durrell, Lawrence 38, 166
  Prospero's Cell 38
Dylan, Bob 120, 311

E

Eakin (Dalton), Robyn 181
  Aunts Up the Cross 181
Eikones 114
Elliott, Ramblin' Jack 120–2, *121*
Embry, Norris 115, 156
Emerson, James 35, 37, 45
Epidaurus 82, 302–4, 308

expatriation
  Greek language   109, 150, 174, 188, 190, 201, 247, 256, 277–8, 303, 316, *389*, 395
  liberal attitudes   xvii, 138, 144, 208, 316, 373
  permanency   7, 18–19, 55–6, 77, 103, 114–5, 128, 148, 156, 317, 372
  women's experiences   95–8

F

Falieros, Spiros   398
Fatouros, Chris   398
Ferguson, George   379
Fermor, Patrick Leigh   167–9, 174, 400
  Mani   169
Ferries   17, 40, 86, 94, 102, 118, 120, 142, 203, 225, 240, 249, 253, 258, 260, 262, 401
Finch, Peter   5, 115
Finer, Leslie   254, 262
  Passport to Greece   254
Fisher, Eddie   240–1
Fitzgerald, F. Scott   116–7, 398
Fitzgerald, Zelda   398
Flower, Cedric   5, 84, 85
Flower, Pat   5, 84, 85, 170
Folke-Olsson, Lena   26, 123, 126–7, 303, *306*
Fonda, Henry   240
For Your Information   2

G

Gardenia, The (cinema)   92
Gassoumis, Athena   68, *69*, 182, *184, 185, 186*, 229, 313, 317
Gassoumis, Carolyn   26–7, 68, *69*, 182, 184–6, *184, 185, 186*, 188, *189*, 190, *194*, 229, *229*, 234, 292, 312–4, 317, *318, 319, 320, 323*, 327–8, *332, 333*, 374–5, 380
Gassoumis, Cassandra   317, *323*
Gassoumis, Demetri   26–7, 68, *69*, 107, *108*, 109, *194, 202*, 209, *211*, 229, *229*, 234, 292, 295, *296, 298*, 312, 313–37, *315, 318, 319, 320, 330, 331, 332, 333*, 374–6, 380
Gassoumis, Kleomenus (Mike)   313
Ghika, Nikos Hadjikriakos-   7, 19, 22, 166–78, *175, 176*, 209–11, *210, 211*, 252, 259, *Plate 2*
Gibbons, Beverly   292–3, 295, *297*
Gibbons, Jim   292–3, 295, *298*
Ginsberg, Allen   15, 17, 115, 120
A *Girl in Black* (film)   239, 255
Go! (magazine)   209, 258–60
Goschen, Angela   9, 26, 123, 147–8, 215
Goschen, Chryssoula   9
Goschen, David   xviii, 9, 18, 19, 26, 123–5, 146–8, *146, 147*, 148, 150, 182–5, *186, 203*, 215, 229, 231, *234*, 322
Goschen, Edward (Sir)   147, 215
Goschen, Mariora   9, 148
Grafos (kafenio)   227, 388
Graves, Robert   344
  Greek Myths   344
Greek Civil War (1945–9)   39, 112, 283
Greek National Tourism Organisation   251, 253
Greek politics   29, 34–7, 39, 105–7, 111–12, 283, 394–5
Greek War of Independence (1821–32)   34–5, 37, 162, 189
Green (Rodriguez), Judith   200
Green, Patricia   268, *268*
Green, William   268, *268*
Greer, Patrick   9, 53, 247
Gropius, Walter   166
Guthrie, Woody   120

H

Hall, Bet   70–1, 198, 354, 375
Hall, Rodney   70–1, 115, 187, 198, 199, 219, 327–8, 353–4, 375
Hammerstein (Shelley), June   120–2, *121*
Hatzimihali, Vanna   *189*

INDEX

Heckstall, Chuck 18, *83*, 151–4, *152, 153, 194*, 229, *229, 230, 232, 234*, 243, *243*
Heidsieck, Christian 7–9, *8*, 123, 400
Hellenic Herald 395
Hennessy, Timothy 181, 182, *Plate 7*
Hepburn, Audrey 29
Hesthamar, Kari 288, 302
Hetherington, John 371, 383
Hicks, Wilson 30
Higham, David 3, 277
Hilton, James 14
Hinks, Roger 169
homosexuality 112, 124–5, 241, 310
Hotel Raya 237–8
Howard, Elizabeth Jane 158
  The Sea Change 158
Hughes, Peter 136
Hulse, Charles ('Chuck') 26, 123–125, 154, *202, 207, 209*, 300, 303, 308, 312, 380, 388, 396, 400
Hutchinson, Barbara 174, 177, 209, *211*
Hydra
  (photographs of) *40, 42, 43, 46, Plate 5*
  agora 45–7, 52, 54, 94, 100, 111, *149*, 159, *159*, 175, 193, 205–6, 249, *251*, 333
  cost of living and house prices 18, 24, 44–5, 58, 97, 128, 131, 137, 142, 150, 153–4, 161, 199–200, 231, 242, 264, 325, 334, 401
  harbour and dockside 40–6, *40, 43, 46*, 98
  history 33–40
  house renovations 63–5, 130–2, 154, 172, 225, 319, 322, 334
  light 49, 51, 104, 252, 354
  sound 48, 113
  views 26, 35, 45, 49–52, *50*, 58, 65, 78, 128–9, 142, 153, 165, 172–3, 201, 245, 271, 274, 317, 334
  volta 46–7, *47*
  water-supply 7, 57–8, 63–4, 79, 95, 172, 313, 321, 325–30, *326, 327, 329*, 332, 335–6

  see also Kala Pigadia, Kamini, Kiaffa, Mandraki, Spilia
Hydriots 28, 34, 37, 44, 87, 118, 127, 166, 180, 212, 240, 260, 401
  and expatriates 55, 60, 68, 74, 103, 105–109, 118, 127, 142, 156, 158–9, 165–192, 203, 218–9, 212, 220, 226, 324, 327–331, 387
  and tourism 251–253, 257, 262, 264–5

I

Ihlen, Marianne xv, *xviii*, 9, 26, 27, 87, *88*, 92, 109, 123–8, 138, *139*, 140, 174, 180, *211*, 215, *216*, 217, 229, *230*, 233, *234*, 236, 237, 271 *272, 273, 274*, 286–91, 289, *289*, 292, 302–4, *306*, 308, *309, 332, 333*, 349, 399, *Plate 7*
Iles Frances (Anthony Berkeley Cox) 342–43
Isaia, Nana 349
Island of Love, The (film) 277
Isle of Wight Festival (1970) 232

J

Jeffrey-Jones, Rhodri 285
Jensen, Axel 9, 26, 115, 123–8, 138, *139*, 140, *141*, 142, 145, 174, 180, *203*, 213, 215, *216*, 217, 229–31, *230, 234*, 286–8, 290, 303
  Doktor Fantastik 142
  Dyretemmerens kors 138
  A Girl I Knew 138, 142, *Plate 12*
  Icarus 138
  Joachim 140
  Line 138
Jensen, Axel Jnr (Tot) *xviii, 203, 211, 216*, 217
Jensen, Marianne *see* Ihlen, Marianne
Johnston, Gae 3, 362
Johnston, George
  (photographs of) *xvi, xviii, 14, 61, 62, 69, 72, 74, 76, 83, 98, 119, 157, 184, 185, 186, 189, 194, 197, 202, 207, 209,*

– 419 –

210, 211, 218, 228, 230, 234, 242, 251, 306, 307, 318, 319, 347, 355, 359, 394, Plate 1, Plate 7
alcoholism 205, 219, 403
arrives on Hydra xv, 6
autobiographical writing 12, 339, 362, 365–6
boats and shipping 85, 86, 292, 310, 312
childhood 2, 363–5
expatriation xvii, 4–7, 39, 55, 77–8, 85, 117, 230, 317, 340–1, 360, 366, 370–2, 381, 383, 398
finances 63, 77, 99, 105, 158–61, 218–20, 341
friendship with Sam Barclay 288–92, 300
friendship with Sidney Nolan 344–6, 372
generosity 24, 379
health 67–8, 102–3, 116, 355–6, 363, 380
house hunting on Hydra 7, 24, 58, 317–19, *318–9*
Hydra, marooned on 116, 118, 358
infidelity 53, 122, 339
insecurity 53, 55, 222, 341, 365, 378
as journalist 1, 2, 338
London 4–5, 51, 53, 56, 60, 63, 66, 81, 83–4, 86, 117, 160, 162, 278, 358
meets Axel Jensen 197–8
meets Charmian Clift 2–3
meets James Burke 13–4
meets Leonard Cohen 196–7
meets Marianne Ihlen 197–8
meets Rodney Hall 198–9
potboilers (Shane Martin novels) 341–43, 344
purchase of Hydra house 7, 58, 60, 63
relationship with Charmian Clift 2–4, 12, 53, 60–1, 74–5, 84, 219, 356–9, 362, 364, 393, 403–5
repatriation 346, 370–1, 376, 382–4, 392, 403–4
reviews 83, 293, 342–3, 363

status on Hydra 207, 222–3, 230, 292–3, 300, 302
studio on Hydra 51–2, 64, 354, *355, 359*
success 22, 293, 370–1, 377–8, 383–4, 390
and tourism *251*, 254, 274
travels 1, 14, 82, 116
work ethic 338–49, 354–9, 362–7
works
 'The Astypalaian knife' 341
 Australia at War 1
 The Australians 392
 Battle of the Seaways 1
 The Big Chariot 6, 83, 338
 A Cartload of Clay 14, 371, 402, 404
 Clean Straw for Nothing 67, 78, 82, 204, 222, 356, 358, 371–2, 403–4
 Closer to the Sun 22, 39, 60, 66, 101–7, 160, 219, 254, 274, 293, 354–5, 356–9, 367, *Plate 14*
 The Cyprian Woman 82, 83, 338
 The Darkness Outside 343
 Death by Horoscope 4
 Death Takes Small Bites 3
 The Far Road 355, 362–63
 Grey Gladiator 1
 High Valley 4, 338
 Meredith trilogy 12, 355, 404
 Moon at Perigee 4
 My Brother Jack 70–2, 85, 219, 346, 355, 363–67, 370–2, 377, 380, 382–3, 389, 390, 392–3, 403
 New Guinea Diary 1
 Pacific Partner 1
 The Serpent in the Rock 277–8
 The Sponge Divers 339–40
 'Vale, Pollini!' 300
 'The Verdict' 356
 see also Shane Martin
Johnston, Jason 1, *47*, 68, *69*, 140, 148, 162, *209*, 289, 384, *386*, 404
Johnston, Martin 1, 4, *57, 62, 69*, 173, *173*, 255–6, 277, 286, 289, 305, *306, 307*, 308, 353, 384, 387, 389, *389*, 404

INDEX

'To Greece Under the Junta' 395
Johnston, Shane 1, 4, *47*, *59*, *69*, *72*, 106, 256, 286, 289, *306*, *311*, 384, *385*, *386*, 395, 404

K

Kala Pigadia 58, 100, 163, 325
Kalergis, Maria 189
Kali, *Kyria* 224
Kalymnos 6, 60, 83–5, 107, 288, 289, 339–41, 361
Kamini 7–8, 37, 54, 79, 128, 166, 242
Kaplan, Robert D. 267
Kardamatis, Ioannis (Wolfgang) 181–2, *Plate 7*
Katsikas (kafenio) *xiv*, *83*, 109, 124, *135*, 193–227, *194*, *195*, *196*, *197*, *202*, *209*, *210*, *211*, *213*, *216*, *218*, 241, 243–4, *244*, 265, *347*, 379
Katsikas, Antony 193–4, 218, 223
Katsikas, Nick 193–4, 201
Katsikas, Polyxena *207*, 218, *218*
Katsimbalis, George 167
Kennedy, Jacqueline (Jackie) 29, 240, 259, 302, *303*
Kerkiraios, Yianni 386
Kerouac, Jack 15, 120
Kiaffa 34, 166
Kingsmill, Anthony 77, 115, 388
Kinnane, Garry 3, 77, 85, 157–8
Kirkus Review 379
Klein, Daniel 49–50
Klein, Yves 181
Kline, Franz 15
Knuckey, Marie 196
Koch, Janice 156
Koch, Katherine 156
Koch, Kenneth 115, 156
Kolve, V. A. (Del) 136–7, 144, 200, 240, 264, 387
de Kooning, Willem 15
Kornetis, Kostis 39
Koussoula, Naya 269
Kovler, Everett 269, *269*

L

Lacarriere, Jacques 135
Ladd, Alan 256, *Plate 9*
Laffin, John 101, 102
 Middle East Journey 101, 102
Lagoudera 235–45, 258
Landery, Charles 283, 286
 Whistling for a Wind 286
Layton, Irving 114
Leatham, John 285
Lederer, William J. 115, 199, 378
 I, Giorghos 379
 The Ugly American 378
Lialios, George 174–5
Liberty 14
Liddell, Robert 258, 259
 The Morea 253
LIFE 13, 17, 20, 21, 30, 31, 111, 134, 144–6, 161, 208, 262, 268, 317, 402
Linton, William 35–7
 The Scenery of Greece and its Islands 35
Loch, Joice 29
 A Fringe of Blue 29
London xv, 4–5, 6, 51, 53, 56, 60, 63–4, 66, 81, 83–4, 86, 90, 95, 103–4, 117, 160–1, 167, 173, 181, 198–9, 230–1, 235, 257–8, 260, 278, 286, 291, 300, 322, 338, 340, 350–1, 353, 371, 383, 387, 392, 395–6, 402
Loren, Sophia 115, 256, *Plate 9*
Lulus (kafenio) 227
Lury, Celia 30

M

MacCallum, Diana 71, 72, *72*, *391*
MacCallum, Mungo Jnr 71–3, *72*, 92–3, *228*, 305, 375, 391–2, *391*
MacCallum, Mungo Snr 71
MacCallum (née McGowan), Sue 71, *72*, 92–3, *228*, 375, *391*
Macintyre, Ben 285
Mack, Lily (Angoulina) 7–9, 123, 400
Mack, Vladimir 7
Mailer, Norman 166

Malouf, David 200
Mandraki 37, 142
Martin, Shane 291, 341–4, 362–3
   Twelve Girls in the Garden 342
   A Wake for Mourning 291, 342–3
   see also George Johnston
Maurice, Jean-Claude 356–7, 362
Maxwell, Robert (Bob) 151–3, *153*, 162, *326*
McGill, Don 122
   Peel Me a Lotus (musical) 122–3
McGregor, Craig 200
McKie, Ronald 170–1
McNay, Ian 375
McNay, Jan 375
Menderes, Adnan 111
Mercouri, Melina 29, 115, 225, 240, *244*, 259, Plate 10
Merkel, Klaus *143*, 144–6, *145*, 148, *194*, 201, 229, *232*, *234*, *252*, 259
Merrick, Gordon 13, 26, 66, 123–125, 154, 156, *207*, *209*, *244*, 300, 303, *303*, 305, *306*, *307*, 308, *309*, 312, 322, 380, 396, 400, 402
   Forth Into Light 13, 66, 67
   The Hot Season 322
   One for the Gods 308–10
   The Strumpet Wind (boat) 308, *309*
Meyer, Jo 340
MI6 284–5, 310
Miaoulis, Andreas 34
Miles Franklin Award 235, 403
Miller, Henry 37–9, 45, 95, 138, 166–7
   The Colossus of Maroussi 37–9, 167, 252, 314
Mingos, Michael 283
Mingos, Vasso ('Rover') 7–12, 17–8, 26, 29, 138, 147, 236, 280–4, 286, 387, 401
Mitchell, Joni 267
Mitford, Nancy 169
Mitrovic, Anna 396
Mitso 164, 288–90, 293–5
modernity 5, 38, 56, 81, 198, 215, 317, 237, 324, 331, 342, 401
   Hydra as refuge from 28–9, 30, 62,
77, 95, 207, 237, 249, 314, 324
Monsell, Joan Eyres 167–8
Moorehead, Alan 29, 344
   Gallipoli 29
Mores, Babis 238–41, 245
Motor Boating 255
Moyer, Donald 136–7

N

Negulesco, Jean 256
Neophytos, Kiki 190
Nereida (ferry) 140, 161
New Yorker, The 211, 344
Niarchos, Stavros 181, 240
Nietzsche, Friedrich 27
Nolan, Cynthia 5, 166–72, *173*, 247, 344, Plate 4
Nolan, Sidney 5, 64–5, 81, 115, 161, 166–73, *173*, 247, 344–7, 372–3, Plate 4

O

Omilos (restaurant-bar) 244
Onassis, Aristotle 29, 181, 240
Osborne, Lawrence 400
   Beautiful Animals 400
Owen, Robert 199, 205, 321–2, 375–6, *377*, 383

P

Paouri, Katerina *21*, 171–92, *183*, *185*, *186*, Plate 6
Paouri, Maria 189, *189*
Papadopoulos, Georgis 111
Papandreaou, Georgis 111
Papastratos, Betty *189*
Papastratos, Doris *189*, 190
Park, Ruth 219
Pedersen (Blair), Dinnie 142, *143*, 144, 188
Pedersen, Simen 142, *143*
Pedersen, Tore 137–8, 140, *141*, 142, *143*, 144, 188, *194*

INDEX

Pelagos Magazine 239
People 62, 116
Perkins, Anthony 115, 240, 243, 259, *Plate 10*
Phaedra (film) 244, 259
photojournalism 15–16, 22, 30, 262, 266–71, 274
Picasso, Pablo 181
Pictures from Greece 7, 138, 236, 280, 284, 286–7
Pinotsis, Kyrio 132
Piper, Michael 140, *197*
Pix 2
Portofino (bar) 242–3, *243*, 258
Poseidon Hotel 82, *83*
post office 203–4, 225
Pownall, William (Bill) 321–2, 374–5
Press, The 24
Private Eye 235
Profitis Ilias (monastery) 271, *274*
Push, The (subculture) 391

Q

Quintos (*kafenio*) 227

R

Rachevsky, Zina *16*
Rand, Chris 210–2, *210, 211*
    Grecian Calendar 211
Randall, Tony 244, *244*
Rauschenberg, Robert 181
Resnick, Martin 15
Reynolds, Anthony 115
Ritsos, Yiannis 112
Roland, Betty 29
    Lesbos 29
Roloi Café 225
Rooks, Conrad 16–7, *16*
Rose Rouge (nightclub) 236
Rothfield, Tom 78
Rothschild, Jacob 174
Rothschild, Victor (Baron) 174
Roussis, Konstantinos *326*

S

Sanfield, Steve 48, 90–3, 109–11, 237, 349, 374
Saronis (ferry) *119*, 263
Saturday Evening Post 14
Schaller, Mark 398
Schneier, Inge 134–6, *135*, 212, *213*, 229, *230, 234*, 271
Schwartz, Gill 9, *10*
Schwartz, Loetitia 9, 138, *139*
Sculthorpe, Peter 168
Seferis, Giorgis 168
Seidemann, Bob 215
Serra, Richard 181
Siddhartha (film) 16
Silverstein, Shel 142
Simmons, Sylvie 45, 91
Simpson, Colin 62, 77, 125, 162, 195, 223, 261–2
Siroco (bar) 242
Sitwell, Osbert 19
Skelton, Barbara 169
Skordoras, Zoe 68, *69*, 74, 158, 387
Slithey Tove, The (boat) 310, *311*
Sofianos, Aristomidos 45, 166
Soraya (Princess) 240, 245, 259
Sotiros, Jorge 29
Spender, Stephen 169
Spetses 29, 34, 280, 344
Speyer, Darthea 132
Speyer, James 18, 132, *133*, 134, 136
Spilia 87, *88, 89*, 144–5, 247, 333
sponge diving 37, 84
Sports Illustrated 253, *Plate 8*
Sriber, Charles 29, 62, 96, 116, 156, 255, 341
    'We'll Never go Back' 156
Sriber, Ruth 29, 96–7, 156–7, 255
Stark, Freya 169
Stein, Gertrude 116–7
Stormie Seas (boat) 280–311, *281, 282, 289, 296, 297, 298, 299, 301, 302*, 310–11, *Plate 11*
Strumpet Wind, The (boat) 308, *309*

– 423 –

Sunday Mirror 384
Sunday Telegraph 235
Sydney Morning Herald 4, 393, 403

T

Tarnower, Herman 268, 269
Tassos (kafenio) *83*, 227
Taylor, Elizabeth 19, 240, 241, 259, 268
Tennant, Emma 235
   A House in Corfu 235
Throckmorton, Peter 311
Tilche, Magda 9, *11*, 106–7, 123, 131, *207*, 236–8, *238*, *306*
Tilche, Paolo 9, *11*, 106–7, 236–8
Tilche, Sandro 9, *11*, 123, *306*
Time 15
Toehold in History (film) 346
Tombazi, Emmanuel 166
Tombazi, Iakovos 34
tourism 11–2, 17, 29–30, 39, 80, 114, 246–79, 333, 400–1
   backpackers 267, 269
   day-trippers 262, 269
   donkey-rides 271–7
   hippies 267, 269, 400
   leisure boating 239, 267
   photography 239, 269–71
Travers, Erica 387
Tunström, Göran 115, 140
   Karantän 140

U

Ungood-Brown, Jasper 18

V

Valaoritis, Nanos *16*
Van Ghent, Dorothy 134, 136
Variety 236
Vogue 395
Votsis, Nicholas 189
Vyzantios, Perikilis 252, *252*

W

Wakeman, Frederick 255
Wallis, Redmond Frankton ('Bim') 18, 23–8, *23*, *25*, 30–1, 41, 49, 54, 64, 68, 73, 79, 90, 95–6, 107, *108*, 110–12, 122, 123–7, 145, 153–4, *155*, 163, 175, 177, 191, 201–2, 206–7, 214, 222, 225, 227, 229, *229*, *232*, *234*, 235, 237, 241, 245, 252, 258, 260, 261, *261*, 271, *272*, 275, 277, 278, 280–2, 284, 291–5, 299–302, 304–305, *306*, 312, 314–7, 319, 321–5, 329, 330–3, 335, 348–9, 350–3, 367, 371, 373–5, 377–82, 387–90, 395, 397, 402–3
   arriving on Hydra 24, 26, 379
   London 24, 154, 257, 291, 300, 350, 353, 396, 402
   returning to Hydra 91, 260, 374
   travel writing 258–60
   Bees on a String 379, 395–6
   The Mills of Space 28
   Point of Origin 28, 352–3, 402, *Plate 13*
   Starbloom 28
   The Submissive Body 379
   The Unyielding Memory 27–8, 31–2, 54, 64, 68, 73, 79, 90, 95–6, 112–3, 122, 162–4, 177, 191–2, 201, 214, 222, 225–6, 235, 241, 245, 278–9, 281–2, 292–5, 305, 312, 314–6, 321–3, 324–5, 333, 335–7, 348–9, 367–9, 378–82, 388–90, 397
Wallis, Robyn 18, 24, *25*, 26–8, 95, *96*, *108*, 110, 123, 153–4, *155*, 199, *202*, *203*, *229*, 258, *261*, 271, *272*, 275, *276*, 291–2, *301*, 304, *306*, 312, 314, 316–7, *332*, *333*, 351–2, 380, 395–6, 402
Wallis, Ruve 154
Warner, Rex 166, 174
The Wastrel (film) 255
Watson, Sheila 402
Welles, Sam 18
Wentworth-MacCallum, Diana 72, *72*
Wheatley, Nadia 65, 70, 185, 310, 362

INDEX

Whelpton, Barbara Crocker 251
Whelpton, Eric 251
White, Patrick 383
Whitman, Rosemary 153, *153*, 242–3, *243*
wine boats *43*, 144, *145*, *385*
winter on Hydra 44, 97, 120, 131, 142, 158, 170–1, 194–96, *197*, 198–9, 203, 226, 246–7, 278–79, 344, 346–7, 353, 363, 376
Winton, Tim 235
   Cloudstreet 235
   The Riders 235

X

Xeri Elia Taverna *see* Douskos Taverna

Y

Yannakopoulos, Kostas 125
Yaros 112

Z

Zander, Clarisse 81–2
Zaraphonitis, Pavlos 78
Zorba the Greek (film) 256